# The Road to the White House 1992

## The Politics of Presidential Elections

# The Road to the White House 1992

## The Politics of Presidential Elections

**Stephen J. Wayne**

*Georgetown University*

**St. Martin's Press**
New York

*Senior editor:* Don Reisman
*Managing editor:* Patricia Mansfield
*Project editor:* Elise Bauman
*Production supervisor:* Alan Fischer
*Text design:* Leon Bolognese and Associates
*Graphics:* Maryland Composition
*Cover design:* CIRCA 86, Inc.

Manufactured in the United States of America.
65432
fedc

For information, write:
St. Martin's Press, Inc.
175 Fifth Avenue
New York, NY 10010

ISBN: 0-312-05195-6
       0-312-05603-6 (pbk.)

**Library of Congress Cataloging-in-Publication Data**

Wayne, Stephen J.
    The road to the White House : the politics of presidential elections / Stephen J. Wayne.—4th ed.
        p.
    Includes bibliographical references.
    ISBN 0-312-05195-6
         0-312-05603-6 (pbk.)
    1. Presidents—United States—Election.   I. Title
JK528.W37   1992
324.973—dc20                                    90-71616
                                                 CIP

**Acknowledgments**
    **Figure 3–2,** "Party Profiles, 1988," copyright © 1988 by The New York Times Company. Reprinted by permission.
    **Table 4–1,** "Proportional Voting and Delegate Allocation," copyright by the American Political Science Association.
    **Table 4–4,** "The Democratic Primary Electorate, 1988," copyright © 1988 by The New York Times Company. Reprinted by permission.
    **Table 4–5,** "The Demography of the National Convention Delegates, 1968–1988," copyright © 1988 by The New York Times Company. Reprinted by permission.

Acknowledgments and copyrights are continued at the back of the book on page 310, which constitutes an extension of the copyright page.

To my mother and father,
Mr. and Mrs. Arthur G. Wayne,
and to the memory of my grandmother,
Mrs. Hattie Marks

# Preface

It is easier to follow a political campaign than to understand it. We read about it in the press, view it on television, and occasionally even see or hear a candidate in person. We observe only what others—the candidates, their advisors, reporters, or a host of other self-interested participants—want us to see, and we are expected to use their views to make a judgment on election day.

There is more, however, to presidential elections than meets the eye. Campaign planners work hard to design a strategy to maximize their vote. They understand the intricacies of the process. They know how the system works, who its beneficiaries are, and where to concentrate their campaign resources. They understand the requirements of finance legislation—how to comply with it, get around it, and take advantage of it. They appreciate the psychological and social motivations of voters and have a feel for which appeals are likely to be most effective most of the time. They are aware of party rules and the ways to build a winning coalition during the nomination period. They can sense the rhythm of conventions and know when events should be scheduled and how various interests can be placated and orchestrated. They know how to organize and plan a general election campaign and how best to present their candidate to the voters. They can usually predict what will happen in the election and interpret the results so as to enhance their political position and governing potential. They may not need to read this book.

On the other hand, people who want to get behind the scenes of presidential campaigns, who want to know the reasons that particular strategies are adopted, certain tactics utilized, which of these strategies and tactics had the desired results, why the election turned out the way it did, and what implications the vote has for the new president and his ability to govern, should benefit from the information contained in this book.

*The Road to the White House, 1992: The Politics of Presidential Elections* is a straightforward "nuts and bolts" discussion of how the system is designed and works. It is primarily concerned with facts, not opinions; with practice, not theory; with implications, not speculations. It summarizes the state of the art and science of presidential electoral politics.

This edition has been thoroughly updated. Like the 1980, 1984, and 1988 editions, it is organized into four main parts. The first discusses the arena in which the election occurs. Its three chapters examine the electoral system, campaign finance, and the political environment. Chapter 1 provides a historical overview of nominations as well as elections, while chapters 2 and 3 examine recent developments. Highlighted are the political considerations that candidates need to consider as they plan and structure their presidential campaigns.

Parts II and III are organized sequentially. They describe the distinct yet related stages of the presidential campaign: delegate selection, nominating conventions, and the general election. Chapter 4 examines reforms in the selection of convention delegates and their impact on voters, candidates, and the parties. Chapter 5 carries this discussion to the nominating convention, describing its purposes, procedures, policies, and politics. In Chapter 6, the organization, strategy, and tactics of the general election are discussed. Chapter 7 describes the projection and targeting of candidate images. It examines how the media cover the campaign, how the candidates try to affect that coverage, and how all of this affects the electorate on election day. Detailed illustrations from the most recent elections are used throughout these chapters.

The fourth part looks at the election and beyond by exploring its implications for the government and for the political system. Chapter 8 discusses and evaluates the presidential vote by asking such questions as: Does it provide a mandate? Does it influence the president's ability to govern? Chapter 9 considers problems in the electoral system and possible reforms. It examines some of the major difficulties that have affected the political system and proposals advanced for dealing with them: how the electoral process can be made more equitable; how it can be made more responsive to popular choice; and how that choice can be conveyed more effectively to elected and appointed officials.

These questions are not easy to answer. Members of Congress, academicians, and other students of the American political system have been debating them for some time, and that debate is likely to continue. Without information on how the system works, we cannot intelligently participate in it or improve it. In the case of presidential politics, ignorance is definitely not bliss.

The road to the White House is long and arduous. In fact, it has become more difficult to travel than in the past. Yet, surprisingly, there are more travelers. Evaluating their journey is essential to rendering an intelligent judgment on election day. However, more is at stake than simply choosing the occupants of the presidential and vice-presidential offices. The system itself is on trial in every presidential election. That is why it is so important to understand and appreciate the intricacies of the process. Only an informed citizenry can determine whether the nation is being well served by the way we go about choosing our president.

Few books are written alone, and this one is no exception. For this edition, I was fortunate to have the wise counsel of Richard G. Niemi of the University of Rochester and my colleague, Clyde Wilcox, of Georgetown University. Their knowledge of the presidential electoral system helped me broaden my understanding of it and saved me from a few serious errors and many more careless mistakes. Eric Pages, a Ph.D. candidate at Georgetown, served as my research assistant. In countless trips to the library, he reviewed and synthesized the new literature, compiled data on the 1988 elections, and aided me in numerous other ways in revising the manuscript. Linda Armstrong and Kevin McNally converted my barely readable handwriting quickly and accurately into a word-perfect format.

I would also like to express my thanks to those political scientists who commented on previous editions of this book: Richard L. Cole, University of Texas at Arlington; Anthony Corrado, Colby College; James W. Davis, Washington University; Gordon Friedman, Southwest Missouri State University; Jay S. Goodman, Wheaton College; Anne Griffin, The Cooper Union; Margorie Randon Hershey, Indiana University; Hugh L. LeBlanc, George Washington University; Kuo-Wei Lee, Pan-American University; James Lengle, Georgetown University; Robert T. Nakamura, State University of New York at Albany; Charles Prysby, The University of North Carolina at Greensboro; Lester Seligman, University of Illinois; Earl Shaw, Northern Arizona University; John W. Sloan, University of Houston; William H. Steward, University of Alabama; and Edward J. Weissman, Washington College.

I also wish to acknowledge with gratitude and thanks the many people at St. Martin's Press who have contributed in numerous ways to the editing, production, and marketing of the four editions of this book. In an era of great instability in college publishing, I feel very fortunate to have been associated with such a stable and first-rate house as St. Martin's.

Finally, everyone makes personal sacrifices in writing a book. My wife, Cheryl Beil, and my sons, Jared and Jeremy, were no exceptions. As always, they gave me lots of encouragement and put up with a lot of weekend work. And although I would have been the last to admit it at the time, they also had to contend with a sometimes tense, intolerant, and grumpy husband and daddy. I thank my family for being so accommodating and especially so understanding.

*Stephen J. Wayne*

# Contents

## 5   The Convention   137

## III   The Campaign   171

## 6   Organization, Strategy, and Tactics   173

# PART
# I

# The
# Electoral
# Arena

# Chapter 1

# Presidential Selection: A Historical Overview

## INTRODUCTION

The road to the White House cannot be traversed in a day. It takes months, often years, to travel. Candidates need to have considerable skill and luck to travel it successfully.

The framers of the Constitution worked for several months on the presidential selection system, and their plan has since undergone a number of constitutional, statutory, and precedent-setting changes. Modified by the development of parties, the expansion of suffrage, the growth of the media, and the revolution in modern technology, the system has become more open and participatory but also more contentious, more circuitous, more structured, and more expensive.

This chapter is about that system: why it was created; what needs it was supposed to serve; what compromises were incorporated in the original plan; how it initially operated; what changes subsequently affected that operation; whom these changes have benefited; and what this suggests about parties, the electorate, and the political system in general.

In addressing these questions, I have organized the chapter into four sections. The first discusses the creation of the presidential election process. It explores the motives and intentions of the delegates at Philadelphia and describes the procedures for selecting the president within the context of the constitutional and political issues of the day.

The second section examines the development of nominating systems. It explores the three principal methods that have been used—partisan congressional caucuses, brokered national conventions, and state primaries and caucuses—and describes the political forces that helped to shape them and, in the case of the first two modes, destroyed them.

The third section discusses presidential elections. It focuses on the most controversial of those decided by the House of Representatives (1800 and 1824), influenced by Congress (1876), unreflective of popular choice (1888) or in which a relatively small number of votes could have changed the outcome (1960, 1968, and 1976). In doing so, the section highlights the evolution of the electoral college.

The final section of the chapter examines the current system. It describes its geographic and demographic bases, whom it benefits, and whom it hurts. The section also discusses the system's major party orientation and its effects on third party candidacies.

## THE CREATION OF THE ELECTORAL COLLEGE

Among the many issues facing the delegates at the Constitutional Convention of 1787 in Philadelphia, the selection of the president was one of the toughest. Seven times during the course of the convention the method for choosing the executive was altered.

The framers' difficulty in designing electoral provisions for the president stemmed from the need to guarantee the institution's independence and, at the same time, create a technically sound, politically effective mechanism that would be consistent with a republican form of government. They were sympathetic with a government based on consent but not with direct democracy. They wanted a system that would choose the most qualified person but not necessarily the most popular. There seemed to be no precise model to follow.

Three methods had been proposed. The Virginia plan, a series of resolutions designed by James Madison and introduced by Governor Edmund Randolph of Virginia, provided for legislative selection. Eight states chose their governors in this fashion at the time. Having Congress choose the president would be practical and politically expedient. Moreover, members of Congress could have been expected to exercise a considered judgment. Exercising a rational judgment was important to the delegates at Philadelphia, since many of them did not consider the average citizen capable of making a reasoned, unemotional choice.

The difficulty with legislative selection was the threat it posed to the institution of the presidency. How could the executive's independence be preserved if his election hinged on his popularity with Congress and his reelection on the legislature's appraisal of his performance in office? Only if the president were to serve a long term and not be eligible for reelection, it was thought, could his independence be protected so long as Congress was the electoral body. But ineligibility also posed problems, as it provided little incentive for the president to perform well and denied the country the possibility of reelecting a person whose experience and success in office might make him better qualified than anyone else. Reflecting on these concerns, Gouverneur Morris urged the removal of the ineligibility clause on the grounds that "it . . . intended to destroy the great motive to good behavior, the hope of being rewarded by a re-appointment."[1] A majority of the states agreed. Once the ineligibility clause was deleted, however, the terms of office had to be shortened to prevent what the framers feared might become almost indefinite tenure. With a shorter term of office and permanent reeligibility, legislative selection was not nearly as desirable, since it could make the president beholden to the legislature.

Popular election was another alternative, although one that did not generate a great deal of enthusiasm. It was twice rejected in the convention by overwhelming votes. Most of the delegates felt that a direct vote by the people was neither desirable nor feasible.[2] Lacking confidence in the public's ability to choose the best-qualified candidate, many delegates also believed that the size of the country and the poor state of its communications and transportation precluded a national campaign and election. The geographic expanse was simply too large to permit proper supervision and control of the election. Sectional distrust and rivalry also contributed to the problem.

A third alternative was some type of indirect election in which popular sentiment could be expressed but would not dictate the selection. James Wilson first proposed this idea after he failed to generate support for a direct popular vote. Luther Martin, Gouverneur Morris, and Alexander Hamilton also suggested indirect popular election through intermediaries. However, it was not until the debate over legislative selection divided and eventually deadlocked the delegates that election by electors was seriously considered. The Committee on Unfinished Business proposed the electoral college compromise on September 4, and it was accepted after a short debate. Viewed as a safe, workable solution to the selection problem, it was deemed consistent with the constitutional and political features of the new government. Popular election was not precluded, but neither was it encouraged by the compromise.

According to the proposal, presidential electors were to be chosen by the states in a manner designated by their legislatures. To ensure their independence, the electors could not simultaneously hold a federal government position. The number of electors was to equal the number of senators and representatives from each state. At a designated time the electors would vote and send the results to Congress, where they would be announced to a joint session by the president of the Senate—

the vice-president. The only limitation on the voting was that the electors could not cast *both* their ballots for inhabitants of their own states.[3]

Under the original plan, the person who received a majority of votes cast by the electoral college would be elected president, and the one with the second highest total would be vice-president. There was no separate ballot for each office. In the event that no one received a majority, the House of Representatives would choose from among the five candidates with the most electoral votes, with each state delegation casting one vote. If two or more individuals were tied for second, then the Senate would select the vice-president from among them. Both of these provisions were subsequently modified by the Twelfth Amendment to the Constitution.

The electoral system was a dual compromise. Allowing state legislatures to establish the procedures for choosing electors was a concession to the proponents of a federal system; having the House of Representatives decide if there was no electoral college majority, was designed to please those who favored a stronger national government. Designating the number of electors to be equal to a state's congressional delegation gave the larger states an advantage in the initial voting for president; balloting by states in the House if the electoral college was not decisive benefited the smaller states.

The large-small state compromise was critical to the acceptance of the electoral college plan. It was argued during the convention debates that in practice the large states would nominate the candidates for president and the small states would exercise the final choice.[4] So great were sectional rivalry and distrust at the time, the prospect of a majority of the college's agreeing on anyone other than George Washington seemed remote.

## THE DEVELOPMENT OF NOMINATING SYSTEMS

While the Constitution prescribed a system for electing a president, it made no reference to the nomination of candidates. Political parties had not emerged prior to the Constitutional Convention. Factions existed, and the framers of the Constitution were concerned about them, but the development of a party system was not anticipated. Rather, it was assumed that electors whose interests were not tied to the national government would make an independent judgment in choosing the best possible person as president.

In the first two elections the system worked as intended. George Washington was the unanimous choice of the electors. There was, however, no consensus on who the vice-president should be. The eventual winner, John Adams, benefited from some discussion and informal lobbying by prominent individuals prior to the vote.[5]

A more organized effort to agree on candidates for the presidency and vice-presidency was undertaken four years later. Partisan alliances were beginning to develop in Congress. Members of the two principal groups, the Federalists and the Anti-Federalists, met separately to recommend individuals. The Federalists chose Vice-President Adams; the Anti-Federalists picked Governor George Clinton of New York.

With political parties evolving during the 1790s, the selection of the electors quickly became a partisan contest. In 1792 and 1796 a majority of the state legislatures chose them directly. Thus, the political group that controlled the legislature also controlled the selection. Appointed for their political views, electors were expected to exercise a partisan judgment. When in 1796 a Pennsylvania elector did not, he was accused of faithless behavior. Wrote one critic in a Philadelphia newspaper: "What, do I chuse Samuel Miles to determine for me whether John Adams or Thomas Jefferson shall be President? No! I chuse him to act, not to think."[6]

Washington's decision not to serve a third term forced Federalist and Anti-Federalist members of Congress to recommend the candidates in 1796. Meeting separately, party leaders agreed among themselves on the tickets. The Federalists urged their electors to vote for John Adams and Thomas Pinckney, while the Anti-Federalists (or Republicans, as they began to be called) suggested Thomas Jefferson and Aaron Burr.

Since it was not possible to indicate the presidential and vice-presidential choices on the ballot, Federalist electors, primarily from New England, decided to withhold votes from Pinckney (of South Carolina) to make certain that he did not receive the same number as Adams (of Massachusetts). This strategy enabled Jefferson to finish ahead of Pinckney with 68 votes compared with the latter's 59, but behind Adams, who had 71. Four years of partisan differences followed between a president who, though he disclaimed a political affiliation, clearly favored the Federalists in appointments, ideology, and policy, and a vice-president who was the acknowledged leader of the opposition party.

Beginning in 1800, partisan caucuses composed of members of Congress met for the purpose of recommending their party's nominees. The Republicans continued to choose candidates in this manner until 1824; the Federalists did so only until 1808. In the final two presidential elections in which the Federalists ran candidates, 1812 and 1816, top party leaders, meeting in secret, decided on the nominees.[7]

"King caucus" violated the spirit of the Constitution. It effectively provided for Congress to pick the nominees. After the decline of the Federalists, the nominees were, in fact, assured of victory—a product of the dominance of the Jeffersonian Republican party as well as the success of the caucus in obtaining support for its candidates.

There was opposition within the caucuses. In 1808, Madison prevailed over James Monroe and George Clinton. In 1816, Monroe overcame a strong challenge from William Crawford. In both cases, however, the electors united behind the successful nominee. In 1820, they did not. Disparate elements within the party selected their own candidates.

Although the caucus was the principal mode of candidate selection during the first part of the nineteenth century, it was never formally institutionalized as a nominating body. How meetings were called, by whom, and when varied from election to election. So did attendance. A sizable number of representatives chose not to participate at all. Some stayed away on principle; others did so because of the choices they would have to make. In 1816 less than half of the Republican members of Congress were at their party's caucus. In 1820 only 20 percent attended, and the caucus had to adjourn without formally supporting President Monroe and Vice-President Daniel D. Tompkins for reelection. In 1824 almost three-fourths of the members boycotted the session.

The 1824 caucus did nominate candidates. But with representatives from only four states constituting two-thirds of those attending, the nominee, William Crawford, failed to receive unified party support. Other candidates were nominated by state legislatures and conventions, and the electoral vote was divided. Since no candidate obtained a majority, the House of Representatives had to make the final decision. John Quincy Adams was selected on the first ballot. He received the votes of 13 of the 24 state delegations.

The caucus was never resumed. In the end it fell victim to the decline of one of the major parties, the decentralization of political power, and Andrew Jackson's stern opposition. The Federalists had collapsed as a viable political force. As the Republican party grew from being the majority party to the only one, factions developed within it, the two principal ones being the National Republicans and the Democratic-Republicans. In the absence of a strong opposition there was little to hold these factions together. By 1830 they had split into two separate groups, one supporting and one opposing President Jackson.

Political leadership was changing as well. A relatively small group of individuals had dominated national politics for the first three decades after the 1787 Constitution. Their common experience in the war, the Constitutional Convention, and the early government produced personal contacts, political influence, and public respect that contributed to their ability to agree on candidates and to generate public support for them.[8]

The framers' successors had neither the tradition nor the national orientation in which to cast their presidential votes. Most owed their prominence and political clout to state and regional areas. Their loyalties reflected these bases of support.

The growth of party organizations at the state and local level affected the nomination system. In 1820 and 1824 it produced a decentralized mode of selection. State legislatures, caucuses, and conventions nominated their own candidates. Support was also mobilized on regional levels.

Whereas the congressional caucus had become unrepresentative, state-based nominations suffered from precisely the opposite problem. They were too representative of sectional interests and produced too many candidates. Unifying diverse elements behind a national ticket proved extremely difficult, although Jackson was successful in 1824 and again in 1828. Nonetheless, a system that was more broadly based than the old caucus and that could provide a decisive and mobilizing mechanism was needed. National nominating conventions filled the void.

The first such convention was held in 1831 by the Anti-Masons. A small but relatively active third party, it had virtually no congressional representation. Unable to utilize a caucus, the party turned instead to a general meeting, which was held in a saloon in Baltimore, with 116 delegates from thirteen states attending. These delegates decided on the nominees as well as on an address to the people that contained the party's position on the dominant issues of the day.

Three months later a second convention was held in the same saloon by opponents of President Jackson. The National Republicans (or Whigs, as they later became known) also nominated candidates and agreed on an address critical of the administration.

The following year the Democratic-Republicans (or Democrats, as they were later called) also met in Baltimore. The impetus for their convention was Jackson's desire to demonstrate popular support for his presidency as well as to ensure the selection of Martin Van Buren as his running mate. In 1836, Jackson resorted to another convention—this time to handpick Van Buren as his successor.

The Whigs did not hold a convention in 1836. Believing that they would have more success in the House of Representatives than in the nation as a whole, they ran three regional candidates, nominated by the states, who competed against Van Buren in areas of their strength. The plan, however, failed to deny Van Buren an electoral majority. He ended up with 170 votes compared with a total of 124 for the other principal contenders.

Thereafter, the Democrats and their opponents, first the Whigs and then their Republican successors, held nominating conventions to select their candidates. The early conventions were informal and rowdy by contemporary standards, but they also set the precedents for later meetings.

The delegates decided on the procedures for conducting the convention, policy statements (addresses to the people), and the nominees. Rules for apportioning the delegates were established before the meetings were held. Generally speaking, states were accorded as many delegates as their congressional representation merited, regardless of the number of actual participants. The way in which the delegates were chosen, however, was left up to the states. Local and state conventions, caucuses, or even committees chose the delegates.

Public participation was minimal. Even the party's rank and file had a small role. It was the party leaders who designated the delegates and made the deals. In time it became clear that successful candidates owed their selection to the heads of the powerful state organizations and not to their own political prominence and organizational support. The price they had to pay, however, when calculated in terms of patronage and other types of political payoffs, was often quite high.

Nineteenth-century conventions served a number of purposes. They provided a forum for party leaders, particularly at the state level. They constituted a mechanism by which agreements could be negotiated and support mobilized. By brokering interests, conventions helped unite the disparate elements within the party, thereby converting an organization of state parties into a national coalition for the purpose of conducting a presidential campaign.

Much of the bartering was conducted behind closed doors. Actions on the convention floor often had little to do with the wheeling and dealing that occurred in the smaller "smoke-filled" rooms. Since there was little public preconvention activity, many ballots were often necessary before the required number, usually two-thirds of the delegates, was reached.

The nominating system buttressed the position of individual state party leaders, but it did so at the expense of rank-and-file participation. The influence of the state leaders depended on their ability to deliver votes, which in turn required that the delegates not exercise an independent judgment. To guarantee their loyalty, the bosses controlled their selection.

Demands for reform began to be heard at the beginning of the twentieth century. The Progressive movement, led by Robert La Follette of Wisconsin and Hiram Johnson of California, desired to break the power of state bosses and their machines through the direct election of convention delegates or, alternatively, through the expression of a popular choice by the electorate.

Florida became the first state to provide its political parties with such an option. In 1904 the Democrats took advantage of it and held a statewide vote for convention delegates. One year later, Wisconsin enacted a law for the direct election of delegates to nominating conventions. Others followed suit. By 1912, fifteen states provided for some type of primary election. Oregon was the first to permit a preference vote for the candidates themselves.

The year 1912 was also the first in which a candidate sought to use primaries as a way to obtain the nomination. With almost 42 percent of the Republican delegates selected in primaries, former President Theodore Roosevelt challenged incumbent William Howard Taft. Roosevelt

TABLE 1–1

**Number of Presidential Primaries and Percentage of Convention Delegates from Primary States, by Party, Since 1912[a]**

| | Democratic | | Republican | |
| --- | --- | --- | --- | --- |
| Year | Number of Primaries | Percentage of Delegates | Number of Primaries | Percentage of Delegates |
| 1912 | 12 | 32.9% | 13 | 41.7% |
| 1916 | 20 | 53.5 | 20 | 58.9 |
| 1920 | 16 | 44.6 | 20 | 57.8 |
| 1924 | 14 | 35.5 | 17 | 45.3 |
| 1928 | 17 | 42.2 | 16 | 44.9 |
| 1932 | 16 | 40.0 | 14 | 37.7 |
| 1936 | 14 | 36.5 | 12 | 37.5 |
| 1940 | 13 | 35.8 | 13 | 38.8 |
| 1944 | 14 | 36.7 | 13 | 38.7 |
| 1948 | 14 | 36.3 | 12 | 36.0 |
| 1952 | 15 | 38.7 | 13 | 39.0 |
| 1956 | 19 | 42.7 | 19 | 44.8 |
| 1960 | 16 | 38.3 | 15 | 38.6 |
| 1964 | 17 | 45.7 | 17 | 45.6 |
| 1968 | 17 | 37.5 | 16 | 34.3 |
| 1972 | 23 | 60.5 | 22 | 52.7 |
| 1976 | 30 | 72.6 | 28 | 67.9 |
| 1980 | 31 | 71.4 | 34 | 76.0 |
| 1984 | 25 | 54.0 | 30[b] | 66.0 |
| 1988 | 37 | 66.6 | 38 | 76.9 |

[a] Includes states holding nonbinding presidential preference primaries except for 1988.

[b] Five of the Republican primaries scheduled for 1984 were actually not held.

*Sources:* 1912–64, F. Christopher Arterton, "Campaign Organizations Confused the Media Political Environment," in *Race for the Presidency,* ed. James David Barber (Englewood Cliffs, N.J.: Prentice Hall, 1978), p. 7; 1968–80, David E. Price, *Bringing Back the Parties* (Washington, D.C.: Congressional Quarterly, 1984), p. 209; 1984, *Congressional Quarterly Weekly Report,* June 16, 1984, p. 1443; 1988, *Congressional Quarterly Weekly Report,* July 9, 1988, p. 1892.

won nine primaries to Taft's one, yet lost the nomination. (See Table 1–1.) Taft's support among regular party leaders who delivered their delegations and controlled the convention was sufficient to retain the nomination. He received one-third of his support from southern delegations, although the Republican party had won only 7 percent of the southern vote in the previous election.

Partially in reaction to the unrepresentative, "boss-dominated" convention of 1912, additional states adopted primaries. By 1916, more than half of them held a Republican or Democratic contest. Although a majority of the delegates in that year were chosen by some type of primary, many of them were not bound to specific candidates. As a consequence, the primary vote did not control the outcome of the conventions.

The movement toward popular participation was short-lived, however. Following World War I the number of primaries declined. State party leaders, who saw these elections as a threat to their own influence, argued against them on three grounds: they were expensive; they did not attract many voters; and major candidates tended to avoid them. Moreover, primaries frequently encouraged factionalism, thereby weakening the party's organizational structure.

In response to this criticism the reformers, who supported primaries, could not claim that their principal goal—rank-and-file control over the party's nominees—had been achieved. Public involvement was disappointing. Primaries rarely attracted more than 50 percent of those who voted in the general election, and usually much less. The minority party, in particular, suffered from low turnout. In some states rank-and-file influence was further diluted by the participation of independents.

As a consequence of these factors, some states that had enacted new primary laws reverted to their former method of selection. Others made the primaries advisory rather than mandatory. Fewer delegates were selected in them. By 1936 only fourteen states held Democratic primaries, and twelve held Republican ones. Less than 40 percent of the delegates to each convention that year were chosen in this manner. For the next twenty years the number of primaries and the percentage of delegates hovered around this level.

Theodore Roosevelt's failure in 1912 and the decline in primaries thereafter made them at best an auxiliary route to the nomination. While some presidential aspirants became embroiled in them, none who depended on them won. In 1920 a spirited contest between three Republicans (General Leonard Wood, Governor Frank Lowden of Illinois, and Senator Hiram Johnson) failed to produce a convention majority and resulted in party leaders' choosing Warren Harding as the standard-bearer. Similarly, in 1952, Senator Estes Kefauver entered thirteen of seventeen presidential primaries, won twelve of them, became the most popular Democratic contender, but failed to win his party's nomination. The reason Kefauver could not parlay his primary victories into a convention victory was that a majority of the delegates were not selected in this manner. Of those who were, many were chosen separately from the presidential preference vote. Kefauver did not contest these separate delegate elections. As a consequence, he obtained only 50 percent of the delegates in states where he actually won the presidential preference vote. Moreover, the fact that most of his wins occurred against little or no opposition undercut Kefauver's claim to being the strongest, most electable Democrat. He had avoided primaries in four states where he feared that he might either lose or do poorly.

Not only were primaries not considered to be an essential road to the nomination, but running in too many of them was interpreted as a sign of weakness, not strength. It indicated a lack of national recognition and/or a failure to obtain the support of party leaders. As a consequence, leading candidates tended to choose their primaries carefully, and the primaries, in turn, tended to reinforce the position of the leading candidates.

Those who did enter primaries did so mainly to test their popularity rather than to win convention votes. Dwight D. Eisenhower in 1952, John F. Kennedy in 1960, and Richard M. Nixon in 1968 had to demonstrate that being a general, a Catholic, or a once-defeated presidential candidate would not be fatal to their chances. In other words, they needed to prove they could win the general election.

With the possible exception of John Kennedy's victories in West Virginia and Wisconsin, primaries were neither crucial nor decisive for winning the nomination until the 1970s. When there was a provisional consensus within the party, primaries helped confirm it; when there was not, primaries were not able to produce it.[9] In short, they had little to do with whether the party was unified or divided at the time of the convention.

Primary results tended to be self-fulfilling in the sense that they confirmed the front-runner's status. Between 1936 and 1968, the pre-convention leader, the candidate who was ahead in the Gallup Poll before the first primary, won the nomination seventeen out of nineteen times. The only exceptions were Thomas E. Dewey in 1940, who was defeated by Wendell Willkie, and Kefauver in 1952, who lost to Adlai Stevenson. Willkie, however, had become the leader in public opinion by the time the Republican convention met. Even when leading candidates lost a primary, they had time to recoup. Dewey and Stevenson, defeated in early primaries in 1948 and 1956, respectively, went on to reestablish their credibility as front-runners by winning later primaries.

This situation changed dramatically after 1968. Largely as a consequence of the tumultuous Democratic convention of that year, whose nominee and platform were allegedly dictated by party "bosses," demands for a larger voice for the party's rank and file increased. In reaction to these demands, the Democratic party began to look into the matter of delegate selection. It enacted a series of reforms designed to ensure broader representation at the convention. To avoid challenges to their delegations, a number of states that had used caucus and convention systems changed to primaries. As Table 1–1 indicates, the number of primaries began to increase as did the percentage of convention delegates chosen from them.

New finance laws, which provided for government subsidies of pre-convention campaigning, and increased media coverage, particularly by television, also added to the incentive to enter primaries. By 1972 both became important. In that year, Senator Edmund Muskie, the leading Democratic contender at the beginning of the process, was forced to withdraw after doing poorly in the early contests, while in 1976, President Gerald Ford came close to being the first incumbent president since Chester A. Arthur in 1884 to be denied his party's nomination. In 1980, President Jimmy Carter was also challenged for renomination. Incumbent-president primaries have changed the quest for the nomination. Today, they are used to build popularity rather than simply reflect it. Challengers can no longer hope to succeed without entering them; incumbents can no longer ignore them.

The impact of primaries has been significant. They have affected the strategies and tactics of the candidates. They have influenced the composition and behavior of the delegates. They have changed the decision-making character of the national conventions. They have shifted power within the party. They have enlarged the selection zone of potential nominees. They have made governing more difficult. Each of these changes will be discussed in the chapters that follow.

## THE EVOLUTION OF THE GENERAL ELECTION

The general election has changed as well. The electoral college no longer operates as it was designed. It now has a partisan coloration. There is greater public participation, although it is still not direct. The system bears a resemblance to its past. While it has become more democratic, it is still not without its biases.

The electoral college system was one of the few innovative features of the Constitution. It had no immediate precedent, although it bore some relationship to the way the state of Maryland selected its senators. In essence, it was invented by the framers, not synthesized from British and American experience. And it is one aspect of the system that has rarely worked as intended.

Initially, the method by which the states chose their electors varied. Some provided for direct election in a statewide vote. Others had the legislatures do the choosing. Two states used a combination of popular and legislative selection.

As political parties emerged around the turn of the nineteenth century, state legislatures maneuvered the selection process to benefit the party in power. This maneuvering resulted in the election of more cohesive groups of electors who shared similar partisan views. Gradually, the trend evolved into a winner-take-all system, with electors chosen on a statewide basis by popular vote. South Carolina was the last state to move to popular selection. It did so after the Civil War.

The development of the party system changed the character of the electoral college. Only in the first two elections, when Washington was the unanimous choice, did the electors exercise a nonpartisan and presumably independent judgment. Within ten years from the time the federal government began to operate, they quickly became the captives of their party and were expected to vote for its candidates. The outcome of the election of 1800 vividly illustrates this new pattern of partisan voting.

The Federalist party supported President John Adams of Massachusetts and Charles C. Pinckney of South Carolina. The Republicans, who had emerged to oppose the Federalists' policies, backed Thomas Jefferson of Virginia and Aaron Burr of New York. The Republican candidates won, but, unexpectedly, Jefferson and Burr received the same number of votes. All electors who had cast ballots for Jefferson also cast them for Burr. Since it was not possible to differentiate the candidates for the presidency and vice-presidency on the ballot, the results had to be considered a tie, though Jefferson was clearly his party's choice for president. Under the terms of the Constitution, the House of Representatives, voting by state, had to choose the winner.

On February 11, 1801, after the results of the electoral college vote were announced by the vice-president—who happened to be Jefferson—the House convened to resolve the dilemma. It was a Federalist-controlled House. Since the winners of the 1800 election were not to take office until March 4, 1801, a "lame-duck" Congress would have to choose the next president.[10] A majority of Federalists supported Burr, whom they regarded as the more pragmatic politician. Jefferson, on the other hand, was perceived as a dangerous, uncompromising radical by many Federalists. Alexander Hamilton, however, was outspoken in his opposition to Burr, a political rival from New York, whom Hamilton regarded as "the most unfit man in the United States for the office of President."[11]

On the first ballot taken on February 11, Burr received a majority of the total votes, but Jefferson won the support of more state delegations.[12] Eight states voted for Jefferson, six backed Burr, and two were evenly divided. This left Jefferson one short of the needed majority. The House took nineteen ballots on its first day of deliberations, and a total of thirty-six before it finally elected Jefferson. Had Burr promised to be a Federalist president, it is conceivable that he would have won.

The first amendment to reform voting procedures in the electoral college was enacted by the new Congress, controlled by Jefferson's party, in 1803. It was accepted by three-fourths of the states in 1804. This amendment to the Constitution—the twelfth—provided for separate voting for president and vice-president. It also refined the selection procedures in the event that the president and/or vice-president did not receive a majority of the electoral vote. The House of Representatives, still voting by states, was to choose from among the three presidential candidates with the most electoral votes, and the Senate, voting by individuals, was to choose from the top two vice-presidential candidates. If the House could not make a decision by March 4, the amendment provided for the new vice-president to assume the presidency until such time as the House could render a decision.

The next nondecisive presidential vote did not occur until 1824. That year, four people received electoral votes for president: Andrew Jackson (99 votes), John Quincy Adams (84), William Crawford (41), and Henry Clay (37). According to the Twelfth Amendment, the House of Representatives had to decide from among the top three, since none had a majority. Eliminated from the contest was Henry Clay, who happened to be Speaker of the House. Clay threw his support to Adams, who won. It was alleged that he did so in exchange for appointment as secretary of state, a charge that Clay vigorously denied. After Adams became president, however, he did appoint Clay to that position.

Jackson was the winner of the popular vote. In the eighteen states that chose electors by popular vote that year (there were twenty-four states in the Union at the time), he received 192,933 votes compared with 115,696 for Adams, 47,136 for Clay, and 46,979 for Crawford. Adams, however, had the backing of more state delegations. He enjoyed the support of the six New England states (he was from Massachusetts), and with Clay's help, the representatives of six other states backed his candidacy. The votes of thirteen states, however, were needed for a majority. New York seemed to be the pivotal state and Stephen Van Rensselaer, a Revolutionary War general, the swing representative. On the morning of the vote, Speaker Clay and Representative Daniel Webster tried to persuade Van Rensselaer to vote for Adams. It was said that they were unsuccessful.[13] When the voting began, Van Rensselaer bowed his head as if in prayer. On the floor he saw a piece of paper with "Adams" written on it. Interpreting this as a sign from the Almighty, he dropped the paper in the box. New York went for Adams by one vote, providing him with a bare majority of states.[14]

Jackson, outraged at the turn of events, urged the abolition of the electoral college. His claim of a popular mandate, however, was open to question. The most populous state at the time, New York, did not permit its electorate to participate in the selection of electors. Rather, the New York legislature made the decision. Moreover, in three of the states in which Jackson won the electoral vote but lost in the House of Representatives, he had fewer popular votes than Adams. He captured the majority of electoral votes in two of these states because the electors were chosen on a district rather than statewide basis.[15]

Opposition to the system mounted, however, and a gradual democratization of the process occurred. More states began to elect their electors directly by popular vote. In 1800, ten of the fifteen used legislative selection. By 1832, only South Carolina retained this practice.

There was also a trend toward statewide election of an *entire* slate of electors. Those states that had chosen their electors within districts converted to a winner-take-all system in order to maximize their voting power in the electoral college. This change, in turn, created the possibility that there could be a disparity between the popular and electoral vote. A candidate could be elected by winning the popular vote in the big states by small margins and losing the smaller states by large margins.

The next disputed election occurred in 1876. Democrat Samuel J. Tilden received the most votes. He had 250,000 more popular votes and 19 more electoral votes than his Republican rival, Rutherford B. Hayes. Nonetheless, Tilden was one vote short of a majority in the electoral college. Twenty electoral votes were in dispute. Dual election returns were received from Florida (4), Louisiana (8), and South Carolina (7). Charges of fraud and voting irregularities were made by both parties. The Republicans, who controlled the three state legislatures, contended that Democrats had forcibly prevented newly freed blacks from voting. The Democrats, on the other hand, alleged that many nonresidents and nonregistered people had participated. The other disputed electoral vote occurred in the state of Oregon. One Republican elector was challenged on the grounds that he held another federal position (postmaster) at the time he was chosen, and thus was ineligible to be an elector.

Three days before the electoral college vote was to be officially counted, Congress established a commission to examine and try to resolve the dispute. The electoral commission was to consist of fifteen members: ten from Congress (five Republicans and five Democrats) and five from the Supreme Court. Four of the Supreme Court justices were designated by the act (two Republicans and two Democrats), and they were to choose a fifth justice. David Davis, a political independent, was expected to be selected, but on the day the commission was created, Davis was appointed by the Illinois legislature to the United States Senate. The Supreme Court justices then picked Joseph Bradley, an independent Republican. Bradley sided with his party on every issue. By a strictly partisan vote, the commission validated all the Republican electors, thereby giving Hayes a one-vote margin of victory.[16]

The only other election in which the winner of the popular vote was beaten in the electoral college occurred in 1888. Democrat Grover Cleveland had a plurality of 95,096 popular votes but only 168 electoral votes compared with 233 for the Republican, Benjamin Harrison. Cleveland's loss of Indiana by about 3,000 votes and New York by about 15,000 led to his defeat.

While all other leaders in the popular vote have won a majority of electoral votes, shifts of just a few thousand popular votes in a few states could have altered the results. In 1860, a shift of 25,000 in New York from Abraham Lincoln to Stephen A. Douglas would have denied Lincoln a majority in the electoral college. A change of less than 30,000 in three states in 1892 would have given Harrison another victory over Cleveland. In 1916, Charles Evans Hughes needed only 3,807 more votes in California to have beaten Woodrow Wilson. Similarly, Thomas E. Dewey could have denied Harry S. Truman a majority in the electoral college with 12,487 more California votes in 1948. In 1960, a change of less than 9,000 in Illinois and Missouri would have meant that John F. Kennedy lacked an electoral college majority. In 1968, a shift of only 55,000 votes from Richard M. Nixon to Hubert H. Humphrey in three states (New Jersey, Missouri, and New Hampshire) would have thrown the election into the House—a House controlled by Democrats. In 1976, a shift of only 3,687 in Hawaii and 5,559 in Ohio would have cost Jimmy Carter the election.[17]

Not only could the results of these elections have been affected by very small voter shifts in a few states, but in 1948, 1960, and 1968 there was the further possibility that the electoral college itself would not be able to choose a winner. In each of these elections, third party candidates or independent electoral slates threatened to secure enough votes to prevent either of the major candidates from obtaining a majority. In 1948, Henry Wallace (Progressive party) and Strom Thurmond (States' Rights party) received almost 5 percent of the total popular vote, and Thurmond won 39 electoral votes. In 1960, fourteen unpledged electors were chosen in Alabama and Mississippi.[18] In 1968, Governor George Wallace of Alabama, running on the American Independent party ticket, received almost 10 million popular votes (13.5 percent of the total) and 46 electoral votes. It was clear that close competition between the major parties, combined with a strong third party movement, provided the electoral college with its most difficult test.

## THE POLITICS OF ELECTORAL COLLEGE VOTING

The electoral college is not neutral. No system of election can be. The way votes are aggregated does make a difference. It benefits some of the electorate and adversely affects others.

The electoral college usually works to the advantage of the majority; more often than not, it has exaggerated the margin of the popular vote leader. Richard Nixon's 301 electoral votes in 1968 provided him with 56 percent of the college; his popular vote percentage was only 43.4 percent. Jimmy Carter's election in 1976 resulted in a smaller disparity. He won 50.1 percent of the popular vote and 55 percent of the electoral vote. In 1980, Ronald Reagan received 51 percent of the popular vote but a whopping 91 percent of the electoral vote.

Although the electoral college has usually expanded the margin of the popular vote winner, it has also from time to time led to the defeat of the candidate with the most popular votes. On three occasions— 1824, 1876, and 1888—the plurality winner was a loser in the electoral college. Even though such an electoral loss would be less likely today because the parties are competitive in more states, it is still possible.

The electoral college contains a number of built-in biases. The most significant of these is the winner-take-all voting that has developed. The presidential and vice-presidential candidates who receive a plurality of the popular vote within the state get in almost every instance all its electoral votes. Naturally this arrangement benefits the largest states, not only because of the number of electoral votes they cast but because the votes are almost always cast in a bloc. Moreover, the advantage that the citizens of the largest states receive increases in proportion to their population. (See Figure 1–1 for the relative advantage large populations

## FIGURE 1–1
### State Size According to Population: The 1992 Electoral Vote[a]

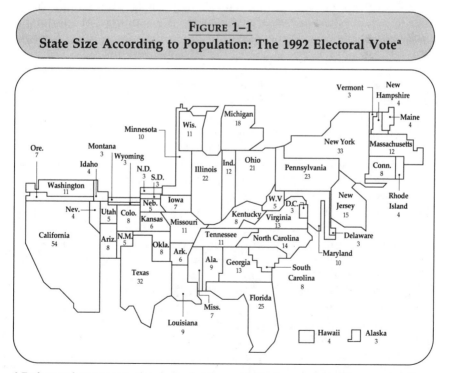

[a] Each state has a vote in the electoral college equal to the number of its representatives plus two.

*Source: New York Times,* December 28, 1990, p. A9.

confer upon the states.) This large-state advantage is why a greater share of campaign time and resources is spent in these states.

By giving an edge to the larger and more competitive states, the electoral college also works to benefit groups that are geographically concentrated within those states and have cohesive voting patterns. Those who live in the central cities and suburbs have a particular advantage. Jews, Hispanics, and urban African-Americans fall into this category. However, the African-American population in general does not because many blacks live in rural and smaller states, particularly in the South. Blue-collar workers and rural dwellers are also disadvantaged.[19]

There is a slight offsetting gain for the very smallest states. That each receives a minimum of three electoral votes regardless of size increases the voting power of sparsely populated states. For example, if Wyoming's population of approximately 456,000 were divided by its three electoral votes, there would be one elector for every 152,000 people. Dividing California's population of 29,839,000 by the 54 electoral votes yields one elector for every 552,574 people.[20]

Additionally, the electoral college works to the benefit of the two major parties and to the detriment of the minor parties. The winner-take-all system within states, when combined with the need for a majority within the college, makes it difficult for third parties to accumulate enough votes to win an election. To have any effect, third party support must be geographically concentrated, as George Wallace's was in 1968 and Strom Thurmond's was in 1948, rather than evenly distributed across the country, as Henry Wallace's was in 1948.

Given the limitations on third parties, their realistic electoral objectives would seem to be to defeat one of the major contenders rather than to elect their own candidate. In 1912, Theodore Roosevelt's Bull Moose campaign split the Republican party, thereby aiding the candidate of the minority party, Woodrow Wilson. In more recent elections, third party and independent candidates have cost the major parties votes but do not appear to have changed the outcome of the elections. Truman's loss of Michigan and New York in 1948 apparently was a consequence of Henry Wallace's Progressive party candidacy, while George Wallace in 1968 probably denied Nixon 46 more electoral votes from the South. However, George Wallace's 11.4 percent of the Missouri vote and his 11.8 percent in Ohio probably hurt Humphrey more than Nixon and may explain the loss of these two states by the Democratic candidate. Ford's narrow victory in Iowa in 1976 (632,863 to 619,931) may be partially attributed to the 20,051 votes Eugene McCarthy received as an independent candidate, votes that very likely would have gone to Carter had McCarthy not run.

The impact on third parties is more than simply a question of numbers. It affects the psychology of voting for a candidate who has little chance of winning a majority of the electoral vote. In 1980, the Carter and Reagan campaigns appealed to voters sympathetic to John Anderson on precisely these grounds. They urged them not to waste their vote on a candidate who could not win. This "wasted vote" appeal undercut Anderson's ability to raise money and garner political support.

## SUMMARY

The quest for the presidency has been and continues to be influenced by the system designed in Philadelphia in 1787. The objectives of that system were to protect the independence of the institution, to ensure the selection of a well-qualified candidate, and to do so in a way that was politically expedient. It was intended to be consistent with the tenets of a republican form of government.

While many of the objectives are still the same, the system has changed significantly over the years. Of all the factors that have influenced these changes, none has been more important than the advent of political parties. This development created an additional first step in the process—the nomination, which has influenced the selection and behavior of the electors and has affected the operation and the beneficiaries of the electoral college itself.

The nomination process is necessary to the parties, whose principal interest is to get their leaders elected. At first, members of Congress, meeting in partisan caucuses, decided on the nominees. On the basis of common friendships and shared perspectives, they reached a consensus and then used their influence to mobilize support for it. In effect, the system provided for legislative selection of the president in violation of the letter and spirit of the Constitution.

The caucus method broke down with the weakening of the parties, the demise of the Federalists, and the factionalization of the Republicans. It was never restored. In its place developed a more decentralized mode of selection reflective of the increasing sectional composition of the parties.

The new nomination process, controlled by state leaders, operated within the framework of a brokered national convention. There was little rank-and-file participation. The wheeling and dealing were done for the party's electorate, not by them. Demands for greater public involvement eventually opened the system, thereby reducing the influence of state leaders and decreasing the dependence of candidates on them. Power eventually shifted from the political leaders to the candidates themselves, with the people making the final judgment.

Similar trends, rooted in the development of parties and the expansion of suffrage, affected the way in which the electors were selected and voted. Instead of being chosen on the basis of their qualifications, electors were selected on the basis of their politics; instead of being elected as individuals, entire slates of electors were chosen; instead of exercising independent judgment, the electors became partisan agents who were morally and politically obligated to support their party's choice. The predictable soon happened: bloc voting by electors in states.

The desire of the populace for greater participation also had an effect. It accelerated the movement to choose the electors directly by the people, which resulted in an increased likelihood of the electoral vote's reflecting, even exaggerating, the popular vote. Only three times in U.S. history was the plurality winner not elected. However, the shift of a very small number of votes in a few states could have altered the results of other elections, most recently in 1960, 1968, and 1976. This situation raises doubts about the adequacy of the system.

The equity of the electoral college itself has come into question. The way it works benefits the larger, more competitive states with the most electoral votes. Within those states, the groups that are better organized and more geographically concentrated seem to enjoy the greatest advantage. Their vote is maximized by the winner's taking all the state's electoral votes and the state's having a larger share of the total electoral college. Candidates keep this size factor in mind when planning and conducting their campaigns.

In summary, the electoral system has been decisive and efficient, but questions about its equity remain. It does not jeopardize the president's independence. In fact, it may do just the opposite; it may isolate the selection of president and vice-president too much from that of other officials for national office. It permits a partisan choice but recently has not contributed to the strength of the party inside or outside the government. It facilitates participation in the nomination process but has not substantially raised the level of public involvement in the general election. The winning candidate often obtains only a bare majority or even plurality of the voters, who, in recent elections, have constituted barely more than half the voting age population—hardly the mandate we might expect in a vibrant democratic society.

## NOTES

1. Gouverneur Morris, *Records of the Federal Convention*, ed. Max Farrand (New Haven: Yale University Press, 1921), 2:33.
2. The first proposal for direct election was introduced in a very timid fashion by James Wilson, delegate from Pennsylvania. James Madison's *Journal* describes Wilson's presentation as follows: "Mr. Wilson said he was almost unwilling to declare the mode which he wished to take place, being apprehensive that it might appear chimerical. He would say however at least that in theory he was for an election by the people; Experience, particularly in N. York & Massts, shewed that an election of the first magistrate by the

people at large, was both convenient & successful mode." Farrand, *Records of the Federal Convention*, 1:68.

3. So great was the sectional rivalry, so parochial the country, so limited the number of people with national reputations, that it was feared that electors would tend to vote primarily for those from their own states. To prevent the same states, particularly the largest ones, from exercising undue influence in the selection of both the president and vice-president, this provision was included. It remains in effect today.

4. George Mason declared, "Nineteen times out of twenty, the President would be chosen by the Senate." Farrand, *Records of the Federal Convention*, 2:500. The original proposal of the Committee on Unfinished Business was that the Senate should select the president. The delegates substituted the House of Representatives, fearing that the Senate was too powerful with its appointment and treaty-making powers. The principle of equal state representation was retained. Choosing the president is the only occasion on which the House votes by states.

5. Thomas R. Marshall, *Presidential Nominations in a Reform Age* (New York: Praeger, 1981), p. 19.

6. Quoted in Neal R. Peirce and Lawrence D. Longley, *The People's President* (New Haven, Conn.: Yale University Press, 1981), p. 36.

7. Marshall, *Presidential Nominations*, p. 20.

8. Ibid., p. 21.

9. Louis Maisel and Gerald J. Lieberman, "The Impact of Electoral Rules on Primary Elections: The Democratic Presidential Primaries in 1976," in *The Impact of the Electoral Process*, ed. Louis Maisel and Joseph Cooper (Beverly Hills, Calif.: Sage Publications, 1977), p. 68.

10. Until the passage of the Twentieth Amendment, which made January 3 the date when members of Congress took their oath of office and convened, every second session of Congress was a lame-duck session.

11. Quoted in Lucius Wilmerding, *The Electoral College* (New Brunswick, N.J.: Rutgers University Press, 1953), p. 32.

12. There were 106 members of the House (58 Federalists and 48 Republicans). On the first ballot, the vote of those present was for Burr, 53–51.

13. Peirce and Longley, *People's President*, p. 51.

14. Marquis James, *The Life of Andrew Jackson* (Indianapolis: Bobbs-Merrill, 1938), p. 439.

15. William R. Keech, "Background Paper," in *Winner Take All: Report of the Twentieth Century Fund Task Force on Reform of the Presidential Election Process* (New York: Holmes and Meier, 1978), p. 50.

16. The act that created the commission specified that its decision would be final unless overturned by both houses of Congress. The House of Representatives, controlled by the Democrats, opposed every one of the commission's findings. The Republican Senate, however, concurred. A Democratic filibuster in the Senate was averted by Hayes's promise of concessions to the South, including the withdrawal of federal troops. Tilden could have challenged the findings in court but chose not to do so.

17. Richard M. Scammon and Alice V. McGillivray, *American Votes 12* (Washington, D.C.: Congressional Quarterly, 1977), p. 15.

18. In Alabama, slates of electors ran against one another without the names of the presidential candidates appearing on the ballot. The Democratic slate included six unpledged electors and five loyalists. All were elected. The

unpledged electors voted for Senator Harry Byrd of Virginia, while the loyalists stayed with the Kennedy-Johnson ticket. In Mississippi, all eight Democratic electors voted for Byrd.

19. Lawrence D. Longley and James D. Dana, Jr., "New Empirical Estimates of
the Biases of the Electoral College for the 1980s," *Western Political Quarterly*
37 (March 1984): pp. 168–70.

20. There are two other, less obvious, biases in the electoral college. The distribution of electoral votes is calculated on the basis of the census, which
occurs every ten years. Thus, the college does not mirror population shifts
within this period. Nor does it take into account the number of people who
actually cast ballots. It is a state's population, not its turnout, that determines
the number of electoral votes it receives, over and above the automatic three.

## SELECTED READINGS

Abbot, David W., and James P. Levine. *Wrong Winner: The Coming Debacle in the
Electoral College.* New York: Praeger, 1991.

Best, Judith. *The Case against Direct Election of the President: A Defense of the Electoral
College.* Ithaca, N.Y.: Cornell University Press, 1975.

Bickel, Alexander M. *Reform and Continuity: The Electoral College, the Convention,
and the Party System.* New York: Harper & Row, 1971.

Chase, James S. *Emergence of the Presidential Nominating Convention, 1789–1832.*
Urbana, Ill.: University of Illinois Press, 1973.

Congressional Quarterly. *Presidential Elections Since 1789.* Washington, D.C.:
Congressional Quarterly, 1991.

Farrand, Max. *The Records of the Federal Convention of 1787.* Vol. 1–5. New Haven:
Yale University Press, 1911.

Longley, Lawrence D., and James D. Dana, Jr. "New Empirical Estimates of the
Biases of the Electoral College for the 1980s." *Western Political Quarterly* 37
(March 1984), 157–173.

Marshall, Thomas R. *Presidential Nominations in a Reform Age.* New York: Praeger,
1981.

Nelson, Michael. "Constitutional Aspects of the Elections," in Michael Nelson
(ed.) *The Elections of 1988.* Washington, D.C.: Congressional Quarterly, 1989,
181–209.

Peirce, Neal R., and Lawrence D. Longley. *The People's President.* New Haven:
Yale University Press, 1981.

Reichley, A. James. "The Electoral System," in A. James Reichley (ed.) *Elections
American Style.* Washington, D.C.: Brookings Institution, 1987, 1–26.

Roseboom, Eugene H. *A History of Presidential Elections.* New York: Macmillan,
1957.

Sundquist, James. *Constitutional Reform and Effective Government.* Washington,
D.C.: Brookings Institution, 1986.

———. Senate, Committee on the Judiciary. *The Electoral College and Direct Election.* Hearings, 95th Cong., 1st sess. Washington, D.C.: Government Printing
Office, 1977.

———. Senate, Committee on the Judiciary. *Hearings on Direct Popular Election
of the President and Vice-President of the United States.* 96th Cong., 1st sess.
Washington, D.C.: Government Printing Office, 1979.

# Chapter 2

# Campaign Finance

## INTRODUCTION

Running for president is very expensive. In 1984, a whopping $325 million was spent by major party candidates in their quest for the nomination and election. In 1988, the amount had escalated to $500 million! Of this, $233.5 million was spent on the preconvention nomination, $42.1 million on the conventions, and $208.3 million during the general election.[1] The phenomenal increase of 54 percent in just four years was triggered by spirited nomination contests in both parties, substantial funding for state and local party organizations, and the spiraling costs of campaigning.

The magnitude of these expenditures poses serious problems for presidential candidates, who must raise considerable sums during the preconvention struggle, monitor their expenses closely, make important allocation decisions, and conform to the intricacies of finance laws during both the nomination and general election campaigns. Moreover, such expenditures raise important issues for a democratic selection process. This chapter will explore some of those problems and issues.

The chapter is organized into five sections. The first details the costs of presidential campaigns, paying particular attention to the huge increase in expenditures since 1960. The next section looks briefly at the contributors, the size of their gifts, and the implications of large donations for a democratic selection process. What happens when the individual's right to give conflicts with government's desire to set limits? Who prevails? Legislative attempts to control spending and subsidize elections are discussed in the third section. The fourth section examines the impact of campaign finance laws on presidential campaigns, revenues, expenditures, and the party system. In the final section, the relationship between campaign spending and electoral success is explored. Can money buy elections? Have the big spenders been the big winners?

## THE COSTS OF CAMPAIGNING

Candidates have always spent money in their quest for the presidency, but it was not until they began to campaign personally across the country that these costs rose sharply. In 1860, Abraham Lincoln spent an estimated $100,000. One hundred years later, John Kennedy and Richard Nixon were each spending one hundred times that amount. In the twelve years following the 1960 general election, expenditures increased sixfold, an increase far outstripping the 41 percent inflation rate during that period. Table 2–1 lists the costs of the major party candidates in presidential elections from 1860 to 1972, the last general election in which campaign spending by major party candidates was not restricted to funds provided by the federal government. (Table 2–5 lists the maximum expenditures by the major party candidates from 1976 to the present.)

Prenomination costs have risen even more rapidly than those in the general election. Until the 1960s, large expenditures were the exception, not the rule, for gaining the party's nomination. General Leonard Wood spent an estimated $2 million in an unsuccessful quest to head the Republican ticket in 1920. The contest between General Dwight D. Eisenhower and Senator Robert A. Taft in 1952 cost about $5 million, a total that was not exceeded until 1964, when Nelson Rockefeller and Barry Goldwater together spent approximately twice that amount.

In recent elections prenomination expenditures have skyrocketed. The increasing number of primaries, caucuses, and candidates has been largely responsible for the rise. In the 1950s these preconvention contests were optional; since the 1970s they have been mandatory. Even incumbent presidents have to enter, and they spend money even when they are not challenged. In 1984, the Reagan campaign committee spent almost $28 million during the prenomination period, much of it on voter registration drives for the general election; in 1988, four candidates (Republicans George Bush, Robert Dole, and Marion Gordon ("Pat") Robertson, and Democrat Michael Dukakis) spent more than $22 million *each*!

To campaign simultaneously in several states requires considerable money to pay for professional services, large organizations, and direct and indirect voter contact. Identifying potential supporters, contacting them, and getting them to the polls are expensive. The need for tele-

TABLE 2–1

Costs of Presidential General Elections, Major Party Candidates,
1860–1972

| Year | Democrats | | Republicans | |
|------|-----------|--|-------------|--|
| 1860 | Stephen Douglas | $50,000 | Abraham Lincoln* | $100,000 |
| 1864 | George McClellan | 50,000 | Abraham Lincoln* | 125,000 |
| 1868 | Horatio Seymour | 75,000 | Ulysses Grant* | 150,000 |
| 1872 | Horace Greeley | 50,000 | Ulysses Grant* | 250,000 |
| 1876 | Samuel Tilden | 900,000 | Rutherford Hayes* | 950,000 |
| 1880 | Winfield Hancock | 335,000 | James Garfield* | 1,100,000 |
| 1884 | Grover Cleveland* | 1,400,000 | James Blaine | 1,300,000 |
| 1888 | Grover Cleveland | 855,000 | Benjamin Harrison* | 1,350,000 |
| 1892 | Grover Cleveland* | 2,350,000 | Benjamin Harrison | 1,700,000 |
| 1896 | William Jennings Bryan | 675,000 | William McKinley* | 3,350,000 |
| 1900 | William Jennings Bryan | 425,000 | William McKinley* | 3,000,000 |
| 1904 | Alton Parker | 700,000 | Theodore Roosevelt* | 2,096,000 |
| 1908 | William Jennings Bryan | 629,341 | William Taft* | 1,655,518 |
| 1912 | Woodrow Wilson* | 1,134,848 | William Taft | 1,071,549 |
| 1916 | Woodrow Wilson* | 2,284,590 | Charles Evans Hughes | 2,441,565 |
| 1920 | James Cox | 1,470,371 | Warren Harding* | 5,417,501 |
| 1924 | John Davis | 1,108,836 | Calvin Coolidge* | 4,020,478 |
| 1928 | Alfred Smith | 5,342,350 | Herbert Hoover* | 6,256,111 |
| 1932 | Franklin Roosevelt* | 2,245,975 | Herbert Hoover | 2,900,052 |
| 1936 | Franklin Roosevelt* | 5,194,741 | Alfred Landon | 8,892,972 |
| 1940 | Franklin Roosevelt* | 2,783,654 | Wendell Willkie | 3,451,310 |
| 1944 | Franklin Roosevelt* | 2,169,077 | Thomas Dewey | 2,828,652 |
| 1948 | Harry Truman* | 2,736,334 | Thomas Dewey | 2,127,296 |
| 1952 | Adlai Stevenson | 5,032,926 | Dwight Eisenhower* | 6,608,623 |
| 1956 | Adlai Stevenson | 5,106,651 | Dwight Eisenhower* | 7,778,702 |
| 1960 | John Kennedy* | 9,797,000 | Richard Nixon | 10,128,000 |
| 1964 | Lyndon Johnson* | 8,757,000 | Barry Goldwater | 16,026,000 |
| 1968† | Hubert Humphrey | 11,594,000 | Richard Nixon* | 25,402,000 |
| 1972 | George McGovern | 30,000,000 | Richard Nixon* | 61,400,000 |

* Indicates winner.

† George Wallace spent an estimated $7 million as the candidate of the American Independent party in 1968.

*Source:* Herbert E. Alexander, *Financing Politics* (Washington, D.C.: Congressional Quarterly, 1984), p. 7. Copyrighted material reprinted with permission of Congressional Quarterly Inc.

vision advertising and the price of purchasing it have increased significantly. As a consequence, preconvention expenditures since 1968 have actually exceeded those in the general elections. Table 2–2 lists the totals spent in the last seven prenomination campaigns.

The media, newspapers, radio, and particularly television, account for much of the spending. This was not always so. When campaigns were conducted in the press, expenses were relatively low. Electioneering, as carried on by a highly partisan press before the Civil War,

TABLE 2–2
## Costs of Presidential Nominations, 1964–1988 (in millions of dollars)

| Year | Democrats | Republicans |
|------|-----------|-------------|
| 1964 | (uncontested) | $10 |
| 1968 | $25 | 20 |
| 1972 | 33.1 | [a] |
| 1976 | 40.7 | 26.1 |
| 1980 | 41.7 | 86.1 |
| 1984 | 107.7 | 28.0 |
| 1988 | 94.0 | 114.6 |

[a] During a primary in which President Richard M. Nixon's nomination was virtually assured, Representative John M. Ashbrook spent $740,000 and Representative Paul N. McCloskey spent $550,000 in challenging Nixon.

*Sources:* 1964–72, Herbert E. Alexander, *Financing Politics* (Washington, D.C.: Congressional Quarterly, 1976), pp. 45–47; 1976–84, Federal Election Commission, "Reports on Financial Activity, 1987–88, *Presidential Pre-Nomination Campaigns,*" (August 1989), Table A–7, p. 10. Herbert E. Alexander, "Financing the Presidential Elections" (Paper presented at the Institute for Political Studies in Japan, Tokyo, Japan, September 8–10, 1989), pp. 4, 10.

had few costs other than for the occasional biography and campaign pamphlet printed by the party and sold to the public at less than cost.

With the advent of more active public campaigning toward the middle of the nineteenth century, candidate organizations turned to buttons, billboards, banners, and pictures to symbolize and illustrate their campaigns. By the beginning of the twentieth century, the cost of this type of advertising in each election exceeded $150,000—a lot then, but a minuscule amount by contemporary standards.[2]

In 1924, radio was employed for the first time in presidential campaigns. The Republicans spent approximately $120,000 that year, while the Democrats spent only $40,000.[3] Four years later, however, the two parties together spent more than $1 million. Radio expenses continued to equal or exceed a million dollars per election for the next twenty years.[4]

Television emerged as a vehicle for presidential campaigning in 1952. Both national party conventions were broadcast by television as well as radio. While there were only 19 million television sets in the United States, almost one-third of the people were regular television viewers. The number of households with television sets rose dramatically over the next four years. By 1956 an estimated 71 percent had television, and by 1968 the figure was close to 95 percent.

The first spot commercials for presidential candidates appeared in 1952. They became regular fare thereafter, contributing substantially to campaign costs. Film biographies, interview shows, political rallies, and election-eve telethons were all seen with increasing frequency.

In 1948 no money was spent on television by either party's candidate. Twenty years later, expenses exceeded $18 million for radio and television combined, approximately one-third of the total cost of the campaign. In 1988 that figure exceeded $100 million.[5] It should be higher in 1992. This amount, while significant, pales by comparison with the amount major corporations such as General Motors, Ford, and Procter and Gamble spend promoting their products.

The use of other modern technology has also increased expenditures. In 1968, Democrats Hubert Humphrey and George McGovern spent $650,000 between them on polling, while in 1972 the Nixon campaign alone spent more than $1.6 million.[6] If anything, these expenses have also increased.

Finally, the costs of fund raising have increased. In the past, candidates depended on a relatively small number of large contributors and could personally solicit the funds they needed. Today, most of them depend on a relatively large number of small contributors. Mass appeals must be made, and candidates must devote increasing time and energy to these activities.

Dwight Eisenhower was the first presidential candidate to make use of the direct mail technique to raise money. His letter to *Reader's Digest* subscribers promising to go to Korea to end the war generated a substantial financial return for his campaign. Unable to obtain support from their parties' regular contributors, Barry Goldwater in 1964 and George McGovern in 1972 targeted appeals to partisans and other sympathizers. Their success, even though they had been well behind in the preelection polls, combined with changes in the law that prohibit large gifts yet ultimately require more spending, has made direct mail solicitation essential for parties and candidates alike.

Three major issues arise from the problems of large expenditures. One pertains to the donors. Who pays, how much can they give, and what do they get for their money? A second relates to the costs. Are they too high, and can they be controlled without impinging on First Amendment freedoms? The third concerns the impact of spending on the election itself. To what extent does it improve a candidate's chances to win? The next section turns to the first of these questions—the private sources of financial support and attempts to regulate them. Later in the chapter the other questions will be addressed.

## THE SOURCES OF SUPPORT

Throughout most of U.S. electoral history, parties and candidates have depended on large contributions. In the midst of the industrial boom at the end of the nineteenth century, the Republicans were able to count on the support of the Astors, Harrimans, and Vanderbilts, while the Democrats looked to financier August Belmont and inventor-industrialist Cyrus McCormick. Corporations, banks, and life insurance companies soon became prime targets of party fund raisers. The most notorious and probably the most adroit fund raiser of this period was Mark Hanna. A leading official of the Republican party, Hanna owed most of his influence to his ability to obtain substantial political contributions. He set quotas, personally assessing the amount that businesses and corporations should give. In 1896, and again in 1900, he was able to obtain contributions of $250,000 from Standard Oil. Theodore Roosevelt personally ordered the return of some of the Standard Oil money in 1904 but accepted large gifts from magnates E. H. Harriman and Henry C. Frick.[7] Roosevelt's trust-busting activities during his presidency led Frick to remark, "We bought the son of a bitch and then he did not stay bought."[8]

Sizable private gifts remained the principal source of party and candidate support until the mid-1970s. The Republicans benefited more than the Democrats from the wealthy contributors known in the campaign vernacular as "fat cats." Only in 1964 was a Democrat—incumbent Lyndon B. Johnson, who enjoyed a large lead in the preelection polls—able to raise more money from large donors than his Republican opponent, Barry Goldwater.

The reluctance of regular Republican contributors to support the Goldwater candidacy forced his organization to appeal to thousands of potential supporters through a direct mailing. The success of this effort in raising $5.8 million from approximately 651,000 people showed the potential of the mails as a fund-raising technique and shattered an unwritten "rule" of politics that money could not be raised by mail. In 1968, Alabama Governor George Wallace, running as a third party candidate, solicited the bulk of his funds in this fashion.

Despite the use of mass mailings and party telethons to broaden the base of political contributors in the 1960s, dependence on large donors continued to grow. In 1964, more than $2 million was raised in contributions of $10,000 or more. Eight years later, approximately $51 million was collected in gifts of this size or larger. Some gifts were in the million dollar range.

The magnitude of these contributions, combined with the heavy-handed tactics of the Nixon fund raisers in 1971–72, brought into sharp focus the difficulty of maintaining a democratic selection process that was dependent on private funding.[9] Reliance on large contributors, who often did not wish their gifts to be made public, the inequality of funding between parties and candidates, and the high costs of campaigning, especially in the media, all raised serious issues. Were there assumptions implicit in giving and receiving? Could elected officials be responsive to individual benefactors and to the general public at the same time? Put another way, did the need to obtain and keep large contributors affect decision making in a manner that was inconsistent with the tenets of a democratic society? Did the high cost of campaigning, in and of itself, eliminate otherwise qualified candidates from running? Were certain political parties, interest groups, or individuals consistently advantaged or disadvantaged by the distribution of funding? Had the presidency become an office that only the wealthy could afford—or, worse still, that only those with wealthy support could seek?

## FINANCE LEGISLATION

Reacting to these issues, Congress in the 1970s enacted far-reaching legislation designed to reduce dependence on large donors, discourage illegal contributions, broaden the base of public support, and control escalating costs at the presidential level. Additionally, the Democratically-controlled Congress that passed these laws wanted to equalize the funds available to the Republican and Democratic nominees. Finally, the legislation was designed to buttress the two-party system, making it more difficult for minority candidates and parties to challenge major party nominees for elective office successfully.

One law, the Federal Election Campaign Act of 1971 (FECA), set ceilings on the amount of money presidential and vice-presidential candidates and their families could contribute to their own campaigns and the amount that could be spent on media advertising; it also established procedures for the public disclosure of all contributions over a certain amount.

A second statute, the Revenue Act of 1971, created tax credits and deductions to encourage private contributions. It also provided, for the first time, federal subsidies for the general election. Financed by an income tax checkoff provision, the fund allowed a taxpayer to designate $1 to a special presidential election account. Figure 2–1 indicates designations to and disbursements from this fund through 1988.

Despite the enactment of the funding provision in 1971, it did not go into effect until the 1976 presidential election. Most Republicans had opposed the legislation. In addition to conflicting with their general ideological position that the national government's role in the conduct of elections be limited, it offset their party's traditional fund-raising advantage. President Nixon was persuaded to sign the bill only after the Democratic leadership agreed to postpone the year in which the law became effective until after 1972, the year Nixon ran for reelection.

There was also a short but critical delay in the effective date for the disclosure provision of the other 1971 campaign finance act. Signed by the president on February 14, 1972, it was scheduled to take effect in sixty days. This delay precipitated a frantic attempt by both parties to tap large donors who wished to remain anonymous. It is estimated that the Republicans collected a staggering $20 million, much of it pledged

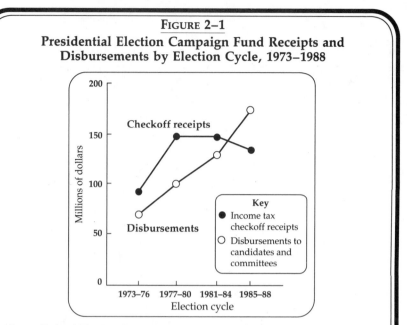

### Figure 2–1
**Presidential Election Campaign Fund Receipts and Disbursements by Election Cycle, 1973–1988**

Checkoff receipts

Millions of dollars

200

150

100

50

0

**Key**
● Income tax checkoff receipts
○ Disbursements to candidates and committees

**Disbursements**

1973–76   1977–80   1981–84   1985–88
Election cycle

*Source:* Federal Election Commission, "Reports on Financial Activity, 1987–88: *Presidential Pre-Nomination Campaigns*," (August 1989), p. 4.

As the figure above indicates, the fund initially produced sufficient revenue to meet the disbursements required by the law, the designated payments to the parties and their candidates during the nomination and the general election. However, a large increase in campaign expenditures in the 1980s and a substantial decrease in the percentage of taxpayers designating money to the fund during this period (from a high of 28.7 percent in 1980 to 19.9 percent in 1989) led the Federal Election Commission in 1990 to warn Congress and the president that there would be insufficient funds available for the 1992 election cycle unless the law were amended or a special appropriation were enacted.* Without enough money in the elections account, candidates for their party's nomination would receive reduced amounts and might not receive them until after the crucial first phase of the nomination process was completed. The reduction in federal funds and delay in payments would adversely affect the Democrats in 1992, particularly lesser-known aspirants who could not raise large amounts of money early in the nomination campaign.

---

* To minimize the effect on candidates, the Federal Election Commission proposed that the Treasury Department disburse money in the fund on the basis of fixed percentages of the total available throughout the nomination phase and calculate the total available by anticipating revenue designated to the fund by taxpayers during the election year. The treasury had proposed a pay-as-you-go rule for disbursements, with funding for the parties' conventions and the general election to be set aside at the beginning of the election year. The treasury proposal would have made less money available for the candidates in the early phases of the nomination process. The Federal Election Commission also engaged in a public relations campaign, urging taxpayers to designate a dollar of their tax to the fund.

beforehand, during this period. Of this money, approximately $1.5 million came in forms that could not be easily traced.

Even after the disclosure provision went into effect, violations were numerous. Moreover, pressure on corporations, particularly by Nixon campaign officials, resulted in a long list of illegal contributions. The spending of funds on "dirty tricks" and other unethical and illegal activities, such as the burglary of the Democratic National Committee's Watergate headquarters, further aroused public ire and eventually resulted in new and more stringent legislation.

Congress responded by amending the Federal Election Campaign Act of 1971. The new provisions, passed in 1974, included public disclosure provisions, contribution ceilings, campaign-spending limits, and federal subsidies for major party candidates in the nomination process and complete funding for them in the general election. A six-person commission was established to enforce the law. Two members of the Federal Election Commission (FEC) were to be appointed by the president and four by Congress.

The amendments were highly controversial. Critics immediately charged a federal giveaway, a robbery of the treasury. Opponents of the legislation also argued that the limits on contributions and spending violated the constitutionally guaranteed right to freedom of speech, that the funding provisions unfairly discriminated against third party and independent candidates, and that appointment of four of the commissioners by Congress violated the principle of separation of powers. One year after the amendments were enacted, the Supreme Court declared some of these portions of the law unconstitutional.

In the landmark decision of *Buckley v. Valeo* (424 U.S. 1, 1976), the Court upheld the right of Congress to regulate campaign expenditures but negated two principal provisions of the law: the overall limits on spending, and the appointment by Congress of four of the six election commissioners. The majority opinion contended that by placing restrictions on the amount of money an individual or group could spend during a campaign, the law directly and substantially restrained freedom of speech, a freedom protected by the First Amendment to the Constitution. However, the Supreme Court did allow limits on contributions to candidates' campaigns and limits on expenditures of those candidates who accepted public funds. In doing so, the Court acknowledged that large, often secret, contributions and rapidly increasingly expenditures did pose problems for a democratic society, problems on which Congress had power to legislate.

The Court's decision required that the election law be amended once again. It took Congress several months to do so. In the spring of 1976, during the presidential primaries, amendments were enacted that continued public funding of the presidential election and subsidizing of the delegate selection process but did so on a voluntary basis. Candidates did not have to accept government funds, but if they did, as in the past, they were limited in how much they could spend. The amount that could be contributed to a candidate was also limited. The Federal Election Commission was reconstituted, with all six members to be nominated by the president and appointed subject to the advice and consent of the Senate.

# Key Provisions of
# Campaign Finance Legislation

*Public Disclosure:* All contributions of $200 or more must be identified. All expenditures of $200 or more must be reported. Campaign committees are also required to file periodic reports before the election and a final report after it.

*Contribution Limits:* In any election, including a primary, contributions from an individual cannot exceed $1,000 to a single candidate, $20,000 to a national political party committee, and $5,000 to other political committees, with the total not to exceed $25,000 in any one year.

Personal contributions from candidates or their immediate families are limited to $50,000 at the prenomination stage and to $50,000 in the general election if a candidate accepts federal funds. Candidates who do not accept federal funds are not limited in what they can contribute to their own campaign. Individuals and political action committees can spend an unlimited amount on their own for candidates of their choice, provided they do not consult or communicate in any way with the candidate's campaign organization.

*Campaign Expenses:* Candidates who accept public funding cannot spend more than $10 million in their quest for the nomination and $20 million in the general election plus a cost-of-living increment calculated from the base year of 1974. In 1988 these limits were $23.1 million in the primaries and caucuses plus an additional 20 percent for fund raising ($4.6 million), a total of $27.7 million, and $46.1 million in the general election. In 1992, the limits will be approximately $28.2 million in the post-convention period plus the 20 percent increment for fund raising ($5.6 million) and $56.5 million in the general election.

In 1979, additional amendments to the Federal Election Campaign Act were passed. Designed to reduce the reporting requirements of the law, they raised the minimum contribution and expenditure that had to be filed. To encourage voluntary activities and higher turnout, the amendments also permitted state and local party committees to purchase an unlimited amount of campaign paraphernalia for candidates for na-

There are also specific spending limits in the states for nomination expenditures. These limits are based on the size of the voting age population in the state. In 1988, they ranged from $444,600 in the smallest states to $7.1 million in the largest state, California. Candidates who do not accept federal funds have no limit on their expenditures. Additionally, the national parties can spend two cents per citizen of voting age in support of their presidential and vice-presidential candidates. However, state and local parties can spend unlimited amounts on voluntary efforts to get out the vote.

*Matching Funds:* Major party contenders who raise $5,000 in twenty states in contributions of $250 or less, a total of $100,000, are eligible to receive matching grants during the prenomination period, which begins January 1 of the year in which the election occurs. Only the first $250 of each contribution will be matched. In 1988, the government provided $67.2 million in matching funds.

*Communication Notices:* All authorized advertisements by candidates' organizations must state the name of the candidate or agent who authorized them. All nonauthorized advertisements must identify the person who made or financed the ad and his or her organizational affiliation, if any.

*Compliance Procedures:* The Federal Election Commission has authority to investigate possible violations, hold hearings, and assess certain civil penalties. Its decision may be appealed to U.S. District Courts. The Justice Department retains the authority for criminal investigation and prosecution.

tional office and to spend an unlimited amount on registration and get-out-the-vote activities. Known as the "soft money" provision, this amendment has created a gigantic loophole in the federal legislation because it permits a party to raise and spend huge sums of money on all its candidates, including its presidential nominees, without being subject to the contribution limits or reporting requirements of the law. Finally, federal financial support for nominating conventions of the major parties was also increased. (See the box entitled "Key Provisions of Campaign Finance Legislation" and Table 2–5.)

## THE IMPACT OF THE LAW

The new legislation has had a significant impact on campaign revenue and expenditures. It has affected the base of contributors, the modes of solicitation, and the objects of spending. It has changed the role of the government, modified the relationship between the party and its nominees, and influenced the strategies and tactics of the campaign.

### *Revenue*

**Individual contributors.** One of the most important objectives of the law was to reduce the influence a small number of large contributors had on the presidential nomination and election. To some extent it has succeeded. No longer can candidates depend on a few wealthy friends to finance their campaigns. The $1,000 limit on individual donors, which is not subject to a cost-of-living adjustment, the $250 ceiling on matching grants, and the eligibility requirements for federal funds have made the solicitation of a large number of contributors absolutely essential. There have, however, been variations in the fund-raising tactics of the candidates and their emphasis on relatively larger or smaller contributors. (See the box entitled "Techniques for Raising Money.") In 1988, for example, Republicans George Bush and Robert Dole and Democrats Bruce Babbitt and Michael Dukakis received the bulk of their donations from the largest gifts permissible by law, $750 to $1,000, while Republican Pat Robertson and Democrat Jesse Jackson obtained most of their money from small contributors, those who gave $500 or less. (See Table 2–3.)

In addition to gifts from individuals, which are the largest single source of campaign revenues, candidates have found other ways to supplement their campaign funds. They can provide some of their own money. There is no restriction on the amount of their personal funds that can be spent in the years prior to the election, until their candidacy

TABLE 2–3

**Prenomination Revenues of Major Party Candidates in Thousands of Dollars, 1988**

| Candidates | Net Receipts[a] | Individual Contributions | Percentage $750 and up | PAC Contributions (Nonparty) | Federal Matching Funds |
|---|---|---|---|---|---|
| *Democrats* | | | | | |
| Bruce Babbitt | 4,349 | 2,265 | 53.6% | 1 | 1,079 |
| Joseph Biden Jr. | 3,981 | 3,779 | 66.8 | — | — |
| Michael Dukakis | 31,237 | 19,401 | 42.5 | — | 9,040 |
| Richard Gephardt | 13,295 | 6,313 | 37.8 | 656 | 2,896 |
| Albert Gore Jr. | 14,958 | 8,016 | 39.0 | 498 | 3,853 |
| Gary Hart | 3,553 | 2,319 | 45.3 | — | 1,084 |
| Jesse Jackson | 26,644 | 12,282 | 7.5 | 46 | 7,608 |
| Lyndon LaRouche Jr. | 3,983 | 3,081 | 23.3 | 5 | 826 |
| Paul Simon | 13,346 | 6,147 | 27.4 | 289 | 3,603 |
| Total | 115,346 | 63,603 | 34.4% | 1,495 | 29,989 |
| *Republicans* | | | | | |
| George Bush | 33,911 | 22,567 | 66.4% | 651 | 8,393 |
| Robert Dole | 28,307 | 17,430 | 51.8 | 810 | 7,618 |
| Pete du Pont | 9,153 | 5,502 | 40.3 | — | 2,550 |
| Alexander Haig Jr. | 2,633 | 1,387 | 60.6 | 22 | 539 |
| Jack Kemp | 20,576 | 10,568 | 22.5 | 65 | 5,877 |
| Pat Robertson | 41,029 | 20,637 | 8.1 | | 9,691 |
| Total | 135,609 | 78,091 | 39.9 | 1,548 | 34,670 |

[a] Includes loans

Source: Federal Election Commission, "Reports on Financial Activity, 1987–88: *Presidential Pre-Nomination Campaigns*," (August 1989), Table A1–A4, pp. 1–5.

is formally established. At the point of candidacy, the $50,000 personal limit is imposed. In the 1988 presidential campaign Democrat Richard Gephardt and Republican Pierre ("Pete") du Pont each contributed the $50,000 maximum; George Bush gave $2,000 to his campaign.[10] Other candidates lent their campaign money. The lending limit for candidates is also $50,000.

Borrowing money from financial institutions is also possible. The law permits candidates to obtain loans (if they can), provided that the terms of payment are clear and that the money is lent in accordance with the regular business practices. With the exception of Bush and Dukakis, every one of the other major party aspirants in 1988 borrowed money, often using the matching funds that they expected to receive from the government as collateral.

Funds raised but not spent by candidates in their campaigns for other offices, such as for the Senate, House of Representatives, or a state governorship, can be used in their quest for the presidential nomination.

## Techniques for Raising Money

Candidates have used two principal methods to raise private contributions. One is to turn to affluent supporters, who have a network of well-to-do personal friends and business associates; the other is to use the services of a firm that specializes in direct mail solicitation. Michael Dukakis successfully employed the first of these techniques, while Pat Robertson raised 90 percent of his private contributions through the second.

At the outset of a presidential campaign, candidates usually find it necessary to gain the support of a number of *collectors* to help finance start-up activities by seeking large contributions. Collectors are not politicians; they are partisans. For them politics is an avocation. Although their motives may vary, most desire access to the candidate as a reward for their political involvement. Some aspire to high government position if their candidate is successful, while others wish to exercise influence, receive social invitations, enjoy the excitement of politics, or help the person they believe is most qualified to win.

In the Dukakis model, collectors were asked to raise at least $10,000 each from their friends and associates. Those who did so (900 people) were named to Dukakis's finance committee; those who raised $25,000 (230 people) were designated as members of the committee's board; those who obtained $100,000 in donations (130 people) were titled *co-chairmen* or *ambassadors* of the committee.[a] George Bush's campaign raised $1,000 from each of 17,000 people, most of them wealthy lawyers, investors, and business entrepreneurs. Members of one large Los Angeles–based law firm contributed a total of $35,000 to Bush.[b]

The direct mail technique is slower and more costly, but it can generate a lot of money. Computerized lists of people who have

Robert Dole had access to almost $2 million collected from his previous Senate campaigns, which he tapped to launch his presidential efforts in 1988.

Although $1,000 is the maximum individual gift, voluntary goods and services are unrestricted. Artists and musicians, in particular, can generate considerable revenue for candidates by offering their time and talent. Concerts, and to a lesser extent art sales, have become excellent sources of revenue. George Bush had considerable success at $1,000 a plate dinners that his campaign organized. In one such dinner, held in Houston, his adopted hometown, he raised $750,000.[11] At the dinner in Washington, D.C., in which he announced his candidacy, his campaign netted $625,000.

made political contributions to like-minded candidates, subscribe to certain magazines, or belong to certain organizations are used in a multistage process. The first of these stages is called *prospecting*. Here the list is employed to identify potential contributors. The rate and size of the contributions from this initial mailing tend to be small. Frequently, the returns will be less than the costs. Jack Kemp reportedly lost $200,000 on his first mailing, but he obtained a file of sympathetic individuals to whom he could make subsequent appeals. In the end the Kemp campaign spent $1.25 for every dollar it raised but came out ahead because of the law, which matched every individual contribution up to $250 with an equal amount from the government.[c]

Michael Dukakis raised $2.4 million in direct mails at a cost of $1.6 million.[d] Pat Robertson raised the most money in this manner. Writing to regular contributors of his 700 Club and to 3 million people who urged him to run for president, Robertson asked his supporters for a contribution of $19.88 per month to join his 1988 club. Forty thousand people responded.[e]

[a] Clyde Wilcox, "Financing the 1988 Prenomination Campaign," in *Nominating the President*, ed. Emmett Buell and Lee Sigelman (Knoxville, Tenn.: University of Tennessee Press, 1991), p. 96.
[b] Charles R. Babcock and Richard Morin, "Bush's Money Machine," *Washington Post*, May 15, 1988, p. A4.
[c] Edward Rollins, quoted in *Campaign for President,: The Managers Look at '88*, ed. David Runkle (Dover, Mass.: Auburn House, 1989) p. 185.
[d] Alexander, "Financing the Presidential Elections, 1988" (Paper presented at the Institute for Political Studies in Japan. Tokyo, September 8–10, 1989), p. 12.
[e] Wilcox, "Financing the 1988 Prenomination Campaign,", p. 98.

**Nonparty groups.** Although the election law prohibits corporations and labor unions from making direct contributions to political campaigns, it does allow their employees, stockholders, or members to form political action committees (PACs) and fund them through voluntary contributions. They can directly affect the presidential selection process in three ways: by giving up to $5,000 to a single candidate, by spending an unlimited amount independently for or against a candidate, and by endorsing a candidate and then using their organization to mobilize and register voters who will support that candidate on election day.

Direct donations are the least important. Money given directly to candidates by PACs in presidential campaigns rarely exceeds 3 percent of the total amount raised during the election year. In 1988 it constituted only 1.4 percent of the total, with the Republican candidates receiving slightly more contributions than the Democrats.[12]

Independent expenditures for PACs as well as those spent by an organization communicating with its members about the candidates, parties, and issues or engaging in public, nonpartisan activities can be significant. Although these expenditures have mushroomed in recent elections, their effect on individual contests is more difficult to evaluate. Groups can be particularly valuable in educating, mobilizing, and turning out voters. The organizing efforts of labor and teacher PACs in the 1984 primaries and caucuses helped produce pluralities for Walter Mondale in several key states; in the 1988 general election many of these same PACs worked hard for the Democratic ticket, spending an estimated $25 million for Dukakis but only $5 million for Bush.[13]

Additionally, PACs can contribute money to state and local political parties in their efforts to turn out a large vote in the general election. Corporations and labor unions may also fund these activities unless prohibited by state law from doing so.

PACs have proven to be so important that presidential candidates now regularly form their own. Known as nonconnected organizations, they have been used primarily to fund organizational activities, build support, and defray travel and other expenses of the candidate in the years between the last election and the actual opening of the current campaign. In addition, some of the budgets of these nonconnected PACs is spent on donations to others during the midterm elections. This money is intended to generate reciprocal support from elected officials for the presidential nominee later on.

A good example of a nonconnected PAC was Citizens for the Republic. Started in 1977, this organization had within a year raised $2.5 million and spent $1.9 million on operations. Most of this money was used for fund raising, travel, and other expenses of the PAC's principal speaker, Ronald Reagan. In the process of raising money, the organization developed a list of more than 300,000 contributors. This list was purchased for a nominal fee by the campaign committee for the reelection of President Reagan. The Reagan PAC became the prototype for other nonconnected organizations.

By the end of 1985 many of the Republican aspirants for the 1988 nomination had already formed PACs that were raising money, building field organizations, and deferring campaign costs on their behalf. This early activity was spurred by the decision of the Michigan Republican party to hold the first round of its selection of delegates to the national nominating convention in August 1986, two years before the meeting. PACs were the vehicle that Republican candidates used to fund most of their campaign activities during this preselection period. Democratic candidates also used PACs to support the initial stages of their campaign. Table 2–4 lists candidate PAC contributions and expenditures for the 1988 nomination process.

The use of nonconnected organizations by presidential aspirants has generated controversy and in the 1984 Democratic primaries got Walter Mondale in trouble. Mondale's campaign had encouraged the formation of delegate committees to provide money and support to slates of individuals who were seeking direct election to the Democratic nominating convention as Mondale delegates. A letter from a Mondale official indicated how such committees could be established and suggested that any legal question concerning support for them be referred to the campaign's legal counsel. As a consequence of these efforts, Mondale delegate committees were organized and raised money in nineteen states. Gary Hart, Mondale's principal opponent, charged that this activity violated the law, which prohibited collusion between the official campaign organization and other nonconnected, nonparty groups. After trying to sidestep the issue, the Mondale campaign was finally pressured to repay the sums his delegate committees had spent—approximately $400,000— from his own campaign fund.

The controversy between the Democrats' two principal contenders in 1984 led some aspirants for the 1988 nomination, including Michael

## TABLE 2–4
### PAC Expenditures and Contributions, 1985–1988

|  | Expenditures | Contributions | Percentage of Contributions |
|---|---|---|---|
| *Democrats* | | | |
| Richard Gephardt | $1,186,224 | $67,596 | 6% |
| Paul Simon | 465,721 | 76,286 | 16 |
| *Republicans* | | | |
| George Bush | $10,795,937 | $860,297 | 8 |
| Robert Dole | 7,553,567 | 419,813 | 6 |
| Jack Kemp | 4,157,478 | 165,815 | 4 |
| Pat Robertson | 674,095 | 37,793 | 6 |

*Note:* PAC activity for 1987–88 cycle is through the end of primary season or until the candidate dropped out of the race. Contributions are to candidates for federal office. Most PACs made additional contributions to candidates at the end of the 1987–88 cycle, and many made contributions to state and local candidates that are not reflected in these figures.

*Source:* Clyde Wilcox, "Financing the 1988 Prenomination Campaign," in *Selecting a President in 1988*, ed. Emmett Buell and Lee Sigelman (Knoxville, Tenn.: University of Tennessee Press, 1991), Table 4.10, p. 116.

Dukakis, to denounce PACs, delegate committees, and other nonparty groups, and seek new ways to fund their prenomination activities. One device used by Gary Hart, Bruce Babbitt, and others, including Republicans Jack Kemp and Pat Robertson, was the creation of a tax-exempt foundation to provide support for research, agenda building, staff, and travel. The foundations also generated valuable donor lists. Pat Robertson's Freedom Council was particularly active in the 1986 stage of the Michigan caucus.

The indirect use of foundations for political activities, however, also generated criticism, not only because it circumvented the election law but because it conflicted with an Internal Revenue Service regulation that tax-exempt foundations cannot engage in political campaigns on behalf of any candidate.

**Matching funds.** In addition to individuals and nonparty groups, a third source of money for the nomination process is the government itself. Individual contributions up to $250 can be matched by an equal amount from the federal election fund in the calendar year of the election, if certain conditions are met. Contributions received in the previous year are also eligible for matching in the election year, provided they were given to the candidate's official campaign committee.

While eligibility for matching funds is not difficult to establish (see the box entitled "Key Provisions of Campaign Finance Legislation"), the maintenance of eligibility is somewhat harder. Candidates for their party's nomination who fail to receive at least 10 percent of the vote in two consecutive primaries in which they are entered lose their eligibility until such a time as they receive at least 20 percent of the vote in a primary. Twice during the 1984 campaign Jesse Jackson lost his eligibility for matching funds, only to regain it later. He remained eligible throughout his 1988 campaign.

Losing eligibility not only stops the flow of government funds; it also casts doubt on the viability of a candidacy in the eyes of the media, politicians, and potential contributors. For these reasons, candidates tend to avoid nonessential contests in which they are not likely to receive the minimum 10 percent of the vote.

There is a catch to accepting matching funds, as noted earlier in this chapter. Candidates are then subject to state and national expenditure limits. These limits tend to be a problem in the early, small caucus and primary states, such as Iowa and New Hampshire, particularly for lesser-known candidates, who need strong showings to establish their credibility and to raise money for the rest of their campaign. The desire to be free of these spending ceilings led one Republican aspirant, John Connally, to reject matching funds in 1980 and another, Pat Robertson, to seriously consider doing so in 1988. With a large donor base and the need to demonstrate his electability at the outset of the nomination process, Robertson initially placed his matching funds in an escrow account to give himself the option of exceeding the spending limits. Although he raised a considerable amount of money during the early stages of the campaign, he spent even more. To make up for the shortfall, he borrowed $5.5 million in January 1988 and $1.9 million in February using his escrowed matching funds as collateral.[14] Whether his use of government funds as collateral for a debt would still have subjected him to the state limits was unclear and quickly became moot when he decided to spend his matching funds. Like the other contenders for their party's nomination, Robertson found that he needed the money. Besides, there were other legitimate ways to skirt the expenditure limits.

On balance, the matching-fund provision has provided greater opportunities for lesser-known aspirants to seek their party's nomination. These opportunities would be seriously curtailed if all or a substantial portion of the matching funds were unavailable at the beginning of the nomination process due to insufficient money in the federal government's election account as may occur in 1992 and subsequent elections.

The availability of matching funds, as provided by the Federal Election Campaign Act, has not completely eliminated the financial advantage that nationally recognized candidates have, especially as the primaries and caucuses get under way. What it does do for all candidates is to encourage them to begin their fund raising well before the election. The need to qualify for funds, the $250 maximum for matching, and the $1,000 contribution limit for individuals require candidates for their party's nomination to build donor lists and solicit personal contributions in the year before the nomination. Conversely, these factors discourage late entrants, even nationally recognized leaders.

The relative importance of individual contributions, nonparty committees, and matching funds are illustrated in Figure 2–2.

**Soft money.** The 1979 amendments to the FECA that permitted state and local parties to spend unlimited amounts of money to get people to vote encourage the parties to solicit large, unreported sums of money from wealthy partisans and distribute that money to their state and local affiliates for get-out-the-vote activities. These activities include the operation of telephone banks, the distribution of campaign literature, and the recruitment of field organizers and other political operatives who supplement the candidate's campaign organization.

In 1988, both parties' presidential candidates depended on the state parties to pay for most of their staff who were based in the states. Only the campaign director for the state and one or two other top officials for each state stayed on the national payroll. This arrangement enabled Bush and Dukakis to operate with very small national staffs. It reduced their administrative overhead and their need to fund large grass-roots organizations and permitted them to devote most of the public funds to media advertising.

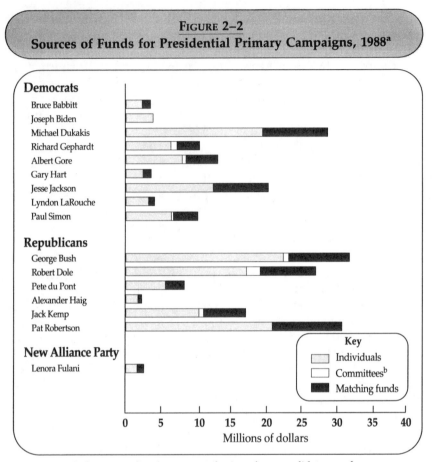

FIGURE 2–2

**Sources of Funds for Presidential Primary Campaigns, 1988[a]**

**Democrats**
- Bruce Babbitt
- Joseph Biden
- Michael Dukakis
- Richard Gephardt
- Albert Gore
- Gary Hart
- Jesse Jackson
- Lyndon LaRouche
- Paul Simon

**Republicans**
- George Bush
- Robert Dole
- Pete du Pont
- Alexander Haig
- Jack Kemp
- Pat Robertson

**New Alliance Party**
- Lenora Fulani

Key
- Individuals
- Committees[b]
- Matching funds

0   5   10   15   20   25   30   35   40
Millions of dollars

[a] Does not include outstanding loans, contributions from candidates, and some miscellaneous receipts.

[b] Includes direct contributions from PACs and other political committees but not internal expenses, such as communicating to its membership or independent expenditures.

*Source:* Federal Election Commission, *Record*, vol. 15, October 1989, p. 12.

The soft money raised and distributed for the 1988 general election was estimated to be more than $130 million, considerably more than the $96.4 million of government money divided equally among the major party candidates.[15] Of this amount, the Republicans enjoyed an almost 2:1 advantage. Total party spending in 1988 was $96.7 million for the Republicans and $50 million for the Democrats, including the $8.3 million each party received from the government to conduct its presidential campaign.[16]

Not only has the discrepancy in party revenue and expenditures, evident also in 1980 and 1984, undercut a principal intent of the FECA to limit and equalize spending, but the pattern of solicitation by both parties has also contravened a basic objective of the law to reduce the influence of large donors. Both parties have turned to wealthy individuals for large contributions to their soft money accounts. In 1988, the Republicans received $100,000 or more from 267 people, while 130 individuals gave the Democrats this amount or more.[17]

The figures for total revenue and expenditure in 1988 indicate how much the law has been modified in practice. Government money accounted for approximately 30 percent of the money raised and spent in the nomination phase in 1988 and 50 percent in the general election.[18]

## *Expenditures*

The additional revenue that soft money has generated combined with the independent spending that the Supreme Court has permitted have also substantially increased the total amount of money spent in U.S. presidential campaigns. If only expenses reported by campaign organizations are considered, expenditures have remained relatively constant over the years. They have been increased by a cost-of-living adjustment (COLA) as indicated in Table 2–5, but that adjustment has not kept pace with the actual rise in campaign expenses such as those for media, air travel, hotel accommodations, and even fund raising. Between 1974, the base year, and 1988, the COLA increased by 123 percent, but television advertising costs rose by even more.

### TABLE 2–5
### Presidential Spending Limits and COLAS, 1976–1988

| | Unadjusted Limit 1974 Base Year | 1976 | 1980 | 1984 | 1988 |
|---|---|---|---|---|---|
| COLA[a] | – | 9.1% | 47.2% | 102% | 123% |
| Primary election limit[b] | $10 million | $10.9 million | $14.7 million | $20.2 million | $23.1 million |
| General election limit | $20 million | $21.8 million | $29.4 million | $40.4 million | $46.1 million |
| Party convention limit | $2 million | $2.2 million | $4.4 million | $8.1 million | $9.2 million |
| Party general election limit (2 cents × VAP[c] adjusted by COLA) | — | $3.2 million | $4.6 million | $6.9 million | $8.3 million |

[a] COLA means the cost-of-living adjustment, which the Department of Labor annually calculates using 1974 as the base year.

[b] Primary candidates receiving matching funds must comply with two types of spending limits: a national limit (listed in the above table), and a separate limit for each state. The state limit is $200,000 or sixteen cents multiplied by the state's voting age population, whichever is greater. (Both amounts are adjusted for increases in the cost of living.) The maximum amount of primary matching funds a candidate may receive is half of the national spending limit.

[c] VAP means voting age population.

*Source:* Federal Election Commission, *Annual Report, 1984* (June 1, 1985), pp. 8–9, updated by author from figures from FEC.

According to Herbert Alexander, a political scientist specializing in campaign finance, the expenditures of the major candidates in nomination contests and general elections, if measured in terms of constant dollars "have increased only by a factor of four, whereas aggregate unadjusted costs have risen almost seventeen-fold from 1960–1988."[19]

From the perspective of campaign managers, the crunch in expenditures represents a real problem, particularly at the initial stages of the nomination process. The need to get a boost or maintain a lead has prompted candidates of both parties to spend much of their money early, even before the first contest is held, and to focus their attention on the states that have these first caucuses and primaries. In 1988 this was the Iowa caucus (held in early February), the New Hampshire primary (held in mid-February), and the states located primarily in the South that conducted their elections during the second Tuesday in March, a day referred to as "Super Tuesday" because of the sixteen primaries and five caucuses held on that day.

The limits on spending in Iowa and New Hampshire, especially, have been insufficient for the emphases the candidates place on these states, the amount of time they and their staff spend in them, and the air time they wish to buy on radio and television. As a consequence, they almost all exceed the limits, employing a variety of tactics, most of which have been approved by the Federal Election Commission. Campaign workers commute to Iowa and New Hampshire from neighboring states, eating, sleeping, and renting cars from outside these states whenever possible so that their expenditures will not be applied to the Iowa and New Hampshire totals. WATTS lines are used instead of in-state phone banks. Television ads, particularly those directed at New Hampshire, are aired on Boston television, where 85 percent of the cost can be allocated to the Massachusetts limit. In 1988, fund-raising appeals were placed at the end of in-state media advertising in Iowa to enable candidates to deduct as much as 50 percent of the cost as a fund-raising expenditure.

In addition to the limits in Iowa and New Hampshire, candidates also have been concerned about their overall spending in the primary process. Thus far, however, the total permissible expenditures have not proven to be a problem because the eventual winner has emerged so early. The spending patterns of the principal contenders for the 1988 Republican and Democratic nominations are presented in Figure 2–3.

George Bush spent about one-third of his legal limit in 1987, about two-thirds by the end of February of the election year, and was within $4 million of his legal limit by the end of March. Dole and Robertson were within $2.5 million of theirs by March 31. Had the contest continued, the candidates would have had to depend increasingly on nonparty groups and free media to conduct their campaign. Total 1988 prenomination expenditures are listed in Table 2–6.

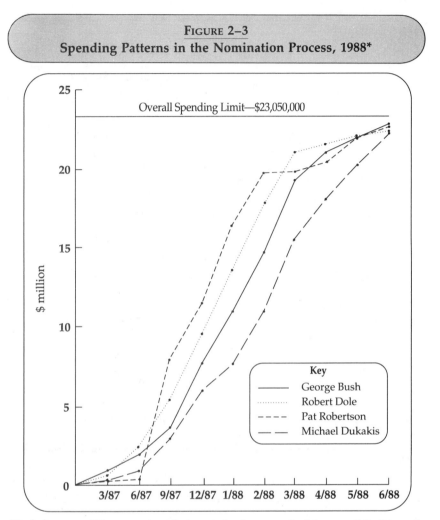

FIGURE 2–3
**Spending Patterns in the Nomination Process, 1988***

* Includes competitive campaigns that most closely approached the overall limit in each election cycle.

*Source:* Federal Election Commission, "Reports on Financial Activity, 1987–88: *Presidential Pre-Nomination Campaigns*," (August 1989), Appendix II.

Another money problem, particularly evident in 1988, was the concentration of primaries and caucuses during the second week of March. The only way for candidates to reach voters in a number of states during the same time period is through advertising on radio, television, and in newspapers. Television advertising, in particular, is one of the most expensive forms of communication. On Super Tuesday alone, Democrats Albert Gore spent $2 million on radio and television and Dukakis spent $1.6 million on television.[20] Bush's media budget for the nomi-

TABLE 2–6
**Prenomination Expenditures of Major Party Candidates, 1988**

| Democrats | Expenditures Subject to Limit |
|---|---|
| Bruce Babbitt | $2,501,148 |
| Joseph Biden | — |
| Michael Dukakis | $22,479,320 |
| Richard Gephardt | $7,970,298 |
| Albert Gore | $10,990,597 |
| Gary Hart | — |
| Jesse Jackson | $15,233,217 |
| Lyndon LaRouche | $3,680,522 |
| Paul Simon | $6,807,114 |
| **Subtotal** | **$69,662,216** |
| | |
| **Republicans** | |
| George Bush | $23,024,993 |
| Robert Dole | $22,459,164 |
| Pete du Pont | $5,082,323 |
| Alexander Haig | $474,854 |
| Jack Kemp | $16,699,406 |
| Pat Robertson | $23,180,885 |
| **Subtotal** | **$90,921,625** |
| **Grand Total** | **$160,583,841** |

*Source:* Federal Election Commission, "Reports on Financial Activity, 1987–88: *Presidential Pre-Nomination Campaigns*," (August 1989), Appendix I.

nation phase of his campaign was $3.4 million.[21] In the general election both major party nominees spent more than 60 percent of their budget on media.

Independent expenditures have also played a significant role in the nomination and general election process. In 1980, $13.7 million was reported to the FEC as being spent independently on the presidential campaign. In 1984, this figure had risen to $17.5 million, with ideological groups spending the bulk of this money.[22] In 1988 total independent spending reported declined slightly.[23] Approximately $4.1 million was spent independently in the nomination stage from January 1988 through the party conventions and $13.8 in the general election.[24]

The Republican party has benefited disproportionately from this independent spending. In 1984, $16.3 million was spent on behalf of Reagan or against Mondale compared with $1.2 expended for Mondale or against Reagan.[25] In 1988 total spending decreased, but the proportions benefiting the Republican nominees were as lopsided as ever—$9.5 mil-

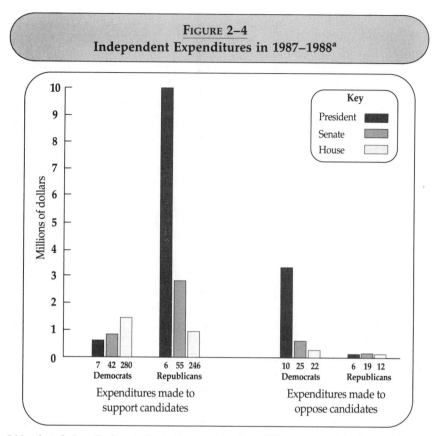

**FIGURE 2–4**
**Independent Expenditures in 1987–1988[a]**

Key
- President
- Senate
- House

Millions of dollars

| 7  42  280 | 6  55  246 | | 10  25  22 | 6  19  12 |
| Democrats | Republicans | | Democrats | Republicans |

Expenditures made to
support candidates

Expenditures made to
oppose candidates

[a] Numbers below the bars indicate the number of candidates supported or opposed with independent expenditures.

*Source:* Federal Election Commission, *Record* (August 1989), p. 9.

lion was spent in activities lauding Bush or criticizing Dukakis, while slightly more than $500,000 was expended in support of Dukakis and in opposition to Bush.[26] Figure 2–4 presents the independent expenditures reported to the FEC for the 1988 presidential election.

## Competition between Parties and Candidates

The FECA created competition between the parties and their nominees. This competition was not the intent of the law, but it has been a consequence. By providing funds directly to individuals who seek the Republican and Democratic nominations, the law facilitates candidacies and candidate organizations within the national parties, thereby factionalizing those parties. The organization of the successful candidate is not dismantled after the nomination; it is expanded and can compete with the regular party organization. On the other hand, the 1979 amendments have encouraged the national parties to mount extensive fundraising operations, soliciting soft money and directing it toward their state and local affiliates. These affiliates, in turn, have used the money to pay for their field operations. The presidential candidates' organizations, specifically the people appointed to be their state coordinators, have thus become dependent on the state parties to turn out *their* candidate's vote.

The law affects the candidates in another way. Once the nomination is won, the incumbent is usually advantaged. Equalizing spending by the candidates at the national level hurts a challenger more than an incumbent. Presidents make the news simply by being president; challengers have to buy time on television to present themselves as serious presidential candidates.

In 1976 the law also seemed to work to the benefit of the Democrats because it eliminated the fund-raising advantage that Republican nominees had enjoyed over the years. However, beginning in 1980 Republicans have benefited more from independent expenditures and soft money, an advantage that is likely to continue for some time.

Finally, the law has adversely affected minor parties by requiring their candidates to obtain at least 5 percent of the presidential vote to be eligible for public funds. Independent candidate John Anderson qualified in 1980, but only after the election was over. He eventually received $4.2 million, enough to pay off his debts, but not enough to have mounted a vigorous campaign.

Since Anderson was not assured of federal funds, he had difficulty borrowing money. Unable to secure large bank loans, he had to depend on private contributions and loans. He raised $12.1 million, mainly through mass mailings. Ironically, having qualified in 1980, Anderson was automatically eligible for funds in 1984 had he chosen to run. Thus the law, despite its intent to bolster the candidates of the major parties, provides an incentive for the continuation of a third party candidacy once that candidacy has been successfully launched in the previous election.

## THE CONSEQUENCES OF SPENDING

Is spending related to electoral success? Have candidates with the largest bankrolls generally been victorious? In the general elections at the presidential level, the answers seem to be yes, but it is difficult to determine precisely the extent to which money contributed to victory or simply flowed to the likely winner.

Between 1860 and 1972, the winner outspent the loser twenty-one out of twenty-nine times. Republican candidates have spent more than their Democratic opponents in twenty-five out of twenty-nine elections. The four times they did not, the Democrats won. The trend has continued. In 1980, 1984, and 1988 considerably more was spent in this way for the Republican nominees than for their Democratic opponents.

What do all these figures suggest? The pattern of greater spending and electoral victories indicates that *the money contributes to success, but potential success also attracts money.* Having more funds is an advantage, but it does not guarantee victory. The fact that heavily favored incumbent Richard Nixon outspent rival George McGovern more than 2:1 in 1972 does not explain McGovern's huge defeat, although it probably portended it. On the other hand, Hubert Humphrey's much narrower defeat by Nixon four years earlier was probably influenced by Humphrey's having spent less than $12 million, compared with more than $25 million spent by Nixon. The closer the election, the more the disparity in funds can be a factor.

Theoretically, campaign spending should have a greater impact on the nomination process than on the general election and at the beginning of the process than at the end. The first need to gain visibility, mobilize support, and develop an effective organization requires a large outlay of funds.

The big spenders in 1988 were the big winners in Iowa, New Hampshire, and on Super Tuesday. Gephardt outspent his Democratic rivals in Iowa and won. Dukakis, the victor in New Hampshire, spent more than his opponents, but his large expenditure of funds was probably less important than his recognition as governor of a neighboring state. On Super Tuesday, Democratic candidates who outspent their opponents won 75 percent of the primaries and caucuses.[27] Only Jesse Jackson, whose expenditures were considerably less than his opponents', did well, winning five states.

After Super Tuesday the relationship between spending and electoral success became murkier on the Democratic side. Jackson spent more than Dukakis in April, May, and June but won only one out of fifteen primaries (the District of Columbia) and three out of six caucuses. Similarly, four years earlier, Hart outspent Mondale in thirty-three out of fifty states. He won nineteen and lost seventeen of them.[28]

Among the Republicans state-by-state spending did not seem to be related to electoral success once the campaign got under way. In Iowa and New Hampshire all three candidates spent approximately the same amount, but on Super Tuesday they did not. George Bush was outspent by his opponents in twelve of thirteen contests yet lost only one of them. For candidates of both parties in 1984 and again in 1988, the big spenders lost more often than they won.[29]

What do the pattern of spending and the results of the 1988 nomination contests suggest about the relationship between money and electoral success? *When* does money matter? According to political scientist

Clyde Wilcox, it matters most when the candidates are least known to the voters, when they do not receive a lot of news coverage, and when paid advertising, which, of course, is expensive, can bring recognition and enhance images.[30] Money tends to matter most at the early stages of the campaign, when the candidates are not as well-known. As the campaign progresses, when candidates are better known to the electorate, as Bush and Jackson were initially in 1988, the expenditure of funds will not be as critical to electoral success. Money buys recognition, but it may not buy much more.

Nor does the expenditure of funds by the candidates seem to be a major factor in the general election. In an examination of campaign advertising spending by Bush, a group of political scientists found an *inverse* relationship between advertising costs and public support for the candidates. They write, "When Bush spent more in one week than he had in the previous week, the size of his lead actually grew smaller."[31]

## SUMMARY

Campaign finance became an important aspect of presidential elections by the end of the nineteenth and the beginning of the twentieth centuries. In recent years, however, it has become even more important as costs have escalated. Expanded use of communications, particularly television, to reach the voters has been primarily responsible for the increase, although other methods of contacting voters and assessing their opinions have also added to the sharp rise in expenditures.

With few exceptions, candidates of both major parties turned to the large contributors, the so-called fat cats, for financial support in the early and mid-twentieth century. Their dependence on a relatively small number of large donors, combined with spiraling costs, created serious problems for the democratic selection process. The 1972 presidential election, with its high expenditures, "dirty tricks," and illegal campaign contributions, vividly illustrated some of these problems and generated support from Congress and the public for rectifying them.

In the 1970s Congress enacted and amended the Federal Election Campaign Act. Its purpose in doing so was to bring donors into the open and to prevent their exercising undue influence on elected officials. By placing limits on contributions, controlling expenditures, and subsidizing the election, Congress hoped to make the selection process less costly and more equitable. It established the Federal Election Commission to oversee compliance and prosecute offenders.

The legislation has achieved only some of its intended goals. It has increased the importance of having a large base of contributors during the preconvention period but has not eliminated the impact of large donors on the parties' efforts in the general election. It has limited the expenditures of candidates in both the nomination and general election but has not reduced the amount of money spent on presidential campaigns. It has produced greater equity by its limits on contributions and expenditures and by its federal subsidies but has not achieved equity among candidates or between parties in either phase of the electoral process. It has provided greater opportunities for those candidates who lack national recognition, but it has not lessened the advantages that such recognition can bring to those who seek their party's nomination. It has benefited major party candidates in the general election but has factionalized the major parties during the nomination. It has weakened the party leadership's control over their nomination process and over their conduct of the general election campaign, but it has also enhanced the strategic value of their fund-raising abilities. It has encouraged the formation and involvement of nonparty groups, but it has also more recently increased the importance of state and local party organizations.

Finally, the law has contributed to knowledge about the conduct of campaigns. Gifts and expenditures of candidates are now part of the public record. This information is used by candidates to develop strategy, by the media to cover the election, and by academicians and other analysts to explain the outcome. The publicizing of actions that violate the letter and spirit of the law has served to discourage such actions. In general, compliance has not been a major problem, although much ingenuity has been spent on legitimately circumventing restrictions on expenditures and contributions.

## NOTES

1. Herbert E. Alexander, "Financing the Presidential Elections, 1988" (Paper presented at the Institute for Political Studies in Japan, Tokyo, Japan, September 8–10, 1989), p. 3.
2. Herbert E. Alexander, "Making Sense about Dollars in the 1980 Presidential Campaigns," *Money and Politics in the United States,* ed. Michael J. Malbin (Washington, D.C.: American Enterprise Institute/Chatham House, 1984), p. 24.
3. Edward W. Chester, *Radio, Television and American Politics* (New York: Sheed & Ward, 1969), p. 21.
4. Herbert E. Alexander, *Financing Politics,* 3rd ed. (Washington, D.C.: Congressional Quarterly, 1984), pp. 11–12.
5. Edward Rogers (Bush campaign) and Susan Estrich (Dukakis campaign), quoted in *Campaign for President: The Managers Look at '88,* ed. David R. Runkle (Dover, Mass.: Auburn House, 1989), p. 190.
6. Herbert E. Alexander, "Spending on Presidential Campaigns" in *Electing the President: A Program for Reform,* ed. Robert E. Hunter (Washington, D.C.: Center for Strategic and International Studies, Georgetown University, 1986), p. 61.

7. This brief discussion of the sources of political contributions is based primarily on Alexander, *Financing Politics*, pp. 55–59.

8. Quoted in Jasper B. Shannon, *Money and Politics* (New York: Random House, 1959), p. 35.

9. In 1972 the chief fund raiser for the Nixon campaign, Maurice Stans, and Richard Nixon's private attorney, Herbert Kalmbach, collected contributions, some of them illegal, on behalf of the president. They exerted strong pressure on corporate executives, despite the prohibition on corporate giving. Secret contributions totaling millions of dollars were received, and three special secret funds were established to give the White House and the Committee to Reelect the President (CREEP) maximum discretion in campaign expenditures. It was from these funds that the "dirty tricks" of the 1972 campaign and the Watergate burglary were financed.

10. Alexander, "Financing the Presidential Elections," p. 16.

11. Clyde Wilcox, "Financing the 1988 Prenomination Campaigns," in *Nominating the President*, ed. Emmett Buell and Lee Sigelman (Knoxville, Tenn.: University of Tennessee Press, 1991), p. 96.

12. Alexander, "Financing the Presidential Elections," p. 17.

13. Ibid., p. 33 and Ronald B. Rapoport, Walter J. Stone, and Alan I. Abramowitz, "Do Endorsements Matter? Group Influence in the 1984 Democratic Caucuses," *American Political Science Review* 85 (1991), pp. 193–203.

14. Wilcox, "Financing the 1988 Prenomination Campaigns," p. 99.

15. Frank Fahrenkopt (Republican National Committee) and Susan Estrich (Dukakis campaign), quoted in *Campaign for President*, p. 190.

16. Ibid.

17. Alexander, "Financing the Presidential Elections," p. 27.

18. Ibid., pp. 4, 10.

19. Ibid., p. 3.

20. Frederick Martin (Gore campaign) and Susan Estrich (Dukakis campaign), quoted in *Campaign for President*, pp. 176–77.

21. Alexander, "Financing the Presidential Elections," p. 14.

22. Federal Election Commission, *Record*, October 1985, p. 5.

23. All spending by non-party groups does not have to be reported to the FEC. For example, the cost of internal communications to a group's membership urging them to vote for a particular candidate, or nonpartisan public activities, such as urging citizens to vote, do not have to be reported as independent expenditures. On the other hand, public partisan activities, such as advertisements for or against a candidate, do have to be reported. Organized labor often spends more internally on its political activities than it does in the public arena.

24. Federal Election Commission, *Record*, August 1989, p. 8.

25. Ibid.

26. Alexander, "Financing the Presidential Elections," p. 33.

27. Wilcox, "Financing the 1988 Prenomination Campaigns," p. 111.

28. Ibid.; and Gary R. Orren, "The Nomination Process: Vicissitudes of Candidate Selection," in *The Election of 1984*, ed. Michael Nelson (Washington, D.C.: Congressional Quarterly, 1985), p. 50.

29. Michael Robinson, Clyde Wilcox, and Paul Marshall, "The Presidency: Not For Sale," *Public Opinion* II (March/April 1989): 51.

30. Wilcox, "Financing the 1988 Prenomination Campaigns," p. 112.

31. Robinson, Wilcox, and Marshall, "Presidency," p. 50.

# SELECTED READINGS

Alexander, Herbert. "Campaign Finance Reform." *Proceedings of the Academy of Political Science* 37 (March 1989): 123–40.

———. *Financing Politics*. 3rd ed. Washington, D.C.: Congressional Quarterly, 1984.

———. "Financing the Presidential Elections, 1988." Paper presented at the Institute for Political Studies in Japan, Tokyo, Japan, September 8–10, 1989.

Heard, Alexander. *The Costs of Democracy*. Chapel Hill, N.C.: University of North Carolina Press, 1960.

Magleby, David B. and Candice J. Nelson. *The Money Chase: Congressional Campaign Finance Reform*. Washington, D.C.: Brookings Institution, 1990.

Malbin, Michael J., ed. *Money and Politics in the United States*. Washington, D.C.: American Enterprise Institute, 1984.

Robinson, Michael J. "The Power of the Primary Purse: Money in 1984." *Public Opinion* 7 (August/September 1984): 49–51.

———, Clyde Wilcox, and Paul Marshall. "The Presidency: Not For Sale." *Public Opinion* II (March/April 1989): 49–53.

Sabato, Larry J. *PAC Power*. New York: W. W. Norton, 1985.

Sorauf, Frank J. *Money in American Elections*. Glenview, Ill.: Scott Foresman, 1988.

Stephenson-Horne, Marilee. "The Road to Hell: Unintended Consequences of Unwise Federal Campaign Finance Reforms." *Northern Kentucky Law Review* 17 (Spring 1990): 547–70.

Wilcox, Clyde. "Financing the 1988 Prenomination Campaigns," in *Nominating the President*, edited by Emmett H. Buell, Jr. and Lee Sigelman, Knoxville, Tenn.: University of Tennessee Press, 1991: 91–118.

*The symbol of the Political Action Committee of the CIO, 1940.*

# Chapter 3

# The Political Environment

## INTRODUCTION

The nature of the electorate influences the content, images, and strategies of the campaign and affects the outcome of the election—an obvious conclusion, to be sure, but one that is not always appreciated. Campaigns are not conducted in ignorance of the voters. Rather, they are calculated to appeal to the needs and desires, attitudes and opinions, and associations and interactions of the electorate.

Voters do not come to the election with completely open minds. They come with preexisting views. They do not see and hear the campaign in isolation. They observe it and absorb it as part of their daily lives. In other words, their attitudes and associations affect their perceptions and influence their behavior. Preexisting views make it important for students of presidential elections to examine the formation of political attitudes and the patterns of social interaction.

Who votes and who does not? Why do people vote for certain candidates and not others? Do campaign appeals affect voting behavior? Are the responses of the electorate predictable? Political scientists have been interested in these questions for some time. Politicians have been interested for even longer.

A great deal of social science research and political savvy have gone into finding the answers. Spurred by the development of sophisticated survey techniques and methods of data analysis, political scientists, sociologists, and social psychologists have uncovered a wealth of information on how the public reacts and the electorate behaves during a campaign. They have examined correlations between demographic characteristics and voter turnout. They have explored psychological motivations, social influences, and political pressures that contribute to voting behavior. This chapter will examine some of their findings.

It is organized into three sections. The first discusses who votes. Describing the expansion of suffrage in the nineteenth and twentieth centuries, the section then turns to recent trends. Turnout is influenced by partisan, economic, and social factors. It is also affected by laws that govern elections and by circumstances of the vote itself, such as the closeness of the contest, interest in the campaign, and even the weather on election day. The impact of these variables on the decision whether to cast a ballot is the principal focus of this section.

The second and third sections of the chapter study influences on the vote. First, the *partisan* basis of politics is examined. How do political attitudes affect the ways people evaluate the campaign and shape their actual voting decision? Models of voting behavior are presented and then used to help explain contemporary voting patterns.

Next, the *social* basis of politics is analyzed. Dividing the electorate into distinct and overlapping socioeconomic, ethnic, and religious groupings, this section deals with the relationship of these groupings to voting behavior. It places primary emphasis on the formation of party coalitions during the 1930s and their evolution into the 1990s.

The final discussion of this section looks to the future. Are the two major parties going through a period of realignment or are they still in a period of dealignment? Are voters becoming more independent in their allegiances and their voting decisions? Recent research provides some answers to these questions.

## TURNOUT

Who votes? In one sense, this is a simple question to resolve. Official election returns indicate the number of voters and the states, even the precincts, in which the votes were cast. By easy calculation, the percentage of those eligible who actually voted can be determined. In 1980, 52.6 percent of the voting-age population cast ballots in the presidential election; in 1984, the figure was 53.1 percent; in 1988, it was 50.2 percent. (See Table 3–1.)

For campaign strategists and political analysts, however, more information is needed. In planning a campaign, it is necessary to design and target appeals to attract specific groups of voters. In assessing the results, it is also essential to understand how particular segments of the electorate responded. By evaluating turnout on the basis of demographic characteristics and partisan attitudes, strategists and analysts alike obtain the information they need to make sophisticated judgments.

TABLE 3–1

Participation in Presidential Elections, 1932–1988

| Year | Resident Population of Voting Age | Total Presidential Vote | % of Voting Age Population |
|------|-----------------------------------|-------------------------|----------------------------|
| 1932 | 75,768,000 | 39,732,000 | 52.4% |
| 1936 | 80,174,000 | 45,643,000 | 56.0 |
| 1940 | 84,728,000 | 49,900,000 | 58.9 |
| 1944 | 85,654,000 | 47,977,000 | 56.0 |
| 1948 | 95,573,000 | 48,794,000 | 51.1 |
| 1952 | 99,929,000 | 61,551,000 | 61.6 |
| 1956 | 104,515,000 | 62,027,000 | 59.3 |
| 1960 | 109,672,000 | 68,838,000 | 62.8 |
| 1964 | 114,090,000 | 70,645,000 | 61.9 |
| 1968 | 120,285,000 | 73,212,000 | 60.9 |
| 1972 | 140,777,000 | 77,719,000 | 55.2 |
| 1976 | 152,308,000 | 81,556,000 | 53.5 |
| 1980 | 164,595,000 | 86,515,000 | 52.6 |
| 1984 | 174,467,000 | 92,653,000 | 53.1 |
| 1988 | 182,628,000 | 91,595,000 | 50.2 |

*Source:* U.S. Department of Commerce, Bureau of the Census, *Statistical Abstract of the United States* (Washington, D.C.: Government Printing Office, 1990), p. 264.

Voting turnout has varied widely over the years. In the first national election, only about 11 percent of the potentially eligible population participated. The presidential vote was even smaller, since most electors were designated by the state legislatures and not chosen directly by the people.

In the early period from the end of the eighteenth century until 1824, voters constituted only about 20–25 percent of those who were eligible to vote in most states. Without parties or a tradition of participation in politics, the public deferred to the more political prominent members of the society.[1] Turnout increased in the 1820s, however, spurred by a political reform movement. Known as Jacksonian democracy, this movement advocated greater public participation in the electoral process. By the 1830s, 50–60 percent of the electorate voted. With the rise of competitive, mass-based parties in the 1840s, turnout increased to 80 percent and remained within the 70–80 percent range for the next fifty years in all regions except for the South.[2] There, the rise of one-party politics following the Civil War and the disfranchisement of blacks after withdrawal of federal troops substantially reduced the proportion of those who voted.

At the turn of the century, turnout began to decline in the nation as a whole, although the number of voters continued to increase. Thousands of immigrants, who initially spoke little English, enlarged the electorate but reduced the proportion of it who voted. Similarly the enfranchisement of women in 1920 had much the same effect.[3]

Although voter turnout grew moderately during Franklin Roosevelt's presidency and the post–World War II period, it has declined since 1960. In the 1988 presidential election, one-half of the electorate did not vote. Only 27 percent of those eligible cast ballots for the winner, George Bush. In off-year elections, turnout is even lower, frequently in the range of 40 percent or less. In 1990 it was only 33 percent.

What is wrong? Does the low turnout indicate voter satisfaction or alienation? Does it contribute to stability or create conditions for instability? What party and which programs benefit and which groups suffer when so many people do not vote? These questions will be addressed in an examination of turnout and its implications for the political system.

## *The Expansion of Suffrage*

The Constitution empowers the state legislatures to determine the time, place, and manner of holding elections for national office. While it also gives Congress the authority to alter such regulations, Congress did not do so until the Civil War. Thus the states were free to restrict suffrage, and most did. In some, property ownership was a requirement for exercising the franchise; in others, a particular religious belief was necessary. In most, it was essential to be white, male, and over twenty-one.

By the 1830s, most states had eliminated property and religious restrictions. The Fifteenth Amendment, ratified in 1870, removed race and color as qualifications for voting. In theory, it enabled all black males to vote. In practice, it enfranchised those in the North and border states but not those in the South. A series of institutional devices such as the poll tax, literacy tests, and restrictive primaries in which only Caucasians could participate (known as "white primaries") combined effectively with social pressure to prevent blacks from voting in the South for another hundred years.

Following the Civil War, both the number of eligible voters and the percentage of actual voters increased. Close competition between the parties contributed to this higher level of participation, as did the absence of registration procedures and the use of secret ballots in some states.

In the twentieth century, the passage of the Nineteenth, Twenty-third, Twenty-fourth, and Twenty-sixth Amendments continued to expand the voting age population. In 1920, women received the right to vote; in 1961, the District of Columbia was granted electoral votes, thereby extending the franchise to its residents in presidential elections; in 1964, the collection of a poll tax was prohibited in national elections;

in 1971, suffrage was extended to all citizens eighteen years of age and older. Previously, each state had established its own minimum age.

Moreover, the Supreme Court and Congress began to eliminate the legal and institutional barriers to voting. In 1944, the Court outlawed the white primary.[4] In the mid-1960s, Congress, by its passage of the Civil Rights Act (1964) and the Voting Rights Act (1965), banned literacy tests in federal elections for all citizens who had at least a sixth-grade education in a U.S. school. Where less than 50 percent of the population was registered to vote, federal officials were sent to facilitate registration. No longer was long and costly litigation necessary to ensure the right to vote. Amendments to the Voting Rights Act have also reduced the residence requirement for presidential elections to a maximum of thirty days.

The expansion of suffrage has produced more voters. It has enlarged the electorate, but it has also contributed to the smaller percentage of that electorate who actually votes.

Take women, for example. Although they received the right to vote in 1920, the proportion of women who exercised this right was less than that of men for another fifty-six years. In 1980 the proportion of women and men who voted was approximately equal. By 1988, women were slightly more likely to vote than men.

The case of women is not unusual. Newly enfranchised voters tend to cast ballots less regularly than those who have previously enjoyed the right to vote. It takes time to develop the habit of voting.

Registration procedures also act as an impediment to voting. These procedures vary from state to state. The period during which people may register, the places where they have to go to do so, even the hours when registration may occur, are controlled by state law. Naturally, the harder the states make it to register, the smaller the vote they can expect.

Registration procedures have a particularly significant effect on a mobile society such as that of the United States. With one-third of the population moving on an average of every two years, the need to re-register to vote effectively decreases the size of the vote. Two political scientists, Raymond E. Wolfinger and Steven J. Rosenstone, estimated that turnout could be increased by as much as 9 percent by making modest adjustments in these laws that would ease registration procedures.[5]

Concern has been voiced about the relatively low turnout of voters in the United States as compared to other democratic countries. Contemporary voting statistics demonstrate that this concern is justified. If the percentage of *eligible* voters in the United States who actually vote is compared to that of twenty-one other democratic countries located primarily in Western Europe, the United States ranks twentieth; if, however, the percentage of *registered* voters who actually vote is the basis for comparison, the United States fares better, ranking eleventh out of twenty-four.[6] And unlike many other countries, the United States does not impose penalties on those who fail to register and vote; nor does it have a national system for automatic registration.

There is another reason that turnout in the United States trails that of many other democratic countries. In the United States most elections are conducted in single-member districts. In these elections the candidate with the most votes wins. Those elections which are conducted in multimember districts and decided on the basis of a proportional vote provide more incentives for those in the minority to turn out to vote than does the winner-take-all system or elections conducted in single-member districts. Since so many national and state elections in the United States are not close, turnout is discouraged by the electoral system itself.

## Psychological and Social Influences on Turnout

In addition to the system and its impact, other influences on whether people vote are their interest in the election, concern over the outcome, feelings of civic responsibility, and sense of political efficacy (their belief that their vote really matters).[7] Naturally, people who feel more strongly about the election are more likely to get involved. Those with more intense partisan feelings are more likely to have this interest, more likely to participate in the campaign, and more likely to vote on election day. Voting, in fact, becomes a habit. The more people have done it in the past, the more likely they will do it in the future.

Table 3–2 provides empirical support for the proposition that turnout increases with age, at least up to a point. In 1988, for example, only 33 percent of those in the youngest cohort (eighteen–twenty years old) voted. Each subsequent age group in that election voted with greater frequency. Although Table 3–2 does not show it, turnout does decrease after age seventy-five. Nonetheless, those over seventy-five still vote more regularly than those under twenty-four.[8]

Other characteristics related to turnout are education, income, and occupational status. As people become more educated, as they move up the socioeconomic ladder, as their jobs gain in status, they are more likely to vote. Education is the most important of these variables. It has a larger impact than any other single social characteristic.[9] As Table 3–2 demonstrates, the higher the level of education, the greater the percentage voting.

The reason education is so important is that it provides the skills for processing and evaluating information, for perceiving differences among the parties, candidates, and issues, and for relating these differences to personal values and behavior. Education also affects personal success. It increases a person's stake in the system, interest in the election, and concern over the outcome. Since the lesson that voting is a civic responsibility is usually learned in the classroom, schooling may

TABLE 3–2

**Voting Turnout by Population Characteristics, 1968–1988**
**(in percentages)**

|                    | 1968  | 1972  | 1976  | 1980  | 1984  | 1988  |
|--------------------|-------|-------|-------|-------|-------|-------|
| SEX                |       |       |       |       |       |       |
| Male               | 69.8% | 64.1% | 59.6% | 59.1% | 59.0% | 56.4% |
| Female             | 66.0  | 62.0  | 58.8  | 59.4  | 60.8  | 58.3  |
| AGE                |       |       |       |       |       |       |
| 18–20              |       | 48.3  | 38.0  | 35.7  | 36.7  | 33.2  |
| 21–24              | 51.0  | 50.7  | 45.6  | 43.1  | 43.5  | 38.3  |
| 25–34              | 62.5  | 59.7  | 55.4  | 54.6  | 54.5  | 48.0  |
| 35–44              | 70.8  | 66.3  | 63.3  | 64.4  | 63.5  | 61.3  |
| 45–64              | 74.9  | 70.8  | 68.7  | 69.3  | 69.8  | 67.9  |
| 65 & over          | 65.8  | 63.5  | 62.2  | 65.1  | 67.7  | 68.8  |
| EDUCATION          |       |       |       |       |       |       |
| 8 years or less    | 54.5  | 47.4  | 44.1  | 42.6  | 42.9  | 36.7  |
| HIGH SCHOOL        |       |       |       |       |       |       |
| 1–3 years          | 61.3  | 52.0  | 47.2  | 45.6  | 44.4  | 41.3  |
| 4 years            |       |       | 59.4  | 58.9  | 58.7  | 54.7  |
| COLLEGE            |       |       |       |       |       |       |
| 1–3 years          | 72.5[a] | 65.4[a] | 68.1 | 67.2 | 67.5 | 64.5 |
| 4 years or more    | 81.2[a] | 78.8[a] | 79.8 | 79.9 | 79.1 | 77.6 |
| RACE               |       |       |       |       |       |       |
| White              | 69.1  | 64.5  | 60.9  | 60.9  | 61.4  | 59.1  |
| Black              | 57.6  | 52.1  | 48.7  | 50.5  | 55.8  | 51.5  |
| Hispanic           | NA    | 37.4  | 31.8  | 29.9  | 32.6  | 28.8  |

[a] Indicates percentage who had completed more than twelve years of schooling.

*Source:* U.S. Department of Commerce, Bureau of the Census, *Statistical Abstract of the United States* (Washington, D.C.: Government Printing Office, 1990), p. 262.

also contribute to a more highly developed sense of responsibility about voting. Finally, education provides the knowledge and confidence to overcome voting hurdles—to register on time, to file absentee ballots properly, and to mark the ballot or use the voting machine correctly on election day.[10]

Given the relationship of education to turnout, it may seem surprising that the rate of turnout should decline in the nation as a whole at a time when the general level of education has risen.[11] One explanation for the decline has been the increasing number of younger voters; another has been the weakening of partisan attitudes; a third has been the growth of political cynicism and apathy among the electorate, particularly among those in the lower socioeconomic groups.

The "baby boomers" born in the mid-1940s and the 1950s entered the electorate in the mid-1960s and 1970s. They enlarged the pool of eligible voters but reduced the proportion of those who vote because young people tend to vote with less regularity than their elders. (See Table 3–2.) They are more mobile; they have fewer economic interests and looser political ties to the community in which they live and vote; and they have not developed the habit of voting or, in some cases, even of identifying with a political party. Similarly, advances in medicine have prolonged life and increased the number of senior citizens, particularly those over seventy-five. They, too, tend to vote less, primarily for reasons of health.

Although the "youthing" and aging of the electorate may have resulted in a lower percentage of voter turnout, it does not explain most of the decline. Most age groups have lower turnout.

Another explanation lies with political attitudes—feelings toward parties. For the last three decades, partisan identities have weakened. Since party loyalty is a motivation for voting, a decline in partisanship decreases turnout. Similarly, parties have become less important influences on the campaign, provide less sturdy linkage to voters, and are less reliable predictors of their candidate's policy positions or their officeholder's policy judgments. As the parties become more personalized and factionalized and as campaigns become more candidate centered, the election becomes more confusing to voters. It is harder to discern whose election is in their own interests. The difficulty of making this calculation has contributed to nonvoting among those with less education, who tend to have less information and less highly developed analytic skills.

People have also become more disillusioned about the political system and, correspondingly, less confident that their vote matters or that they can change the way government works or public officials behave. This lower sense of efficacy has also depressed the vote. In a recent study, three political scientists, Paul R. Abramson, John H. Aldrich, and David W. Rohde, calculated that 62 percent of the decline in turnout can be attributed to the combined effects of weaker partisan affiliation and feelings of less political effectiveness.[12]

There is also a class bias in voting, which appears to be related to negative feelings people have about their own ability to affect events and the trust they place in political leaders. The decline in turnout has been greatest among those in the lowest socioeconomic groups and therefore, on a proportional basis, among the nonwhite population more than among the white population. The bias produces a tragic irony in American politics. Those who are most disadvantaged, who have the least education, and who need to change conditions the most actually participate the least. Those who are the most advantaged, who benefit from existing conditions and presumably from public policy, vote most often. These trends in voting behavior work to reflect, even perpetuate, the status quo.

## Turnout and Partisanship

The decrease in turnout has had partisan political implications as well. Since the Democratic party draws more of its electoral support from those in the lower socioeconomic groups, those with less formal education, and those with fewer professional opportunities, the decline has hurt the Democrats more than the Republicans. In 1988, for example, Dukakis would have gained 2.6 million votes if black and Hispanic voters turned out with the same frequency as the rest of the population.[13] Still, he would have fallen 4.3 million votes short of Bush's winning margin. Moreover, nonvoters surveyed after the 1988 election indicated that they preferred Bush to Dukakis by approximately 6 percent, slightly less than Bush's popular vote majority. Declining turnout, in short, has contributed to the Democratic party's presidential woes in the 1970s and the 1980s, although it has not been the Democrats' only problem.

To improve the turnout of those more likely to vote Democratic, the party has employed a "sweep" strategy, trying to register as many people as possible, particularly in areas of Democratic strength. This strategy is based on the assumption that the greater the turnout, the more Democratic candidates will benefit.

Lower turnout has also affected the Republicans, but not as much as the Democrats. The primary reason that the Republicans have been less adversely affected than the Democrats is that they receive more of their support from those in the higher socioeconomic brackets, those who tend to vote more regularly. Moreover, the Republican party has also benefited from greater financial resources, which have enabled it to mount more effective efforts to identify and register new voters.

Unlike the Democrats, the Republicans have employed an individualized targeting approach to voter registration. Traditionally, they have used a variety of lists of potential Republican voters and depended on elaborate communications technology to reach them.

Both parties conducted massive registration drives in 1984, with the result that turnout in the general election increased marginally. By most estimates the Republicans were more successful than the Democrats that year in registering new voters. In 1988 neither party mounted as large or costly a registration effort as it did four years earlier. The failure to do so may have contributed to the decrease in turnout in the 1988 general election.

# THE PARTISAN BASIS OF POLITICS

In addition to who votes, the partisan basis of politics affects why people vote as they do. Considerable research has been conducted on the attitudes and behavior of the U.S. voter. Initially, much of it was done under the direction of the Center for Political Studies at the University of Michigan. Beginning in 1952, the center began conducting nationwide surveys during presidential elections.[14] The object of these surveys has been to identify the major influences on voting behavior. A random sample of the electorate is interviewed before and after the election. Respondents are asked a series of questions designed to reveal their attitudes toward the parties, candidates, and issues. On the basis of the answers, researchers try to explain voting behavior of the U.S. electorate.

## *A Model of the U.S. Voter*

One of the earliest and most influential theories of why people vote as they do was presented in a book entitled *The American Voter* (1960). The model on which the theory is based assumes that individuals are influenced by their partisan attitudes and social relationships in addition to the political environment in which the election occurs. In fact, these attitudes and those relationships condition the impact of that environment on individual voting behavior.

According to the theory, people develop attitudes early in life, largely as a consequence of interacting with their families, particularly their parents. These attitudes, in turn, tend to be reinforced by neighborhood, school, and religious associations. The reasons they tend to be reinforced lie in the psychological and social patterns of behavior. Psychologically, it is more pleasing to have beliefs and attitudes supported than challenged. Socially, it is more comfortable to associate with "nice," like-minded people—those with similar cultural, educational, and religious experiences—than with others. This desire to increase one's "comfort level" in social relationships explains why the environment for most people tends to be supportive much of the time.[15]

Attitudes mature and harden over the years. Older people become less amenable to change and more set in their ways. Their behavior is more predictable.[16] Political attitudes are no exception to this general pattern of attitude formation and maintenance. They, too, are developed early in life, are reinforced by association, grow in intensity, and become more predictable with age.

Of all the factors that contribute to the development of a political attitude, an identification with a political party is one of the most important. It affects how people see the campaign and how they vote.

Party identification operates as a conceptual mechanism, a lens through which people evaluate the campaign. It provides cues for interpreting the issues, for judging the candidates, and for deciding whether and how to vote. The stronger these attitudes, the more compelling the cues; conversely, the weaker the attitudes, the less likely they will affect perceptions during the campaign and influence voting on election day.[17]

When identification with party is weak or nonexistent, other factors, such as the personalities of the candidates and their issue positions, will be correspondingly more important. In contrast to party identification, which is a long-term stabilizing factor, candidate and issue orientations are short term, more variable influences that differ from election to election. Of the two, the image of the candidate has been viewed as more significant most of the time.

Candidate images turn on personality and policy dimensions. People tend to form general impressions about candidates on the basis of what they know about their leadership capabilities, decision-making capacity, and personal traits. For an incumbent president seeking reelection, accomplishments in office provide much of the criteria for an evaluation—how well the president has done. Other characteristics, such as trustworthiness, integrity, and candor, are also important. For the challenger, it is the potential for office as demonstrated by experience, knowledge, confidence, and assertiveness, plus a host of personal qualities that help determine qualifications for a leadership position such as being president.[18]

Candidates' stands on the issues, however, seem less critical to the proponents of this voting behavior model than do their partisanship and performance in office. The principal explanation for downgrading the importance of issues has been the low level of information and awareness that much of the electorate possesses. To be important, issues must be salient. They must attract attention; they must hit home. Without personal impact, they are unlikely to be primary motivating factors in voting. To the extent that issue positions are not known or distinguishable between the principal candidates, the candidates' experience, particularly their performance in office, becomes a stronger influence on the vote.

Ironically, that portion of the electorate which can be more easily persuaded—weak partisans and independents—tends to have the least information.[19] Conversely, the most committed tend to be the most informed. They use their information to support their partisanship.

The relationship between degree of partisanship and amount of information has significant implications for a democratic society. The traditional view of a democracy holds that information and awareness are necessary to make an intelligent judgment on election day. However, the finding that those who have the most information are also the most committed, and that those who lack this commitment also lack the incentive to acquire information, has upset some of the assumptions about the motivation for acquiring information and using it to vote intelligently on election day.

## A Refined Theory of Voting

The model of voting behavior presented in 1960 has engendered considerable controversy. Critics have charged that the theory presumes that most of the electorate is uninformed and vote habitually rather than rationally. One well-known political scientist, the late V. O. Key, even wrote a book dedicated to "the perverse and unorthodox argument . . . that voters are not fools."[20] Key studied the behavior of three groups of voters between 1936 and 1960: switchers, stand-patters, and new voters. He found those who switched their votes to be interested in and influenced by their own evaluation of policy, personality, and performance. In this sense, Key believed that they exercised an intelligent judgment when voting.

Key's conclusion that most voters were not automatons and that most of their voting decisions were not solely or even primarily the product of their psychological dispositions and social pressures was carried a step further by Morris Fiorina in his provocative study, *Retrospective Voting in American National Elections* (1981). Utilizing a rational-choice model adopted from economics, Fiorina argued that voting decisions are calculations people make on the basis of their accumulated political experience. They make these calculations by assessing the past performance of the parties and their elected officials in the light of the promises they made and political events that have occurred. Fiorina calls this a *retrospective evaluation*.[21]

Retrospective evaluations are not only important for influencing voting in a given election; they are also important for shaping partisan attitudes, which Fiorina defines as "a running tally of retrospective evaluations of party promises and performance."[22] These attitudes, in turn, influence voting. In other words, it is a two-way street. Political attitudes, especially partisanship, shape and are shaped by the political environment in which they occur. Although political attitudes do not change quickly, they do change. The discussion that follows will examine the principal changes that have taken place in the last three decades and their impact on voting behavior.

## Partisan Voting Patterns

The initial model of voter behavior was based on research conducted in the 1950s. Since that time, the U.S. electorate has experienced a divisive, unsuccessful war in Southeast Asia, a cohesive, successful one in the Persian Gulf, a major scandal (Watergate) that led to the resignation of a president, other smaller scandals involving public officials, large-scale social movements for equal rights and opportunities involving racial minorities and women, and periods of economic recession, inflation, and prosperity. Naturally these events and the reaction of public officials to them have had an impact on the partisan attitudes of the electorate.

Three major trends stand out. First, there has been a reduction in the number of people who identify with a party and, conversely, an increase in the number of self-proclaimed independents. Second, there has been a decline in the strength of partisan identities. Third, there has been a shift in partisan loyalties, with the Democratic party losing adherents and the Republican party gaining them. Each of these changes has important long- and short-term implications for U.S. electoral politics.

Table 3–3 lists the percentage of party identifiers and independents. As the table indicates, between 1952 and 1988 there was a 10 percent decline in people who identify with a political party and a 15 percent increase in the number of self-proclaimed independents. Most of the shift occurred after 1964. The table also suggests that the decline was

### TABLE 3–3
### Party Identification, 1952–1988[a] (in percentages)[b]

| Party Identification | 1952 | 1956 | 1960 | 1964 | 1968 | 1972 | 1976 | 1980 | 1984 | 1988 |
|---|---|---|---|---|---|---|---|---|---|---|
| *Democrat* | | | | | | | | | | |
| Strong | 22 | 21 | 20 | 27 | 20 | 15 | 15 | 18 | 17 | 18 |
| Weak | 25 | 23 | 25 | 25 | 25 | 26 | 25 | 23 | 20 | 18 |
| *Independent[c]* | | | | | | | | | | |
| Leaning Democrat | 10 | 6 | 6 | 9 | 10 | 11 | 12 | 11 | 11 | 12 |
| Nonpartisan | 6 | 9 | 10 | 8 | 11 | 13 | 15 | 13 | 11 | 11 |
| Leaning Republican | 7 | 8 | 7 | 6 | 9 | 11 | 10 | 10 | 12 | 13 |
| *Republican* | | | | | | | | | | |
| Weak | 14 | 14 | 14 | 14 | 15 | 13 | 14 | 14 | 15 | 14 |
| Strong | 13 | 15 | 16 | 11 | 10 | 10 | 9 | 9 | 12 | 14 |
| *Apoliticals* | | | | | | | | | | |
| "Don't know" | 4 | 4 | 3 | 1 | 1 | 1 | 1 | 2 | 2 | 2 |

[a] The survey question was, "Generally speaking, do you usually think of yourself as a Republican, a Democrat, an Independent, or what?" If Republican or Democrat, "Would you call yourself a strong (R) (D) or a not very strong (R) (D)?" If Independent, "Do you think of yourself as closer to the Republican or Democratic party?"

[b] Percentages may not equal 100 due to rounding.

[c] The people who fall into this category are those who declare themselves to be independent, but in follow-up questions indicate that they lean in a partisan direction.

*Source:* Center for Political Studies, University of Michigan

principally in the strong partisan category through the 1970s. The increase in this category in the 1980s, particularly among Republicans, may augur a reversal of this trend.

In general, partisanship has weakened among most population groups. Many strong partisans have become weak partisans, and many weak partisans now consider themselves independent. How independently they behave on election day is another matter. Truly independent voting has increased far less rapidly than independent identification. In other words, a sizable portion claim that they are independent but continue to vote for candidates of the same party. They appear in Table 3–3 as independent but leaning in a partisan direction.

The decline in partisanship and the growth of independents have produced a more volatile and manipulable electorate. With weaker partisan allegiances and more independent identifiers, the campaign, the candidates, and the issues have become more important influences on the vote.

## *Partisan Deviations*

There has been a dramatic rise in split-ticket voting. According to Arthur H. Miller and Martin P. Wattenberg, about three times as many people divide their vote today as did in the 1950s.[23] The defections come primarily from weak partisans. Figure 3–1 presents the rates of defection among party identifiers from 1952 to 1988.

Defections from partisan voting patterns have helped the Republicans more than the Democrats. Without votes from Democratic defectors, the GOP could not have won seven presidential elections since 1952. Much of the help, however, has been short term. Although the Republicans have won all but one election at the presidential level since 1968, they still do not command the loyalty of a majority of the electorate.

The gap between the Republicans and Democrats has narrowed, however. In 1952 the Democrats enjoyed a 20 percent advantage in the party identification of the electorate. Twenty years later that advantage had declined to 18 percent. The 1980s have seen an even greater reduction in the differential between Democratic and Republican party identification. In the 1988 preelection survey conducted by the National Elections Center at the University of Michigan, the Democratic lead in party identifiers was only 8 percent. If those who indicated they were independent but leaned in a partisan direction were taken into account, the gap narrowed to about 7 percent. When turnout of party identifiers and leaners are considered, the difference was only 1 percent.[24] Since 1988, and particularly following the successful military operation in the Persian Gulf in 1991, the Democrats' partisan advantage has eroded. They no longer command the allegiance of a majority or perhaps even a plurality. Gallup polls conducted between 1989 and 1991 show the parties at parity, each commanding the support of about one-third of the electorate.

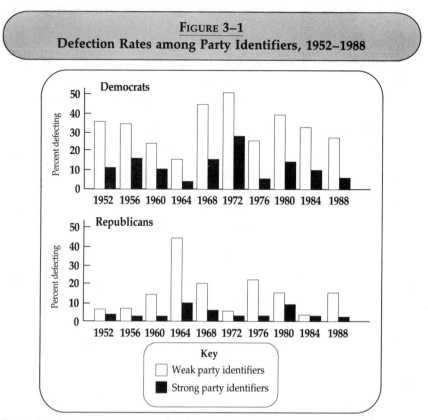

FIGURE 3–1
Defection Rates among Party Identifiers, 1952–1988

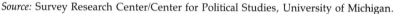

*Source:* Survey Research Center/Center for Political Studies, University of Michigan.

Partisan ties have also become weaker than they were thirty or even twenty years ago. The weakening of partisan loyalties, in turn, has produced more candidate-oriented voting and, to a lesser extent, more issue-oriented voting, especially at the presidential level. Partisanship, although still relevant, has decreased in importance. Why?

The reaction to Vietnam and Watergate, to the credibility gaps and political abuses of the so-called imperial presidents, generated feelings of mistrust and hostility that were directed at politicians. Those who became eligible to vote during this period were less willing to identify with a political party. Moreover, the salience of social and cultural issues rendered the traditional partisan alliances, which had been built on economic ties, much less relevant.

A second reason for the drop in partisan identification has been the lowering of the voting age to eighteen. Over the last thirty years, the percentage of the electorate twenty-four years of age and under has nearly doubled. Since party identification tends to develop and harden over time, the youthing of the electorate contributed to the decline in partisanship and growth of independents. This trend may change as the electorate gets older.

A third factor has to do with contemporary modes of campaigning and the declining role of the party in that capacity. In the past, the political party came between the voter and the candidate. Political parties provided the organization, planned the campaign, and made the partisan appeal. In doing so, they trumpeted their own cause. Today, much of the information comes directly from the candidate's organization via television. The party no longer mediates as it did in the pretelevision age.

Nonetheless, it is premature to write an obituary for partisanship and its impact on the electorate. In 1988 there was a stronger relationship between partisanship and presidential voting than in any of the last six presidential elections.[25] This relationship did not extend, however, to voting for Congress.

What seems clear today is that partisanship is no longer as good a predictor of the vote as it was in the past. It is not as strong an influence on how people evaluate the candidates or the issues and ultimately, on how they vote. Partisan ties have weakened, but they have not been eliminated, nor have they been replaced. The impact that the weakening of these ties has on the parties' electoral coalitions is discussed in the next section.

## THE SOCIAL BASIS OF POLITICS

### *The New Deal Realignment*

Political coalitions develop during periods of partisan realignment. The last time such a realignment occurred was in the 1930s. Largely as a consequence of the Great Depression, the Democrats emerged as the dominant party.[26] Their coalition, held together by a common economic concern that the government play a more active role in dealing with the nation's economic problems, supported Franklin Roosevelt's New Deal program. Those who saw government involvement as a threat to the free enterprise system opposed much of Roosevelt's domestic legislation. They remained Republican in attitude and voting behavior.

The Democrats became the majority party during this period by expanding their coalition. Since the Civil War, the Democrats had enjoyed southern support. White Protestants living in rural areas dominated the southern electorate; blacks were largely excluded from it. Only in the election of 1928, when Al Smith, the Catholic governor of New York, ran as the Democratic candidate, was there a sizable southern popular and electoral vote for a Republican candidate at the presidential level. Being a Catholic and an opponent of prohibition made Smith unacceptable to many white Protestant fundamentalists who lived in the South.

Roosevelt maintained the expanded southern support across the socioeconomic spectrum. Poor as well as wealthy southerners backed his candidacy. In each of his four presidential races, Roosevelt received well over two-thirds of the southern vote.[27]

Catholics, as a group, also voted Democratic before the 1930s. Living primarily in the urban centers of the North, Catholics became increasingly important to the Democrats as their numbers grew. Poor economic and social conditions, combined with the immigrant status of many Catholics, made them dependent on big-city bosses, who were able to deliver a sizable Democratic vote. In 1928, for the first time, a majority of the cities in the country voted Democratic. Catholic support for Smith and the Democratic party figured prominently in this vote.

The harsh economic realities of the Great Depression enabled Roosevelt to expand Democratic support in urban areas still further, particularly to those in the lower socioeconomic strata. Outside the South, Roosevelt's political coalition was differentiated along class lines. It attracted people with less education and income and those with lower-status jobs.[28] Organized labor, in particular, threw its support to Roosevelt. Union members became a core group in the Democratic coalition.

In addition to establishing a broad-based, lower-class party, Roosevelt also lured specific racial and ethnic groups, such as blacks and Jews, from their Republican affiliation. Blacks voted Democratic primarily for economic reasons, while Jews supported Roosevelt's liberal domestic programs and his anti-Nazi foreign policy. Neither of these groups provided the Democratic coalition of the 1930s with a large number of votes, but their loyalty to the party and long-term impact on it have been significant.

In contrast, during the same period the Republican party shrank. Not only were Republicans unable to attract new groups to their coalition, but they were unable to prevent the defection of some supporters whose economic situation affected their partisan loyalties and influenced their vote. Although the Republicans did retain the backing of a majority of business and professional people, they lost the support of much of the white Protestant working class. Republican strength remained concentrated in the Northeast, particularly in the rural areas.[29]

## *Evolving Political Coalitions*

The coalition that formed during the New Deal held together, for the most part, until the 1960s. During this period, blacks and Jews increased their identification with and support of the Democratic party and its candidates. Catholics tended to remain Democratic, although they fluctuated more in their voting behavior at the presidential level. Nonsouthern white Protestants continued to support the Republicans.

There were some changes, however, mainly along socioeconomic lines. Domestic prosperity contributed to the growth of a larger middle class. Had such a class identified with the Republicans for economic reasons, the Democratic majority would have been threatened. This identification did not occur, however. Those who gained in economic and social status did not, as a general rule, discard their partisan loyalties. The Democrats were able to hold on to the allegiance of a majority of this group and improve their position with the professional and managerial classes, which had grown substantially during this period. The Republicans continued to maintain their advantage with those in the upper socioeconomic strata. The economic improvement in the country had the effect of muting the class distinctions that were evident during the 1930s and 1940s.[30]

Partisan attitudes, however, were shifting in the South. White southerners, particularly those who first voted after 1940, began to desert their party at the presidential level, largely over civil rights issues. In 1948, Harry Truman won 52 percent of the southern vote, compared with Roosevelt's 69 percent four years earlier. Although Adlai Stevenson and John Kennedy carried the South by reduced margins, the southern white Protestant presidential vote went Republican for the first time in 1960. Had it not been for the growth of the black electorate in the South and its overwhelming support for Democratic candidates, the defection of the southern states from the Democratic camp would have been even more dramatic.

Major shifts in the national electorate began to be evident in the mid-1960s and have continued into the 1990s. (See Table 3–4.) One of the most significant and enduring of these changes has been the continued defection of southern white Protestants to the Republican party at the presidential level. This shift has occurred at other levels as well. In 1940, Roosevelt won 80 percent of the southern white Protestant vote. Thirty-six years later Jimmy Carter, a southern white Protestant himself, was not able to carry the southern white Protestant vote. In 1984 and 1988 southern whites were less apt to vote Democratic than were whites in any other region of the country. Dukakis received only 37 percent of the Southern, white vote.[31]

Party identification of southern whites has changed as well. Since 1952 there has been a substantial decline in the partisan loyalty that the Democrats have enjoyed. In that year 85 percent of southern whites considered themselves Democrats; by 1988 that proportion had shrunk to 46 percent. The ratio of Democrats to Republicans in the South has gone from 6:1 to less than 2:1.

Another potentially important shift has been the movement of new voters, particularly youth, to the Republican party. After being more Democratic than their elders in the five previous presidential contests,

## TABLE 3–4
## Vote by Groups in Presidential Elections, 1952–1988 (in percentages)

| | 1952 | | 1956 | | 1960 | | 1964 | | 1968 | | |
|---|---|---|---|---|---|---|---|---|---|---|---|
| | Adlai Steven- son | Dwight Eisen- hower | Adlai Steven- son | Dwight Eisen- hower | John Ken- nedy | Richard Nixon | Lyndon John- son | Barry Gold- water | Hubert Hum- phrey | Richard Nixon | George Wallace |
| National total, by sex | 44.6% | 55.4% | 42.2% | 57.8% | 50.1% | 49.9% | 61.3% | 38.7% | 43.0% | 43.4% | 13.6% |
| Male | 47 | 53 | 45 | 55 | 52 | 48 | 60 | 40 | 41 | 43 | 16 |
| Female | 42 | 58 | 39 | 61 | 49 | 51 | 62 | 38 | 45 | 43 | 12 |
| Race: | | | | | | | | | | | |
| White | 43 | 57 | 41 | 59 | 49 | 51 | 59 | 41 | 38 | 47 | 15 |
| Nonwhite | 79 | 21 | 61 | 39 | 68 | 32 | 94 | 6 | 85 | 12 | 3 |
| Education: | | | | | | | | | | | |
| College | 34 | 66 | 31 | 69 | 39 | 61 | 52 | 48 | 37 | 54 | 9 |
| High school | 45 | 55 | 42 | 58 | 52 | 48 | 62 | 38 | 42 | 43 | 15 |
| Grade school | 52 | 48 | 50 | 50 | 55 | 45 | 66 | 34 | 52 | 33 | 15 |
| Occupation: | | | | | | | | | | | |
| Professional and busi- ness | 36 | 64 | 32 | 68 | 42 | 58 | 54 | 46 | 34 | 56 | 10 |
| White collar | 40 | 60 | 37 | 63 | 48 | 52 | 57 | 43 | 41 | 47 | 12 |
| Manual | 55 | 45 | 50 | 50 | 60 | 40 | 71 | 29 | 50 | 35 | 15 |
| Age (years): | | | | | | | | | | | |
| Under 30 | 51 | 49 | 43 | 57 | 54 | 46 | 64 | 36 | 47 | 38 | 15 |
| 30–49 | 47 | 53 | 45 | 55 | 54 | 46 | 63 | 37 | 44 | 41 | 15 |
| 50 & older | 39 | 61 | 39 | 61 | 46 | 54 | 59 | 41 | 41 | 47 | 12 |
| Religion: | | | | | | | | | | | |
| Protestant | 37 | 63 | 37 | 63 | 38 | 62 | 55 | 45 | 35 | 49 | 16 |
| Catholic | 56 | 44 | 51 | 49 | 78 | 22 | 76 | 24 | 59 | 33 | 8 |
| Politics: | | | | | | | | | | | |
| Republican | 8 | 92 | 4 | 96 | 5 | 95 | 20 | 80 | 9 | 86 | 5 |
| Democrat | 77 | 23 | 85 | 15 | 84 | 16 | 87 | 13 | 74 | 12 | 14 |
| Independent | 35 | 65 | 30 | 70 | 43 | 57 | 56 | 44 | 31 | 44 | 25 |
| Region: | | | | | | | | | | | |
| East | 45 | 55 | 40 | 60 | 53 | 47 | 68 | 32 | 50 | 43 | 7 |
| Midwest | 42 | 58 | 41 | 59 | 48 | 52 | 61 | 39 | 44 | 47 | 9 |
| South | 51 | 49 | 49 | 51 | 51 | 49 | 52 | 48 | 31 | 36 | 33 |
| West | 42 | 58 | 43 | 57 | 49 | 51 | 60 | 40 | 44 | 49 | 7 |
| Members of labor union families | 61 | 39 | 57 | 43 | 65 | 35 | 73 | 27 | 56 | 29 | 15 |

[a] Less than 1 percent.

*Source:* "Gallup Opinion Index," November 1988, pp. 6–7. Reprinted with permission.

younger voters (ages eighteen–twenty-nine) supported Ronald Reagan in his reelection bid just as strongly as did those over thirty. (See Table 3–4.) Their support of George Bush was even greater. Beginning in the 1980s, more new voters identified with the Republicans than the Democrats. If this trend continues, the long-term implications will be significant and may affect the balance between the major parties.

While Democrats have lost the allegiance of southern whites at the presidential level and may be losing that of the youth, they have also seen support from several of their key coalition groups decline. Organized labor is a good example. In six of the eight presidential elections between 1952 and 1976, this group favored the Democratic candidate by an average of nearly 30 percentage points. In 1984, the results were much closer. Four years later Dukakis regained the Democrats' advan-

## TABLE 3–4  (*cont.*)

| 1972 | | 1976 | | | 1980 | | | 1984 | | 1988 | |
|---|---|---|---|---|---|---|---|---|---|---|---|
| George Mc-Govern | Richard Nixon | Jimmy Carter | Gerald Ford | Eugene Mc-Carthy | Jimmy Carter | Ronald Rea-gan | John Ander-son | Walter Mon-dale | Ronald Rea-gan | Michael Dukakis | George Bush |
| 38% | 62% | 50% | 48% | 1% | 41% | 51% | 7% | 41% | 59% | 46% | 54% |
| 37 | 63 | 53 | 45 | 1 | 38 | 53 | 7 | 36 | 64 | 44 | 56 |
| 38 | 62 | 48 | 51 | a | 44 | 49 | 6 | 45 | 55 | 48 | 52 |
| 32 | 68 | 46 | 52 | 1 | 36 | 56 | 7 | 34 | 66 | 41 | 59 |
| 87 | 13 | 85 | 15 | a | 86 | 10 | 2 | 87 | 13 | 82 | 18 |
| 37 | 63 | 42 | 55 | 2 | 35 | 53 | 10 | 39 | 61 | 42 | 58 |
| 34 | 66 | 54 | 46 | a | 43 | 51 | 5 | 43 | 57 | 46 | 54 |
| 49 | 51 | 58 | 41 | 1 | 54 | 42 | 3 | 51 | 49 | 55 | 45 |
| 31 | 69 | 42 | 56 | 1 | 33 | 55 | 10 | 34 | 66 | — | — |
| 36 | 64 | 50 | 48 | 2 | 40 | 51 | 9 | 47 | 53 | — | — |
| 43 | 57 | 58 | 41 | 1 | 48 | 46 | 5 | 46 | 54 | — | — |
| 48 | 52 | 53 | 45 | 1 | 47 | 41 | 11 | 40 | 60 | 37 | 63 |
| 33 | 67 | 48 | 49 | 2 | 38 | 52 | 8 | 40 | 60 | 45 | 55 |
| 36 | 64 | 52 | 48 | a | 41 | 54 | 4 | 41 | 59 | 49 | 51 |
| 30 | 70 | 46 | 53 | a | 39 | 54 | 6 | 39 | 61 | 42 | 58 |
| 48 | 52 | 57 | 42 | 1 | 46 | 47 | 6 | 39 | 61 | 51 | 49 |
| 5 | 95 | 9 | 91 | a | 8 | 86 | 5 | 4 | 96 | 7 | 93 |
| 67 | 33 | 82 | 18 | a | 69 | 26 | 4 | 79 | 21 | 85 | 15 |
| 31 | 69 | 38 | 57 | 4 | 29 | 55 | 14 | 33 | 67 | 43 | 57 |
| 42 | 58 | 51 | 47 | 1 | 43 | 47 | 9 | 46 | 54 | 51 | 49 |
| 40 | 60 | 48 | 50 | 1 | 41 | 51 | 7 | 42 | 58 | 47 | 53 |
| 29 | 71 | 54 | 45 | a | 44 | 52 | 3 | 37 | 63 | 40 | 60 |
| 41 | 59 | 46 | 51 | 1 | 35 | 54 | 9 | 40 | 60 | 46 | 54 |
| 46 | 54 | 63 | 36 | 1 | 50 | 43 | 5 | 52 | 48 | 63 | 37 |

tage, winning two votes for every one that Bush received from members of union families. Although Dukakis's labor vote reflects the continuing support Democrats have received from union members, the decline of blue-collar workers in the population, and particularly the decreasing proportion of union members, has made labor a smaller and hence less important component of the electorate.

Catholic allegiance to the Democratic party has also weakened. The Democratic vote of this group has declined from its high of 78 percent in 1960 to a low of 39 percent in 1984. Dukakis recovered some of this loss in 1988, receiving a slight majority of the Catholic vote (2 percent). The bad news for the Democrats is that the proportion of Catholics identifying with the Republican party has doubled in the past decade, although a plurality of Catholics still consider themselves Democrats.

Jewish voters have evidenced a much smaller decline in their Democratic partisan sympathies. They have become more independent in their voting behavior, however. Carter received 72 percent of the Jewish vote in 1976 but only 47 percent in 1980—the first election since World War II when a majority of Jews did not vote Democratic. Dissatisfaction with Carter led Jews to give John Anderson 14 percent of their vote in that election. In 1984 and 1988, however, Jews returned to their traditional voting patterns, with approximately two-thirds of this group supporting the Democratic presidential candidates.

Although the Democrats have lost support from some of their key New Deal groups, they have retained and even increased the support of others, notably blacks and Hispanics. In recent decades, blacks have become even more loyal to the Democratic party than they were in the past. Few Republican identifiers are left among black voters, in contrast to the late 1950s, when almost 25 percent considered themselves Republican. In presidential elections since 1964, between 85 and 90 percent of the black vote has gone to the Democratic candidate. (See Table 3–4.) In 1984, one out of every four Mondale voters was black; in 1988, one out of five Dukakis voters was black.

Hispanic voters have also increased their support of the Democrats and have become an important component of that party's electoral coalition. With the exception of Cuban Americans, a largely business and professional, middle-class group concentrated in south Florida, approximately two-thirds of Hispanic voters identify with the Democratic party and vote for its candidates.[32] The lower socioeconomic status of many of these voters works to reinforce their Democratic inclinations but also to lower their turnout.

Additionally, since 1980, there have been discernible differences in the partisan identities and electoral voting patterns of men and women. This differential has produced what some have referred to as a "gender gap," with women more likely to identify and vote Democratic and men more likely to prefer the Republican party and its candidates. The gap has been in the range of 4–8 percent. It is larger among whites than nonwhites, larger among those in the higher socioeconomic brackets than in the lower groups, and larger among those with more formal education than less.[33] It is also greater between those who are unmarried than those who are married.

In the light of these shifts, how can the Democratic party's electoral coalition be described today? The Democrats have become the party of ethnic and racial minorities. They still receive overwhelming support from minority racial groups, those with the lowest incomes, and those who live in the central cities. (See Figure 3–2.) However, the relatively small size of the latter two groups compared to the general population and their lower turnout make them less important components of the total electorate than they were in the past. On the other hand, the traditional Democratic-oriented groups—union families, Catholics, and Jews—have weakened in their backing of Democratic candidates. Southern whites seem to have deserted the party entirely at the presidential level. Additionally, young voters in the 1980s have not identified with the Democratic party in anywhere near the proportion that they did a decade or two ago.

Although the Democratic New Deal coalition has eroded, the groups within that coalition with the exception of southern whites have not become Republican. They have simply provided less support for the Democrats. While the Republican party has gained adherents, it has not done so by virtue of a direct exodus of groups from the Democrats.

As an electoral coalition, the Republicans have become more white, more middle class, and more suburban. They have gained support in the South and Southwest, the so-called Sunbelt. They have maintained their traditional Protestant loyalties and gained adherents from Christian fundamentalist groups, which had supported Democratic candidates through 1976. George Bush received 80 percent of the votes of this group. The contemporary Republican party thus consists of those in racial and religious majorities, those in the higher socioeconomic groups, and those in the professional and managerial positions.

What conclusions can we draw about the social basis of politics today? It is clear that the old party coalitions have changed and, in the Democrats' case, have weakened. While class, religion, and geography are still related to party identification and voting behavior, they are not as strongly related as they were in the past. Voters are less influenced by group cues. They exercise a more independent judgment on election day, a judgment that is less predictable and more subject to be influenced by the campaign itself. These changes explain why the Republicans' chances have improved. Although they have not become a majority of the electorate, they have, however, reduced the Democrats' advantage and eliminated it at the presidential level.

## A New Republican Majority?

Are Republican gains evidence of a new realignment of voters? Will the GOP soon emerge as the partisan majority? The answer is still unclear, but two basic trends stand out: one relates to the contemporary dealignment of the partisan attitudes of the electorate; the other pertains to the decreasing gap between Democratic and Republican party identifiers. Both of these trends favor the Republicans.

**Dealignment.** Dealignment is a weakening in the attachment people feel toward political parties. It has produced more split-ticket voting, which has helped Republican presidential candidates more than Democratic candidates. It has also led more people to think of themselves

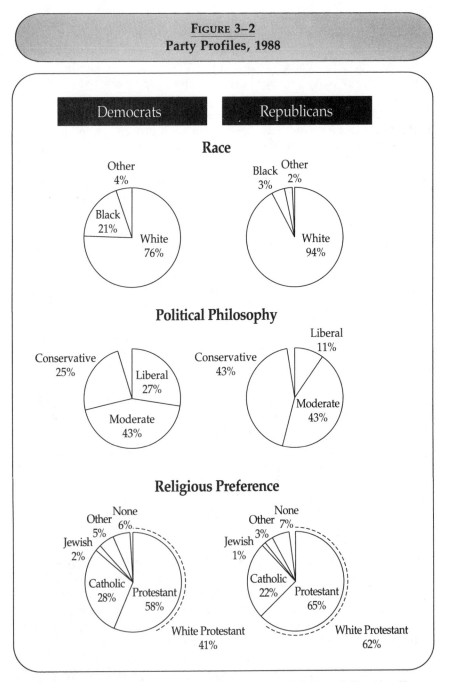

**FIGURE 3–2**
**Party Profiles, 1988**

Democrats | Republicans

**Race**

Democrats:
- Other 4%
- Black 21%
- White 76%

Republicans:
- Black 3%
- Other 2%
- White 94%

**Political Philosophy**

Democrats:
- Conservative 25%
- Liberal 27%
- Moderate 43%

Republicans:
- Liberal 11%
- Conservative 43%
- Moderate 43%

**Religious Preference**

Democrats:
- Other 5%
- None 6%
- Jewish 2%
- Catholic 28%
- Protestant 58%
- White Protestant 41%

Republicans:
- Other 3%
- None 7%
- Jewish 1%
- Catholic 22%
- Protestant 65%
- White Protestant 62%

Based on telephone interviews in three New York Times/CBS News Polls with self-identified Democrats and Republicans who said they were registered to vote. A total of 1,177 Democrats and 994 Republicans were interviewed in three surveys conducted July 5–8, May 9–12, and March 19–22. Those giving no answer are not shown.

*Source:* New York Times/CBS News Poll, *New York Times,* July 17, 1988, p. 17.

FIGURE 3–2 (*cont.*)

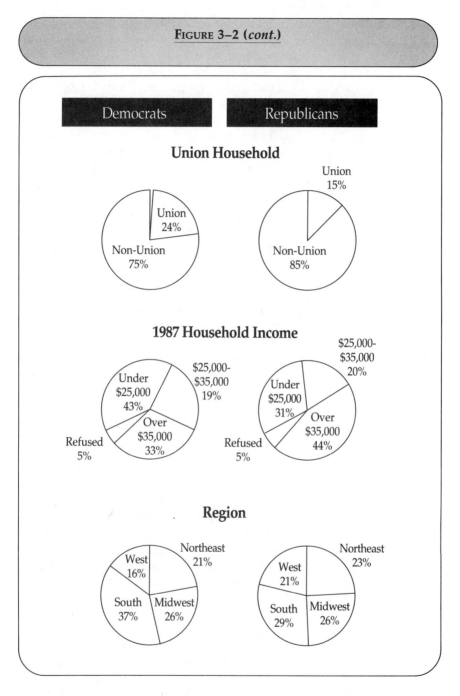

Democrats            Republicans

### Union Household

Democrats:
- Union 24%
- Non-Union 75%

Republicans:
- Union 15%
- Non-Union 85%

### 1987 Household Income

Democrats:
- Under $25,000 43%
- $25,000-$35,000 19%
- Over $35,000 33%
- Refused 5%

Republicans:
- Under $25,000 31%
- $25,000-$35,000 20%
- Over $35,000 44%
- Refused 5%

### Region

Democrats:
- Northeast 21%
- West 16%
- South 37%
- Midwest 26%

Republicans:
- Northeast 23%
- West 21%
- South 29%
- Midwest 26%

as independents. The Republicans have been the beneficiaries of their vote as well.

Dealignment, in short, has enabled the Republicans to win an electoral majority in five of the last six presidential elections, receiving 265.3 million votes compared to 216.1 million for the Democrats—a difference of more than 49.2 million.

Not only have the Republicans won the popular vote, but they have maintained and seemingly enlarged their electoral college advantage. Twenty-one states have voted for the Republican candidate in each of the last six presidential elections. These states had 187 electoral votes in the 1980s, 69 percent of the number needed for victory. In 1992, they will have 191 as a result of reapportionment based on the 1990 census. By contrast, only the District of Columbia has given its support to all recent Democratic nominees. Thus the Democratic candidate begins the campaign with a considerably smaller base of support in the electoral college than does the Republican.

**Realignment.** There is some evidence that a gradual partisan realignment may also be occurring. It may, however, be less meaningful than the one that took place in the 1930s. With the exception of white southerners at the presidential level, this realignment does not involve wholesale shifts from one electoral coalition to another. Nor does it involve overwhelming proportions of new voters who ally themselves with one party. Rather it consists of a gradual weakening of support among voters for the Democrats and a small but continuing preference of newer voters for the Republicans. If these trends persist, they could result in a Republican majority in the future.

However, a partisan realignment that occurs during an era of weaker partisan attachments for adherents to both parties may not have the same effect as one in which partisan loyalties were stronger and more predictive of the vote. If people have generally less confidence in parties and weaker partisan allegiances, then their affiliation is not likely to matter as much. In the words of Martin Wattenberg, a keen student of partisan attitudes and behavior, "such a realignment is hollow when the two parties involved continue to have a weak image in the public mind and an uncertain role in the future of American government."[34]

## SUMMARY

The electorate is not neutral. People do not come to campaigns with completely open minds. Rather, their preexisting attitudes and accumulated experiences color their perceptions and affect their judgment, much as stimuli from the campaign affect those attitudes and experiences.

Of the political beliefs people possess, partisanship has the strongest impact on voting behavior. It provides a perspective for evaluating the campaign and for deciding whether and how to vote. It is also a motive for being informed, for being concerned, and for turning out to vote on election day.

Since the 1960s there has been a substantial decline in the proportion of the population voting. This decline can be partially attributed to the weakening of party ties, to the increasing proportion of younger voters, and to the cynicism and apathy of the electorate, a cynicism and apathy that has been particularly evident among those in the lower socioeconomic groups, those with the least formal education.

Partisan attitudes have also eroded since the 1960s. The percentage of people identifying with a party has declined. One consequence has been the increasing importance of short-term factors in campaigning. A second has been more split-ticket voting. The weakening of partisan ties has produced a vote that either party can win. It has produced a presidential vote that has less carryover to congressional and state elections. And it has produced an electorate that is more volatile at the presidential level. All of these shifts have worked to the Republicans' advantage.

Group ties to the parties have also loosened. Their coalitions have shifted. The Democratic party, which became dominant during the New Deal period, has lost the support of a majority of southern whites in presidential elections and has suffered defections from other groups. That some of these groups have also declined as a proportion of the population or have lower than average turnout has further aggravated the Democrats' problem. Only minorities, such as blacks and Hispanics, have retained their loyalty to the Democrats.

Naturally, the Republicans have benefited from the fraying of the Democrats' electoral coalition. Looser partisan ties have given them greater electoral opportunities. That they have been much more successful in taking advantage of these opportunities at the presidential level than at other levels indicates that weakening group loyalties do not easily or quickly convert to new partisan allegiances.

The Republicans have gained in the South, benefited from the increased social and economic conservatism of a growing middle and upper-middle class, and made potentially significant strides among younger voters. They have won five of the last six presidential elections but have not thus far been able to expand their electoral coalition to a partisan majority.

These changes within the political environment have important implications for presidential politics. The decline in turnout, the weakening of partisan attitudes, and the splintering of the New Deal coalitions augur a new era in electoral politics. It is clear that a dealignment has occurred. It is not clear whether a permanent realignment is taking place or, if it is, how important that realignment will be to the future of Amer-

————, and James A. Stimson. *Issue Evolution: Race and the Transformation of American Politics*. Princeton N.J.: Princeton University Press, 1990.

Edsall, Thomas B. *The New Politics of Inequality*. New York: W. W. Norton, 1984.

Fiorina, Morris, P. *Retrospective Voting in American National Elections*. New Haven, Conn.: Yale University Press, 1981.

Ladd, Everett Carll, Jr., with Charles D. Hadley. *Transformations of the American Party System*. 2nd ed. New York: W. W. Norton, 1978.

Nie Norman H., Sidney Verba, and John R. Petrocik. *The Changing American Voter*. Cambridge, Mass.: Harvard University Press, 1976.

Niemi, Richard G., and Herbert F. Weisberg. *Controversies in Voting Behavior*. 3rd ed. Washington, D.C.: Congressional Quarterly, 1992.

Piven, Frances Fox, and Richard A. Cloward. *Why Americans Don't Vote*. New York: Pantheon, 1988.

Smith, Eric. *The Unchanging American Voter*. Berkeley, Ca.: University of California Press, 1990.

Stanley, Harold W., and Richard G. Niemi. "Partisanship and Group Support, 1952–1988." Paper presented at the annual meeting of the American Political Science Association, Atlanta, Georgia, August 31–September 3, 1989.

Teixeira, Ruy A. "Registration and Turnout." *Public Opinion* 11 (January/February 1989): 12–13, 56–58.

Wattenberg, Martin P. *The Decline of American Political Parties: 1952–1988*. Cambridge, Mass.: Harvard University Press, 1990.

Wolfinger, Raymond E., and Steven J. Rosenstone. *Who Votes?* New Haven, Conn.: Yale University Press, 1980.

# PART II

# The Nomination

# Chapter 4

# Delegate Selection

## INTRODUCTION

Presidential nominees are selected by the delegates to their party's national convention. The way those delegates are chosen can influence the choice of nominees. It can also affect the influence of the state and its party leadership.

Procedures for delegate selection are determined by state law. Today, these procedures also have to conform to general guidelines and rules established by the national party. In the past, they did not. Rather, statutes passed by the state legislature reflected the needs and desires of the political leaders who controlled the state. Naturally, these laws were designed to buttress that leadership and extend its influence.

Primary elections in which the party's rank and file chose the delegates were discouraged, co-opted, or even circumvented. Favorite son candidates, tapped by the leadership, prevented meaningful contests in many states. Other states held primaries but made them advisory, with the actual selection of the delegates left to caucuses, conventions, or committees, which were more easily controlled by party officials. There were also impediments to potential delegates' getting on the ballot: high fees, lengthy petitions, early dates for filing. Winner-take-all provisions gave a great advantage to the organization candidate, as did rules requiring delegates to vote as a unit.

Not until the 1970s was popular participation in the selection of convention delegates encouraged. It was a national party, the Democrats, that took the lead by adopting a series of reforms affecting the period during which delegates could be selected, the procedures for choosing them, and ultimately their behavior at the convention. While these rules limited the states' discretion, they did not result in uniform primaries and caucuses. Considerable variation still exists in how delegates are chosen, how the vote is apportioned, and who participates in the selection.

This chapter will explore these rules and their consequences for the nomination process. It is organized into four sections. The first details the changes in party rules. The second considers the legal challenges to these rules and the Supreme Court's decisions on these challenges. The third section examines the impact of the rules changes on the party and the electorate, while the fourth discusses how they have affected the candidates and their campaigns.

# REFORMING
# THE NOMINATION PROCESS

Historically, states enacted their own rules for delegate selection with relatively little guidance from the national party. Some discouraged popular participation; others encouraged it but made no effort to translate public opinion of the candidates into delegate support for them. In very few states was the delegation as a whole representative, demographically or ideologically, of the party's electorate within that state.

Democratic party reforms have attempted to change this situation. The party had two primary objectives in altering its rules to promote more internal democracy. Democrats wanted to encourage greater rank-and-file participation and to select delegates who were more representative of the rank and file. The problem has been how to achieve these goals and still win elections. Judging by the Democrats' lack of success at the presidential level since 1968, they have not as yet found a satisfactory solution.

The Democratic party has gone through two stages in reforming its delegate selection procedures. During the first, 1968–80, it adopted a highly structured set of national rules and sought to impose them on the states. Since that time the party permitted its state affiliates greater flexibility in determining how their delegations were to be chosen in 1984 and 1988 but limited that discretion in 1992. Unlike the Democrats, the Republican party has not mandated national rules on its state parties. However, Republican state parties have been affected by Democratic reforms, particularly in states whose legislatures are controlled by the Democrats.

## Democratic Rules, 1968–1980

The catalyst for the rules changes was the tumultuous Democratic convention of 1968, in which Senator Hubert Humphrey won the nomination although he had not entered one single primary. Yet the primaries of that year were very important. They had become the vehicle by which Democrats could protest the Johnson administration's conduct of the war in Vietnam.

Senator Eugene McCarthy, the first of the antiwar candidates, had challenged Lyndon Johnson in the New Hampshire primary. To the surprise of many political observers, McCarthy received 42.4 percent of the vote, almost as much as the president, who got 49.5 percent. Four days after McCarthy's unexpectedly strong showing, Senator Robert Kennedy, brother of the late president and political rival of Johnson, declared his candidacy for the nation's highest office. With protests against the war mounting and divisions within the Democratic party intensifying, Johnson bowed out, declaring that he did not want the country's involvement in Southeast Asia to become a political issue.

Johnson's withdrawal cleared the way for Hubert Humphrey, the vice-president, to become a candidate. Humphrey, however, waited almost a month to announce his intentions. His late entrance into the Democratic nomination process precluded his running in the primaries. Like Johnson, Humphrey did not want to become the focal point of antiwar protests. Nor did he have the grass-roots organization to match McCarthy's and Kennedy's. What he did have was the support of many Democratic leaders, including the president.

The last big-state primary was in California. In it, Kennedy scored a significant victory, but during the celebration that followed, he was assassinated. His death left McCarthy as the principal antiwar candidate, but he was far short of a convention majority. Despite the last-minute entrance of Senator George McGovern, who hoped to rally Kennedy delegates to his candidacy, Humphrey won the nomination easily. To make mattes worse for those who opposed Humphrey and the administration's war efforts, an amendment to the party platform calling for an unconditional end to the bombing of North Vietnam was defeated. McCarthy and Kennedy delegates felt victimized by the process and the result. They were angry. They demanded reform.

Compounding the divisions within the convention were demonstrations outside of it. Thousands of youthful protestors, calling for an end to the war, congregated in the streets of Chicago. The police, under orders from Mayor Richard Daley to maintain order, used strong-arm tactics to disperse the crowds. Clashes between police and protestors followed. Television news crews filmed these confrontations, and the networks showed them during their convention coverage. The spectacle of police beating demonstrators further inflamed emotions and led to calls for reform, not only from those who attended the convention but from those who watched it on television.

After the election, the Democratic party responded to these protests. A commission, chaired initially by Senator George McGovern, was appointed to study procedures for electing and seating convention delegates and to propose ways of improving them. The commission recommended that delegate selection be tuned more closely to popular sentiment within the state and, implicitly, less to the wishes of state party leaders. Rules to make it easier for individuals to run as delegates, to limit the size of the districts from which they could be chosen, and, to require that the number of them who were elected be proportional to the popular vote that they or the candidates to whom they were pledged received, were approved by the party.

Additionally, Democrats tried to prevent independents and, especially, partisans of other parties, from participating in the selection of their delegates. The difficulty, however, was to determine who was a Democrat, since some states did not require or even permit registration by party. When implementing this rule, the party adopted a very liberal interpretation of Democratic affiliation. People identifying themselves as Democrats at the time of voting, or who requested Democratic ballots, were viewed as Democrats. This process of identification effectively permitted *crossover* voting, allowing Republicans or independents to cross over and vote in the Democratic primary. The only primaries that the Democratic rules effectively prohibited were *open primaries*, those in which voters are given the ballots of both major parties, discard one, and vote the other.

In addition to translating public preferences into delegate selection, the other major objective of the reforms was to equalize representation on the delegations themselves. Three groups in particular—blacks, women, and youth—had protested their underrepresentation on party councils and at the conventions. Their representatives and others who were sympathetic to their plight pressed hard for more power and better representation for minorities. The reform commission reacted to these protests by proposing a rule requiring that all states represent these particular groups in reasonable relationship to their presence in the state population. Failure to do so was viewed as *prima facie* evidence of discrimination. In point of fact, the party established quotas.

Considerable opposition to the application of this rule during the 1972 nomination process developed, and it was subsequently modified to require that states implement affirmative action plans for those groups that had been subject to past discrimination.[1] The party went one step further with respect to women. It required that, beginning with its 1980 nominating convention, each state delegation be equally divided between the sexes.

One consequence of these Democratic rules was to make primaries the preferred method of delegate selection. Moreover, primary voting became more closely tied to delegate selection than it had been in the past, a trend that has continued. The number of advisory primaries, in which the popular vote is not tied to the selection of delegates, declined, while the number of binding primaries, in which it is tied, increased.[2] This shift gave the party's electorate a more direct voice in choosing the nominee.

Caucuses were still permitted, but they, too, were redesigned to encourage rank-and-file participation. No longer could a state party

# The Iowa Caucus:
## How It Works

| DATE | STAGES |
|---|---|
| February | 1. Caucuses are held in precincts to choose delegates to county conventions. |
| March | 2. Conventions are held in counties to choose delegates to congressional district conventions. |
| May | 3. Conventions held in congressional districts to elect district-level delegates to national party conventions. The same delegates also attend the state convention. |
| June | 4. State conventions elect at-large delegates to national party convention. Democrats also select their state party and elected official delegates. |

**Procedures for the first-round precinct caucuses:**

*Democrats.* Only registered Democrats who live in the precinct and can vote may participate. Attendees are asked to join preference groups for candidates. A group must consist of at least 15 percent of those present to be viable. Nonviable groups are dissolved, and those who were members of them may join other viable groups. Much lobbying occurs at this stage of the meeting. Delegates are allocated to candidates strictly on the basis of the group's proportion to the caucus as a whole.

*Republicans.* Attendees cast a presidential preference vote by secret ballot. Delegates to the county convention are then selected by whatever method the caucus chooses, either by direct election (winner take all) or proportionally on the basis of the straw vote.

leader cast a large number of proxies for the delegates of his choice. Caucuses had to be publicly announced with adequate time given for campaigning. Moreover, they had to be conducted in stages, and three-fourths of the delegates had to be chosen in districts no larger than those for members of Congress.

Other consequences, not nearly so beneficial to the goal of increased participation, were lengthening of the process, escalating its costs, fatiguing its candidates, boring the public, and dividing the party. Since the contests at the beginning of the quest for the nomination received the most attention from the media, candidates, and public alike, states moved their primaries forward, "front-loading" the process and forcing candidates to start their campaigns even earlier than in the past, another trend that has continued.

Primaries and caucuses affected the type of delegate selected as well. They made it more difficult for elected officials and party leaders automatically to attend the nominating conventions. The absence of these members of the party's governing elite generated and extended cleavages between the nominees and their electoral coalitions and the party's organization and its leadership.

These cleavages created serious problems for the Democrats. Put simply, they adversely affected the chances of its nominees winning the general election, and if successful, of governing. During the presidential campaign, the divisiveness impaired a unified organizational effort, tarnished the images of party candidates, and increased defections from straight partisan voting. After the election, it delayed agenda and coalition building.

In short, party reforms produced unintended consequences. These consequences—the proliferation of primaries, the lengthening of the process, the divisiveness within the party, the poor representation of elected leaders, and, most important, the failure to win elections and govern successfully—prompted the Democrats to reexamine and modify their rules for delegate selection during the 1980s.

## *Democratic Rules, 1981–Present*

Three commissions, each appointed after the presidential election and composed of a cross section of party officials, interest group representatives, and supporters of leading candidates for the nomination met and proposed a series of rule changes to rectify the negative effects of past reforms. The new reforms were designed to strengthen the party and improve the chances of its nominees without at the same time undermining the democratic goals of *fair reflection* and *equal representation*.

The rule modifications fall into three categories: those that affect the time frame and procedures of the selection process, those that affect the representation of public officials and party leaders, and those that govern the behavior of delegates at the convention itself.

The objective of the original reforms in the 1970s was to encourage participation by rank-and-file party supporters and to reflect their sentiment in the allocation of delegates. Three problems in particular impeded the achievement of these objectives.

1. The states that held their primaries and caucuses early seemed to exercise disproportionate influence. This situation created a tendency by states to front-load the process, by candidates to expend most of their resources at the beginning or as soon as they got them, and by participants to turn out more regularly in March than in May.
2. The relatively small percentage of the vote needed to receive delegates (known as a *threshold*) encouraged candidacies. Not only did a low threshold factionalize the party; it also provided an incentive for those without national experience, reputation, and even party ties, to run. By obtaining the votes of as little as 15 percent of those who participated in a primary or caucus, relatively unknown candidates could win delegates, gain recognition, and use this recognition to build a constituency and become a national figure.
3. The application of the proportional voting rule in some instances did not fairly reflect the popular vote. Moreover, even in instances in which it did reflect the popular vote, it produced unintended and undesirable consequences for the national party, for its state affiliates, and for the candidates seeking the nomination. For the national party, proportional voting extended the nomination process, disadvantaging it and its nominees in the general election. For the state parties, proportional voting diffused power and reduced the collective influence of party officials. For the candidates, proportional voting discouraged them from investing resources in districts that were highly competitive and from which they could gain only minimal advantage and encouraged them to concentrate on less competitive districts where they enjoyed the most support. This concentration of resources adversely affected turnout and representation.

To modify the first of these problems, the party has tried to impose a "window" period during which primaries and caucuses could be held. In 1988 the official period extended from the second Tuesday in March to the second Tuesday in June. In 1992 it will begin one week earlier, the first Tuesday in March, and extend until the second Tuesday in June.

What to do with those states, such as Iowa and New Hampshire, whose laws require that they choose their delegates before others, has been a perennial issue. Believing that it could not conduct its own selection process in these states, the national party decided that the best it could do was establish the window and grant these states an exception but require them to hold their contests closer to the designated period than in the past. In 1988 Iowa was permitted to schedule its contest three weeks before the window opened, New Hampshire's primary two weeks before, and the Maine and Wyoming caucuses a few days before. However, the states of Iowa and New Hampshire moved their contests one week earlier than the exception permitted when South Dakota and Vermont also scheduled their primaries before the window opened and thereby challenged the exclusive exemptions that Iowa and New Hampshire had been given. (See "The Iowa Caucus: How It Works.") The party acceded to these changes rather than contest them. In 1992, it sought to reimpose its 1988 exceptions, allowing Iowa to hold its caucus no more than fifteen days before the others, New Hampshire seven days before, and Maine two days before.

Front-loading still remains a problem, however, more so now than ever. In 1984, 6 percent of the delegates were chosen in primaries or caucuses before March, and 36 percent during that month. In 1988, 5 percent were chosen before March and more than 40 percent by the end of that month. During Super Tuesday week alone, approximately one-third of the Democratic delegates and 37 percent of the Republicans had been selected.

Another change has been the modifications to the so-called fair reflection rule. One modification affects the minimum percentage of the vote necessary to be eligible for delegates; the other pertains to the methods by which the primary vote is converted into delegates. Both have been controversial.

In 1984 the Democrats raised the minimum vote needed to obtain delegates to 20 percent in caucuses and up to 25 percent in primaries. This change was designed to advance nationally known candidates such as Walter Mondale and reduce the factionalizing effect that a large number of people contesting for the nomination can have on the party. Democrats hoped the change would enable the eventual winner, preferably someone of national prominence, to emerge earlier and be better positioned to challenge the Republicans in the general election.

Naturally, these changes disadvantaged those who were not as well-known. They also hurt minority candidates such as Jesse Jackson. With his supporters concentrated in heavily black areas, Jackson was unable to reach the minimum percentage needed in many predominantly white districts. Although he received 19 percent of the vote in primaries, he obtained only 10 percent of the delegates selected in them. Bending to pressure from Jackson and others, the Democrats lowered the threshold in 1988 to 15 percent in primaries and caucuses and will continue it at that level in 1992.

Jackson was also victimized by another rule governing the delegate selection process—the formulas states were permitted to use when converting the popular vote into delegate support. Instead of adhering strictly to a straight proportional vote, the Democrats also allowed states to elect individual delegates directly within the districts or give a bonus of one delegate to the candidate who received the most popular votes within a district.

Both of these variations on the proportional voting theme advantaged front-runners. The first, often referred to as the winner-take-all primary, creates the possibility that the popular vote leader could get all the delegates within a district by winning only a plurality of the votes (as few as 35–45 percent, depending on the number of other candidates running). Losing candidates could be shut out entirely, even though their delegates received a substantial portion of the vote. In 1984 Walter Mondale won 40 percent of the popular vote and 53 percent of the delegates in this type of primary. In 1988 Michael Dukakis pulled a similar feat, winning 49 percent of the vote and 62 percent of the delegates. Jackson, on the other hand, suffered. In 1984 he received 18 percent of the vote but only 7 percent of the delegates in winner-take-all districts. In 1988 it was more of the same. With 30 percent of the vote in states that held winner-take-all primaries, he received only 14 percent of the delegates.[3] Is it any wonder that Jackson criticized the system as unfair and urged that it be changed?

In 1980 only two states conducted winner-take-all primaries within electoral districts. In 1984, after the rules were changed, seven elected to do so; in 1988, five did so. The incentive for states to conduct winner-take-all primaries is that they tend to produce a more cohesive delegation, thereby maximizing the state's influence on the nominees and the platform.

The other type of acceptable formula for allocating delegates, the winner-take-more or bonus plan, had much the same effect: it benefited the front-runners. In 1984 Mondale converted 41 percent of the popular vote he received in bonus primary states to 53 percent of the delegates. In 1988 Dukakis converted his 43 percent of the popular vote to 54 percent of the delegates.[4] (See Table 4–1.)

Although both allocation formulas disadvantaged lesser-known candidates, they did not alter the probable outcome or produce an undemocratic result. In 1984 and again in 1988 the candidate who received the most popular votes won. Had there been straight proportional voting in 1984 and 1988, Jackson would have done better, but he would still have fallen short of the numbers needed to win the nomination.

Nonetheless, the conversion of popular votes into delegate totals, which undercut the fair reflection rule and reduced Jackson's delegate support, prompted him to demand an end to these alternative formulas for proportional voting. In 1988 the rules committee of the Democratic National Convention complied. For 1992, delegates selected in all Democratic primaries will be apportioned on the basis of a straight proportional vote within the districts in which they are elected.

This change for 1992 has produced criticism, however. Some party leaders believe that it will further weaken the party and reduce the

TABLE 4–1

**Proportional Voting and Delegate Allocation, 1984 and 1988**

| | 1984 Proportion of Votes (Proportion of Delegates) | | | 1988 Proportion of Votes (Proportion of Delegates) | | | |
|---|---|---|---|---|---|---|---|
| | Walter Mondale | Gary Hart | Jesse Jackson | Michael Dukakis | Jesse Jackson | Albert Gore | Others |
| *Allocation rule* | | | | | | | |
| Direct election (winner take all) | 40 (53) | 36 (32) | 18 (7) | 49 (62) | 30 (14) | 4 (0) | 17 (24) |
| Bonus system (winner take more) | 41 (53) | 32 (33) | 21 (14) | 43 (54) | 29 (30) | 12 (8) | 16 (8) |
| Proportional representation | 32 (38) | 39 (45) | 17 (11) | 39 (44) | 30 (35) | 18 (16) | 13 (4) |
| *Total* | 39 (49) | 36 (36) | 19 (10) | 42 (50) | 30 (30) | 13 (11) | 15 (9) |

*Source:* 1984, Gary R. Orren, "The Nomination Process: Vicissitudes of Candidate Selection," in *The Election of 1984*, ed. Michael Nelson (Washington, D.C.: Congressional Quarterly, 1985), p. 39; 1988, Jerry W. Calvert, "Rules That Count: Voter Choice, Party Rules and the Selection of National Convention Delegates in 1988" (Paper presented at the annual meeting of the American Political Science Association, Washington, D.C., September 1–4, 1988), p. 26.

chances of its nominees in the general election. They fear that proportional voting will provide an added incentive for candidates to extend their quest for the nomination, make a consensus more difficult to achieve, and give the party less time to unify the factions that have developed and endured during the primary process.

Another reform of the 1980s has been the addition of new leadership delegates. The party had been unhappy with the decreasing number of its elected officials who attended the convention as delegates in the 1970s. The absence of these officials, it was thought, contributed to the lack of support that the nominees received during the campaign and after the election. Jimmy Carter's difficulties in dealing with Congress were cited as evidence of the need for closer cooperation between party leaders and their presidential standard-bearer.

To facilitate closer ties, the Democrats established two new categories of party leader and elected official delegates. Those in the first category, equal to 15 percent of the state's delegation, were to be pledged and allocated to candidates on the same basis as the rest of the delegation. Those in the second category, known as superdelegates, were to be officially unpledged. Chosen from a group consisting of all the Democratic governors, all the members of the Democratic National Committee, four-fifths of the Democratic members of Congress, and a small number of distinguished elected officials, these superdelegates might be in a position to hold the balance of power in a divided convention.

In 1984 and again in 1988, the superdelegates were not in such a position. They have had an impact on the delegate selection process, however, by reinforcing the front-runner's advantage. This impact was particularly evident in 1984, when the superdelegates were selected before the caucus and primaries had begun, an arrangement that gave front-runner Walter Mondale a tremendous advantage in influencing who were chosen as superdelegates and in winning their support. Complaints that the popular vote had been preempted and that nonestablishment candidates were disadvantaged by the early selection of members of Congress led the party to move the selection of superdelegates for 1988 to the middle of the nomination cycle, after Michael Dukakis had established a sizable and seemingly unbeatable lead. Although unpledged, they supported the apparent winner.

The tendency of superdelegates to provide a national perspective and be more inclined to back nationally recognized political leaders for the nomination has incurred criticism from those who desire the selection process to be open and not dominated by national legislators and party officials. Here, too, Jesse Jackson tried to reduce the influence of superdelegates, who have given him much less support than he has received from the Democratic electorate. The party's Rules Committee, at its 1988 convention, agreed to a Jackson-sponsored proposal to decrease the number of superdelegates by eliminating the automatic inclusion of all members of the party's National Committee. This decision, however, was reversed by the National Committee two years later. In 1992 there will be 686 superdelegates, 16 percent of the total. In 1988 there were 644, 15.5 percent of the entire convention. Those who are not automatically delegates by virtue of their position will be chosen between April 15 and May 1, 1992.

Finally, the Democrats have reversed the rule adopted by the convention in 1980 that delegates who are publicly committed must vote for the candidate to whom they are pledged. Democratic delegates today can vote their consciences, although their initial selection as delegates must still have the approval of the candidate to whom they are committed. It is unlikely under the circumstances that many delegates will change their minds at the convention, unless their candidate encourages them to do so.

## *Republican Rules*

The Republicans have not changed their rules after each recent national convention as have the Democrats. Nor can they. It is the Republican convention itself that approves the rules for choosing delegates for the next Republican convention. Under normal circumstances, these rules cannot be altered by the Republican National Committee or by special commissions the party creates.

Republicans, however, have been affected by the Democratic rules changes. Since state legislatures enact laws governing party nominations, and since the Democrats have controlled most of these legislatures, they have literally forced some of their reforms on the Republicans. Moreover, the Republicans have also made changes of their own. A Committee of Delegates and Organizations, appointed in 1969, recommended that delegate selection procedures encourage greater participation in states that used conventions to pick their delegates; that more information about these procedures be promulgated to the party's electorate; and that voting by proxy be prohibited. These recommendations, adopted by the 1972 Republican convention, remain in effect today.

Unlike the Democrats, the Republicans have not chosen to mandate national guidelines for their state parties. Although they do not have a window period during which all primaries and caucuses must be held, their nominations process is front-loaded. The first Republican contest for the 1988 nomination occurred in 1986 and the first round of caucus selection took place in January 1988, even before the Iowa caucus.

Whereas the Democrats prescribe a minimum threshold to receive delegate support, the Republicans do not. In 1988 their threshold varied per state, from 20 percent in Rhode Island and South Dakota to zero in three states.[5] Whereas the Democrats impose some form of proportional voting, the Republicans do not. In 1988, only fourteen states and the District of Columbia allocated Republican delegates in direct proportion to the popular vote, while nineteen states directly elected them on the basis of a winner-take-all vote within the district or within the state. This situation greatly advantaged George Bush. With nine of the fourteen southern states holding some type of winner-take-all vote on Super Tuesday, Bush won 59 percent of the popular vote in these states and 97 percent of the delegates. After winning the winner-take-all Illinois primary the following week, Bush had 69 percent of the delegates he needed to win the nomination, forcing his principal rival, Robert Dole, to drop out of the contest. Had the delegates been elected on the basis of a straight proportional vote, Bush would have had only 46 percent compared to Dole's 22 percent, perhaps enabling Dole to continue a little longer.

Finally the Republicans do not have special categories of delegates for party and elected officials, although their state and national leaders have traditionally attended Republican conventions in greater proportion than their Democratic counterparts. (See Table 4–6.) Nor do the Republicans require that 50 percent of each state delegation be women. In the 1980s women have constituted between 29 and 44 percent of the delegates at Republican conventions.

Table 4–2
Delegate Selection Rules for 1992

| | Democrats | Republicans |
|---|---|---|
| Rank-and-file participation | Open to all registered or self-declared Democrats. | No national rule.[a] |
| Apportionment of delegates within states | 75 percent of base delegation elected at congressional district level or lower; 25 percent elected at-large on proportional basis. | No national rule; may be chosen at-large. |
| Party leader and elected official delegates | Members of National Committee, governors, former presidents and vice-presidents, congressional leadership, 80 percent of members of Congress. | None. |
| Composition of delegations | 50 percent men, 50 percent women. No discrimination. Affirmative action plans required. | No gender rule or quota, but each state is asked to try to achieve equal representation of men and women. No discrimination. "Positive action" to achieve broadest possible participation required. |
| Time frame | First Tuesday in March to second Tuesday in June. Exceptions: Iowa, New Hampshire, and Maine. | No national rule. |
| Allocation of delegates | By proportional vote. Only in caucuses and primaries. | May be selected by primary, caucuses, or state committee on basis of proportional vote or direct election within districts or at-large. |
| Threshold | 15 percent. | No national rule. |
| Delegate voting | May vote their conscience. | No national rule. |
| Enforcement | Automatic reduction in state delegation size for violation of time frames, allocation, or threshold rules. | Each state party to enforce its own rules, although certain types of disputes may be appealed to the national party. |

[a] Republican national rules prescribe that selection procedures be in accordance with the laws of the state.

A summary of delegate selection rules for the 1992 nomination appears in Table 4–2.

## THE LEGALITY OF PARTY RULES

As previously mentioned, party reforms, to be effective, must be enacted into law. Most states have complied with the new rules. A few have not, resulting in confrontation between these states and the national party. When New Hampshire and Iowa refused to move the dates of their respective primary and caucuses into the Democrats' window period in 1984, the national party backed down. But previously, when Illinois chose its 1972 delegates in a manner that conflicted with new Democratic rules, the party sought to impose its rules on the state.

In addition to the political controversy that was engendered, the conflict between the Democratic National Committee and Illinois also presented an important legal question: which body—the national party or state—was the higher authority? In its landmark decision, *Cousins v. Wigoda* (419 U.S. 477, 1975), the Supreme Court sided with the party. The Court stated that political parties were private organizations with rights of association protected by the Constitution. States could not abridge these rights unless there were compelling constitutional reasons to do so. While states could establish their own primary laws, the party could determine the criteria for representation at its national convention.

The *Cousins v. Wigoda* decision provided an additional incentive for states to change their laws when they conflicted with party rules. The number of challenges declined. They were not, however, eliminated entirely. The issue of crossover voting as practiced in the open primary prompted another court test and decision in favor of the party.

Democratic rules prohibited open primaries. Four states had conducted this type of election in 1976. Three voluntarily changed their law for 1980. The fourth, Wisconsin, did not. State law permitted voters who participated in the primary to request the ballot of either party. The national party's Compliance Review Commission ordered the state party to design an alternative process. It refused. The case went to court.

Citing the precedent of *Cousins v. Wigoda*, the Supreme Court held in the case of *Democratic Party of the U.S. v. Wisconsin ex. rel. La Follette* (450 U.S. 107, 1981) that a state had no right to interfere with the party's delegate selection process unless it demonstrated a compelling reason to do so. It ruled that Wisconsin had not demonstrated such a reason; hence, the Democratic party could refuse to seat delegates who were selected in a manner that violated its rules.

A more recent decision by the Supreme Court, also involving open primaries, has further enhanced the power of parties, in this case state parties, to establish rules for nominating candidates. In December 1986 the Supreme Court, in the case of *Tashjian v. Republican Party of Connecticut* (107 S. Ct. 544, 1986), voided a Connecticut law that prohibited open primaries. Republicans, who were in the minority in Connecticut, had favored such a primary as a means of attracting independent voters. Unable to get the Democratic-controlled legislature to change the law, the state Republican party went to court, arguing that the statute violated First Amendment rights of freedom of association. In a 5–4 ruling, the Supreme Court agreed, and struck down the legislation.

Although these Court decisions have given the political parties the legal authority to design and enforce their own rules, the practicality of doing so is another question. Other than going to court if a state refuses to change its election law, a party, particularly a national party, has only two viable options: require the state party to conduct its own delegate selection process in conformity to national rules, or grant the state party an exemption so that it can abide by the law of the state. In 1984 the Wisconsin Democratic party was forced by the national Democratic party to adopt a caucus mode of selection since the Republican-controlled legislature refused to change the state's open primary system. Turnout declined in the Wisconsin caucus. In 1988 the Democrats gave Wisconsin and Montana, the only other state with a tradition of open primaries, exemptions to the closed primary rule. Other states are still precluded from switching to an open primary.

While the procedures for choosing convention delegates have not engendered major political or legal controversies within the Republican party, the formula for apportioning the delegates has. The Republicans determine the size of each delegation on the basis of three criteria: statehood (six delegates), House districts (three per district), and support for Republican candidates elected within the previous four years (one for a Republican governor, one for each Republican senator, one if the Republicans won at least half of the congressional districts in one of the last two congressional elections, and a bonus of four and one-half delegates plus 60 percent of the electoral vote if the state voted for the Republican presidential candidate in the last election).

This apportionment formula effectively discriminates against the larger states in two ways. First, it awards many of the bonus delegates to a state without regard to its size. Thus, the voting strength of the larger states is proportionally reduced by the bonuses, while that of the smaller states is increased. Second, since the larger states are more competitive, they are less likely to be awarded bonus delegates on a recurring basis. Particularly hard hit are states in the Northeast and Midwest, such as New York and Pennsylvania, and smaller states, such as Massachusetts and Minnesota.

The Ripon Society, a moderate Republican organization, has twice challenged the constitutionality of this apportionment rule, but it has not been successful. The first of these challenges, initiated in the form of a lawsuit, was declared moot when a decision was delayed until after the 1972 Republican convention. A second case, begun in 1975, challenged the formula on the grounds that it violated the Supreme Court's "one person, one vote" rule. This argument was rejected by the U.S. Court of Appeals for the District of Columbia, and the Supreme Court refused to intervene. The society has continued to contest the rules within the party, but to no avail.

The Democratic apportionment formula has also been subject to some controversy. Under the plan used since 1968 and modified in 1976,

TABLE 4–3
### Delegate Apportionment, 1988 and 1992

| State | Democrats | | Republicans | |
|-------|-----------|------|-------------|------|
| | *1988* | *1992* | *1988* | *1992* |
| Alabama | 61 | 62 | 38 | 38 |
| Alaska | 17 | 18 | 19 | 19 |
| Arizona | 40 | 47 | 33 | 37 |
| Arkansas | 43 | 43 | 27 | 27 |
| California | 336 | 382 | 176 | 201 |
| Colorado | 51 | 54 | 36 | 37 |
| Connecticut | 59 | 61 | 35 | 35 |
| Delaware | 19 | 19 | 17 | 19 |
| District of Columbia | 24 | 29 | 14 | 14 |
| Florida | 146 | 160 | 82 | 97 |
| Georgia | 86 | 88 | 48 | 52 |
| Hawaii | 25 | 26 | 20 | 13 |
| Idaho | 23 | 24 | 22 | 22 |
| Illinois | 187 | 183 | 92 | 85 |
| Indiana | 85 | 86 | 51 | 51 |
| Iowa | 58 | 57 | 37 | 23 |
| Kansas | 43 | 42 | 34 | 30 |
| Kentucky[a] | 60 | 62 | 38 | 35 |
| Louisiana[a] | 71 | 69 | 41 | 38 |
| Maine | 27 | 30 | 22 | 22 |
| Maryland | 78 | 80 | 41 | 42 |
| Massachusetts | 109 | 107 | 52 | 38 |
| Michigan | 151 | 148 | 77 | 72 |
| Minnesota | 86 | 87 | 31 | 32 |
| Mississippi[a] | 45 | 45 | 31 | 32 |
| Missouri | 83 | 86 | 47 | 47 |
| Montana | 25 | 22 | 20 | 20 |
| Nebraska | 29 | 31 | 25 | 24 |
| Nevada | 21 | 23 | 20 | 21 |

[a] May be increased by 1 if a Republican governor is elected in 1991.

[b] Members of Congress to be chosen by May 1, 1992.

the Democrats have allotted 50 percent of each state delegation on the basis of the state's electoral vote and 50 percent on the basis of its average Democratic vote in the last three presidential elections. The rule for apportionment was challenged in 1971 on the grounds that it did not conform to the "one person, one vote" principle, but the Court of Appeals asserted that it did not violate the equal protection clause of the Fourteenth Amendment. The Democratic formula results in even larger conventions than the Republican. Table 4–3 lists the apportionment of Republican and Democratic convention delegates for 1988 and 1992.

## TABLE 4–3
## Delegate Apportionment, 1988 and 1992 (*cont.*)

| State | Democrats | | Republicans | |
|---|---|---|---|---|
| | *1988* | *1992* | *1988* | *1992* |
| New Hampshire | 22 | 24 | 23 | 23 |
| New Jersey | 118 | 117 | 64 | 60 |
| New Mexico | 28 | 33 | 26 | 25 |
| New York | 275 | 268 | 136 | 100 |
| North Carolina | 89 | 93 | 54 | 57 |
| North Dakota | 20 | 20 | 16 | 17 |
| Ohio | 174 | 167 | 88 | 83 |
| Oklahoma | 51 | 52 | 36 | 34 |
| Oregon | 51 | 53 | 32 | 23 |
| Pennsylvania | 193 | 188 | 96 | 90 |
| Rhode Island | 26 | 28 | 21 | 15 |
| South Carolina | 48 | 50 | 37 | 36 |
| South Dakota | 19 | 20 | 18 | 19 |
| Tennessee | 77 | 77 | 45 | 45 |
| Texas | 198 | 214 | 111 | 121 |
| Utah | 27 | 28 | 26 | 27 |
| Vermont | 19 | 19 | 17 | 19 |
| Virginia | 85 | 92 | 50 | 54 |
| Washington | 72 | 80 | 41 | 35 |
| West Virginia | 44 | 38 | 28 | 16 |
| Wisconsin | 88 | 91 | 47 | 35 |
| Wyoming | 18 | 19 | 18 | 20 |
| American Samoa | 4 | 5 | 4 | 4 |
| Democrats abroad | 9 | 10 | | |
| Guam | 4 | 5 | 4 | 4 |
| Puerto Rico | 56 | 57 | 14 | 14 |
| Virgin Islands | 4 | 5 | 4 | 4 |
| Unassigned superdelegates[b] | 253 | 262 | | |
| Totals | 4,160 | 4,286 | 2,227 | 2,203 |

## THE IMPACT OF THE RULES CHANGES

The new rules have produced some of their desired effects. They have opened up the nomination process by allowing more people to participate. They have increased minority representation at the conventions. But they have also decreased the influence of state party leaders over the selection of delegates and ultimately weakened the power of party leaders in the presidential electoral process.

### *Turnout*

One objective of the reforms was to involve more of the party's rank and file in the delegate selection process. This goal has been achieved. Turnout has increased. In 1968, before the reforms, only 12 million people participated in primaries, approximately 11 percent of the voting age population (VAP). In 1972, the first nomination contest after changes were made, that number rose to 22 million. It has climbed steadily since then, declining only in 1984, when Ronald Reagan ran unopposed for the Republican nomination. In 1988 with two contested nominations, turnout increased to almost 37 million, approximately 21 percent of the voting age population.

While more people have participated in their party's nomination, the level of participation has not been uniform. It has been greater in primaries than in caucuses. In 1988 about 35 million people voted in the primaries (24.4 percent of the VAP) compared to only 1 million who participated in the caucuses (1.6 percent of the Democrats and 2 percent of the Republicans).[6] Turnout has tended to be greater in states that hold the first elections such as Iowa and New Hampshire than in those which hold them toward the end of the cycle. In the 1988 Iowa caucus, for example, Republican turnout exceeded that of any other of the party's caucuses and in fact, constituted about one-half of all those who participated in Republican caucuses that year. For the Democrats more people voted in Iowa than in all of the party's other caucuses except for the much larger state of Michigan. As a percentage of the party's electorate, turnout in Iowa was higher than in Michigan. Similarly, in New Hampshire the percentage turning out to vote, 32 percent for the Republicans and 38 percent for the Democrats, was higher than each party's average primary turnout (22 percent for the Republicans and 34 percent for the Democrats). In California, for example, which held its contest on June 7, only 22 percent of the Republicans and 29 percent of the Democrats voted.

There have been variations in levels of participation among groups within the electorate as well. The better-educated, higher-income, older members of the society vote more often in these nomination contests than do those who lack these characteristics. In general, the lower the turnout the greater the demographic differences between voters and nonvoters. Although this pattern of participation has persisted in recent elections, the success of the Jackson campaigns in 1984 and 1988 in attracting minority voters and, to a much lesser extent, that of the campaign of Pat Robertson in appealing to certain white, evangelical Protestants, especially Pentecostals and charismatics, have muted some of the differences that had existed between primary voters and their party's electorate.

There have also been claims that primary voters tend to be more ideologically extreme in their political beliefs than the average party voter, with Democrats more liberal and Republicans more conservative than their party as a whole. Strong empirical evidence has not been found to support this contention. Primary voters do not appear to be more ideologically extreme than people who voted in the general election but not in the primaries.[7] (See Table 4–4 for a profile of the Democratic party's primary electorate in 1988.)

## *Representation*

A principal goal of the reforms was to make the national nominating convention more representative of those who identify with the party. Before 1972, the delegates were predominantly white, male, and well educated. Mostly professionals whose income and social status placed them considerably above the national mean, they were expected to pay their own way to the convention. Large financial contributors, as well as elected officeholders and party officials, were frequently in attendance.

In 1972 the demographic profile of convention delegates began to change. The proportion of women rose substantially. Youth and minority participation, especially in Democratic conventions, also increased. Since 1976, when that party changed from a quota system to an affirmative action commitment, the representation of minorities has remained fairly constant. The percentage of women has increased, largely as a consequence of the initiation of a quota of 50 percent by the Democrats. But attendance by those under age thirty, who have been removed from the specified minorities list, has declined.

Despite the changes in composition, the income and educational levels of the delegates have remained well above the national average. In 1988, 16 percent of the Democratic delegates and 27 percent of the Republican delegates had family incomes over $100,000. Similarly, most of the delegates had much more formal education than did their party's rank and file. Forty-two percent of the Republicans and slightly over 50 percent of the Democrats had undergraduate degrees and had completed some postgraduate work.[8] Clearly the 1988 convention delegates

TABLE 4–4

The Democratic Primary Electorate, 1988

| | Proportion of Primary Voters | Michael Dukakis | Jesse Jackson | Others |
|---|---|---|---|---|
| Total votes | 22.7 million | 9.7 million | 6.6 million | 6.4 million |
| % of vote | 100 | 43 | 29 | 28 |
| Men | 47% | 41% | 29% | 30% |
| Women | 53 | 43 | 30 | 26 |
| White | 75 | 54 | 12 | 35 |
| Black | 21 | 4 | 92 | 4 |
| Hispanic | 3 | 48 | 30 | 20 |
| 18–29 years | 14 | 35 | 38 | 27 |
| 30–44 | 31 | 37 | 36 | 26 |
| 45–59 | 25 | 42 | 30 | 28 |
| 60 and older | 30 | 53 | 19 | 29 |
| Liberal | 27 | 41 | 41 | 19 |
| Moderate | 47 | 47 | 25 | 28 |
| Conservative | 22 | 38 | 23 | 38 |
| Democrat | 72 | 43 | 33 | 24 |
| Independent | 20 | 44 | 20 | 34 |
| Catholic | 30 | 60 | 18 | 22 |
| White Protestant | 36 | 43 | 10 | 47 |
| Jewish | 7 | 75 | 8 | 17 |

*Note:* This table, which constructs a Democratic primary electorate for the nation, combines vote totals and exit poll percentages from thirty-three primary states where delegates were selected from February to June. Vote totals are from secretaries of state. Sources of exit poll percentages: ten from New York Times/CBS News, fourteen from CBS News alone, five from ABC News, and one from NBC News. No exit polls were available in Montana, Oregon, or Washington, D.C.

*Source: New York Times*, 13 June, 1988, p. B7.

enjoyed a much higher standard of living and much greater educational opportunities than did most Americans. Their status was reflected to some extent by a greater emphasis on middle-class issues and less attention to the concerns of the poor and the less educated.

It is more difficult to determine the extent to which ideological and issue perceptions of recent delegates differed from those of their predecessors and from the electorate as a whole. In general, convention delegates tend to be more conscious of issues than their party's rank and file. Moreover, they display a greater degree of ideological consistency in their attitudes than other party sympathizers. Republican delegates have been found to be more conservative than Republicans as a whole, and Democrats more liberal than Democrats as a whole.

Surveys of the ideological perspectives of convention delegates at recent conventions reveal clear distinctions between the delegates of the parties. Most Republican delegates consider themselves conservative, and most Democrats consider themselves liberal. (See Table 4–5.) Moreover, the issue stands of the delegates tend to confirm their ideological cleavage, with Republican and Democratic delegates consistently taking more conservative and liberal positions, respectively, on a range of policy matters.[9] If these positions were plotted on an ideological continuum, they would appear to be more consistent (or ideologically pure) than the electorate they represented and much more consistent (or pure) than the general public.

The delegate selection process seems to have contributed to the purity of these perspectives by encouraging activists, who have less of a tie to the party and more of a tie to a candidate and his or her issue positions, to get involved and run for delegate. To the extent that this trend has resulted in the election of more issue purists and fewer partisan pragmatists, compromise has become more difficult and party unity more elusive. One object of the creation of superdelegates by the Democrats was to reverse this trend.

In short, despite the reforms, there continue to be differences between the ideological and demographic characteristics of convention delegates and those of their parties and of the electorate as a whole. Convention delegates reflect some demographic characteristics of their party's rank and file more accurately than in the past, but they are not necessarily more ideologically representative. In fact, delegates have tended to exaggerate the differences between the beliefs and attitudes of Republicans and Democrats. Whether this trend makes contemporary conventions more or less representative is difficult to say. One thing is clear: it is difficult to achieve representation, reward activism, maintain an open process, unite the party, and win elections, all at the same time.

## *Party Organization and Leadership*

While increasing turnout and improving representation were two desired effects of the reforms, weakening the state party structures and their leadership were not. Yet these two developments seem to have been an initial consequence of the increasing number of primaries. By promoting internal democracy, the primaries helped devitalize party organizations already weakened by new modes of campaigning and party leadership already weakened by the loss of patronage opportunities and growth of social services.[10] Although it was hoped that the growth of participatory caucuses might strengthen the parties by en-

Table 4-5

The Demography of the National Convention Delegates, 1968–1988

| | 1968 | | 1972 | | 1976 | | 1980 | | 1984 | | 1988 | |
|---|---|---|---|---|---|---|---|---|---|---|---|---|
| | Dem. | Rep. | Dem. | Rep. | Dem. | Rep. | Dem. | Rep. | Dem. | Rep. | Dem. | Rep. |
| Women | 13% | 16% | 40% | 29% | 33% | 31% | 49% | 29% | 49% | 44% | 48% | 33% |
| Blacks | 5 | 2 | 15 | 4 | 11 | | 15 | 3 | 18 | 4 | 23 | 4 |
| Under thirty | 3 | 4 | 22 | 8 | 15 | 7 | 11 | 5 | 8 | 4 | 4 | 3 |
| Median age (years) | (49) | (49) | (42) | | (43) | (48) | (44) | (49) | (43) | (51) | (46) | (51) |
| Lawyers | 28 | 22 | 12 | | 16 | 15 | 13 | 15 | 17 | 14 | 16 | 17 |
| Teachers | 8 | 2 | 11 | | | 4 | 15 | 4 | 16 | 6 | 14 | 5 |
| Union members | | | 16 | | 21 | 3 | 27 | 4 | 25 | 4 | 25 | 3 |
| Attending first convention | 67 | 66 | 83 | 78 | 80 | 78 | 87 | 84 | 78 | 69 | 65 | 68 |
| College graduate | 19 | | 21 | | 21 | 27 | 20 | 26 | 20 | 28 | 21 | 26 |
| Postgraduate[a] | 44 | 34 | 36 | 34 | 43 | 38 | 45 | 39 | 51 | 35 | 52 | 42 |
| Protestant | | | 42 | | 47 | 73 | 47 | 72 | 49 | 71 | 50 | 69 |
| Catholic | | | 26 | | 34 | 18 | 37 | 22 | 29 | 22 | 30 | 22 |
| Jewish | | | 9 | | 9 | 3 | 8 | 3 | 8 | 2 | 7 | 2 |
| Liberal | | | | | 40 | 3 | 46 | 2 | 48 | 1 | 43 | 0 |
| Moderate | | | | | 47 | 45 | 42 | 36 | 42 | 35 | 43 | 35 |
| Conservative | | | | | 8 | 48 | 6 | 58 | 4 | 60 | 5 | 58 |

[a] Includes those in the category of college graduates.

Source: 1968–80, CBS News/New York Times Delegate Surveys; 1984–1988, Martin Plissner and Warren J. Mitofsky, "The Making of the Delegates, 1968–1988," Public Opinion 11 (September/October 1988): 4, and supplemental data appearing in the New York Times, August 14, 1988, p. 32.

larging the pool of citizens, who by virtue of their attendance at the caucuses would be more likely to engage in other party activities, this outcome has not occurred.

Another consequence of the rules changes is that seeking the nomination has become a self-selection process. When combined with government subsidies during the primaries, the reforms have encouraged the proliferation of candidates. This proliferation, in turn, has led to the creation of separate electoral organizations that can rival the regular party organization.

The power of elected party leaders has also been weakened. No longer able to control their state's delegation, party officials now have to compete with the supporters of the successful candidate for influence over the campaign. And prior to the creation of delegate slots for party leaders and elected officials, they had to run in the primaries and caucuses and win to ensure their attendance at the national conventions. Table 4–6 indicates the decreasing proportion of these VIPs who became delegates from 1968 through 1976, particularly at Democratic conventions.

State party organizations and state party leaders seem to be making a comeback, although most have not attained the preeminent position they enjoyed prior to the rules changes. Moreover, their control over soft money raised by the national committee to get out the votes for its candidates has given them some of the additional leverage that they had lost in the 1970s. The increasing importance of state and local committees in providing funds and organizational support for the general election has also benefited these state party officials.

## TABLE 4–6
### Representation of Major Elected Officials at National Conventions, 1968–1988[a] (in percentages)

|  | 1968 | 1972 | 1976 | 1980 | 1984 | 1988 |
|---|---|---|---|---|---|---|
| *Democrats* | | | | | | |
| Governors | 96% | 57% | 44% | 74% | 91% | 100% |
| U.S. senators | 61 | 28 | 18 | 14 | 56 | 85 |
| U.S. representatives | 32 | 12 | 14 | 14 | 62 | 87 |
| *Republicans* | | | | | | |
| Governors | 92 | 80 | 69 | 68 | 93 | 82 |
| U.S. senators | 58 | 50 | 59 | 63 | 56 | 62 |
| U.S. representatives | 31 | 19 | 36 | 40 | 53 | 55 |

[a] Figures represent the percentages of Democratic or Republican officeholders from each group who served as delegates.

*Source:* Figures provided by the Democratic and Republican National Committees.

In the past, candidates carefully chose the primaries they would enter and concentrated their efforts where they thought they would run best. Today, they have much less discretion. By allocating delegates on the basis of a proportional primary vote or multistage convention system, the nomination process now provides incentives for campaigning in a larger number of states.

Strategy and tactics have naturally changed. There are now new answers to the old questions: when to declare, where to run, how to organize, what to claim, and how to win. Before 1972, it was considered wise to wait for an opportune moment in the spring of the presidential election year before announcing one's candidacy. Adlai Stevenson did not announce his intentions until the Democratic convention. John F. Kennedy made his announcement two months before the New Hampshire primary. It was considered wise to restrict primary efforts, obtain the backing of the state party leaders, and work through their organizations. The successful candidates were those who could unify the party. They took few chances. The object of their campaign was to maintain a winning image.

## Basic Strategic Guidelines

**Plan far ahead.** Much conventional wisdom is no longer valid. Today it is necessary for all candidates to plan their campaigns early. Creating an organization, devising a strategy, and raising the amount of money necessary to conduct a national campaign all take time. These needs prompted George McGovern to announce his candidacy for the 1972 presidential nomination in January 1971, almost a year and one-half before the Democratic convention, and Jimmy Carter to begin his quest in 1974, two years before the 1976 Democratic convention.

Regardless of the date the official announcement is made, it is now common practice to begin campaigning several years before the nomination. Republicans George Bush, Jack Kemp, and Pat Robertson had field organizations contesting for delegates in the first stage of the Michigan caucuses in the summer of 1986, two full years before the Republican convention. Similarly, Democratic contenders for their party's nomination traditionally take numerous trips to Iowa and New Hampshire before their caucuses and primary selection.

The quest for the 1992 nomination, however, did not begin as early as previous elections. The war in the Persian Gulf muted partisan politics for the latter half of 1990 and the first half of 1991. Moreover, the presence of a popular incumbent seeking reelection markedly reduced the incentive for candidates to mount the hustlings and campaign for their party's nomination in order to challenge President Bush in the general election. It was not until April 30, 1991, that the first candidate for the Democratic nomination, Paul E. Tsongas, announced his candidacy.

**Concentrate efforts in the early contests.** Doing well in the initial caucuses and primaries and qualifying for matching grants are the principal aims of most candidates today. The early contests are particularly important for lesser-known aspirants, less for the number of delegates they can win than for the amount of publicity they can generate and the public recognition they can gain as a consequence.

The initial round of the Iowa caucuses has received extensive coverage in recent years. As the first "official" contest for convention delegates, it has assumed importance far beyond the numbers of people who participate or number of delegates who are chosen. Jimmy Carter in 1976, George Bush in 1980, and Gary Hart in 1984 got great boosts from their unexpected showings in this state. Conversely, Ronald Reagan in 1980, John Glenn in 1984, and George Bush in 1988 were hurt by their performances in Iowa.

Doing well in Iowa can boost the fortunes of a lesser-known candidate. A good example was Gary Hart's performance in 1984. He received only 16.5 percent of the Democratic vote, compared to front-runner Walter Mondale's 48.9 percent, former nominee George McGovern's 10.3 percent, and Senator John Glenn's 3.5 percent.[11] But Mondale's victory was expected; Hart's second-place finish was not. As a consequence, Hart shared the media spotlight with Mondale but profited from more laudatory coverage.

Pat Robertson's surprising second-place finish ahead of Bush in 1988 generated substantial media coverage that was initially favorable. Robertson's gain was Bush's loss. But it also reduced the attention given to Robert Dole's victory in that state. Robertson received more television coverage than Dole following the Iowa caucus.[12] The surprising Republican results combined with the close but expected Democratic ones also muted some of the afterglow for the Democratic winner. With the media focusing on Robertson's strength, Bush's weakness, and Dole's coequal front-running status, Democratic winner Richard Gephardt did not receive the boost from Iowa that Carter had in 1976 or Gary Hart had in 1984. He did increase in the polls, but his rise proved to be short-lived.

The Carter, Bush (1980), and Hart victories inflated the importance of Iowa for non-front-running candidates of both parties in 1988. Moreover, with New Hampshire following only eight days later, and Super Tuesday two weeks after that, the winners did not have sufficient time to maximize their wins by raising a lot of money and building deep organizations in the states that were soon to hold their nomination contests. The other problem, which the winners of Iowa have traditionally faced, is that the expectations of their future performance increase, but their media coverage also becomes more critical. In general, front-runners receive more negative coverage than do non-front-runners.[13]

The losers often find themselves in the opposite position, with decreased expectations but more favorable media coverage. Bush's best media occurred after his Iowa loss and before the New Hampshire primary.[14] Thus, although Dole and Gephardt gained as a consequence of their Iowa wins, they discovered, as Gary Hart had four years earlier and as Pat Robertson found out in 1988, that winning early or doing better than expected can be a mixed blessing.

The winners of the New Hampshire primary in 1988, George Bush and Michael Dukakis, fared better than did those in Iowa. For Bush, New Hampshire offered the comeback from his Iowa loss and the bounce into Super Tuesday. For Dukakis, doing well in New Hampshire reaffirmed his strength in a neighboring state and positioned him well for the contests that were to follow. However, had either Bush or Dukakis lost New Hampshire, it could have been a death knell.

New Hampshire is traditionally important because it is the first state to hold a primary in which the entire electorate participates. It is thus the first popular test of a candidate's electability. Naturally candidates who do surprisingly well in this primary have benefited enormously. Eugene McCarthy in 1968, George McGovern in 1972, and Jimmy Carter in 1976 all gained visibility and credibility from their New Hampshire performances, even though none had a majority of the vote and only Carter had even a plurality.

Winning New Hampshire after his surprising finish in Iowa propelled Gary Hart onto the front page and into the nightly news. He became a topic of intense interest. He gained recognition. Before Iowa, less than half the electorate had ever heard of him and only 3 percent of the Democrats wanted him as their nominee. After New Hampshire, 90 percent had heard of him and 33 percent wanted him to be the Democratic candidate.

Like Iowa, New Hampshire also receives much media attention. Together with Iowa, it accounted for 34 percent of all the prenomination television coverage on the national news in 1988. According to television analyst S. Robert Lichter and his associates, "If only extensive discussions of the state contests are counted, there were more analyses of Iowa and New Hampshire than of *all* other states combined."[15] That is why it is so important for candidates to run in these early contests.

For non-front-runners, there are few options. The Iowa caucus and New Hampshire primary provide a chance to gain national recognition and establish credentials. Having less money, a smaller organization, and fewer volunteers and partisan supporters, non-front-runners have great incentive to compete. The stakes are high, but the odds are not good. The failure to stand out may force them to drop out. On the other hand, winning is no guarantee of future success; it is simply an opportunity to continue.

Democrat Albert Gore, a senator from Tennessee, and Republican Alexander Haig, former general and secretary of state, adopted a variation of the Iowa–New Hampshire strategy in 1988. With private surveys indicating that they did not enjoy much support in Iowa, both chose to de-emphasize that state and concentrate on other ones—in Haig's case

New Hampshire and in Gore's the southern regional primaries. Their principal danger in utilizing this strategic approach was to stay in the news in February while media coverage focused on those candidates who were competing in Iowa.

Jesse Jackson also did not concentrate his campaign resources in Iowa. With a small minority population in an agricultural state, Jackson's social message was not expected to receive much support. However, unlike Haig and Gore, who needed to conserve their resources and build a core of supporters by demonstrating their electability, Jackson had different objectives. In the words of one of his campaign officials, Richard Hatcher:

> Our largest job in the campaign . . . was to have enough money to keep the plane that Jesse was on in the air. That was a major challenge of the campaign. We learned very quickly that people who did not like Jesse Jackson were probably not inclined to vote for him under almost any circumstance. We found that people like that underwent a change if they saw him or heard him in person. In fact, in some instances, they would even become workers in the campaign. We knew it was really important to us that he be exposed to as many people as possible.[16]

For front-runners, the needs and opportunities are different. The initial caucuses and primaries present a situation in which their superior resources can be used to eliminate or preclude competition, demonstrate electability, perhaps even invulnerability, and build a delegate lead. Winning confirms the front-runner's status; losing jeopardizes it, but recovery is possible, as Ronald Reagan showed in 1980, Walter Mondale in 1984, and George Bush in 1988. However, an early loss can raise questions about a front-runner's viability, as it did for Bush in 1988.

**Raise and spend big bucks early.** The candidates who plan far ahead, concentrate their efforts in the early contests, and do better than expected can reap significant fund-raising advantages. Bush and Dukakis pursued an early big bucks strategy in 1988 with considerable success. Each desired to raise as much as possible as early as possible to maximize his government-issued matching funds, to outspend his opponents, and to pay for his large organization.

Bush's strategy was to raise $10 million to begin the quest for the nomination. According to Edward Rogers, one of Bush's financial managers:

> Our goal was to have $10 million in the bank, with virtually no liabilities, on January 1. We knew early on, it was common sense, that if we would lose one of the early primaries, money would dry up. . . . Part of the discipline was, having put that money into the bank, not to spend it and not to nickel and dime county conventions and hospitality receptions at Republican events. It adds up. There was a lot of discipline not to spend that money.[17]

Other Republican candidates devoted equally intense efforts to building a war chest. Their performance in Iowa and New Hampshire dictated whether this chest could be replenished. The general consensus among campaign managers was that each Republican candidate needed $8–$10 million to get to Super Tuesday and $16–$17 million to get through it. Democrats calculated that they needed a slightly smaller amount.

Having a solid financial base is a strategic imperative. It allows a presidential campaign to plan ahead, to decide where to establish its field organizations, how much media advertising to buy, and where to focus it (and on whom) in order to do the most good.

Of all the Democratic candidates in 1988, Michael Dukakis gained the most as a consequence of his superior fund raising. He used his money to build and staff large organizations in New Hampshire and key southern states, develop and target his media to key groups, and focus his personal efforts on campaigning, whereas Richard Gephardt, his principal early opponent, had to devote nearly all his resources to Iowa and then use much of the period following his victory to raise additional funds. By the time Gephardt got to Super Tuesday, he had relatively little money left to do polling, buy advertising, and pay campaign workers.

Senator Albert Gore had a different problem. His decision not to compete in Iowa or New Hampshire hurt his fund raising. Needing to establish his credibility as a candidate and also to obtain delegates, Gore was forced to spend $3 million to blanket the South with radio and television advertising on Super Tuesday, compared to Dukakis's $1.6 million, which was effectively targeted to win delegates, not popular votes. Gore emerged with victories in four southern states and 28.4 percent of the delegates selected on Super Tuesday. Dukakis, however, maintained his lead with wins in five states, three of which were in the South. He received almost 32 percent of the delegates elected on this day.

Another advantage of having money up front is that the news media interpret it as a sign of strength in the prenomination period prior to caucuses and primaries. The campaign's organization and financial resources are seen as indicators of its electoral potential. In 1988, according to Lichter and his associates, "organizational and financial strength underlay Robertson's image as a viable candidate despite his status as a political novice. The Bush and Dukakis campaigns enjoyed a steady stream of praise for organization and financial resources. Conversely, financial and organizational problems took the sheen off the efforts of Hart, Dole, and Simon."[18]

The need to have large sums early is exacerbated by the front-loading of the nomination process. To take advantage of any boost that Iowa or New Hampshire may provide, it is necessary to fund simultaneous media campaigns in a number of states.

Two principal consequences follow from the need for early money: the financial campaign in the years before the nomination has assumed greater importance than in the past, and non-front-runners are disadvantaged even more than they were previously. The odds against a little-known outsider using Iowa and New Hampshire as a stepping stone to the nomination have increased in recent years. Candidates also have to be concerned about a countervailing problem—staying within the overall spending limits for the primary period. As it was, Bush, Robertson, and Dole almost "maxed-out" (that is, used all of their permissible expenditures) before the primaries ended.

**Develop a deep and wide organization.** The concentration of primaries and caucuses requires that candidates create a deep and wide organization, one that can attend to the many facets of the campaign and do so in many states simultaneously. In the past, getting the endorsements of state party leaders and using their organizations to run campaigns was regarded as the surest and easiest course of action. An effective state organization could be expected to turn out the faithful.

The rules changes, however, have weakened but not eliminated the influence of state party leaders. George Bush cashed in some of his political capital, built up as chair of his party's national committee and vice-president, to buttress his support in the South. He depended on the governors and their organizations in New Hampshire, South Carolina, and Illinois to win these critical states. New Hampshire was the comeback state after Iowa; South Carolina, coming three days before Super Tuesday, was the springboard into the South; and midwestern Illinois was the final victory that sealed Dole's defeat.

Four years earlier Walter Mondale had also used his position as former vice-president and a longtime national Democratic leader to build a strong organization with the help of the party and elected officials around the country. Although no Democratic candidate in 1988 began with as much organizational support as Mondale had in 1984, Dukakis's superior financial position enabled him to have more paid staff and make more effective use of campaign resources than did any of the other Democrats seeking the nomination. His organization sustained him in Iowa and three important southern states: Florida, Texas, and Maryland.

The major task of any organization is to mobilize voters. Telephone banks must be established, door-to-door canvassing undertaken, and appropriate material mailed or hand delivered. It is also necessary to create the impression of public support and generate excitement. These activities involve a large volunteer effort. A major assumption of the Robertson campaign in 1988 was that the 3 million people who signed petitions urging him to run for president would be a continuing source for voluntary campaign activities and for fund raising.

Eugene McCarthy and George McGovern recruited thousands of college students to help in 1968 and 1972. Jimmy Carter had his "Peanut

Brigade," a group of Georgians who followed him from state to state, in 1976. Mondale benefited from the support of organized labor in 1984. Jesse Jackson effectively used black churches to recruit volunteers and raise money. His victory in the Michigan caucuses can be attributed in large part to his mobilization of minority and student supporters in a state that permitted on-site registration.

**Monitor public opinion.** With intentions clear, money in hand, and an organization in place, it is necessary to ascertain public sentiment, appeal to it, and perhaps manipulate it. To achieve the first step, polling is essential.

The use of polls by candidates is fairly recent. Thomas E. Dewey was the first to have private polling data available to him when he tried unsuccessfully to obtain the Republican nomination in 1940. John F. Kennedy was the first candidate to engage a pollster in his quest for the nomination. Preconvention surveys conducted by Louis Harris in 1960 indicated that Hubert Humphrey, Kennedy's principal rival, was vulnerable in West Virginia and Wisconsin. On the basis of this information, the Kennedy campaign decided to concentrate time, effort, and money in these Protestant states. Victories in both helped demonstrate Kennedy's broad appeal, thereby improving his chances for the nomination enormously.

Today, all major presidential candidates commission polls. These private surveys are important for several reasons. They provide information about the beliefs and attitudes of voters, their perceptions of the candidates, and the kinds of appeals that are apt to be most effective. Michael Dukakis used polls effectively in developing and targeting an appeal on Super Tuesday.

Poll results are also used to build momentum, increase morale, raise money, and affect media coverage. By indicating who can win and who should be taken seriously, polls affect the amount of attention candidates receive. Television coverage of a candidate is closely related to that candidate's position in the polls. Front-runners get more coverage, although that coverage is also apt to be more critical. The only exception in 1988 was Jesse Jackson, whose capacity to attract media attention did not seem to relate to his popular support. His coverage was also more favorable than other Democratic front-runners with the exception of Bruce Babbitt.[19]

The tendency of the media to follow the polls is not surprising given the emphasis placed on the competition between candidates, the "horse race." Moreover, each of the major networks and major news organizations now conducts or commissions surveys throughout the campaign, and the results are presented as news to its viewers or readers.

The relationship between poll position and media coverage places lesser-known candidates at a competitive disadvantage and reinforces their need to enter the early contests and win or do better than expected. Their only other option, which is not nearly as effective, is to say or do something out of the ordinary, take an extreme position, or make a symbolic gesture to get on the news. For lesser-known candidates, the worst news is no news.

The amount of coverage is important because the more coverage candidates have, particularly during the early months, the more volunteers they can attract and the more money they can raise. The benefits of appearing to be popular and electable suggest why candidates have also used their private polls for promotional purposes. Releasing favorable surveys is a standard stratagem. Nelson Rockefeller, in fact, tied his quest for the Republican nomination in 1968 to poll data. Since he did not enter the primaries, Rockefeller's aim was to convince Republican delegates that he, not Richard Nixon, would be the strongest candidate. Private surveys conducted for Rockefeller in nine large states, five important congressional districts, and the nation as a whole one month before the Republican convention indicated that he would do better against potential Democratic candidates than Nixon. Unfortunately for Rockefeller, the final Gallup preconvention poll, fielded two days after former President Dwight Eisenhower endorsed Nixon, did not support these findings. The Gallup results undercut the credibility of Rockefeller's polls as well as of another national poll that had Rockefeller in the lead and thus effectively ended his chances for the nomination.

While polls directly affect a candidate's strategy and tactics, their impact on the general public is less direct. Despite the fear of many politicians, there are few empirical data to suggest that polls create a bandwagon effect, a momentum for a candidate which causes people to jump on board. There is, however, some evidence of a relationship between a candidate's standing in the polls, success in the primaries, and winning the nomination. Whether the public opinion leaders win because they are more popular or whether they are more popular initially because they are better known and ultimately because they look like winners is unclear.

**Design and target a distinctive appeal.** The information obtained from polls is used to create and shape leadership images and to target these images to sympathetic voters. In designing an appeal, candidates must first establish their credentials, then articulate a general approach, and finally discuss specific policy problems and solutions. For lesser-known candidates the initial emphasis must be on themselves and their relevant political experience. This emphasis was particularly important for the Democrats in 1988, since only two contenders, Gary Hart and Jesse Jackson, had national recognition. The others, referred to in the media as the "seven dwarfs" (there was no Snow White) had to present their qualifications for the nation's highest office at the outset of the campaign. Richard Gephardt did this with considerable success in Iowa by repeatedly showing his campaign biography on television. In the words of his campaign manager, William Carrick,

> The bio ads were not exciting, didn't get on the nightly news, but they were extremely important to a virtually unknown candidate. We had good bio ads, and when we were able to use them early, they made a big difference. In terms of Iowa, we were doing it the day after Christmas in places where we were able to lay an early foundation with the biographical ads. You could pivot on that and go to tough issue ads on trade or whatever else.[20]

The Dukakis campaign utilized a similar tact. According to manager Susan Estrich,

> We used our bio spot everywhere. Just a funny story: Our New York people said that under no circumstances did they want this bio spot. They wanted a special ad for New York and whatnot. So we put together a focus group and showed them all our spots and all of everybody's spots. The spot they liked best was the bio one because, I think, it conveyed information and because we were in a race of unknowns, none of whom except Gary [Hart] had been around the track. We used that bio spot all the way through.[21]

Once the foundation had been laid, the Democratic candidates tried to make appeals that distinguished themselves from their opponents. Taking the theme of new ideas that Gary Hart had articulated in 1984 and in 1988 until he was forced out of the race, Dukakis indicated that he had the competence and on-the-job experience to carry them out. He appealed primarily to middle-class, white-collar Democrats as well as to Hispanic voters. Dukakis spoke Spanish fluently. Gephardt selected a populist theme, emphasizing his opposition to unfair trading practices and his leadership position in the House of Representatives. He targeted his message to organized labor and to those hurt by foreign competition. Gore hewed a more conservative line in appealing to traditional southern conservatives as well as Democrats elsewhere who wanted their party to take a tougher, more militant stand in foreign affairs. He stressed his Senate role in the national security arena. Simon, also a senator, painted himself as an old-fashioned activist, a Harry Truman Democrat. He wore a bow tie and horn-rimmed glasses to reinforce his Truman image. Like Gephardt, Simon directed his message toward blue-collar workers, party activists, and lower-middle-class Democrats. Bruce Babbitt, former governor of Arizona, tried to be a nontraditional candidate stating unpopular positions such as the need for more taxes and doing so in a halting, unpolished way. Jesse Jackson focused on the economic and social issues that he had raised in his 1984 campaign and continued to attract the support of his rainbow coalition. Jackson's liberal posture and Gore's conservative stance positioned other Democrats in the middle of their party's political spectrum.

On the Republican side in 1988, Bush emphasized his experience; Dole, his leadership; and Robertson, his basic Christian values. For Bush, the initial problem was to establish his conservative credentials given the orientation of the Republican primary electorate. In the words of campaign manager Lee Atwater:

> I felt strongly there were only two things that George Bush needed to do other than stick with Reagan that would preempt anybody from ever being able to get him on the right. One was to be hardcore on taxes, which as you all know he was. Number two was to be hard-core on the anti-communist cluster of issues. If he did those two things, no one could ever move out on him on the right.[22]

Robert Dole had a different need—to establish a reason for Republicans to switch from Bush to Dole. While the Dole campaign had no difficulty presenting its candidate as a strong leader, the campaign was never able to convince Republicans that Bush was not also such a leader. Robertson's initial problems were high negatives; he was viewed as less acceptable by mainstream Republicans. Thus his task was to present himself as a traditional Republican with a nontraditional background. To do so, he articulated Reagan themes and talked very specifically about issues. However, several careless statements on which the media focused undercut his competence in the eyes of the voters. The other Republicans—Pete du Pont, Alexander Haig, and Jack Kemp—were never able to establish themselves and identify distinctive issue positions that appealed to the party's electorate.

Once images are created and constituencies targeted, the appeal must be communicated. The mass media have become the principal mechanism through which communication is accomplished. In the nomination period candidates tend to concentrate on the local press—making themselves available to reporters and editors, timing speeches and announcements to receive maximum press coverage, buying advertisements to be broadcast on the radio during rush hours and on television during the evening's prime time. High costs limit candidates' use of the national media.

Recent nominations have seen their share of creative sloganing. Bush criticized Reagan's economic proposals in 1980 as "voodoo economics." Mondale attempted to reveal the emptiness of Hart's "new agenda" with the line, "Where's the beef?" In 1988 there were fewer of these memorable phrases. Robert Dole hurt his image when he accused George Bush of lying about his record. Media commentators recalled

Dole's mean and nasty reputation and his role as a political hatchet man in the 1976 presidential campaign when he was the Republican vice-presidential nominee. In 1984 a similar offhanded comment haunted Jesse Jackson. His reference to Jews as "Hymies" in an informal conversation with a black reporter created a stir that forced Jackson to deny repeatedly that he was anti-Semitic.

All of these factors—timing, finance, organization, and communications—affect the quest for delegates. They help shape the candidates' strategies and tactics for the nomination. Generally speaking, there have been two successful contemporary prototypical strategies, one for the lesser-known aspirant, the other for the front-runner. Jimmy Carter used the first of these strategies successfully in his initial quest for the nomination in 1976. In his second run four years later, Carter adopted the second. Since that time most of the principal contenders have employed one of these strategies or a variation of them in their attempts to win their party's nomination.

## *The Non-Front-Runner Strategy: Stepping Stones to Prominence*

The Carter strategy in 1976 was to run hard and fast at the outset. Stress was placed on the early caucuses and primaries. Since Carter had a name recognition problem, a major objective of his early campaign was to attract media attention.

Hamilton Jordan, Carter's campaign manager, designed the basic game plan two years before the election. He described the early preconvention strategy as follows:

> The prospect of a crowded field coupled with the new proportional representation rule does not permit much flexibility in the early primaries. No serious candidate will have the luxury of picking or choosing among the early primaries. To pursue such a strategy would cost that candidate delegate votes and increase the possibility of being lost in the crowd. I think that we have to assume that everybody will be running in the first five or six primaries.
>
> A crowded field enhances the possibility of several inconclusive primaries with four or five candidates separated by only a few percentage points. Such a muddled picture will not continue for long as the press will begin to make "winners" of some and "losers" of others. The intense press coverage which naturally focuses on the early primaries plus the decent time intervals which separate the March and mid-April primaries dictate a serious effort in all of the first five primaries. Our "public" strategy would probably be that Florida was the first and real test of the Carter campaign and that New Hampshire would just be a warm-up. In fact, a strong, surprise

showing in New Hampshire should be our goal which would have tremendous impact on successive primaries.[23]

The goal was achieved. Dubbed the person to beat after his victories in the Iowa caucuses and New Hampshire primary, Carter, with his defeat of George Wallace in Florida, overcame a disappointing fourth place in Massachusetts a week earlier and became the acknowledged front-runner.

The efficiency of the Carter organization, the effectiveness of his personal style of campaigning, and the lack of strong opposition helped him to win eight of the next nine primaries. These victories gave him approximately 35 percent of the delegates selected by early May, more than double that of his nearest competitor. Although Carter lost ten out of the last seventeen primaries, he was able to continue to build a delegate lead over the field. By the end of the primaries, his nomination had become a foregone conclusion.

The Carter effort in 1976 became the model for George Bush in 1980 and Gary Hart in 1984 and for most of the Democratic contenders in 1988. Concentrating their efforts in Iowa and New Hampshire, candidates campaigned vigorously in these states and used the media, particularly local media, to increase their name recognition. They visited the states frequently and tried to build deep organizations.

Iowa activities paid off, at least initially. Bush's victory in 1980, Hart's surprising second-place finish in 1984, and Gephardt's win in 1988 elevated them overnight to serious contenders. New Hampshire, however, burst Bush's and Gephardt's bubble. Both were unable to meet heightened expectations and unable to defeat the front-running Ronald Reagan (1980) and Michael Dukakis (1988). For Hart, however, New Hampshire had precisely the opposite effect. His defeat of Walter Mondale propelled him to the position of front-runner.

The front-loading of the selection process, particularly the holding of a southern regional primary in 1988, has reduced the "bump" that Iowa can give to a victorious non-front-runner. Lesser-known candidates enter the Iowa caucuses because they lack the name recognition, financial backing, and the organizational base that nationally recognized candidates can have. A win in Iowa gives them the potential for developing these necessary criteria for gaining their party's nomination.

Carter used Iowa as his first stepping stone in 1976. Gephardt attempted to take a similar route in 1988, but scheduling changes made it more difficult. Facing a popular Massachusetts governor in neighboring New Hampshire eight days later and with twenty Super Tuesday contests only two weeks away, he was not able to gain as much leverage from his Iowa win as Carter had twelve years earlier. Although Gephardt's standing among Democrats in New Hampshire increased by 14 percent following Iowa, he still trailed Dukakis in that state. More-

# Non-Front-Runner Strategies in 1988: The Campaign Managers Speak

## DEMOCRATS

*Bruce Babbitt.* We tried to present Babbitt as the uncandidate, the antipolitician, the truth-teller; not slick on TV; not racked up with a lot of endorsements; but a man pushing unpopular ideas which we felt most of the public instinctively knew were right and correct and were the ideas that were coming but did not yet have common currency in public opinion. We attempted to challenge the voters, and what happened was—well, we got blown out. I think somewhere in the Bible it says. "The truth shall set you free," and in our case it did that very quickly.

Our failure in Iowa was based on a couple of things. First, the Dukakis campaign eclipsed a great part of our positioning. Second, I think that we never were able to establish a long-term calendar credibility—not enough money, not enough base. . . . Third, I think the 15 percent threshold in Iowa served to plummet us down rather than up, and I think the threshold has that effect in both directions. And funny, and most important, I think ideas are kind of like aging wine. They get better with age. They take a little time to breathe. We pursued a set of ideas that, while advancing them very successfully, we were not successful in making them credible enough or popular enough to establish a base around them and turn that into a viable campaign.

*Frederick DuVal (p. 6)*

*Richard Gephardt.* By the time he [Gephardt] announced we had an impressive group of veteran Iowa organizer activists behind the Gephardt candidacy, we also had made less impressive, but significant, efforts in New Hampshire. Theoretically, we were positioned to finish a decent second in Iowa to then prohibitive-favorite Gary Hart. Then the events of May unfolded and Gary Hart fell out of the sky. The next thing we knew was that *The Des Moines Register* poll had Dick Gephardt a two-to-one favorite in Iowa over the next closest contender, which I think at that time was Bruce Babbitt.

*Source:* David R. Runkel, ed., *Campaign for President: The Managers Look at '88* (Dover, Mass.: Auburn House, 1989).

The news media unloaded on Gephardt from Iowa to Super Tuesday. After finishing second in Iowa, Simon defined his future survival as dependent on a second-place finish in New Hampshire. We got a dose of negative advertising in New Hampshire from Simon and Dukakis. Instead of being in the classic position of the Iowa winner against the New Hampshire favorite, a Dukakis-Gephardt confrontation, we ended up having a donnybrook with Paul Simon for second place. Dukakis was sort of our elder statesman, above the fray.

. . . The high point for us was South Dakota, where we conducted a week-long campaign, spending $65,000 to buy 2,000 rating points. We went from 11 points down to win by 12 points and did that in the course of seven or eight days. That was the high point.

From then on we got caught in a cross fire between Gore and Dukakis on Super Tuesday. They spent substantial advertising dollars attacking Gephardt in the South and destroyed our Super Tuesday prospects. We were low on money and could not counterattack. After a failed attempt to revive the Gephardt campaign in Michigan, Dick withdrew from the race.

*William Carrick (pp. 3–5)*

*Albert Gore.* The strategy was to try to use the new calendar and take advantage of 20 states casting their votes on the same day, on the 8th of March—two-thirds of them in the South—to win a bunch of those states. We thought we had a good chance to do so with a candidate from the South. We also believed that if we were successful, we would then be present for a side-by-side comparison and close scrutiny alongside the one or two others who remained. We thought there would be only two or three remaining on the 9th of March as strong and viable candidacies.

*Frederick Martin (p. 21)*

## REPUBLICANS

*Pierre ("Pete") du Pont.* He [du Pont] thought there was a reasonable chance someone could beat George Bush in Iowa and New Hampshire, and he felt that if Bush were defeated in both Iowa and

*(cont.)*

## Non-Front-Runner Strategies in 1988: The Campaign Managers Speak (*cont.*)

New Hampshire, he would be mortally wounded and would not be a viable candidate after that point. Pete himself felt that he didn't have the resources to win in either Iowa or New Hampshire—certainly not in Iowa—but thought he did have the resources and the ability to come in a strong third in Iowa and perhaps higher in New Hampshire.

Our goal was to get 15 percent in Iowa and come in third, and we hoped Bush would not get more than 25 percent and that he would come in second. We hoped that would give us a lift and that our position would improve in New Hampshire, not necessarily to second but to above 20 percent. Bush would again come in second, and whoever came in first would not do significantly better—ideally a little worse—than he did in Iowa. The result would be that we would become the alternative to whoever had beaten Bush in Iowa and New Hampshire.

*Allan B. Hubbard (pp. 1–2)*

*Alexander Haig.* Starting late, we knew we had to front-load and that meant doing well in Iowa and New Hampshire. Super Tuesday looked good to us because we felt that we could do well in the South if we were able to move beyond New Hampshire.

Second, while we had this strategy, we knew we'd have to look to events beyond our control for something special, something different, to cause voters to consider the Haig dark-horse candidacy seriously, and which anticipated an atmosphere in which voters would say, "We aren't satisfied with the status quo and business as usual. We have to turn away from the front-runners to a Haig (or to another candidate). . ."

Third, because we were a small low-budget operation, we needed someone else's troops on the ground. We needed one of the other candidates—but probably not one of the two front-runners—to bow out of the race relatively early so we could siphon off some of that support to help us in building a staff and an organization. As it happened, when the [Paul] Laxalt campaign ended we did pick up some staffers, but it was far too late to really help us.

*Daniel Mariaschin (pp. 10–11)*

over, because he had devoted so many resources to winning Iowa, Gephardt found his campaign organizationally and financially disadvantaged. Robert Dole also did not get the boost he needed from Iowa, although his popularity among New Hampshire Republicans went up 14 percent in the days following his Iowa win.

New Hampshire's importance, however, has not decreased. It is essential to non-front-runners because it is the first popular election in the nomination cycle. No one who has not won the New Hampshire primary has been elected president since 1952, the year that primaries began to be an important route to the nomination.

Not only does New Hampshire generate a lot of publicity, but coming right before the window on primaries and caucuses opens, it is a launching pad for the elections that follow even though it may not be able to generate the money and organizational support it once produced for non-front-runners.

To summarize, the task for lesser-known aspirants is to increase their public recognition and, at the same time, to demonstrate their effectiveness as candidates. A win in the early caucuses and primaries, no matter how slight, confounds the odds, surprises the media, embarrasses the front-runner, and energizes the non-front-runner's candidacy. Media coverage expands; fund raising is made easier; volunteers join the organization; endorsements become more likely; and momentum can be generated, at least in the short run.[24] In the 1992 campaign most of the Democratic candidates can be expected to try to follow this route to the nomination. (See the box entitled "Non-Front-Runner Strategies in 1988.")

## *Another Non-Front-Runner Approach: Using the Campaign Pulpit*

Jesse Jackson was not a typical non-front-runner in 1984 and 1988, and, to some extent, Pat Robertson was not in 1988. Jackson did not employ the prototypical strategy although Robertson did. Jackson did not have a large paid organization or extensive paid media advertisements. Robertson did. Both, however, lacked political experience. Although each had a core of supporters who could be mobilized for effective action, neither began the campaign with broad-based public support. Both had high negatives: a lot of voters did not like them. Why then, with little realistic chance of being their party's nominees, did they seek the nomination?

Each had several overlapping objectives: to use the campaign as a pulpit for presenting their ideas and as a vehicle for mobilizing their constituencies to promote the interests of those who were not well represented in the party and its hierarchy, to be considered as a member of that hierarchy with considerable political power, and to influence the

# Pulpit Strategies in 1988:
# The Campaign Managers Speak

## DEMOCRAT

*Jesse Jackson.* We went into the year with a commitment that we would run in every state. We did not intend to avoid a single state regardless of the composition of the citizenry of that state. We also made a commitment that we would remain in the campaign to the end. We were not going to drop out under any circumstances.

. . . We saw Iowa and New Hampshire as simply legitimizing primaries, that is, as simply showing that we were serious and major players in the campaign. We did not do very well in Iowa and New Hampshire, and yet it was clear that we were viable.

. . . It was our strategy to get to Super Tuesday. Obviously Super Tuesday had been planned as the Waterloo for a candidate like Jesse Jackson. The whole idea was to produce a moderate nominee for the Democratic party. We saw Super Tuesday as really being made to order for Jesse Jackson. It was a situation where we felt he was going to do extremely well. As it turned out, he did. He won more states on Super Tuesday than any other candidate and for the first time, our campaign began to be competitive in terms of delegates. Then the campaign turned north. . . .

*Richard Hatcher (pp. 24–25)*

## REPUBLICAN

*Pat Robertson.* We had to compete everywhere if we were to maintain credibility—every state, every primary. We had to organize completely from outside the party. The Robertson campaign was a grass-roots, precinct campaign.

*(cont.)*

party and its platform. As the 1988 campaign progressed and Jackson remained as Dukakis's only opponent, he voiced an additional goal— that he be seriously considered for the Democratic vice-presidential nomination.

To achieve these objectives, Jackson and Robertson needed the campaign. They also needed to demonstrate their political strength by winning elections if they were to remain active candidates. Jackson continued to the convention even though Dukakis had built up a huge delegate lead. Robertson dropped out after the southern regional primaries, when the Republican nomination was effectively over.

Further, we determined that we must maximize spending. This wasn't something that we just hoped for; it was a basic tenet of the strategy. You must raise it and spend it judiciously according to the plan. We had to have it on time, and we had to have it early.

Lastly, it was imperative that we win a few small states that were open ballot primaries, and we had to win one big state. You can look at the spending reports and determine which large state we targeted. It was Texas. From this strategy and those dictated tactics, there were three organizational strategies: compete in all the caucus states, which represented about 24 percent of the delegates to the Republican National Convention; compete in certain congressional districts for the three-per-district winner-take-all delegates, another 24 percent of the total delegates; and win three small state primaries and one big state.

We targeted 125 congressional districts mainly in nontraditional Republican areas where very few votes captured the district and the three district delegates. Alabama, Georgia, and Mississippi were the small states we targeted to win and Texas was the large state. Following Super Tuesday, it was anticipated that our support would accelerate as other candidates dropped out.

*R. Marc Nuttle (pp. 27–28)*

*Source:* David R. Runkel, ed., *Campaign for President: The Managers Look at '88* (Dover, Mass.: Auburn House, 1989).

Others have also used the campaign to focus attention on themselves and their ideas. Ellen McCormick ran as an antiabortion candidate for the Democratic nomination in 1976. Lyndon LaRouche has used the Democratic primaries in 1980 and 1984 as a pretext for expounding his philosophy and increasing his supporters. George McGovern entered the 1984 nomination sweepstakes and Gary Hart reentered in 1988 in large part to participate in the public forum generated by the campaign. With television being the primary vehicle for conducting a large-scale nomination campaign, and with candidates such as Jackson and Robertson attracting attention by their distinctive perspectives and appeals,

# Front-Runner
# Strategies in 1988: The
# Campaign Managers Speak

## DEMOCRATS

*Michael Dukakis.* Our imperative was to survive Iowa credibly enough to hold that lead in New Hampshire. Our great concern obviously was that if we lost badly in Iowa, we wouldn't go to New Hampshire as a credible candidate. New Hampshire, as many of us know, has a way of turning on its friends and neighbors. We were able to succeed in part because of a very strong organization on the ground in both states.

We went into Super Tuesday with a four-corner strategy. I think some of the reforms that the party put into effect clearly did not have their intended effect. We were able to win the delegates on Super Tuesday and turn it into a victory by winning Texas and Florida, where we'd gone in and organized early; by winning in the West; by winning in Maryland; and by winning in the Northeast.

*Susan Estrich (pp. 7–8)*

*Gary Hart.* We always looked at the primary process as full cycle, not that he [Hart] would be the front-runner going into Iowa and New Hampshire and win the election very easily. We saw that Gephardt was doing very well in Iowa. We knew Dukakis, being so near New Hampshire, had great support there. In those early states, we knew we had to do well—first, second, or third—well enough to stay in it.

We had a good financial base. We were prepared to see it through Super Tuesday. We thought the real race would start after Super Tuesday.

The field would narrow after Super Tuesday, we guessed, to four or five people, and then the real race would begin. Our strategy was to try to maneuver the message throughout that year, to try to make the ability to govern the cutting issue and in the end to win because that would be the criteria by which the Democratic candidate was chosen.

Our strategy was to be strong financially, husband our resources, and come out strong after Super Tuesday. Then we thought it would be a battle all the way to California.

*Susan Casey (p. 18)*

## REPUBLICANS

*George Bush.* I didn't see how we could win in Iowa. We decided that we should never say that publicly and that we should fight hard in Iowa but we had to be prepared to lose Iowa. We thought there would be a very short attention span. In 72 hours, regardless of what happened in Iowa, if we ran a good campaign on the ground, we could prevail in New Hampshire. If we could get South Carolina 72 hours before the rest of Super Tuesday, we could get 8 or 10 points just off a good victory in South Carolina. . . .

We also made a decision to really concentrate on three governors that I felt had strong enough organizations in their states—if we could get them lined up early—to bring about a win no matter what else happened. They were John Sununu in New Hampshire, Carroll Campbell in South Carolina, Jim Thompson in Illinois.

*Lee Atwater (p. 34)*

*Robert Dole.* Politically, we had a big advantage, and that advantage was Iowa. We always knew we would be strong there. We realized, if we had Iowa, what we would have to do to step beyond that. When we started getting back survey data from the South at the end of 1987, we saw the kinds of leads and strengths and all of the attributes and characteristics that the vice-president had. We knew immediately that we could no longer simply win early and win often, say, finish strongly in New Hampshire but not win it. We knew at this point we had to win New Hampshire.

. . . One of the problems we had in New Hampshire, among many, was that a lot more voters there really believed that George Bush was the conservative candidate in the race. We were never really able to overcome that.

*William Lacy (p. 37)*

media candidates are likely to continue to use the nomination for their own purposes even when they have little chance of being their party's nominee. (See "Pulpit Strategies in 1988," above.)

## The Front-Runner Strategy: Amassing Delegates

Front-runners have more flexibility in designing their strategy. They do not need to gain recognition or establish their credentials. They do need to maintain their credibility and electability and extend their constituencies. And like everyone else, they need to acquire delegates.

The principal advantages front-runners have occur at the beginning of the process. A key element of their strategy must be to maximize these advantages. They need to make use of the benefits of a superior organization, financial base, media coverage, political endorsements, and volunteer efforts to overwhelm their opposition. The front-loading of the primaries provides added impetus to strike a knockout blow in the early rounds, when the lesser-known opponents are least able to compete with them.

Walter Mondale pursued this strategy in 1984, and George Bush did so in 1988. Robert Dole and Michael Dukakis used varieties of this approach. They all competed in Iowa and New Hampshire. They also spent heavily up front. They developed organizations with paid staffs in as many states as possible.

Once the initial rounds have been completed, the key for the front-runner is to amass as many delegates as possible. The proportional voting rules in the Democratic contests dictate that almost all primaries and caucuses be entered, regardless of the prospects of winning. The effect of these rules will be particularly evident in 1992. The same rules, however, encourage unequal resource allocation, roughly in proportion to the number of delegates who can realistically be won.

For the front-runner the name of the game is delegates. Winning is nice, an early roll is beneficial, but in the end it is the acquisition of delegates that provides a hedge against future losses and a mechanism for maintaining current position within the party and among its electorate. In 1980 both Carter and Reagan easily survived large-state losses by virtue of their big delegate lead and the proportion of delegates they gained even in defeat. In 1984 Mondale held on to his position as front-runner despite Hart's victories in both large and small states, because with each contest the former vice-president got closer and closer to the magic number needed to win the nomination. In 1988 George Bush practically eliminated rival Robert Dole on Super Tuesday by virtue of his large delegate lead. Michael Dukakis won more delegates than either of his competitors on Super Tuesday, positioning himself well for the remainder of the contests. (See the box entitled "Front-Runner Strategies.")

# SUMMARY

The delegate selection process has changed dramatically since 1968. Originally dominated by state party leaders, it has become more open to the party's rank and file as a consequence of the reforms initiated by the Democratic party. These reforms, designed to broaden the base of public participation and increase the representation of the party's electorate at its nominating convention, have affected the Republicans as well, even though the GOP has not chosen to mandate national guidelines for its state parties, as the Democrats have. Supreme Court decisions that give the national parties the authority to do so, new state laws that conform to these rules, and public pressure to reflect popular sentiment and improve representation have led to a greater number of primaries and more delegates selected in them for both parties.

Public participation has increased although turnout levels have varied with the date of the contest, the level of intraparty competition, the amount of money spent, and other candidate-related factors. The delegates have been demographically more representative than those of the prereform era. Larger percentages of women and minorities have been chosen. Attitudinally, however, the delegates remain more ideologically conscious, consistent, and extreme in their views than do rank-and-file partisans.

There have been other effects not nearly so beneficial to the parties. Candidacies have proliferated. Opportunities for outsiders have increased. The parties, particularly the Democrats, have become more factionalized at the national level. These unintended consequences have generated still other reforms (imposition of a window period, creation of new delegates, and until recently, formulas for proportional voting) designed to produce more cohesiveness within the party without abolishing the original goals. They have also been designed to strengthen the influence of party leaders and elected officials.

The strategy for seeking delegates has also been affected by the rules changes. The basic tenets of this strategy include:

1. Plan far ahead.
2. Concentrate efforts in the early contests.
3. Raise and spend big bucks early.
4. Create a deep and wide organization.
5. Monitor public opinion.
6. Design and target a distinctive appeal.

Tactical decisions on how to mobilize and allocate sufficient resources to build and maintain delegate support depend on the particular circumstances of individual candidates.

In general, there have been two successful prototypes to winning the nomination: the come-from-nowhere approach of the non-front-runner, and the heavy and continuous pounding strategy of the leading candidates.

Non-front-runners need stepping stones to the nomination. Their initial goal must be to establish themselves as viable candidates. At the outset, the key is recognition. Over the long haul, it is momentum. Recognition is bestowed by the media on those who do well in the early caucuses and primaries; momentum is achieved through a series of pre-nomination victories that demonstrate their electability. Together, recognition and momentum compensate for what the non-front-runners lack in reputation and popular appeal. That is why non-front-runners must concentrate their time, efforts, and resources in the first few contests. They have no choice. Winning will provide them with opportunities; losing will confirm their secondary status.

For the front-runners, the task is different. They have to maintain their position as likely nominees, not establish it. This purpose provides them with a little more flexibility at the outset, but it also requires a broad-based campaign with major resources raised and spent early. Front-runners must take advantage of their organizational and financial base to build a quick and insurmountable lead.

In the end, it is the ability to generate a popular appeal among the party's electorate that is likely to be decisive. Only one person in each party can amass a majority of the delegates, and that is the individual who can build a broad-based coalition. While specific groups may be targeted, if the overall constituency is too narrow, the nomination cannot be won. That is why candidates tend to broaden and moderate their appeal over the course of the prenomination process even before they begin the general election campaign.

# NOTES

1. The groups that were initially singled out were native Americans, blacks, and youth. Subsequently, the list of affected groups has been altered by the addition of Hispanics, Asian/Pacific Americans, and women, and by the deletion of youth. In 1992 the party has also added those with physical handicaps to the groups protected against discrimination.
2. Some states hold a presidential preference vote with a separate election of convention delegates by a convention. Others connect the presidential vote and delegate selection on an at-large or district basis. By voting for a particular candidate and/or delegates pledged to that candidate, voters may register their presidential choice and delegate selection at the same time and by the same vote. The number of these primaries has increased as a consequence of the rules changes. A third alternative is to cast separate votes for president and for convention delegates.
3. Jerry W. Calvert, "Rules That Count: Voter Choice, Party Rules and the Selection of the National Committee Delegates in 1988" (Paper presented at the annual meeting of the American Political Science Association, Washington, D.C., September 1–4, 1988), pp. 26, 27.
4. Ibid., p. 26.
5. Ibid., p. 16.
6. Barbara Norrander, "Turnout in Super Tuesday Primaries: The Composition

of the Electorate" (Paper presented at the annual meeting of the American Political Science Association, Atlanta, Georgia, August 31–September 3, 1989), p. 2.

7. Barbara Norrander, "Ideological Representativeness of Presidential Primary Voters," *American Journal of Political Science* 33 (August 1989), pp. 570–587.

8. "Convention Delegates: Who They Are and How They Compare," *New York Times*, August 14, 1988, p. A32.

9. Warren J. Mitofsky and Martin Plissner, "The Making of the Delegates, 1968–1980," *Public Opinion* (October/November 1980): 40–42; John S. Jackson, Barbara Brown, and David Bositis, "Herbert McCloskey and Friends Revisited: 1980 Democratic and Republican Party Elites Compared to the Mass Public," *American Politics Quarterly* 10 (1982): 158–80; Martin Plissner and Warren J. Mitofsky, "The Making of the Delegates, 1968–1988," *Public Opinion* (September/October 1988): 46.

10. Howard L. Reiter maintains that the reforms routinized and legitimized long-term changes that were occurring to the party system. Of these changes he mentions "the advent of the electronic media, civil service reforms which undercut the patronage system, the rise of the educated middle class and assimilation of immigrants, government social welfare programs, new campaign techniques, and the nationalization of politics." "The Limitations of Reform: Changes in the Nominating Process," *British Journal of Political Science* 15 (1985): 399–417.

11. The vote itself was small. Only 85,000 people attended the caucuses, out of 500,000 who usually can be expected to vote for the Democratic candidate in the presidential election. Hart received the votes of 12,500 of this group. William C. Adams, "Media Coverage of Campaign '84: A Preliminary Report," *Public Opinion* 7 (April/May 1984): 11.

12. S. Robert Lichter, Daniel Amundson, and Richard E. Noyes, *The Video Campaign: Network Coverage of the 1988 Primaries* (Washington, D.C.: American Enterprise Institute, 1988), pp. 95–96, 53.

13. Michael J. Robinson and Margaret Sheehan, *Over the Wire and on TV: CBS and UPI in Campaign '80* (New York: Russell Sage Foundation, 1983), p. 243.

14. Lichter, Amundson, and Noyes, *Video Campaign*, p. 104.

15. Ibid., p. 12.

16. Quoted in *Campaign for President: The Managers Look at '88*, ed. David R. Runkel (Dover, Mass.: Auburn House, 1989), p. 24.

17. Quoted in ibid., p. 184.

18. Lichter, Amundson, and Noyes, *Video Campaign*, p. 65.

19. Ibid., p. 72.

20. Quoted in *Campaign for President*, p. 144.

21. Quoted in ibid., p. 6.

22. Quoted in ibid., p. 34.

23. Hamilton Jordan, Memorandum to Jimmy Carter, August 4, 1974, in Martin Schram, *Running for President, 1976* (New York: Stein & Day, 1977), pp. 379–80.

24. According to Larry M. Bartels, momentum is a product of personal preferences that are projected onto expectations. Bartels argues that momentum can best be achieved by a little-known candidate who scores unexpected successes in situations where there is no clear front-runner. What happens is that people who have little substantive information about this candidate project their own desires for an ideal candidate onto this new winner. This result increases expectations and contributes to momentum. "Expectations

and Preferences in Presidential Nominating Campaigns," *American Political Science Review* 79 (1985): 804–815.

## SELECTED READINGS

Aldrich, John H. *Before the Convention.* Chicago: University of Chicago Press, 1980.

Bartels, Larry M. *Presidential Primaries and the Dynamics of Public Choice.* Princeton, N.J.: Princeton University Press, 1988.

Buell, Emmett H., Jr., and Lee Sigelman, eds. *Nominating the President.* Knoxville, Tenn.: University of Tennessee Press, 1991.

Crotty, William, and John S. Jackson III. *Presidential Primaries and Nominations.* Washington, D.C.: Congressional Quarterly, 1985.

Greer, John G. *Nominating Presidents: An Evaluation of Voters and Primaries.* New York: Greenwood, 1989.

Jackson, John S., Barbara Brown, and David Bositis. "Herbert McCloskey and Friends Revisited: 1980 Democratic and Republican Party Elites Compared to the Mass Public." *American Politics Quarterly* 10 (1982): 158–80.

Lichter, S. Robert, Daniel Amundson, and Richard E. Noyes. *The Video Campaign: Network Coverage of the 1988 Primaries.* Washington, D.C.: American Enterprise Institute, 1988.

Norrander, Barbara. "Ideological Representativeness of Presidential Primary Voters." *American Journal of Political Science* 33 (August 1989): 570–587.

Orren, Gary R. "The Nomination Process: Vicissitudes of Candidate Selection." In *The Election of 1984*, ed. Michael Nelson, pp. 27–82. Washington, D.C.: Congressional Quarterly, 1985.

Plissner, Martin, and Warren J. Mitofsky. "The Making of the Delegates, 1968–1988." *Public Opinion* 3 (September/October 1988): 45–47.

Polsby, Nelson W. *The Consequences of Party Reform.* New York: Oxford University Press, 1983.

Reiter, Howard L. "The Limitations of Reform: Changes in the Nominating Process." *British Journal of Political Science* 15 (1985): 399–417.

Runkel, David R., ed. *Campaign for President: The Managers Look at '88.* Dover, Mass.: Auburn House, 1989.

Shafer, Byron E. *Quiet Revolution: The Struggle for the Democratic Party and the Shaping of Post-Reform Politics.* New York: Russell Sage Foundation, 1983.

# Chapter 5

# The Convention

## INTRODUCTION

Theoretically, national conventions perform four basic functions. The first and most important is to choose the presidential and vice-presidential nominees. As the party's supreme governing body, they also determine its rules and regulations, decide on its platform, and provide a forum for unifying the party and for launching its presidential campaign. In practice, however, conventions often ratify previously made decisions. The choice of a presidential candidate is frequently a foregone conclusion, and the selection of a running mate is, in reality, the presidential nominee's. Similarly, drafts of party platforms are formulated before the convention and are either accepted by the delegates with little or no change or shape the character of the debate at the convention.

Prior to 1956, conventions were decision-making bodies. Majorities were constructed within them to nominate presidential candidates. Party leaders, who exercised considerable control over the selection of their state delegation, debated among themselves. Once they agreed on the candidates, they cast the votes of their delegates in favor of their particular choice.

The last brokered conventions occurred in 1952.[1] In that year Democratic and Republican leaders wheeled and dealed in "smoke-filled rooms" to select Governor Adlai Stevenson of Illinois and General Dwight Eisenhower as their respective nominees. Since that convention, the delegate selection process has dictated the nominees.

Another indication of the decline of the brokered convention has been first ballot phenomena that have characterized all recent conventions. In fact, since 1924, when the Democrats took 103 ballots to nominate John W. Davis, there have been only four conventions (two Democratic and two Republican) in which much more than one ballot has been needed. In 1932 the Democrats held four roll calls before they agreed on Franklin Roosevelt, and three in 1952 to nominate Adlai Stevenson. In 1940, Republican Wendell Willkie was selected on the eighth ballot, breaking a deadlock among Thomas Dewey, Arthur Vandenberg, and himself. Eight years later, Dewey was nominated on the third ballot.

A variety of factors have reduced the convention's decision-making capabilities. State party leaders no longer control the composition or behavior of their delegations. The involvement of the party's rank and file in the selection process enhances the prospects that the delegates will be publicly committed to a candidate and that their votes for the nominee will be known long before they are cast in the convention. In fact, the major television networks, newsmagazines, and newspapers regularly conduct delegate counts during the preconvention stage of the nomination process and forecast the results.

The broadcasting of conventions by radio and later, television has also detracted from the delegates' ability to bargain and cajole. It is difficult to compromise before a television camera, especially during prime time. Public exposure has forced negotiations off the convention floor and even out of "leaky" committee rooms.

Size is another factor that has affected the proceedings. Conventions used to be relatively small. In 1860, 303 delegates nominated Democrat Stephen Douglas, while 466 chose Republican Abraham Lincoln. Today, the participants run into the thousands. Table 5–1 lists the number of delegate votes at Democratic and Republican conventions since 1940. When alternates and delegates who possess fractional votes are included, the numbers grow even more. In 1992 the Republicans, swelled by the bonus given states that went for the GOP in 1988, will have around 2,203 delegates, while the Democrats, augmented by the bonus delegates of elected and party officials, will have 4,286 delegates.

Because of the large number of delegates, divisions within the party have been magnified. There is more desire from minorities to be heard. These pressures, in turn, have produced the need for more efficient organizations, both within the groups desiring recognition and by party officials and candidate representatives seeking to maintain order and to create the image of a unified party. For the party leaders and the prospective nominee, the task has become one of orchestration, and the goal is to conduct a huge pep rally replete with ritual and pomp—a made-for-television production. From the perspective of the party and its nominees, the convention now serves primarily as a launching pad for the general election campaign.

TABLE 5–1
Delegate Votes at Nominating Conventions,
1940–1992[a]

| Year | Republicans | Democrats |
|------|-------------|-----------|
| 1940 | 1,000 | 1,100 |
| 1944 | 1,059 | 1,176 |
| 1948 | 1,094 | 1,234 |
| 1952 | 1,206 | 1,230 |
| 1956 | 1,323 | 1,372 |
| 1960 | 1,331 | 1,521 |
| 1964 | 1,308 | 2,316 |
| 1968 | 1,333 | 2,622 |
| 1972 | 1,348 | 3,016 |
| 1976 | 2,259 | 3,008 |
| 1980 | 1,994 | 3,331 |
| 1984 | 2,234 | 3,933 |
| 1988 | 2,277 | 4,160 |
| 1992 | 2,203 | 4,286 |

[a] The magic number, the number of votes needed for nomination, equals one more than half.

*Source:* Richard C. Bain and Judith H. Parris, *Convention Decisions and Voting Records*, 2d ed. (Washington, DC: Brookings Institution, 1973), Appendix C. Updated by author.

This chapter explores that pep rally goal and the tension it has created, tension between the party and its nominees on one hand and media representatives, activist delegates, and defeated candidates on the other. The first part of the chapter describes the official convention, the one in which the delegates participate. Here the issues that most frequently divide the convention and must be resolved by it are examined. The first section outlines the official procedures; the second surveys the credentials, rules, and platforms; and the third details the selection of the nominees. Throughout these discussions procedural, substantive, and personnel issues are presented as barometers of party cohesiveness and as indicators of the support the nominees can expect to receive from their own party in the general election.

The mediated convention—the one the people of the United States see on television—serves as the prime focus of the fourth section of the chapter. The principal questions that are discussed in this section include how the parties script and stage their show and how the media react to that orchestration. The impact the convention has on the electorate and ultimately on the government is the subject of the final section.

# THE OFFICIAL CONVENTION

Preliminary decisions on the convention are made by the party's national committee, usually on the recommendation of its chair and the appropriate convention committees. An incumbent president normally exercises considerable influence over many of these decisions: the choice of a convention city, the selection of temporary and permanent convention officials, and the designation of the principal speakers. These decisions are rarely challenged by the convention. Both the Democrats and the Republicans have traditionally turned to national party leaders, primarily members of Congress, to fill many of the positions.

## *Organizing the Meeting*

Over the years, a standard agenda has been followed by both parties. (See Table 5–2.) The first day is devoted to welcoming speeches and usually the keynote address. Given during prime viewing hours to a large home and convention audience, this speech is designed to unify the delegates, smoothing over the divisions that may have emerged during the preconvention campaign, and to rouse them and the public for the coming election. The address ritually trumpets the achievements

**TABLE 5–2**
**Agenda of National Nominating Conventions**

| First Day | Third Day |
|---|---|
| Opening ceremonies | Opening ceremonies |
| Welcoming speeches | Nominations of presidential candidates |
| Election of convention officers | Roll call for presidential nomination |
| Treasurer's report | |
| National chair's report | |
| Keynote address | |

| Second Day | Fourth Day |
|---|---|
| Opening ceremonies | Opening ceremonies |
| Credentials Committee report[a] | Nominations of vice-presidential candidates |
| Rules Committee report[a] | Roll call for vice-presidential nomination |
| Platform Committee report[a] | Acceptance speeches: |
| |    Vice-presidential nominee |
| |    Presidential nominee |
| | Adjournment |

[a] These reports are often interspersed with short speeches by party and public officials.

# Planning for the Convention

The city where the convention is to be held is usually chosen a year or two in advance of the convention. The Democrats announced their selection of New York for their 1992 meeting in the summer of 1990 while the Republicans chose Houston in January 1991. A number of factors are usually considered when deciding upon the best possible site. They include the size and availability of the convention hall, its suitability for television, the number of hotel rooms, local transportation to and from the hall, the political atmosphere of the city, its symbolic value, and most important, the financial concessions it makes to host the meeting.

The size of modern conventions requires large meeting halls to seat the delegates and alternates and to accommodate the thousands of others who wish to attend. For example, in 1992 the Republicans specified that their convention hall seat 20,000. Each party has also required the host city to have approximately 25,000 first-class hotel rooms, including suites, plus adequate transportation and press facilities for the conventioneers.

In recent years security has also become a major concern. The 1968 demonstrations at the Democratic convention in Chicago have led leaders of both parties to take elaborate precautions to prevent potentially disruptive activities. The cost of this security as well as for the preparation of the hall can be extremely high.

Cities and principal corporations within them normally subsidize these costs. In 1988 Atlanta underwrote $1.5 million of the costs of the Democratic convention, while local business kicked in another $750,000 for the official parties. New Orleans, host of the 1988 Republican convention, raised almost $7 million from private and public donations. Both New York and Houston have pledged approximately $110 million toward convention expenses.

Each party is also given money from the federal election campaign fund to conduct its national convention. In 1988 this amount was $9.2 million. In 1992 it will be about $10.8 million.

The political atmosphere is also important in selecting a convention site. Parties and their prospective nominees prefer to launch their campaign among supporters. Being nominated in Chicago in 1860 helped Abraham Lincoln almost as much as it hurt Hubert Humphrey 108 years later. Cities can have symbolic significance as well. One reason the Democrats ruled out New Orleans in 1992 was the passage of a restrictive abortion bill by the Louisiana legislature. New York, in contrast, will provide a more hospitable environment for liberal groups within the party, while party fund raisers will tap its financial community for contributions. Houston, adopted home of George Bush, should be equally advantageous for raising money and launching the president's reelection campaign.

of the party, eulogizing its heroes and criticizing the opposition for its ill-conceived programs, inept leadership, and general inability to cope with the nation's problems. The keynoter for the party that does not control the White House sounds a litany of past failures and suggests in a not-so-subtle way that the country needs new leadership.

The tone of the speech, however, can vary considerably. In 1984 Governor Mario Cuomo of New York, the Democratic keynoter, sounded a sober theme. Describing the United States as a tale of two cities, he chided the Reagan administration for pursuing policies that benefited the rich at the expense of the poor. In contrast, Ann Richards, then treasurer of Texas, who gave the 1988 keynote address, was more folksy, upbeat, and humorous. Praising traditional Democratic New Deal beliefs and policies, she criticized George Bush for being aloof, insensitive, and uncaring. "Poor George," she said sarcastically, "he can't help it. He was born with a silver foot in his mouth."[2]

Naturally, the keynoter for the party in office reverses the blame and praise. Noting the accomplishments of the administration and its unfinished business, the speaker urges a continuation of the party's effective leadership.[3] Continuation is what New Jersey's Governor Thomas Keen preached in his address to the 1988 Republican convention. Mocking Democratic liberalism as a recipe for big government and more taxes, he lauded Republican politics and policies.

In a departure from previous conventions, the keynote address was given on the second night of the Republican convention in 1988. The first day was devoted to paying a tribute to President Reagan with speeches praising his administration, a movie highlighting its achievements, and an address by the president comparing the gains of his eight years in office with the failings of the Carter years that preceded them. Reagan credited Vice-President Bush with major contributions and reiterated his strong support of him and other Republicans in the forthcoming elections. The president's promise to do all he could to help Bush get elected contrasted with the lukewarm backing departing President Dwight Eisenhower gave his vice-president, Richard Nixon, in 1960.

Reagan's speech continued the recent practice of allowing party leaders, including former presidents, to address the convention during prime time. With the convention's promotional activities for the party and its nominees eclipsing its decision-making functions, prime time exposure has become one of its most treasured prizes. In recent conventions the Democrats have even traded this exposure to unsuccessful candidates in exchange for their public commitment to support the ticket in the election. That was the deal given Edward Kennedy in 1980, Jesse Jackson and Gary Hart in 1984, and Jackson again in 1988. In the case of Jackson, his speeches attracted more viewers than any other convention event, including the acceptance addresses by the nominees.

The second day of the convention is usually consumed by reports from the major committees (Credentials, Rules, and Platform). Often the product of lengthy negotiations, these reports to the convention represent the majority's voice on the committees. For a minority to present its views, 25 percent of the committee in question must concur in the minority report. Membership on the committees tends to reflect support for the candidates in the convention as a whole.

The third day is devoted to the presidential nomination and balloting. In an evenly divided convention, this period is clearly the most exciting. Much ritual has surrounded the nomination itself. In early conventions, it was customary for delegates simply to rise and place the name of a candidate in nomination without a formal speech. Gradually, the practice of nominating became more elaborate. Speeches were lengthened. Ritual required that the virtues of the candidate first be extolled before his identity was revealed. Today, with public speculation beginning months before and the selection of the nominee a foregone conclusion, the practice of withholding the name has been abandoned. The achievements of the prospective candidate are still lauded, however.

Demonstrations normally follow the nomination. The advent of television, however, has changed the character of these demonstrations. No longer spontaneous, they are now carefully staged and timed to indicate enthusiasm for the nominee but also to keep convention events moving during the prime time viewing hours.

Once all nominations have been made, the balloting begins. The secretary of the convention calls the roll of states in alphabetical order, with the chair of each delegation announcing the vote. A poll of the delegation may be requested by any member of that delegation. In 1988 the Democrats installed an electronic system to ensure a fast and accurate count. After the delegation is polled, the chair records the vote of the state on a terminal connected to the podium.

Vice-presidential selection, followed by the nominees' acceptance speeches, are the final order of business. They occur on the last day of the convention. In their early years, nominating conventions evidenced some difficulty in getting candidates to accept the vice-presidential nomination. Because of the low esteem in which the office was held, a number of prominent individuals, including Henry Clay and Daniel Webster, actually refused it. In Webster's words, "I do not propose to be buried until I am really dead and in my coffin."[4]

Today, the vice-presidency is coveted. Its increased significance, especially as a stepping stone to the presidency, has generated a desire to be nominated to this office. In the twentieth century six vice-presidents have become president through succession (either death or resignation); two, Richard Nixon and George Bush, have been elected to the presidency (although Nixon was not elected directly from the vice-presidency); and two others, Hubert Humphrey and Walter Mondale, have been presidential candidates.

Despite the appeal of the vice-presidency, it is almost impossible to run for it directly. There are no vice-presidential primaries and no government matching funds for vice-presidential candidates. Only one "vote" really counts—the presidential nominee's. Since the prospective nominee normally has sufficient delegates to control the convention, the presidential standard-bearer can dictate the selection. Although most delegates accept the recommendation, there have been a sprinkling of protest votes over the years by delegates who do not like the person selected or who use the vice-presidential nomination to signify opposition to a policy position or perspective that the presidential nominee has adopted.

Only once in recent history, however, has the convention had to make more than a pro forma decision on the vice-presidential nomination. In 1956, Democrat Adlai Stevenson professed to have no personal preference. He allowed the convention to choose between Estes Kefauver and John Kennedy. The convention chose Kefauver, the most popular Democrat in the public opinion polls at the time of his nomination.

Since the choice of a vice-presidential nominee is usually not difficult or particularly controversial, a great deal of time is not set aside for it. Moreover, the convention vote on the nomination is frequently made on the afternoon of the last day, to leave the prime viewing hours for the acceptance speeches of the vice-presidential and presidential candidates. These speeches are intended to be the crowning event of the convention. They are the time for displays of enthusiasm and unity. They mark the beginning of the party's presidential campaign.

## Articulating the Themes

The custom of giving acceptance speeches was begun in 1932 by Franklin Roosevelt. Before that time, conventions designated committees to inform the presidential and vice-presidential nominees of their decisions. Journeying to the candidate's home, the committees would announce the selection in a public ceremony. The nominee, in turn, would accept in a speech stating his positions on the major issues of the day. The last major party candidate to be told of the nomination in this fashion was Republican Wendell Willkie in 1940.

Today, acceptance speeches can be occasions for great oratory: they are both a call to the faithful and an address to the country. They articulate the principal themes for the general election.

Harry Truman's speech to the Democratic convention in 1948 is frequently cited as one that helped to fire up the party. Truman chided the Republicans for obstructing and ultimately rejecting many of his legislative proposals and then adopting a party platform that called for some of the same social and economic goals. He electrified the Democratic convention by challenging the Republicans to live up to their convention promises and pass legislation to achieve these goals in a special session of Congress that he announced he was calling. When the Republican-controlled Congress failed to enact that legislation, Truman was able to pin a "do-nothing" label on it and make that the basic theme of his successful presidential campaign.

In 1984 Democratic candidate Walter Mondale made a mammoth political blunder in his acceptance speech. Warning the delegates about the United States budget deficit that had increased dramatically during Reagan's first term, Mondale said that he would do something about it if he were elected president: "Let's tell the truth. Mr. Reagan will raise taxes, and so will I. He won't tell you. I just did."[5] Democratic delegates cheered his candor, directness, and boldness; the public did not. He and his party were saddled with the tax issue throughout the *entire* campaign.

Michael Dukakis used his speech in 1988 to emphasize his character and competence. Describing himself as the product of an American dream, the son of immigrant parents, in a not-so-subtle contrast to Bush's privileged background, Dukakis stressed his public service and his hands-on experience. "This election isn't about ideology; it's about competence," he said.[6] George Bush in his speech reiterated the goals and promised to complete the vision of the Reagan years, but he also tried to distinguish himself from his predecessor by noting values and objectives that the Reagan administration had been criticized for neglecting: the building of "a kinder and gentler America."[7]

## CREDENTIALS, RULES, AND PLATFORMS

There have been frequent challenges at national party conventions. In one way or another they involve the leadership and the successful nominees and concern the delegates pledged to these nominees, the rules that got them there and will enable them to control the proceedings, and the policies they have advocated and are likely to pursue. Those who initiate the challenges are the unsuccessful candidates and their supporters. Desiring to exercise influence in a convention in which they are the minority, they use these challenges as a means of forcing the leadership and the nominees to acknowledge their claims and to give them something in exchange for their support in the forthcoming election. These challenging delegates, who are likely to be activists and who represent others with similar views and desires, do not want to leave the convention empty-handed, even though they have lost the nomination.

### *Challenging Credentials*

All delegates must present proper credentials to participate at national nominating conventions. Disputes over credentials have occurred from

Ford won the presidential vote 1,187–1,070—a margin almost identical to that of his rules victory.

An even more acrimonious division over party rules occurred in 1980 at the Democratic convention. At issue was a proposed requirement that delegates vote for the candidate to whom they were publicly pledged at the time they were chosen to attend the convention. Trailing Jimmy Carter by about six hundred delegates, Ted Kennedy, who had previously supported the requirement, urged an open convention in which delegates could vote their consciences rather than merely exercise their commitments. This change in the rules would have required rejection of the pledged delegate rule. Naturally, the Carter organization favored the rule and lobbied strenuously and successfully for it. By a 600-vote margin the convention accepted the binding rule, thereby assuring President Carter's renomination. The Democrats have subsequently repealed this rule, requiring instead that delegates reflect in good conscience the sentiments of those who elected them.[8]

## Drafting the Platform

Traditionally, the platform has been the object of most of the challenges and controversies. The ideological orientation of activist delegates and the pragmatic political needs of the leadership and the party's nominees make controversy almost inevitable. Two often-conflicting aims lie at the heart of the platform-drafting process. One has to do with winning the election, and the other with pleasing the party's coalition. To maximize the vote, platforms should attract, not alienate. They should permit people to see what they want to see. This goal of accommodation has been accomplished by moderating the language and, occasionally, by increasing the level of ambiguity on the most controversial and emotionally charged issues. When appealing to the party's coalition, on the other hand, traditional images have been presented and "bread-and-butter" positions stressed.

The tension resulting from "the electoral incentives to fudge and the coalition incentives to deliver"[9] has caused real problems for platform drafters. The resulting documents contain high-sounding rhetoric, self-praise, and unrealistic goals that open them to criticism that they are substantially meaningless and politically unimportant, that they bind and guide no one. There may be some truth to these criticisms, but they also overstate the case.

**Promises and performance.** While platforms contain rhetoric and self-praise, they also consist of goals and proposals that differentiate them from one another. In an examination of the Democratic and Republican

| Domestic Issues | Democrats | Republicans |
| --- | --- | --- |
| Minimum wage | Proposes to increase the incomes of working poor through income tax credit. | Supports indexed minimum wage. |
| Women's rights | Supports Equal Rights Amendment. | Opposes Equal Rights Amendment. |

**Foreign and Defense Issues**

| | | |
| --- | --- | --- |
| Central America | Supports peace plan devised by Central American governments. | Seeks to provide humanitarian and military aid to the Contras in Nicaragua. |
| Middle East | Calls for new leadership to pursue peace, building on the framework of the Camp David Accords; notes special relationship with Israel. | Opposes the establishment of a Palestinian state; notes special relationship with Israel. |
| South Africa | Declares South Africa a terrorist state and supports imposition of comprehensive sanctions on its economy. | Deplores apartheid but warns that pressures on the government may adversely affect economic condition for blacks. |
| Strategic Defense Initiative (SDI) | Opposes weapons in outer space. | Supports deployment of system. |

*Source:* The Democratic Party Platform, 1988 and The Republican Party Platform, 1988.

erable influence, while supporters of the leading candidate ultimately control the final product.[12]

**Accommodations and disagreements.** The platform-drafting process has traditionally been designed to accommodate outside interests in such a way as to maximize the leadership's control over the final document. In the first stage the party holds public meetings and invites individuals and group representatives to present their ideas and make their claims. On the basis of these hearings, an initial draft is then written by the staff and presented to the Platform Committee when it convenes, approximately one week before the convention begins. To some extent the committee repeats this exercise. Subcommittees, organized on the basis of policy areas, hold hearings, revise the draft, and present it to the full committee, which, in turn, reviews its subcommittees' reports. After the committee has adopted a completed platform, it reports it to the convention for its approval.

Between 1944 and 1960, conventions made few significant changes in their platform committees' reports. The exception during this period was in 1948, when a major dispute over the civil rights section of the Democratic platform led to a walkout of delegates from several southern states. Beginning in the 1960s, however, the acquiescence that had greeted earlier party platforms has frequently been replaced by acrimonious debate. In 1964, Republicans Nelson Rockefeller and George Romney proposed platform amendments that condemned extremism and urged a stronger civil rights position. Goldwater partisans soundly defeated these challenges. The 1968 Democratic convention witnessed an emotional, four-hour debate on United States policy in Vietnam. Although the convention voted to sustain the majority position, which had the approval of President Lyndon Johnson, the discussion reinforced the image of a divided party to millions of home viewers.

A variety of factors have contributed to the increasing number of platform disputes in recent years. The development of ideological, ethnic, and racial groups within the parties has generated additional demands on the party and requests for specific platform planks. Changes in the selection process have also resulted in the election of more issue-oriented delegates who are less dependent on and loyal to party leadership and are more extreme in their ideological views. These issue activists tend to gravitate to the Platform Committee and, specifically, to the subcommittee considering "their" issues. This trend has tended to exaggerate rather than minimize the policy differences among the delegates.

Television has also magnified the problem (at least from the perspective of the party) by providing publicity for platform challenges. Even if groups cannot get their goals adopted and incorporated into the platform, they can attract attention by just stating their positions and making demands. The publicity enables them to gain new members, retain old ones, and take in more contributions. It also provides public "proof" that the leadership is working for its membership. And it pressures the successful nominee not to move too far to the political center so as to appease the more moderate general electorate.

Although the platform-drafting process has become more open and more divisive in recent years, it has not affected the parties equally. The Republicans—the more homogeneous of the two parties—have suffered less than the Democrats.

# PRESIDENTIAL AND VICE-PRESIDENTIAL SELECTION

## *Strategies and Tactics*

There are a number of prizes at nominating conventions. The platform contains some of them. The rules can also be important, but the big prize is the presidential nomination itself. When that is in doubt, all the efforts of the leading contenders must be directed at obtaining the required number of votes to be nominated. When it is not in doubt, the leading contenders can concentrate on uniting the party and converting the convention into a huge campaign rally for themselves. In 1976 the Reagan organization focused its attention on winning the nomination; in 1980 it sought to present a united front; in 1984 it orchestrated a coronation ceremony that was repeated four years later by George Bush.

In recent Democratic conventions the front-runners have tried to heal the wounds of the nomination contest by appealing to disaffected delegates to join them and the party for the fall campaign. This is precisely what Michael Dukakis did in 1988. Making peace with his principal opponent, Jesse Jackson, Dukakis conceded the rules changes and some of the platform proposals Jackson wanted in exchange for Jackson's public support of the Democratic ticket at the convention and during the campaign.

A key to success, regardless of the objective, is organization. Recent conventions have seen the operation of highly structured and efficient candidate organizations. Designed to maximize the flow of information, regulate floor activity, and anticipate and control roll call votes, these organizations usually have elaborate communications systems linking floor supporters to a command center outside the convention hall. Key staff members at the command center monitor reports, articulate positions, and make strategic decisions.

Here is how *Washington Post* reporters Dan Balz and David Broder described the Dukakis floor operation in 1988:

> The crowded trailer is where the campaign makes it happen. Inside are the young delegate trackers who are responsible for segments of 275 to 300 delegates and are linked directly to their whips on the convention floor through identical blue point-to-point phones. In an adjacent "boiler room" other top campaign officials watch the action. The boiler room has five television sets, a computer and direct phones to the podium and to Dukakis' suite in the Hyatt Regency hotel.[13]

In addition to having an effective organization, candidates need a general strategy, the contours of which are shaped by the aspirant's status at the time of the convention. The object for leading candidates is to maintain the momentum, win on the first ballot, and prepare for the general election. For those who are behind, the goal is to challenge the certainty of the initial balloting, despite public predictions to the contrary, and to demonstrate the ability to win the nomination and the election. Thus, although Gary Hart trailed Walter Mondale by hundreds of delegates going into the 1984 convention, he continued to maintain the possibility of his receiving the Democratic nomination until the actual balloting put Walter Mondale over the top. Jesse Jackson did not claim that he would win the nomination in his public statements prior to the 1988 Democratic convention. He knew he would not be the nominee but felt an obligation to his delegates and those they represented to stay in until the end to permit them to cast their votes during the official roll call.

Front-runners must avoid taking unnecessary risks. Ford followed this strategy in 1976, as Carter did in 1980, Mondale in 1984, and Dukakis in 1988. They compromised where possible on policy and other issues but held their ground on those challenges that could have jeopardized their nomination or injured their presidential campaign.

Although it may be necessary for front-runners to show their strength, they must be careful not to flaunt it and accentuate divisions created by the nomination process. Once the nomination is assured, the object of front-runners is to unify the faithful and present a united front for the general election. Achieving unity requires the victorious candidate to reach out to disaffected members of his party.

For non-front-runners still seeking the nomination, there are two immediate needs: to indicate the vulnerability of the front-runner, and to emphasize their own capacity to win. Two tactics have been employed by challengers to accomplish these ends. One is to release polls showing the strength of the non-front-runner and the weakness of the convention leader in the general election. The objective here is to play on the delegates' desire to nominate a winner. The Rockefeller campaign adopted such a strategy for the 1968 Republican convention but had to abandon it when the final preconvention polls showed his opponent, Richard Nixon, to be the more popular Republican. Gary Hart also toyed with the possibility of using polls to wrest the Democratic nomination from Mondale in 1984 when a nationwide survey conducted after the final primary showed him running 10 percentage points ahead of Mondale in a hypothetical election against President Reagan. But in the end, Hart was unable to persuade Mondale delegates to desert their candidate.

A second tactic is to create an issue before the presidential balloting and win on it. If the issue affects the rules that affect the vote, so much the better. Reagan in 1976 and Kennedy in 1980 tried this ploy without success. Their defeats on key votes confirmed their status as also-rans and forced them to focus on the platform to influence the party and its nominee, to save face, and to position themselves for the next battle in four years.

## *Characteristics of the Nominee*

The nominations of relatively obscure governors by the Democrats in 1976 and 1988 and a former movie actor and California governor by the Republicans in 1980 also indicate that changes in the preconvention process may have affected the kind of people chosen by their parties. In theory, many are qualified. The Constitution prescribes only three formal criteria for the presidency: a minimum age of thirty-five, a four-teen-year residence in the United States, and native-born status. Naturalized citizens are not eligible for the office.

In practice, a number of informal qualifications have limited the pool of potential nominees. Successful candidates have usually been well-known, active in politics, and held high government positions. Of all the positions from which to seek the presidential nomination, the presidency is clearly the best. Only five incumbent presidents (three of whom were vice-presidents who had succeeded to the office) have failed in their quest for the nomination. It should be noted, however, that several others were persuaded to retire rather than face tough challenges. An incumbent president's influence over his party (especially before 1972), his record as president (which his party cannot easily disavow), and the prominence of his office all contribute to his renomination potential.

Over the years, there has been a variety of paths to the White House. When the congressional caucus system was in operation, the position of secretary of state within the administration was regarded as a stepping stone to the nomination if the incumbent chose not to seek another term. When national conventions replaced the congressional caucus, the Senate became the incubator for most successful presidential candidates. After the Civil War, governors emerged as the most likely contenders, particularly for the party that did not control the White House. Governors of large states in particular possessed a political base, a prestigious executive position, and leverage by virtue of their control over their delegations.

The position of governors as potential candidates weakened with the development of national television networks in the 1950s. With most statehouses not located in major population centers, governors did not get as much exposure as Washington-based officials. Lacking national media coverage in an age of television and national political experience at the time the role of government in Washington was expanding, most governors also did not possess the staffing resources that the White House and Senate provided. It is no wonder that between 1960 and 1972 all party nominees came from the upper legislative chamber or the White

House.[14] The nominations of Carter, Reagan, and Dukakis have broken this trend. While the rules changes and finance legislation have once again increased the opportunities for governors, they have not reduced the advantage a national reputation and Washington experience can provide as an apprenticeship for the presidency, as the nomination of George Bush in 1988 attests.

There are other informal criteria, although they have less to do with qualifications for office than with public prejudices. Only white males have ever been nominated by either of the major parties. Until 1960, no Catholic had been elected, although Governor Alfred E. Smith of New York was chosen by the Democrats in 1928. Michael Dukakis was the first candidate whose ancestry could not be traced to northern Europe, a surprising commentary on a country that has prided itself on being a melting pot.

Personal matters, such as health and family life, can also be factors. After Alabama governor, George Wallace, was crippled by a would-be assassin's bullet, even his own supporters began to question his ability to withstand the rigors of the office. Senator Thomas Eagleton was forced to withdraw as the Democratic vice-presidential nominee in 1972 when his past psychological illness became public. Today, presidential and vice-presidential candidates are expected to release detailed medical reports on themselves.

Family ties have also affected nominations and elections. There have been only two bachelors elected president, James Buchanan and Grover Cleveland.[15] During the 1884 campaign, Cleveland was accused of fathering an illegitimate child. He was taunted by his opponents: "Ma, Ma, Where's my Pa?/Gone to the White House/Ha! Ha! Ha!" Cleveland admitted responsibility for the child, even though he was not certain he was the father.

Until 1980 no person who was divorced had ever been elected. However, Andrew Jackson married a divorced woman, or at least a woman he thought was divorced. As it turned out, she had not been granted the final court papers legally dissolving her previous marriage. When this information was revealed during the 1828 campaign, Jackson's opponents asked rhetorically, "Do we want a whore in the White House?"[16] Jackson and Cleveland both won.

In more recent times, candidates have been hurt by marital problems, allegations of sexual misconduct, or other personal frailties. The dissolution of Nelson Rockefeller's marriage and his subsequent remarriage seriously damaged his presidential aspirations in 1964. That Adlai Stevenson was divorced also did not improve his chances, particularly after his former wife spoke out against him. Senator Edward Kennedy's marital problems and his driving accident on Chappaquiddick Island, off the coast of Massachusetts, in which a young woman riding with the senator was drowned, were serious impediments to his

## TABLE 5–3
## Democratic Party Conventions and Nominees, 1900–1992

| Year | City | Dates | Presidential Nominee | Vice-Presidential Nominee | Number of Presidential Ballots |
|---|---|---|---|---|---|
| 1900 | Kansas City | July 4–6 | William Jennings Bryan | Adlai Stevenson | 1 |
| 1904 | St. Louis | July 6–9 | Alton Parker | Henry Davis | 1 |
| 1908 | Denver | July 7–10 | William Jennings Bryan | John Kern | 46 |
| 1912 | Baltimore | June 25–July 2 | Woodrow Wilson | Thomas Marshall | 1 |
| 1916 | St. Louis | June 14–16 | Woodrow Wilson | Thomas Marshall | 43 |
| 1920 | San Francisco | June 28–July 6 | James Cox | Franklin Roosevelt | 103 |
| 1924 | New York | June 24–July 9 | John Davis | Charles Bryan | 1 |
| 1928 | Houston | June 26–29 | Alfred Smith | Joseph T. Robinson | 4 |
| 1932 | Chicago | June 27–July 2 | Franklin Roosevelt | John Garner | Acclamation |
| 1936 | Philadelphia | June 23–27 | Franklin Roosevelt | John Garner | 1 |
| 1940 | Chicago | July 15–18 | Franklin Roosevelt | Henry Wallace | 1 |
| 1944 | Chicago | July 19–21 | Franklin Roosevelt | Harry Truman | 1 |
| 1948 | Philadelphia | July 12–14 | Harry Truman | Alben Barkley | 3 |
| 1952 | Chicago | July 21–26 | Adlai Stevenson, Jr. | John Sparkman | 1 |
| 1956 | Chicago | August 13–17 | Adlai Stevenson, Jr. | Estes Kefauver | 1 |
| 1960 | Los Angeles | July 11–15 | John Kennedy | Lyndon Johnson | 1 |
| 1964 | Atlantic City | August 24–27 | Lyndon Johnson | Hubert Humphrey | Acclamation |
| 1968 | Chicago | August 26–29 | Hubert Humphrey | Edmund Muskie | 1 |
| 1972 | Miami Beach | July 10–13 | George McGovern | Thomas Eagleton[a] Sargent Shriver[a] | 1 |
| 1976 | New York | July 12–15 | Jimmy Carter | Walter Mondale | 1 |
| 1980 | New York | August 11–14 | Jimmy Carter | Walter Mondale | 1 |
| 1984 | San Francisco | July 16–19 | Walter Mondale | Geraldine Ferraro | 1 |
| 1988 | Atlanta | July 18–21 | Michael Dukakis | Lloyd Bentsen | 1 |
| 1992 | New York | July 13–16 | | | |

[a] The 1972 Democratic convention nominated Thomas Eagleton, who withdrew from the ticket on July 31. On August 8 the Democratic National Committee selected Sargent Shriver as the party's candidate for vice-president.

*Source:* Updated from *National Party Conventions, 1831–72* (Washington, D.C.: Congressional Quarterly, 1976), pp. 8–9. Copyrighted material reprinted with permission of Congressional Quarterly, Inc.

**TABLE 5-4**

**Republican Party Conventions and Nominees, 1900–1992**

| Year | City | Dates | Presidential Nominee | Vice-Presidential Nominee | Number of Presidential Ballots |
|---|---|---|---|---|---|
| 1900 | Philadelphia | June 19–21 | William McKinley | Theodore Roosevelt | 1 |
| 1904 | Chicago | June 21–23 | Theodore Roosevelt | Charles Fairbanks | 1 |
| 1908 | Chicago | June 16–19 | William Taft | James Sherman | 1 |
| 1912 | Chicago | June 18–22 | William Taft | James Sherman / Nicholas Butler[a] | 1 |
| 1916 | Chicago | June 7–10 | Charles Evans Hughes | Charles Fairbanks | 3 |
| 1920 | Chicago | June 8–12 | Warren Harding | Calvin Coolidge | 10 |
| 1924 | Cleveland | June 10–12 | Calvin Coolidge | Charles Dawes | 1 |
| 1928 | Kansas City | June 12–15 | Herbert Hoover | Charles Curtis | 1 |
| 1932 | Chicago | June 14–16 | Herbert Hoover | Charles Curtis | 1 |
| 1936 | Cleveland | June 9–12 | Alfred Landon | Frank Knox | 1 |
| 1940 | Philadelphia | June 24–28 | Wendell Willkie | Charles McNary | 6 |
| 1944 | Chicago | June 26–28 | Thomas Dewey | John Bricker | 1 |
| 1948 | Philadelphia | June 21–25 | Thomas Dewey | Earl Warren | 3 |
| 1952 | Chicago | July 7–11 | Dwight Eisenhower | Richard Nixon | 1 |
| 1956 | San Francisco | August 20–23 | Dwight Eisenhower | Richard Nixon | 1 |
| 1960 | Chicago | July 25–28 | Richard Nixon | Henry Cabot Lodge, Jr. | 1 |
| 1964 | San Francisco | July 13–16 | Barry Goldwater | William Miller | 1 |
| 1968 | Miami Beach | August 5–8 | Richard Nixon | Spiro Agnew | 1 |
| 1972 | Miami Beach | August 21–23 | Richard Nixon | Spiro Agnew | 1 |
| 1976 | Kansas City | August 16–19 | Gerald Ford | Robert Dole | 1 |
| 1980 | Detroit | July 14–18 | Ronald Reagan | George Bush | 1 |
| 1984 | Dallas | August 20–23 | Ronald Reagan | George Bush | 1 |
| 1988 | New Orleans | August 15–18 | George Bush | George Bush | 1 |
| 1992 | Houston | August 17–21 | George Bush | Dan Quayle | 1 |

[a] The 1912 Republican convention nominated James Sherman, who died on October 30. The Republican National Committee subsequently selected Nicholas Butler to receive the Republican electoral votes for vice-president.

*Source:* Updated from *National Party Conventions, 1831–72* (Washington, D.C.: Congressional Quarterly, 1976), pp. 8–9. Copyrighted material reprinted with permission of Congressional Quarterly, Inc.

presidential candidacy in 1980. Similarly, Gary Hart's alleged "womanizing" forced his withdrawal in 1988, while the length of the period between Pat Robertson's marriage and the birth of his first son raised some eyebrows and was a topic of conversation and concern among some of his religious supporters. Senator Joseph Biden was also pressured to withdraw his candidacy for the Democratic nomination in 1988 after it was revealed that he had used excerpts of a speech delivered by a British Labour leader without attribution and has made false claims about his record as a student.

The informal qualifications of the presidential nominee have in general been matched by those of the vice-presidential candidate as well. However, the nomination of a woman, Geraldine Ferraro, by the Democrats in 1984 may remove or reduce sex as a barrier and make it easier for candidates from minority groups to be nominated as well.

The vice-presidential search has also been affected by the perceived need for geographic and ideological balance. Presidential aspirants have tended to choose vice-presidential candidates primarily as running mates and only secondarily as governing mates. Despite statements to the contrary, most attention is given to how the prospective nominee would help the ticket.

The choice of Dan Quayle is a good example. Needing to bolster his standing among conservative Republicans and to appeal to younger voters, Vice-President Bush, sixty-four years old, born and raised in Connecticut, who had moved to Texas and has a vacation home in Maine, chose a forty-one-year-old senator from the Midwest (Indiana) on the advice of his media and polling consultants.[17] Similarly, Governor Michael Dukakis of Massachusetts selected Senator Lloyd Bentsen of Texas to broaden his support in the South and Southwest, particularly among more moderate Democratic voters. Dukakis was undoubtedly hoping that Bentsen, who had defeated Bush for the Senate in 1970, would help him as much as Texas Senator Lyndon Johnson had helped Massachusetts Senator John Kennedy in 1960. (For lists of Democratic and Republican party conventions and nominees, see Tables 5–3 and 5–4.)

## THE MEDIATED CONVENTION

Radio began covering national conventions in 1924. Television broadcasting commenced in 1956. Since conventions in the 1950s were interesting and unpredictable events in which important political decisions were made, and since most Americans had never actually seen one of them (they may have read about them), convention coverage immediately attracted a sizable audience, one which increased rapidly as the number of households having television sets expanded. During the 1950s and 1960s about 25 percent of the potential viewers watched the conventions, with the numbers swelling to 50 percent during the most significant part of the meeting. The sizable audience made conventions important for fledgling television news organizations, which were beginning to rival newspapers for news coverage during this period.

Initially, the three major networks provided almost gavel-to-gavel coverage. They focused on the official events—what went on at the podium. Commentary by network correspondents was kept to a minimum. With conventions much longer than they are today, this coverage was extensive. The 1952 Democratic and Republican conventions each had ten sessions and lasted more than forty hours.

The changes in the delegate selection process that occurred in the 1970s and 1980s had a major impact on the amount and type of television coverage as well as the size of the viewing audience. As the decision-making capabilities of conventions declined, their newsworthiness decreased, as did the proportion of households that tuned in. Table 5–5 indicates the declining ratings that conventions have received through 1984, a decline that continued in 1988. It also notes the decreasing percentages of the proceedings that are carried live on the major networks through 1984.

Not only has the incentive for the commercial networks to provide gavel-to-gavel coverage decreased, but the absence of real news at the convention has forced them to be more inventive, even manipulative, to *find* news to maintain their viewing audience. This new network orientation, which highlights the more dramatic and entertaining aspects of the convention rather than broadcasting its official, predictable, and frequently boring proceedings, has interfered with the party's desire to

### TABLE 5–5
### Mediated Conventions, 1960–1988

| Year | Official Sessions (in minutes) | Convention Network Coverage | Percentage of Households Watching the Convention | Average Entertainment Rating |
|------|------|------|------|------|
| 1960 | 2,755 | 3,054 | 21.2 | 38.8 |
| 1964 | 2,486 | 3,364 | 23.4 | 39.6 |
| 1968 | 3,148 | 4,133 | 27.8 | 40.3 |
| 1972 | 2,999 | 3,345 | 22.0 | 43.6 |
| 1976 | 2,944 | 3,365 | 23.9 | 42.3 |
| 1980 | 3,818 | 2,557 | 22.6 | 40.7 |
| 1984 | 2,884 | 1,361 | 21.3 | 34.7 |
| 1988 | —— | 3,535 | 20.8 | 30.0 |

*Source:* 1960–84, Byron E. Shafer, *Bifurcated Politics: Evolution and Reform in the National Party Convention* (Cambridge, Mass.: Harvard University Press, 1988), Tables 8.1 and 8.7, pp. 265, 278; 1988, updated by author.

present a united front and to use the convention to launch the president's campaign. As a result, party leaders have gone to elaborate lengths to orchestrate their meetings, while the networks have gone to elaborate lengths to circumvent that orchestration and present the seamier side of conventions—the problems, disharmonies, and other events less beneficial to the party and its nominees.

## Scripting the Convention as Theater

Assuming that the more unified the convention, the more favorable its impact, party leaders take television coverage into account when planning, staging, and scheduling national party conventions. The choice of a convention site, the selection of speakers, and the instructions to the delegates are all made with television in mind. Even the decorations of the hall are carefully crafted by media experts. Here's how Frances Marcus described the stage that was being set for the 1988 Republican convention:

> Republican officials indicated the stage has been designed to eliminate any jarring shades and sharp angles. Corners have been rounded, and a technologically advanced lighting system will give the television audience flattering views of the speakers' complexions, eye colors and clothing. An elevator lift will automatically adjust each speaker's height so that camera angles will not have to be changed. And cosmetics experts will be on hand to add their bit.
> While the upper face of the stage will be red, white and blue, the lower part behind the speakers will be covered in a soft gray-blue material, a curtain of "cool colors," said Mark Goode, program producer for the convention.[18]

With a color-coordinated stage; a band playing upbeat, patriotic music; speakers carefully timed, rehearsed, and designed to heighten the campaign themes; balloons set to fall like rain on the nominees and the delegates dressed in all types of garb, the result was pure theater. The Democrats, of course, did the same thing. Hiring a Hollywood producer to stage their convention, they also tried to carefully orchestrate events. In the words of *New York Times* correspondent R. W. Apple, Jr.:

> The platform in the Omni convention hall has been repainted in tele-visual colors such as ecru; a humorist, Garrison Keillor, was hired to sing the national anthem along with a gaggle of schoolchildren and to read touching letters from other children, and a script as detailed as that for any Hollywood production has been written. All this comes from a party that used to balk at wearing blue shirts for black-and-white television and sneer at Richard M. Nixon's "media events."[19]

Movie stars regularly make appearances. Films about the party and its recent presidents are shown. Entertaining while they inform, these films provide an additional benefit for the party: they require a darkened hall, which makes it more difficult for the networks to interview the unhappy delegates. The newspeople are forced to carry the movie on their networks or to talk from the quiet of anchor booths. Either way, what is being broadcast minimizes the divisiveness that a variety of opinions often suggests and the turmoil that thousands of people milling about on the convention floor can convey.

The films themselves have exacerbated the tension between party officials who want to inform the electorate about the achievements of their officeholders or the qualifications of their nominees and the network managers who view such visual presentations as propaganda, not news. In 1984 a film designed to introduce President Reagan by citing the accomplishments of his administration was not carried by two of the three major networks on precisely these grounds.

Conventions have also become faster-paced than in the past, primarily because the three major commercial networks have cut back on the amount of coverage they give to the conventions. The general rule the networks followed in 1988 was that they would give prime time coverage to significant events, thereby forcing convention planners to fit their significant events into prime time. With less airtime, tedious reports and roll calls have been reduced. There are fewer candidates placed in nomination, and the speeches themselves are shorter and rehearsed in advance to improve their delivery to the television audience. Michael Dukakis visited the Atlanta convention hall on the day of his nomination at 8:30 A.M. to have technicians adjust the stage, teleprompters, lighting, and sound system for him. His managers did not want him to appear shorter than Jesse Jackson, who made his address earlier in the week.[20] Even the delegate demonstrations are now scripted, timed, and controlled offstage by the convention planners. Democrats allocated five minutes for the music and delegate cheers that greeted nominee Michael Dukakis and fifteen minutes for the "spontaneous" reaction that was arranged to follow his thirty-minute address.

Major addresses are now scheduled only during prime time. A 10:30 P.M. (Eastern Daylight Saving Time) acceptance speech is considered ideal and is now standard fare. In 1972, however, a debate over party rules and the nomination of several candidates for the Democratic vice-presidential nomination delayed McGovern's speech until 2:48 A.M., prime time only in Hawaii and Guam!

While major unifying events are timed to increase the number of viewers, potentially disruptive and discordant situations are scheduled to minimize them. Raucous debates, likely to convey the image of a divided party, are delayed, if possible, until after the evening viewing hours. In the 1964 Republican convention, for example, when Goldwater partisans got wind of a series of minority platform amendments favored by Nelson Rockefeller and George Romney, they arranged to have the majority report read in its entirety to postpone the amendments until early morning in the East, when most potential supporters of the minority position would not be watching. In the 1964 Democratic convention, President Johnson rescheduled a movie paying tribute to President John Kennedy until after the vice-presidential nomination had been concluded, to preclude any bandwagon effect for Robert Kennedy for that position. In 1984 and again in 1988, the Democrats scheduled debate on minority platform planks introduced by Jesse Jackson for the afternoon, before the major networks were to begin their coverage.

## Covering the Convention as News

Initially, conventions were considered newsworthy events. Their decisions on personnel and policy were significant for the party, the electorate, and the country. As those decisions became preordained by the delegate selection process, the networks reduced their convention coverage and changed their emphasis. In 1988 the three major networks provided about sixty hours of evening coverage over the eight days the Democratic and Republican conventions met.[21] However, only about half of this coverage was devoted to the official, orchestrated convention—the speeches, films, reports, and votes. The remainder focused on the delegates, the party, the unsuccessful and successful nominees, and the general election. Those who subscribed to cable television could have seen the entire convention. The Cable News Network (CNN) provided gavel-to-gavel coverage, as did C-Span, the public service channel, which broadcast the official proceedings with no commentary.

As an action medium, television constantly scans the floor for dramatic events and human interest stories. Delegates are pictured talking, eating, sleeping, parading, even watching the convention on television. Interviews with prominent individuals, rank-and-file delegates, and family and friends of the prospective nominee are conducted. To provide a balanced presentation, supporters and opponents are frequently juxtaposed. To maintain the audience's attention, the interviews are kept short, usually focusing on reactions to actual or potential political problems. This kind of coverage creates the impression of division, often making the convention seem more fractured to the viewer than to the participant.

A variety of factors heightens this discordant effect: the simultaneous picturing of multiple events, the compactness of the interviews, the crowd of delegates pressed together or milling around the hall. When compared with the calm of the anchor booth, the floor appears to be a sea of confusion.[22]

Where there is little discord, the media and even the convention organizers and its presidential nominee may try to create tension as a device to hold the audience. The most frequent unresolved question is, Who will be the party's vice-presidential nominee? Unless an incumbent president and vice-president are seeking renomination, the vice-presidential recommendation of the presidential nominee has often not been revealed until the morning of the final day. Lyndon Johnson went so far as to heighten the drama by asking the two most likely candidates to join him in Washington for the helicopter trip to the convention in Atlantic City, New Jersey.

The vice-presidential charade reached new heights in 1980. Throughout the first three days of the Republican convention, network correspondents speculated on who Reagan's running mate would be. On the second day of the convention, unbeknownst to the public, officials of the Reagan organization approached former President Gerald Ford, who had expressed interest in the vice-presidential nomination. As private talks were being conducted, Ford indicated his willingness to consider the vice-presidency during a television interview. This interview immediately fueled public speculation and turned the media focus from the convention proceedings on the platform to the Reagan-Ford negotiations. To follow these negotiations the delegates had to watch television from the convention floor. So great were the expectations for this so-called dream ticket that when it failed to materialize, Reagan had to come to the convention himself to whip up support for his second choice, George Bush.

For a variety of reasons, including the desire for suspense, presidential candidates have not made in-depth inquiries about their running mates. This lack of examination had serious repercussions in 1972, when Thomas Eagleton, the Democratic vice-presidential nominee, was forced to leave the ticket after his history of mental depression became known. George McGovern had not been aware of Eagleton's past illness when he picked him. The Democrats were also hurt in 1984 when allegations of campaign irregularities and incomplete financial disclosures by Geraldine Ferraro in her congressional campaigns were made at the start of the general election campaign. Similarly in 1988, the critical scrutiny that Republican vice-presidential nominee, Dan Quayle, received diverted attention from the convention and raised questions about Bush's judgment. After the firestorm subsided, however, Bush's choice of Quayle resulted in only minor damage to the ticket.

The media tend to inflate the coverage of the vice-presidential nomination in the absence of other news. Such inflating was particularly evident in 1988, when vice-presidential designee Dan Quayle received more coverage during the Republican convention than did presidential nominee Bush and twice as much as President Reagan.[23]

Even more controversial than television coverage *in* recent conventions has been the networks' coverage *outside* the conventions. Television's reporting of the 1968 Chicago demonstrations in particular generated considerable public and party criticism. Not only were the networks charged with overemphasizing the disruptions to the detriment of their convention coverage; they were seen as helping to incite the demonstrators by the mere presence of their live cameras in the streets. Claiming that the events were newsworthy and certainly not of their own creation, the networks responded by denying that the demonstrations received disproportionate coverage. CBS News reported that it had devoted only thirty-two minutes to these events out of more than thirty-eight hours of total convention coverage.[24]

## ASSESSING THE CONVENTION'S IMPACT

Does coverage such as the kind the Democrats received in 1968 have an impact? Was it partially responsible for the party's defeat? Do conventions affect voting behavior? Do they influence the electorate's perception of the candidates and their evaluations of their messages?

The answer to these questions is a qualified yes. There seems to be a relationship between convention unity and electoral success. Since 1968 the party that has had the most harmonious convention has emerged victorious.[25] However, it is difficult to say how much or even whether the unity contributed to the result or simply reflected the partisan environment that fostered the particular outcome.

In the short run, conventions almost always boost the popularity of their nominees and decrease that of their opponents. Only George McGovern in 1972 did not gain as a consequence of the Democratic convention coverage. The boost, however, may be short-lived. Several months afterward, the impact of the convention is harder to discern. Table 5–6 indicates the levels of support for recent nominees before and after the Democratic and Republican nominating conventions.

Political scientists have suggested three major effects of conventions on voters: (1) they heighten interest, thereby increasing turnout; (2) they arouse latent feelings, thereby raising partisan awareness; (3) they color perceptions, thereby affecting personal judgments of the candidates and their issue stands.[26] Studies have also shown that convention watchers tend to make their voting decisions earlier in the campaign.[27] About one-fifth claim that they make them at the time of the convention.

This number of people is sufficiently large for convention planners to take no chances and not to question the assumption on which contemporary campaigns rest: that an upbeat, harmonious, enthusiastic convention improves the political environment for the party's nominees in the fall. Conventions can have a powerful psychological impact on their viewers, making them more inclined to follow the campaign and vote for a party's candidates. They can energize participants, making them more likely to work for the party's candidates. Finally, they can

TABLE 5–6
**Impact of Conventions on Candidate Popularity,[a] 1976–1988**

| | Before Both Conventions | After Democratic Convention | After Republican Convention |
|---|---|---|---|
| **1976** | | | |
| Democrat (Jimmy Carter) | 53 | 62 | 50 |
| Republican (Gerald Ford) | 36 | 31 | 37 |
| Other/Undecided | 11 | 7 | 13 |
| **1980** | | | |
| Democrat (Jimmy Carter) | 37 | 39 | 29 |
| Republican (Ronald Reagan) | 41 | 38 | 45 |
| Independent (John Anderson) | 15 | 13 | 14 |
| Other/Undecided | 7 | 10 | 12 |
| **1984** | | | |
| Democrat (Walter Mondale) | 39 | 46 | 37 |
| Republican (Ronald Reagan) | 53 | 48 | 56 |
| Other/Undecided | 8 | 6 | 7 |
| **1988** | | | |
| Democrat (Michael Dukakis) | 47 | 54 | 44 |
| Republican (George Bush) | 41 | 37 | 48 |
| Other/Undecided | 12 | 9 | 8 |

[a] In all years shown except 1980 the Democratic conventions preceded the Republican conventions.

*Source:* Gallup polls taken right before and right after conventions, as published in *The Gallup Poll* (Wilmington, Del.: Scholar Resources, 1977, 1981, 1985, and 1989). Published with permission.

have an organizational impact, fostering cooperation among the different and frequently competing groups within the party, encouraging them to submerge their differences and work toward a common goal.

## SUMMARY

Presidential nominating conventions have existed since the 1830s. Picking the party's nominees, determining its platform, and unifying the party remain the principal tasks. There have been changes, however. Caused primarily by the reforms in the delegate selection process and, secondarily, by media coverage of the conventions, these changes have resulted in greater emphasis placed on the public aspects of conventions and less on internal party matters.

National nominating conventions continue to be marred with controversy, which is not surprising considering that they are composed of delegates chosen in a divisive selection process to represent different preferences and perspectives within the party. Although the big prize, the presidential nomination, is usually preordained by the results of the primaries and caucuses, the other prizes, the party's rules and its policy positions, are not. Disputes on the credentials of the delegates, the rules of selection, or procedures of the convention are usually fought among candidate organizations and affect the presidential vote, if not at the current meeting, then during the delegate selection four years hence. Platform issues, on the other hand, tend to reflect infighting within the party's electoral coalition. These policy-oriented controversies have increased in recent years largely as a consequence of the increasing institutionalization of organized interests within the parties and the desire of these interests to obtain recognition and their policy goals.

The tension between the needs of these groups and the goals of the party has increased the tasks that party leaders face at the nominating conventions. In the past, state party officials made the principal demands. In most cases, their object was to extend their political influence rather than to achieve substantive policy goals. Today, the reforms have weakened the influence of state leaders and strengthened candidate organizations. These changes have made compromise more difficult and more necessary if the party is to mount a unified effort. The hope of winning the nomination and the election is still the most compelling reason for giving in—witness Ford's acquiescence on foreign policy planks in 1976, Carter's on economic issues in 1980, and Dukakis's on party rules in 1988.

Tension has also been created between the media and party leaders. To attract and maintain their viewing audience, the media need a newsworthy convention. They find it in the drama and conflict they emphasize. To launch its general election campaign, the party needs an interesting, convincing, and unified convention. Its organizers attempt to achieve these objectives by orchestrating their meeting, emphasizing campaign themes, giving podium opportunities to their candidates, and using various theatrical devices such as made-for-convention movies.

The results of the party's efforts can be measured in the short run by the boost their nominees receive in public approval following the conventions. But many things can happen between the convention and election day that can mute or reinforce the themes and images presented in and projected by the convention. As the first major event of a presidential campaign, conventions affect the start of the race but do not determine the outcome.

Finally, the changes in the delegate selection process have enlarged the selection zone for potential nominees. It is unlikely that a Democratic convention before 1972 would have chosen a McGovern, Carter, or Dukakis or that a Reagan would have come as close as he did to defeating an incumbent president in 1976. Moreover, the selection of a woman by the Democrats in 1984 indicates that sex may no longer be a major consideration—at least for second place on the ticket. Other barriers such as those of race and religion may be less important as well.

To party professionals especially, the best evidence of future success is past success. Factors that might detract from such success, whether political, ideological, or personal, lessen the odds of getting the nomination. As a result, many presidential nominees possess very similar social and political attributes. In politics, the norm is often considered the ideal.

# NOTES

1. Byron E. Shafer, *Bifurcated Politics: Evolution and Reform in the National Party Convention* (Cambridge, Mass.: Harvard University Press, 1988), pp. 17–18.
2. Ann Richards, address to the Democratic convention, Atlanta, Georgia, July 18, 1988, *Congressional Quarterly*, 46 (July 23, 1988), p. 2024.
3. Perhaps the most famous of all keynote addresses was William Jennings Bryan's. A relatively unknown political figure, Bryan at the age of thirty-six electrified the Democratic convention of 1896 with his famous "Cross of Gold" speech. His remarks generated so much enthusiasm that the delegates turned to him to lead them as standard-bearer. He did, and lost.
4. Quoted in Malcolm Moos and Stephen Hess, *Hats in the Ring* (New York: Random House, 1960), pp. 157–158.
5. Walter Mondale, address to the Democratic convention, San Francisco, California, July 19, 1984 as reprinted in *The New York Times*, July 20, 1984, p. A.12.
6. Michael Dukakis, address to the Democratic convention, Atlanta, Georgia, July 21, 1988 reprinted in *The New York Times*, July 22, 1988, p. A10.
7. George Bush, address to the Republican convention, News Orleans, Louisiana, August 18, 1988, reprinted in *The New York Times*, August 19, 1988, p. A14.
8. This requirement means in essence that the convention will not force pledged delegates to exercise their pledges. However, presidential aspirants still have the right to approve delegates identified with their candidacies. Once the delegates have been approved, however, they cannot be removed if they threaten to vote against the candidate to whom they were committed.
9. This marvelously descriptive phrase comes from Jeff Fishel, "Agenda-Building in Presidential Campaigns: The Case of Jimmy Carter" (Paper presented at the annual meeting of the American Political Science Association, Washington, D.C., September 1–4, 1977), p. 20.
10. Gerald M. Pomper, "Control and Influence in American Politics," *American Behavioral Scientist* 13 (1969): 223–228; Gerald M. Pomper with Susan S. Lederman, *Elections in America* (New York: Longman, 1980), p. 161.
11. Naturally, the party controlling the White House has an advantage in accomplishing its goals. According to Pomper, between 1944 and 1968 the party in office achieved about four-fifths of its program, but even the losers gained some of their objectives. During the Nixon administration, the Democrats actually fulfilled more of their pledges than did the Republicans. Pomper with Lederman, *Elections in America*, p. 161.
12. The head of the Platform Committee is appointed by the chair of the National

Committee, usually with the concurrence of the leading candidates. That head, in turn, chooses the staff, invites the testimony of witnesses, negotiates disputes, and generally oversees the process. The committee members, chosen by the state delegations, reflect sentiment within the convention. At least a plurality of the committee tend to support the winning nominee.

13. Dan Balz and David S. Broder, "From Command Trailer, Dukakis Team Keeps Control," *Washington Post*, July 20, 1988, pp. A17, A19.

14. The House of Representatives has not been a primary source. Only one sitting member of the House, James A. Garfield, has ever been elected president, and he was chosen on the thirty-fifth ballot. In recent nomination contests however, a number of representatives have sought their party's nomination. Representative Morris Udall finished second to Jimmy Carter in 1976; Representative John Anderson competed for the Republican nomination in 1980 before running as an independent candidate in the general election. In 1988 Representatives Jack Kemp (Republican) and Richard Gephardt (Democrat) were candidates for the nomination.

15. Historian Thomas A. Bailey reports that in his quest for the presidency, Buchanan was greeted by a banner carried by a group of women that read, "Opposition to Old Bachelors." *Presidential Greatness* (New York: Appleton-Century-Crofts, 1966), p. 74.

16. Ibid.

17. George Bush chose Dan Quayle for another reason. In the words of his son, George Bush, Jr., "Dad felt comfortable with him." The implication here is that he didn't feel as comfortable with other Republicans such as Senate leader Robert Dole; his wife, Elizabeth Dole, who was a cabinet secretary during the Reagan administration; Jack Kemp, member of the House of Representatives and popular among conservatives; or some of the big-state Republican governors who were mentioned as possible vice-presidential nominees. After standing in Reagan's shadow for eight years, Bush wanted a vice-president who would do the same for him. He did not want a prominent Republican with his or her own political base detracting attention or decreasing support from his leadership in his administration. Quayle fit the bill.

18. Frances Frank Marcus, "GOP Designs a Colorful Convention," *New York Times*, May 28, 1988, p. A24.

19. R. W. Apple, Jr., "A Lesson in Imagery," *New York Times*, July 20, 1988, p. A21.

20. Maureen Dowd, "Dukakis in Character Awaiting Spotlight," *New York Times*, July 21, 1988, p. A21.

21. S. Robert Lichter and Linda S. Lichter, "Covering the Convention Coverage," *Public Opinion* 11 (September/October 1988): 41.

22. David L. Paletz and Martha Elson, "Television Coverage of Presidential Conventions," *Political Science Quarterly* 91 (1976): 124–27.

23. Lichter and Lichter, "Covering the Convention Coverage," p. 41.

24. "Republicans Orchestrate a Three-Night TV Special," *Broadcasting*, August 28, 1972, p. 12.

25. Shafer, *Bifurcated Politics*, p. 161.

26. Thomas E. Patterson, *The Mass Media Election* (New York: Praeger Publishers, 1980), pp. 72–74.

27. Ibid., p. 103.

## SELECTED READINGS

Davis, James W. *National Conventions in an Age of Party Reform*. Westport, Conn.: Greenwood Press, 1983.

Lichter, S. Robert, and Linda S. Lichter. "Covering the Convention Coverage." *Public Opinion* 11 (September/October 1988): 41–44.

Malbin, Michael J. "The Conventions, Platforms, and Issue Activists." In *The American Elections of 1980*, edited by Austin Ranney, pp. 99–141. Washington, D.C.: American Enterprise Institute, 1981.

Paletz, David L., and Martha Elson. "Television Coverage of Presidential Conventions." *Political Science Quarterly* 91 (1976): 109–31.

Shafer, Byron E. *Bifurcated Politics: Evolution and Reform in the National Party Convention*. Cambridge, Mass.: Harvard University Press, 1988.

Sullivan, Denis, Robert T. Nakamura, Martha Wagner Weinberg, F. Christopher Arterton, and Jeffrey L. Pressman. "Exploring the 1976 Republican Convention." *Political Science Quarterly* 92 (Winter 1977–78): 633–82.

———, Jeffrey Pressman, and F. Christopher Arterton, *Exploration in Convention Decision Making*. San Francisco: Freeman, 1976.

PART
# III

# The Campaign

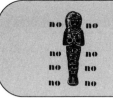
*Left, the symbol of the American Party—The Know Nothings—in the 1856 presidential elections. When asked about their motives or the platform of their organization, party members would respond, "I know nothing." Their candidate, former President Millard Fillmore, placed third behind James Buchanan (Dem.) and John Fremont (Rep.).*

# Chapter 6

# Organization, Strategy, and Tactics

## INTRODUCTION

Elections have been held since 1789, but campaigning by presidential candidates is a more recent phenomenon. For much of United States history, major party nominees did not themselves run for office. Personal solicitation was viewed as demeaning and unbecoming of the dignity and status of the presidency.

The parties did, however, mount campaigns, which were often quite extensive. They included many of the features of modern elections: the creation of party and candidate images, the presentation of these images in friendly newspapers and party literature, and the staging of political rallies, parades, and celebrations. The campaign of 1840 is frequently cited as the first to use these techniques. Replete with parades, slogans, jingles, testimonials, and much party propaganda, the Democratic and Whig campaigns of that year exalted their candidates' qualifications and lampooned their opponents in an attempt to reach the general public and mobilize grass-roots enthusiasm for their ticket. They even made attempts to manipulate the press. This campaign, best remembered for the Whig slogan, "Tippecanoe and Tyler too," became the prototype for subsequent presidential contests.

The tradition of nonparticipation by the presidential nominees was broken in 1860. Senator Stephen A. Douglas, Democratic candidate for president, spoke out on the slavery issue in an attempt to heal the split that had developed within his party. However, he also denied his own ambitions while doing so. "I did not come here to solicit your votes,"

**173**

he told a Raleigh, North Carolina, audience. "I have nothing to say for myself or my claims personally. I am one of those who think it would not be a favor to me to be made President at this time." Abraham Lincoln, Douglas's Republican opponent, refused to reply, even though he had debated Douglas two years earlier in their contest for the Senate seat from Illinois, a contest Douglas won. Lincoln even felt that it was not proper to vote for himself. He cut his own name from the Republican ballot before he cast it for other officials in the election.[1]

Douglas did not set an immediate precedent. Presidential candidates remained on the sidelines, with party supporters organizing campaigns on their behalf, for the next eight elections. It was not until 1896 that another divisive national issue, this time free silver, galvanized the country and elicited a public discussion by a presidential candidate.[2] Again it was the Democratic nominee who took to the stump. William Jennings Bryan, who had received the nomination following his famous "Cross of Gold" speech,[3] pleaded his case for free silver to groups around the country. By his own account, he traveled more than eighteen thousand miles and made more than six hundred speeches, and, according to press estimates, he spoke to almost 5 million people.[4]

Bryan's opponent that year, William McKinley, was the first Republican candidate to campaign, albeit from his own front porch. Anxious not to degrade the office to which he aspired, yet desirous of replying to Bryan's speeches, McKinley spoke to the throngs who came to his Canton, Ohio, home. The Republican party ensured that there would be large and responsive audiences by recruiting and in some cases transporting many of the 750,000 who came to hear their candidate speak.[5]

In 1912, Theodore Roosevelt campaigned actively on the Progressive, or "Bull Moose," ticket. Republican candidates, however, did little more than "front porch" campaigning until the 1930s. Democrats were more active. Woodrow Wilson and Alfred Smith personally took their appeals to the public in 1912 and 1928, respectively. Wilson, a former university professor and president, spoke on a variety of subjects, while Smith, governor of New York and the first Roman Catholic to run for president, tried to defuse the religious issue by addressing it directly.

Radio was first used in a presidential campaign in 1928. Smith's heavy New York accent and rasping voice were faithfully captured on the airwaves, probably to his detriment; the thunderous applause he received in a famous speech given in Oklahoma City on the subject of his religion was not nearly as clear. The applause and shouts sounded like a disturbance. Listeners could not tell whether Smith was being cheered or jeered.[6]

Franklin Roosevelt was a master of radio, and he employed it effectively in all his presidential quests. He also utilized the "whistle stop" campaign train, which stopped at stations along the route to allow the candidate to address the crowds who came to see and hear him. In 1932, Roosevelt traveled to thirty-six states—some thirteen thousand miles. His extensive travels, undertaken in part to dispel a whispering campaign about his health (he had polio as a young man, which left him unable to walk or even stand up on his own), forced President Herbert Hoover onto the campaign trail.[7]

Instead of giving the small number of speeches he had originally planned, Hoover logged more than ten thousand miles, traveling across much of the country. He was the first incumbent president to campaign actively for reelection. Thereafter, with the exception of Franklin Roosevelt during World War II, personal campaigning became standard for incumbents and nonincumbents alike.

Harry Truman took incumbent campaigning a step further. Perceived as the underdog in the 1948 election, Truman whistle-stopped the length and breadth of the United States, traveling thirty-two thousand miles and averaging ten speeches a day. In eight weeks, he spoke to an estimated 6 million people.[8] While Truman was rousing the faithful by his down-home comments and hard-hitting criticisms of the Republican-controlled Congress, his opponent, Thomas Dewey, was promising new leadership but providing few particulars. His sonorous speeches contrasted sharply and unfavorably with Truman's straightforward attacks.

Unlike the Roosevelt years, when voter reactions to the president were known long before the campaign began, Dewey's unexpected loss suggested that campaigns could affect election outcomes. The results of the election illustrated not only the need for incumbents to campaign but also the advantage of incumbency in campaigning, a lesson that was not lost on future presidents.

The end of an era in presidential campaigning occurred in 1948. Within the next four years television came into its own as a communications medium. By 1952 the number of sets and viewers had grown sufficiently to justify, in the minds of campaign planners, a major television effort. The Dwight Eisenhower presidential organization budgeted almost $2 million for television, while the Democrats promised to use both radio and television "in an exciting, dramatic way."[9]

Television made a mass appeal easier, but it also created new obstacles for the nominees. Physical appearance became more important. Styles of oratory changed. Instead of just rousing a crowd, presidential aspirants had to make a more personal appeal to television viewers. Attention began to focus more on the images candidates projected both of themselves and of their opponents and less on the positions they presented.

Public relations techniques that took advantage of the new means of mass communications began to influence how campaigns were planned and who planned them, what messages could be conveyed, and when and by what means. Large, complex campaign organizations were created. Carefully calculated strategies and tactics based on the fundamentals of market research and positive and negative advertising were employed by candidates of both parties.

The participants were also affected. Public relations experts were called on to apply the new techniques. Pollsters and media consultants regularly supplemented savvy politicians in designing and executing presidential campaigns. Even the candidates seemed a little different. With the possible exception of Lyndon Johnson and Gerald Ford, who succeeded to the presidency through the death or resignation of their predecessors, incumbents and challengers alike reflected in their appearances the grooming and schooling of the age of mass communications, particularly television. And where they did not, as in the case of Walter Mondale, they fared poorly.

This chapter and the one that follows discuss these aspects of modern presidential campaigns. Organization, strategy, and tactics serve as the principal focal points of this chapter, while image creation, projection, and impact are addressed in the next one.

The following section describes the structures of modern presidential campaigns and the functions they perform. It examines attempts to create hierarchical campaign organizations but also notes the decentralizing pressures. The tensions between candidate organizations and the regular party structure are discussed as well.

The basic objectives that every strategy must address are explored next. These include designing a basic appeal, dealing with incumbency (if that is relevant), highlighting relevant themes, and building a winning coalition. The last section of the chapter deals with tactics. It begins by describing the techniques for communicating the message, then turns to the targeting and timing of appeals during the campaign, and finally considers turning out the voters on election day. Examples from past contests are used to illustrate some of these tactics of presidential campaigning.

## ORGANIZATION

Running a campaign is a complex, time-consuming, nerve-racking venture. It involves coordinating a variety of functions and activities. These include advance work, scheduling, press arrangements, issue research, speech writing, polling, media advertising, finances, and party and interest group activities. To accomplish these varied tasks, a large, specialized campaign organization is necessary.

All recent presidential campaigns have had such organizations. The organizations have similar features. There is a director who orchestrates the effort and acts as a liaison among the candidate, the party, and the campaign; a manager charged with supervising day-to-day activities;

usually an administrative head of the national headquarters; division chiefs for special operations; and a geographic hierarchy that reaches to the state and local levels.

Within this basic structure, organizations have varied in style and operation. Some have been very centralized, with a few individuals making most of the major strategic and tactical decisions; others have been more decentralized. Some have worked through or in conjunction with national and state party organizations; others have disregarded these groups and created their own field organizations. Some have operated from a comprehensive game plan; others have adopted a more incremental approach. In some, the nominee has assumed an active decision-making role; in others, he has deferred to his principal advisers.

The Barry Goldwater organization in 1964, the Richard Nixon operation in 1972, the Ronald Reagan effort of 1984, and the George Bush campaign of 1988 exemplify the tight, hierarchical structure in which a few individuals control decision making and access to the candidate. In Goldwater's case, his chief advisers were suspicious of top party regulars, most of whom did not support the senator's candidacy. They opted for an organization of believers, one that would operate in an efficient military fashion.[10] This structure and the people chosen to run it produced tension between the regular Republican organization and the citizen groups that had helped Goldwater win the nomination.

There are tensions in every campaign between the candidate's and the party's organizations, between the national headquarters and the field staff, and between the research and operational units. Some of these tensions are the inevitable consequence of ambitious people operating under severe time constraints and pressures. Some are the result of the need to coordinate a large, decentralized party system for a national campaign. Some result from limited resources and the struggle over who gets how much. In Goldwater's case, however, the tensions were aggravated by his circumvention of party regulars, by his concentration of decision making in the hands of a few, and by his attempt to operate with two separate campaign organizations in many states.

The same desire for control and for circumventing the party was evident in Richard Nixon's reelection campaign in 1972. Nixon's organization, larger than Goldwater's, had a staff of 337 paid workers and thousands of volunteers. Completely separated from the national party, even in title, the Nixon Reelection Committee (known as CREEP) raised its own money, conducted its own public relations (including polling and campaign advertising), scheduled its own events, and even had its own security division. It was this division, which operated separately from the Republican party, that harassed the Democratic campaign of George McGovern by heckling his speeches, spreading dishonest rumors, and perpetrating other illegal acts including the attempted wiretapping of the Democratic National Committee headquarters at the Watergate Office Building. The excesses of this division illustrate both the difficulty of overseeing all the aspects of a large campaign organization and the risk of placing nonprofessionals in key positions of responsibility. Had the more experienced Republican National Committee exercised more of an influence over the Nixon campaign, there might have been less deviation from accepted standards of behavior.

The Reagan and Bush efforts in 1984 and 1988 operated more closely with state Republican party organizations than had either Goldwater's or Nixon's. Both were directed by separate campaign organizations, but each was linked to the party at both the national and the state levels. Fund-raising efforts and grass-roots activities were primarily party affairs, while the presidential campaign exercised most of the control over the basic strategy, thematic content of the campaign, relations with the media, resource allocation, and the scheduling and appearances of the presidential and vice-presidential candidates.

The Bush organization has received considerable praise for its tight-knit structure and efficient operating style. A small circle of advisers, each with designated areas of responsibility, ran the campaign and interacted with the nominee. (See Figure 6–1.)

George Bush himself played an important role. Kept aware of on-going campaign activities, he was involved in most of the important strategic decisions. When he was in Washington, Bush met with his senior staff daily. When he was on the road, one or two of them would join him on the campaign plane.[11] Ronald Reagan, in contrast, had much less input into the major strategic and tactical decisions of his campaign. He was more willing to limit his role to speech making and television appearances.

Democratic campaign organizations have tended to be looser in structure and more decentralized in operation than Republican organizations. For many years the Democrats had stronger state parties and a weaker national financial base. As a consequence, their presidential candidates relied more heavily on state party organizations. This is no longer the case.

In recent years Democratic candidates, like their Republican counterparts, have established separate organizations to run their presidential campaigns. They have used their regional and state coordinators to oversee activities, creating some tension with party regulars in the process.[12] Moreover, there has been little coordination with the national committee or with congressional campaign committees. Major decisions have been made by the presidential candidate and his inner circle of advisers.

In 1984 and 1988 the organizations of Walter Mondale and Michael Dukakis had difficulty carrying out coordinated campaign efforts. Their problems were partially structural. Mondale, who knew many party and elected officials, consulted with a wide range of policy experts and cam-

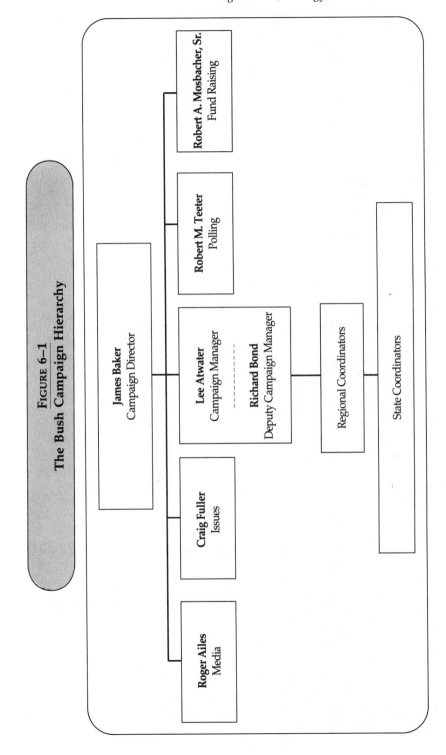

FIGURE 6–1
The Bush Campaign Hierarchy

James Baker
Campaign Director

Roger Ailes
Media

Craig Fuller
Issues

Robert M. Teeter
Polling

Robert A. Mosbacher, Sr.
Fund Raising

Lee Atwater
Campaign Manager

Richard Bond
Deputy Campaign Manager

Regional Coordinators

State Coordinators

paign supporters, often changing directions and reversing previous decisions in midstream. Michael Dukakis had the opposite problem. His campaign organization was too insular for too long. Democrats who had worked in other presidential campaigns were not quickly recruited and integrated into the Dukakis organization. Dukakis himself slowed the effort of his campaign to reach out to other Democrats by insisting that he personally interview all potential aides.[13] It was not until the beginning of September, after Dukakis had fallen behind in the polls, that he rehired the architect of his successful nomination strategy, John Sasso, who had resigned under fire during the early stages of the campaign.[14] Sasso attempted to restructure the organization and invigorate it with veterans of past Democratic campaigns. Valuable time had been lost, however; the candidate's lead was squandered, and a perception of disarray clouded the Dukakis effort for the remainder of the campaign. Ties with the party and some of its principal constituencies were also strained.

The relationship between the candidate's organization and the party's organization is important not only for winning the election but for governing. Candidates who circumvent their party in the planning and conduct of their presidential campaigns, as Richard Nixon did in 1972 and Jimmy Carter in 1976, find it more difficult to mobilize the partisan support needed to bridge the separation of powers and govern effectively. They have less inclination to build a strong national organization and more incentive to convert it into a personal following, responsive to their needs, particularly reelection. Frequently what happens is that key party leaders are replaced by loyal supporters of the successful nominee. When that nominee leaves office, however, these supporters lose their patron and ultimately their position although they may reappear in other campaigns or other administrations. When the party loses a presidential campaign, the candidate's organization disintegrates, and the party, blamed in part for the defeat, must try to rebuild itself. Not only does this situation contribute to frequent turnover among national party leaders, but it weakens the party for the next election.

Candidates who develop and maintain closer ties to the party, as Reagan did in 1980 and 1984 and Bush did in 1988, who are sensitive to their party's organizational needs, are more apt to benefit from the party in their election and during their presidencies. The price they pay is the deference they are forced to give to the party's traditional positions and to its established leadership.

## STRATEGIC OBJECTIVES

All campaigns must have strategies. Most are articulated before the race begins; others develop during the election itself. In 1984, Reagan strategists designed an elaborate plan well before the Republican convention.

The Bush plan was also designed over the summer of 1988 before the Republicans met to nominate him. In contrast, Humphrey's 1968 strategy and Dukakis's strategy twenty years later emerged after their nominations.

Certain decisions cannot be avoided when developing an electoral strategy. These decisions stem from the rules of the system, the costs of the campaign, and the character of the electorate. Each of them involves identifying objectives, allocating resources, and monitoring and adjusting that allocation over the course of the campaign. That is what a strategy is all about: it is a plan for developing, targeting, and tracking campaign resources.

## Designing a Basic Appeal

The first step in constructing a campaign strategy is to design a basic appeal. The appeal is presented as the reason for voting for a particular candidate and cited as the explanation of that vote. It has two primary components: one consists of the emphasis placed on partisan affiliation and partisan issues; the other is the personal leadership dimension of the candidates and their opponents.

**Partisanship.** The partisan disposition of the electorate has been considered important in designing an appeal. All things being equal, the candidates of the larger party have an advantage which they try to maximize by emphasizing their partisan affiliation, lauding their partisan heroes, and making a partisan appeal. Democratic candidates have traditionally clothed themselves in the garb of their party since the realignment of the 1930s. Republican candidates, initially, did not. They avoided partisan references and instead lauded the individual qualifications of their candidates and stressed certain types of issues. Dwight Eisenhower campaigned as a national hero. Richard Nixon separated his entire presidential campaign from his party's efforts for other Republicans. Gerald Ford's official campaign poster contained only his picture. As the gap between the two parties has narrowed, Republican candidates have become more willing to label themselves as Republicans. Both Reagan and Bush pointed to their partisan affiliation and their party's policy positions as reasons for supporting them in the election.

Identifying or not identifying with the party is only one way in which the partisan orientations of the electorate are activated and enforced. Recalling the popular images of the party is another. For the Democrats, common economic interests are still the most compelling link uniting the party's electoral coalition. Perceived as the party of common folks, the party that got the country out of the Great Depression, the party of labor and minority groups, Democrats have tended to do better when economic issues are salient. This connection explains why their candidates for president underscore the "bread-and-butter" issues: low unemployment, high minimum wage, maximum social security and medicare benefits, and placing the heavier burden of taxes on the rich. They contrast their sympathy for the average American with Republican ties to the rich and especially to big business.

For the GOP, the task used to be to downplay economic issues. However, the increasing size of the upper middle class and its concern with high taxes and particularly with inflation, as well as the prosperity that occurred during the Reagan years, indicate that the Republicans may no longer be disadvantaged by pocketbook issues. In 1980 Reagan pointed to the economic failures of the Carter administration, promising new policies and new leadership. In 1984 he contrasted the results of those policies and his leadership with the performance of the previous administration. Bush continued the comparison in his 1988 campaign. The recession, which the country encountered midway through Bush's first term, will, however, make a similar economic appeal more difficult in 1992.

Although the Republicans have gone a long way toward shedding their image as the party responsible for the Great Depression, they have not been as successful in altering the perception that they are the party of the rich. President Bush's support for a reduction of taxes on capital gains, which would have provided greater benefits for the wealthy members of the society, and his opposition to increased taxes on those with incomes exceeding $200,000 during the budget crisis of 1990 have reinforced the class distinctions that many voters perceive between the economic policies of the two parties.

Future Republican nominees are likely to continue to target their general economic message to the growing upper-middle and middle class rather than to lower-income voters. Democrats, in contrast, will continue to refer to the unfairness of the government's revenue and expenditure policies in appealing to the concerns of those in the lower and middle socioeconomic strata and to the social conscience of the more affluent sectors of the electorate.

Whereas economic matters have tended to unite the Democrats, social issues, since the 1970s, have divided them, often pitting groups within the party against one another. Republican presidential candidates have successfully exploited these divisions. By focusing on such high-intensity issues as crime, welfare, busing, racial quotas, and other government-imposed solutions to social problems, they have not only appealed to the fears and frustrations of conservative Democrats but have reaffirmed their support for traditional American values of individual initiative, family responsibility, and local autonomy.

When foreign and national security issues have been salient, Republican candidates have traditionally done better. By emphasizing their competence to deal with national security matters, Republican nominees rekindle the more favorable perception their party has enjoyed in the foreign policy area. In the process they also reduce the impact of partisanship on voting, since international issues have traditionally not engendered the same degree of partisan differences that domestic issues have.

Dwight Eisenhower and Richard Nixon stressed their competence in foreign affairs. In 1952 Eisenhower campaigned on the theme "Communism, Corruption, and Korea," projecting himself as the candidate most qualified to end the war. Nixon took a similar tact in 1968, linking Humphrey to the Johnson administration and the war in Vietnam. Four years later, Nixon varied his message, painting George McGovern as the "peace at any price" candidate and himself as the experienced leader who could achieve peace with honor. Gerald Ford, though, was not nearly so successful in conveying his abilities in foreign affairs, in part because he was overshadowed by the expertise and statesmanship of his secretary of state and national security adviser, Henry Kissinger. In 1980 Reagan pointed to the Soviet invasion of Afghanistan and to the Iranian hostage situation to criticize the foreign policy of the Carter administration and to urge greater expenditures for defense; in 1984, he pointed to the increased defense capacity of the United States and to its success in containing the expansion of communism. Four years later Bush cited his experience in foreign affairs and his personal acquaintance with many world leaders as superior (to his opponent, Michael Dukakis) qualifications for a job in which making and conducting foreign policy were a key component. Bush's successful prosecution of the Persian Gulf war combined with the opposition of a majority of congressional Democrats to the president's use of force in January 1991 will undoubtedly be highlighted by the Republicans during their 1992 campaign.

The perception that the Democrats are weaker in foreign and military affairs has prompted some of their recent standard-bearers to talk even tougher than their opponents. In his 1976 campaign, Carter vowed that an Arab oil embargo would be seen by his administration as an economic declaration of war. In 1984, Walter Mondale supported the buildup of United States defenses, including Reagan's Strategic Defense Initiative. He even criticized the president for proposing to give this new technology to the Soviets. In 1988, Dukakis spoke about the need for the United States to be more competitive within the international economic arena. The Democratic candidate in 1992 can be expected to hew a similar line, emphasizing economic competition, military preparedness, and the vigorous pursuit of U.S. interests within the international arena.

**Leadership.** Regardless of their partisan affiliation, ideological orientation, and issue emphases, candidates for the presidency must stress their own abilities. They must project an image of leadership. In the past, projecting this image was more difficult and important for the Republicans, given the partisan disadvantage they had within the electorate. Today, it may be more difficult and important for the Democrats, given the heterogeneous nature of their party, the perceptions of their party's competence and resolve in foreign affairs, and recent electoral college voting patterns that disadvantage the Democrats. (See Table 6–1.)

The increasing number of independents and those who have only weak links to a political party, the declining number of issues that differentiate the parties or emphasize their past distinctions, and the growing importance of television, which focuses heavily on character issues, all point to leadership as the critical component of any campaign appeal.

Candidates must appear presidential. They must demonstrate the personal characteristics and leadership qualities necessary for the office. In 1988, Dukakis emphasized his competence, while Bush stressed his experience, including his association with a popular administration. (See "Michael Dukakis's General Election Strategy.")

Naturally, candidates can be expected to raise questions about their opponents. These questions assume particular importance if the public's initial image of the candidates is fuzzy, as it was in 1988 with Dukakis, and to a lesser extent with Bush.

**The 1988 campaign.** Public opinion research by the Bush campaign revealed Dukakis's image problems early in the summer preceding the election. Groups of voters, asked a series of questions about the candidates and the issues, indicated that they knew little about Dukakis, were more concerned with social than economic matters, and were more conservative than liberal in their ideological orientation. A strategy was immediately formulated by the senior Bush advisers to take advantage of this situation.

The objective of the strategy was to define Dukakis in ways that would discredit him and, parenthetically, to present Bush as a strong, mainstream, conservative candidate. The strategy was based on the premise that the higher the negative perceptions of a candidate, the less likely that candidate would win.[15] At the time the strategy was devised, Bush's negatives were very high (in the range of 40 percent) and Dukakis's were not (approximately 15 percent).[16] Bush had been made the butt of jokes at the Democratic convention.

To implement the strategy, it was decided that the candidate himself should take the offensive against his Democratic rival, in contrast to other presidential campaigns in which surrogates of the candidate did most of the personal criticizing. There were two reasons for having Bush initiate the attacks. First, it would ensure media coverage, since what the candidates say is more likely to be the focus of attention than what

## Michael Dukakis's
## General Election Strategy

Our strategy for the general election had three basic points. The first was that Michael Dukakis cares about people like you. We highlighted this by trips in the summer to mid-sized communities, focusing on jobs and drugs and housing. . . . [by] a convention that focused on Michael Dukakis, the man of American roots and a product of the American dream. And finally, . . . that Michael Dukakis was on your side. I think we did our best at this prong of our strategy, which obviously built on the traditional strengths of a Democrat, but that's not enough to win the general election.

The second point of our strategy had to be to make the case for change. We had to turn the election into an election about the next four years, not the last eight, about America's place in the world economically, about the future, not the past. We did not succeed in that argument . . . because we didn't make it with enough edge or power, and we made mistakes along the way. . . . Even more, I think, we were undermined by external economic conditions, which if there ever was a broad constituency for change in this country, undermined it.

The final element of our strategy . . . was the whole issue of leadership and character and how that was to play out. We began by thinking that that would be an important element of our fall strategy, that we would emphasize not only competence, not ideology from the convention speech, but the value of integrity. . . . On these issues we ended up on the defensive.

The governor was hurt by attacks on him—the mental health rumors, the attacks on patriotism, the harbor and furlough issues—and perhaps most of all by the perception that he had failed to fight back, which went to his character.

Susan Estrich
Campaign Manager

*Source:* David R. Runkel, ed., *Campaign for President: The Managers Look at '88* (Dover, Mass.: Auburn House, 1989), pp. 8–9.

their supporters say. Moreover, being the attacker was designed to help Bush overcome his "wimp" image, the perception that was current in the media that Bush was not strong enough or tough enough to be president.[17]

Following the Republican convention in August, when the public was just beginning to compare the candidates and form their initial impression of the nominees, Bush unleashed his negative campaign. He painted Dukakis as a free-spending liberal, soft on crime, weak on defense, and short on experience, a Democrat in the tradition of such unsuccessful and discredited Democratic candidates as George McGovern, Jimmy Carter, and Walter Mondale.

Dukakis chose not to reply to Bush's attacks initially. His failure to do so compounded his image problem and allowed the Republicans to define the issues, control the tempo, and shape initial public perceptions. By the time Dukakis did respond, his lead in the polls had all but vanished, his "negatives" approached those of Bush, and his campaign organization seemed to be in disarray. All these outcomes undercut his claim of being the more competent of the two candidates. The Dukakis experience will undoubtedly serve as a lesson to future Democratic standard-bearers.

## Dealing with Incumbency

Claiming or criticizing an image of leadership when an incumbent is running requires a different script. Normally the incumbent is advantaged. The best testimony to the power of incumbency is the success of incumbent presidents who have sought election or reelection. In the twentieth century, fifteen incumbent presidents have run for election, and eleven of them have won. Franklin Roosevelt was reelected three times. (See "The Incumbency Advantage.").

Three Republican presidents—William Howard Taft, Herbert Hoover, and Gerald Ford—and one Democratic incumbent—Jimmy Carter—lost in the twentieth century. Extraordinary circumstances help explain the Republicans' defeats. The Bull Moose candidacy of Theodore Roosevelt in 1912 divided the larger Republican vote between Roosevelt (4.1 million) and Taft (3.5 million). Woodrow Wilson's 6.3 million was thus sufficient to win. The growing depression of the 1930s and the seeming incapacity of the Hoover administration to cope with it swung Republican and independent votes to Franklin Roosevelt. The worst political scandal in the nation's history and the worst economic recession in forty years adversely affected Ford's chances, as did his pardon of the person who had nominated him for the vice-presidency, Richard Nixon. Nonetheless, Ford almost won.

Having a record in office helps to generate an image of leadership. Clearly, a good record tends to benefit incumbents. But a bad record, or especially a lack of achievement, can be harmful. Carter's inability to obtain the release of the Iranian hostages illustrates how inaction can adversely affect a president's image. Moreover, bad times can hurt an incumbent. Rightly or wrongly, the public places responsibility for economic conditions, social relations, and foreign affairs on the president. That he may actually exercise little control over some of these external factors seems less relevant to the electorate than do public perceptions of the conditions, the desire that they be improved, and the expectation that the president should do something about them.

Incumbency is a two-edged sword. It can strengthen or weaken a claim to leadership. That is why incumbents point to their accomplishments, note the work that remains, and sound a "let us continue," "stay the course" theme. Challengers, in contrast, argue that it is time for a change and that they can do better, while at the same time alluding to their own presidential qualities. In the end the advantage seems to be with the incumbent if conditions are generally favorable and if a sufficient number of grievances have not accumulated.

What implications does the advantage of incumbency have for governance? It promotes continuities in presidential policy and in executive personnel. It maximizes the benefits that personal relations and political and policy expertise can bring to presidential decision making and consensus building. It provides a stabilizing element that fosters international cooperation and serves to reinforce the desire for predictability in leadership.

The disadvantages are twofold. First, the new ideas and leadership potential of the challenger may never be realized. Second, after reelection, an incumbent frequently finds himself in a weakened position, less able to provide the kind of leadership he did his first term. Ineligible for reelection (a lame duck), facing a more independent and frequently more hostile Congress, and heading a party that will become more divided as the next election nears and over which he is likely to exercise less influence, the president finds himself with fewer allies, growing opposition, and, obviously, more difficulty in achieving his objectives. On the other hand, expectations of his performance remain high, enlarged in part by his first-term successes and his reelection. Reagan faced all these problems at the beginning of his second term.

Whereas incumbent presidents have an advantage seeking reelection, incumbent vice-presidents seeking election as president have not. The benefits of being vice-president stem from the recognition and status the office provides and the organizational and financial support it usually engenders. Bush used his political connections and cashed in his partisan "IOUs" to help him win the Republican nomination in 1988.

Being vice-president, however, is not necessarily an advantage in the general election. It is difficult to establish leadership credentials from a position of followership. The number two person is not free to dissent from unpopular, unwise, or unsuccessful administration policies; nor can he take credit for popular, wise, and successful ones. Thus the vice-president is in the worst of two worlds, unlikely to receive support from

# The Incumbency Advantage

The advantage of incumbency stems from the visibility of the office, the esteem it engenders, and the influence it provides. Being president guarantees recognition. The president is almost always well known. A portion of the population usually has difficulty at the outset in identifying his opponent, although the primaries have contributed to the name recognition of the challenger.

Another benefit of incumbency is the credibility and respect that the office usually engenders. Naturally these qualities rub off on the president. In the election, the incumbent's strategy is obvious: run as president. Create the impression that it is the president against some lesser-known and less-qualified individual. In the words of Peter Dailey, Nixon's chief media adviser in 1972: "Our basic effort was to stay with the President and not diffuse the issue. We thought that the issue was clearly defined, that there were two choices—the President (and I mean that distinction—not Richard Nixon, but the President) and the challenger, the candidate George McGovern. We wanted to keep the issue clearly defined that way."[a]

The ability of a president to make news, to affect events, and to dispense the "spoils" of government can also magnify the disparity between an incumbent and a challenger. Presidents are in the limelight and can maneuver to remain there. The media focus is always on the president. In the spring of 1984 the media extensively covered President Reagan's travels to Europe and Asia. These visits allowed Reagan to dominate the news on his own terms and made it unnecessary to purchase commercial time to run his own advertisements. He benefited enormously from the contrast of the dignified head of state representing all citizens of the country with the bickering Democratic candidates battling for their party's nomination. Bush can be expected to use the trappings of the presidency in 1992.

Presidents have another advantage. Presumably, their actions can influence events. Economic recoveries are usually geared to election *(cont.)*

[a] Quoted in *Campaign '72*, ed. Ernest R. May and Janet Fraser (Cambridge, Mass.: Harvard University Press, 1973), p. 244.

those who dislike the administration and unlikely to inherit automatically the votes of those who do. A vice-president must convince voters that he has presidential leadership qualities, and he must do so on his own.

Bush dealt with his vice-presidency by binding himself to Reagan, years. In 1984 the economy's performance peaked as election day neared. Foreign policy decisions can also be timed to maximize or minimize their electoral impact. In October 1984 President Reagan held a White House meeting with Soviet Foreign Minister Andrei Gromyko, thereby blunting Mondale's charge that Reagan was not interested in pursuing an arms control agreement with the Russians.

Incumbents are generally perceived as more experienced and knowledgeable, as leaders who have stood the tests *of* the office *in* the office. From the public's perspective, this quality creates a climate of expectations that works to the incumbent's benefit most of the time. Since security is one of the major psychological needs that the presidency serves, the certainty of four more years with a known quantity is likely to be more appealing than the uncertainty of the next four years with an unknown one—provided the past years are viewed as acceptable.

Translated into strategic terms, the public's familiarity and comfort with the incumbent permits that incumbent to highlight his opponent's lack of experience, and contrast it with his own experience and record in office. Carter used a variation of it in 1980. He emphasized the arduousness of the job to contrast his energy, knowledge, and intelligence with Reagan's. Bush can be expected to stress his contacts and success in foreign and national security affairs in his campaign for reelection.

Finally, being president provides an incumbent with the capacity to benefit certain individuals, groups, and areas of the country. The timing of grants, the making of appointments, and the supporting of legislation have political impact. White House staff and cabinet officials, acting as surrogates for the president, can be used effectively to promote the president's programs and policies around the country. While these activities occur throughout an administration, they are more newsworthy and potentially more influential during a campaign. A president can damage his reputation, however, if his actions appear to be solely or primarily for political purposes, as did Ford's pardon of Nixon in 1974 and Carter's announcement of grants during his 1980 reelection campaign.

refusing to indicate positions he had taken or advice he had given to the president when he was vice-president. He cast his fate with his popular predecessor, forcing the electorate to judge him on the basis of the performance *of* the administration rather than his performance *within* it.

6–1 shows each party's electoral base. Twenty-one states, which currently have a total of 191 electoral votes, have voted for the Republican candidate in each of the last six presidential elections. During the same period only the District of Columbia, with 3 votes, has shown the same loyalty to the Democrats. Thus, other things being equal, the Republican candidate begins the campaign with a considerably larger geographic base of support than does his Democratic opponent.

The Republican base has not always been so imposing. In 1964, Goldwater was ready to concede the East and concentrate his efforts on the rest of the country. His basic strategy was to go for the states Nixon had won in 1960 plus several others in the South and Midwest. As one of Goldwater's aides put it: "It was a regional strategy based on the notion that little campaigning would be needed to win votes in the South, no amount of campaigning could win electoral votes in New England and on the East Coast, but that votes could be won in the Midwest and on the West Coast. As the Senator said, 'Go hunting where the ducks are.'"[19]

In 1968, Nixon strategists set their sights on ten battleground states—the big seven (California, Illinois, Michigan, New York, Ohio, Pennsylvania, and Texas) plus New Jersey, Wisconsin, and Missouri, where Humphrey provided the main opposition—and on five peripheral southern states, where George Wallace was the principal foe. Together, these states had 298 electoral votes. Nixon needed to win at least 153 of them, which combined with his almost certain 117 electoral votes from other states, would make the electoral college majority of 270. He actually won 190 electoral votes from the states he targeted.

Nixon's strategy of targeting the industrial states contrasted sharply with that of his previous presidential campaign. In 1960, he had promised to visit all fifty states, a promise he was to regret. On the day before the vote, he had to fly to Alaska to keep his campaign pledge, while Kennedy visited five East Coast states and ended with a torchlight parade in Boston.

In 1976, Ford found himself in a situation that required a broad-gauged national effort. Because the Democrats had nominated a southerner, he could not count on the South or on as many other states as the Republicans had captured in previous years. In fact, his strategists saw only 83 electoral votes from fifteen states as solidly Republican at the beginning of the campaign. Assuming these states to be theirs, and conceding ten states and the District of Columbia (87 electoral votes) to Carter, Ford's planners proposed a nationwide media effort to win the necessary 187 votes from the remaining twenty-five states.

In contrast, Carter's strategy in 1976 was to retain the traditional Democratic states and regain the South. His goal was to win at least 71 votes from the large industrial states. He achieved each of these objectives, but only in the South was his performance really impressive. Not

## TABLE 6–1
## Voting Blocks in the Electoral College, 1968–1988

### Number of Elections

#### States Voting Democratic since 1968

| Four | | Five | | Six | |
|---|---|---|---|---|---|
| Hawaii | 4 | Minnesota | 10 | District of Columbia | 3 |
| Massachusetts | 12 | | | | |
| Rhode Island | 4 | | | | |
| West Virginia | 5 | | | | |
| Total | 25 | | | | |

#### States Voting Republican since 1968

| Six | | Five | | Four | |
|---|---|---|---|---|---|
| Alaska | 3 | Arkansas | 6 | Alabama | 9 |
| Arizona | 8 | Connecticut | 8 | Louisiana | 9 |
| California | 54 | Delaware | 3 | Mississippi | 7 |
| Colorado | 8 | Florida | 25 | Pennsylvania | 23 |
| Idaho | 4 | Iowa | 7 | Texas | 32 |
| Illinois | 22 | Kentucky | 8 | Washington | 11 |
| Indiana | 12 | Maine | 4 | Wisconsin | 11 |
| Kansas | 6 | Michigan | 18 | Total | 102 |
| Montana | 3 | Missouri | 11 | | |
| Nebraska | 5 | North Carolina | 14 | | |
| Nevada | 4 | Ohio | 21 | | |
| New Hampshire | 4 | Oregon | 7 | | |
| New Jersey | 15 | South Carolina | 8 | | |
| New Mexico | 5 | Tennessee | 11 | | |
| North Dakota | 3 | Total | 151 | | |
| Oklahoma | 8 | | | | |
| South Dakota | 3 | | | | |
| Utah | 5 | | | | |
| Vermont | 3 | | | | |
| Virginia | 13 | | | | |
| Wyoming | 3 | | | | |
| Total | 191 | | | | |

*Note:* A majority of the electoral college, needed to elect a president, is 270 votes.

since 1960 had a majority of states from this region gone Democratic. In 1980, Carter failed to hold his 1976 coalition together. Four years later, Democrat Walter Mondale suffered an even greater electoral college defeat, winning only in his home state of Minnesota and the District of Columbia.

Reagan's strategy in both 1980 and 1984 was to rely on Republican support in the South and West and concentrate his efforts on the industrial heartland, specifically Michigan, Illinois, and Ohio.[20] By saturating several key midwestern states with money, media, and appearances by the candidates and well-known boosters, the Reagan campaign hoped to make it impossible for the Democratic ticket to obtain a majority in the electoral college. Winning Ohio and Michigan meant, for all intents and purposes, that the election was over.

The Reagan strategies in 1980 and 1984 provided the operational model for Bush in 1988: retain the South and the Republican strongholds in the West and concentrate campaign resources in a half-dozen pivotal states, including Ohio, Michigan, Illinois, and, in 1988, New Jersey. The Bush plan was designed to enable the Republican ticket to gain a substantial electoral college victory without winning either of the two largest states, California or New York.

Following the Democratic convention, the Dukakis campaign promised a fifty-state strategy, pointing to the popularity of Texan Lloyd Bentsen as evidence of the seriousness with which they intended to compete in the South. In actuality, however, the Democrats realized that winning the southern states would be extremely difficult. Yet they did not want the Republican to take the South for granted and thus be able to concentrate the bulk of their resources in states the Democrats needed to win to obtain a majority in the electoral college, as they had in previous elections.

As the campaign progressed, polls commissioned by both parties indicated that the Republicans were comfortably ahead in all of the South (including Texas and Florida) and in the Rocky Mountain areas. The results of these surveys forced the Democrats—and permitted the Republicans—to spend resources in the other large, competitive states. In the end the Democrats adopted an eighteen-state strategy that would have produced a 2-vote electoral college victory if successful. They won ten states plus the District of Columbia with 112 electoral votes, compared to forty states and 426 electoral votes for their Republican opponents.

The mathematics of the electoral college should continue to plague the Democrats in 1992 and subsequent elections. (See Table 6–1.) The party seems to have only three options: nominate a southern candidate who could put together a variation of Carter's winning coalition in 1976; nominate a western candidate who might appeal to those on the Pacific Coast and in other states in the Southwest and West that have grown in population and will have more electoral votes in 1992 than they had in 1988; or nominate a candidate with broad national standing who is not a politician and is not associated with a particular region (such as General Norman H. Schwarzkopf) and thus could appeal to independent voters in states in which these voters constitute a sizable portion of the population.

## TACTICAL CONSIDERATIONS

Whereas the basic objectives set the contours of the campaign strategy, tactical considerations influence day-to-day decisions. Tactics are the specific ways by which the ends are achieved. They involve techniques to communicate the message and the targets and timing of that message: how appeals will be made, to whom, and when. Unlike strategy, which can be planned well in advance, tactics change with the environment and events. The circumstances, in short, dictate different tactical responses.

### *Communicating Techniques*

There are a variety of ways to convey a political message. They include door-to-door canvassing, direct mail, and media advertisements. At the local level especially, door-to-door campaigning may be a viable option. Obviously, presidential candidates and their national staffs cannot directly engage in this kind of activity in the general election, even though they may have in some of the primaries. They can, however, encourage these efforts by others.

The Kennedy organization in 1960 was one of the first to mount such a campaign on the local level. Using the canvass as a device to identify supporters and solicit workers, Kennedy's aides built precinct organizations out of the newly recruited volunteers. The volunteers, in turn, distributed literature, turned out the voters, and monitored the polls on election day. They were instrumental in Kennedy's narrow victory in several states.

Personal contact is generally considered to have a greater impact on voters than any other kind of campaign activity. It is most effective in stimulating voting. To a lesser extent, it may also influence the decision on how to vote. The problem with personal contact is that it is time-consuming, volunteer intensive, and, with limited funds available, not cost-effective at the presidential level. Increasingly, presidential campaigns have depended on their national parties to raise the soft money that will enable their state and local parties to perform these activities for the entire party ticket. This practice has made the success of the presidential campaign more dependent on local party efforts than it has been in the last twenty years.

Direct mail, a technique frequently used in fund raising, has also been employed to distribute information about the candidate and the party. Personalized letters can be targeted to specific groups and individuals and tailored to address specific issues. The Republicans effectively employed direct mail in 1988. The party's extensive files of registered voters identified potential Republican supporters. Aides canvassed these people by telephone to determine their candidate preferences as well as their issue concerns. Letters signed by George Bush addressing the issue with which they were most concerned were then sent to each of these potential Republican voters. Lacking the information base that the Republicans had, the Democrats were forced to conduct mass mailings directed toward those who lived in key swing precincts or those areas populated by an ethnic, racial, or occupational group that was likely to support its nominees.

For conveying a substantive message to a specific audience, direct mail can be extremely efficient, although its effectiveness varies with the level of education of the group. It tends to have greater impact on those who are less educated, particularly those who do not receive a lot of other mail.

Another option is television. Although costly and impersonal, it has many benefits. Television can reach large numbers of people. It is less taxing on the candidate than extensive personal campaigning. It facilitates control over the political environment. While messages cannot be tailored as precisely as they can in individualized letters, they can be designed to create and project favorable images and can be targeted regionally and, on non–English language cable stations, ethnically. The reach of television, the size of its potential audience, and the ability to direct a message to those who might be sympathetic to it explain why an increasing proportion of expenditures by the campaigns of the presidential candidates are on the production and airing of television advertising. In 1976, total spending on all forms of media accounted for approximately half the campaign budget; in 1984 and 1988 it was almost two-thirds.

But no matter how extensive a candidate's use of television may be, a certain amount of personal campaigning has always been necessary. Appearances by presidential hopefuls create news, often becoming media events themselves. They promote a sense of unity in the party, make the candidates seem real to the voters, and testify to the candidates' concern for the people. No area or group likes to be taken for granted.

The problem with personal appearances is that they are personally wearing, have limited impact, cost a lot of money, and can be dangerous. Making arrangements is itself a complex, time-consuming venture. The work of experts is required to make certain that everything goes smoothly from scheduling to physical arrangements to the rally itself.

Jerry Bruno, who "advanced" Democratic presidential campaigns in the 1960s, described his tasks as an advance man, tasks that have not changed over the years:

> It's my job in a campaign to decide where a rally should be held, how a candidate can best use his time getting from an airport to that rally, who should sit next to him and chat with him quietly in his hotel room before or after a political speech, and who should be kept as far away from him as possible.
>
> It's also my job to make sure that a public appearance goes well—a big crowd, an enthusiastic crowd, with bands and signs, a motorcade that is mobbed by enthusiastic supporters, a day in which a candidate sees and is seen by as many people as possible—and at the same time have it all properly recorded by the press and their cameras.[21]

Bruno's efforts are indicative of the extensive preparations that characterize modern-day campaigns. Advance people go to great lengths to prevent things from marring a speech or event. It is the general practice of most campaigns to issue tickets to partisans for seats near the stage to get supporters close to the candidate and potential demonstrators further away.[22] In one rally in 1988 the Bush campaign tried to minimize the disruptive effect of demonstrations by positioning a line of buses in front of them.

Even with all the advance preparations, public appearances may have a limited impact—or, even worse, a negative one. If the crowds are thin, if the candidate is heckled, if a prominent public figure refuses to be on the platform with the candidate or a controversial one does appear, or if the candidate makes a verbal slip, then the appearance may do more harm than good. Mondale got off to an embarrassing start in 1984 when an early hour Labor Day parade in which he was to appear drew relatively few onlookers. The news was the absence of spectators. Television cameras pictured Mondale walking down near-empty streets in New York City.

The arduous and exhausting schedules of modern campaigns have also contributed to displays of emotion by candidates that have embarrassed them and damaged their public image. One of the most highly publicized of these incidents occurred during the 1972 New Hampshire primary. Senator Edmund Muskie, the Democratic front-runner, seemed to break into tears when defending his wife from the attacks of William Loeb, publisher of the state's *Manchester Union Leader*. In the minds of some, the incident made Muskie look weak and not presidential. It raised the question whether he could withstand the pressures of the presidency. George McGovern, who benefited from the Muskie episode, expressed his own frustration toward the end of his presidential campaign. When passing a vociferous heckler at an airport reception, McGovern told his critic, "Kiss my ass!" The press dutifully reported the senator's comment. George Bush made a similar off-color remark when addressing a group of supporters following his 1984 debate with vice-presidential candidate Geraldine Ferraro. He stated that he had intended "to kick ass" during the debate. The comment, obviously designed to show Bush's forcefulness as a candidate, was greeted with enthusiasm by his supporters.[23]

In recent campaigns each of the major party candidates have made questionable statements that were highlighted by the media. In the midst of the Democratic primaries in 1976, Carter stated that he saw nothing wrong with people trying to maintain the "ethnic purity" of their neighborhoods. After some people interpreted his remarks as racist, Carter indicated that he had made an error in his choice of words, promptly retracted them, and apologized.[24] During his second debate with Carter, President Ford asserted that the Soviet Union did not dominate Eastern Europe. His comment, picked up and repeated by the media, led critics to wonder whether he really understood the complexities of international politics, much less appreciated the influence of the Soviet Union. Ronald Reagan's much-quoted reference to trees as being a primary source of pollution, made before his 1980 campaign, brought him considerable ridicule during it. Some one-liners have worked to the candidate's advantage, at least in the short run. When Republican vice-presidential nominee Dan Quayle compared his Senate experience with John F. Kennedy's in his debate with Lloyd Bentsen, the Democratic candidate shot back, "I served with Jack Kennedy; I knew Jack Kennedy; Jack Kennedy was a friend of mine. Senator, you are no Jack Kennedy."[25] Quayle, shaken by Bentsen's blunt reply, remained on the defensive for the remainder of the debate. Bush's "Read my lips" pledge not to raise taxes enhanced his popularity during the campaign but made it more difficult for him to find an acceptable solution to the problem of the budget deficit once in office.

## Targeting Messages

Candidates are normally very careful about their public utterances. Knowing that the press focuses on inconsistencies and highlights controversies, presidential candidates tend to stick to their articulated public positions. Moreover, they try to control the thematic content of the campaign.

The plan of the Reagan organization in 1984 was to introduce a new theme every ten days to two weeks. All presidential speeches and appearances were to be keyed to this theme. Situations that might have distracted public attention or confused it were carefully controlled.

Speeches are frequently tailored for specific groups. In appealing to ethnic voters, Dukakis referred to his Greek heritage and to his parents' immigration to the United States. "If this son of immigrants can seek and win the presidency with your help," he told voters, "then your kids and your grandkids, the kids and grandkids of immigrants all over this country, from every community, can do the same."[26] The general practice is to tell the audience what they want to hear. Naturally, such an approach creates a favorable response that, in turn, helps to project a positive image when covered by the media.

Occasionally, however, candidates will use the opposite tactic. To exhibit their courage and candor, they will announce a policy to an unsympathetic audience. Carter made such an announcement in 1976 when he told an American Legion convention of his intention, if elected, to issue a blanket pardon to Vietnam draft dodgers. To emphasize the purity of his conservative convictions, Goldwater made a speech in Appalachia criticizing Lyndon Johnson's War on Poverty as phony, and in Tennessee he suggested the possibility of private ownership of the Tennessee Valley Authority. While the senator did not win many converts, he did succeed in maintaining his image as a no-nonsense conservative.

A third approach when discussing issues is simply to be vague. Vagueness allows potential supporters to see what they want to see in a candidate's position. Dwight Eisenhower succeeded with this approach in 1956, as did Reagan in 1984, but Thomas Dewey, eight years before Eisenhower, did not. Dewey lacked the popularity and credibility that Eisenhower and Reagan were both to enjoy after their first four years in office. Both Bush and Dukakis were careful not to offend voters when discussing economic and social issues in 1988.

## Timing Appeals

In addition to the problem of whom to appeal to and what to say, decisions surrounding when to make the appeal are important. Candidates naturally desire to build momentum as their campaigns progress. This goal usually dictates a phased effort, especially for the underdog.

Goldwater's campaign of 1964 illustrates the plight of the challenger. Having won the Republican nomination after heated primary contests against Nelson Rockefeller, the senator initially had to reunite the party. The first month of his campaign was directed toward this end. Endorsements were obtained; the party was reorganized; traditional Republican positions were articulated. Phase two was designed to broaden Goldwater's electoral support. Appeals to conservative Democratic and independent voters were made on the basis of ideology. The third phase was the attack. Goldwater severely criticized President Johnson, his Great Society program, and his liberal Democratic policies. In phase four, the Republican candidate enunciated his own hopes, goals, and programs for America's future. Finally, at the end of the campaign, perceiving that he had lost, Goldwater adhered to his views and became increasingly uncompromising in presenting his conservative beliefs.

In 1988, George Bush's strategy was also phased. The first stage of his campaign during the Republican convention was to establish his own qualifications for the office as an experienced national leader and a loyal vice-president but also a person with his own ideas. Cutting Dukakis down to size was the focus of stage two. Like Goldwater, Bush also trailed his Democratic rival in the polls during the summer preceding the election. Unlike Goldwater, he was able to overcome the gap by pointing to Dukakis's political vulnerabilities as a liberal Democrat. In the third part of his campaign, Bush sought to accentuate the positive. His speeches and advertisements stressed the achievements of the Republican administration of which he was a part and his priorities for the future. The theme of his ads—"peace and prosperity"—was designed to generate and maintain a positive feeling in the last month of the campaign.

## Turning Out Voters

When all is said and done, it is the electorate that makes the final judgment. Who comes out to vote can be the critical factor in determining the winner in a close election. Although turnout is influenced by a number of variables, including the demographic characteristics and political attitudes of the population, registration laws and procedures, the kind of election and its competitiveness, and even the weather, it can also be affected by the campaign itself.

On balance, lower turnout has tended to hurt the Democrats more than the Republicans, because a larger proportion of their party identifiers have been less likely to vote. Thus a key element in the strategy of most Democratic candidates since Franklin Roosevelt has been to maximize the number of voters by organizing large registration drives.

Traditionally the party organizations at the state and local levels, not the candidate's central headquarters, mount the drive. A party divided at the time of its convention can seriously damage its chances in the general election. A case in point was the Humphrey campaign of 1968. Humphrey received the nomination of a party that took until late October to coalesce behind his candidacy, too late to register a large number of voters for the November election. Had it not been for organized labor's efforts in registering approximately 4.6 million voters, Humphrey probably would not have come as close as he did to winning the presidency.

Whereas Humphrey's loss in 1968 can be attributed in part to a weak voter registration drive, Carter's victory in 1976 resulted in part from a successful one. The Democratic National Committee coordinated and financed the drive. With the support of organized labor, Democrats out-registered Republicans. Labor's efforts in Ohio and Texas contributed to Carter's narrow victory in both states. A successful program to attract black voters also helped increase Carter's margin of victory. In 1980, Carter's lukewarm support from labor and his party's weak financial position adversely affected Democratic registration efforts.

One of the most sophisticated registration efforts by either party occurred in 1984. The Reagan-Bush organization used the prenomination period to identify potential unregistered supporters. Lists of people, grouped precinct by precinct, were supplied to state and local Republican committees for the purposes of enlarging the potential Republican vote. In contrast, the Democrats lacked the organizational mechanism and financial support to match the Republican effort. They fell far short of their goal of registering 5–6 million new voters.

Voter registration declined by slightly over 2 percent in 1988. Neither party mounted as successful a registration effort as it had four years earlier despite the almost $150 million raised and spent on get-out-the-vote activities.

## SUMMARY

Campaigning by presidential nominees is a relatively recent phenomenon. Throughout most of the nineteenth century, presidential campaigns were fairly simple in organization and operation and rather limited in scope. With the exception of William Jennings Bryan, there was little active involvement by the candidates themselves.

Changes began to occur in the twentieth century. Largely the consequences of advances in transportation and communications that enabled candidates to campaign across the entire country and reach millions of voters directly, these developments made campaigning more complex, more expensive, and more sophisticated. They required more activity by the candidates and their staffs. Campaign strategy and tactics became more highly geared to the mass media.

Campaign organizations have increased in size and expertise. Supplementing the traditional cadre of party professionals are the professionals of the new technology: pollsters, media consultants, direct mailers, lawyers, accountants, and a host of other specialists. Their inclusion in the candidate's organization has made the coordination of centralized decision making more difficult and more necessary. It has also produced two separate organizations, one very loosely coordinated by the party's national committee and the other more tightly controlled by the candidates and their senior aides.

The job of campaign organizations is to produce a unified and coordinated campaign effort. Most presidential campaigns follow a general strategy based on the prevailing attitudes and perceptions of the electorate, the reputations and images of the nominees and their parties, and the geography of the electoral college. The strategy includes a basic appeal, usually with a partisan and personal dimension, and a resource allocation component.

In designing an appeal, Democratic candidates emphasize their link to the party and those bread-and-butter economic issues that have held their majority coalition together since the 1930s. Republican candidates, on the other hand, focus on foreign policy and on national security matters. In the last three elections, however, they have also used economic issues to their advantage, contrasting domestic conditions during the Carter and Reagan administrations.

Nominees of both parties also try to project images of leadership, trumpeting their own strengths and exploiting their opponent's weaknesses. Negative campaigning can be particularly effective when candidates are not well-known to the general public. When they have an established record, particularly presidents seeking reelection, that record and their performance in office shape much of the leadership imagery.

Generally speaking, incumbents have an advantage in conveying their capacity to lead. Being president—making critical decisions, exercising the powers of the office—is evidence of the leadership that presidential candidates have to demonstrate. Psychologically, the electorate generally finds it safer to keep a known commodity in office than gamble with an unknown one unless times are bad, a national problem persists, or personal factors about the candidates dictate a change.

When allocating resources, the geography of the electoral college must be considered. In recent years Democratic candidates have found themselves at a disadvantage in obtaining an electoral majority. With the South and the West voting more heavily Republican at the presidential level, the Democrats can afford to lose fewer of the large states in which both parties concentrate the bulk of their resources.

The candidates' strategies influence the conduct of their campaigns, but their tactics tend to have greater and more direct effects on day-to-day events. Key tactical decisions include what techniques will be used, when, and by whom. They also include what appeals will be made, how, when, and to whom.

Other than that flexibility is essential, it is difficult to generalize about tactics. Much depends on the basic strategic plan, the momentum of the campaign, and the unfolding of events. In the end, the methods that mobilize the electorate by getting people excited about a candidate are likely to be of the greatest benefit in turning out and influencing the vote. Image creation, production, and projection lie at the heart of this process. The next chapter explores these aspects of campaigning.

# NOTES

1. Quotation and other details in Marvin R. Weisbord, *Campaigning for President* (New York: Washington Square Press, 1966), pp. 45, 5.
2. In 1893 the country suffered a financial panic and slid into a depression. Particularly hard hit were the farmers and silver miners of the West. Angered at the repeal of the Sherman Silver Purchase Act, which had required the government to buy a certain amount of silver and convert it into paper money, farmers, miners, and other western interests wanted new legislation to force the government to buy and coin an unlimited amount of silver. Eastern financial interests opposed the free coinage of silver, as did President Grover Cleveland. Their opposition split the Democratic party at its convention of 1896 and in the general election of that year.
3. The speech was made during the platform debate. Bryan, arguing in favor of the free and unlimited coinage of silver, accused eastern bankers and financiers of trying to protect their own parochial interests by imposing a gold standard. "You shall not press down upon the brow of labor this crown of thorns, you shall not crucify mankind upon a cross of gold," he shouted at the end of his remarks. Bryan's speech moved the convention. Not only did the free silver interests win the platform fight, but Bryan himself won the presidential nomination on the fifth ballot.
4. William Jennings Bryan, *The First Battle* (1896; reprint, Port Washington, N.Y.: Kennikat Press, 1971), p. 618.
5. Keith Melder, "The Whistlestop: Origins of the Personal Campaign," *Campaigns and Elections* 7 (May–June 1986): 49.
6. Weisbord, *Campaigning for President*, p. 116.
7. Franklin Roosevelt had been crippled by polio in 1921. He wore heavy leg braces and could stand only with difficulty. Nonetheless, he made a remarkable physical and political recovery. In his campaign, he went to great lengths to hide the fact that he could not walk and could barely stand. The press generally did not report on his disability. They refrained from photographing, filming, or describing him struggling to stand with his braces.
8. Cabell Phillips, *The Truman Presidency* (New York: Macmillian, 1966), p. 237.
9. Quoted in Stanley Kelley, *Professional Public Relations and Political Power* (Baltimore: Johns Hopkins Press, 1956), pp. 161–62.
10. Karl A. Lamb and Paul A. Smith, *Campaign Decision-Making: The Presidential Election of 1964* (Belmont, Calif.: Wadsworth, 1968), pp. 59–63.
11. Lee Atwater, quoted in David R. Runkel, ed., *Campaign for President: The Managers Look at '88* (Dover, Mass.: Auburn House, 1989), p. 91.
12. In 1988, Michael Dukakis chose to keep his campaign headquarters in Boston, Massachusetts, rather than move it to Washington, D.C., for symbolic as well as practical reasons. A Boston address underscored the competence image Dukakis desired to project as a working governor and made it more difficult for Washington-based Democrats to interfere with the conduct of his campaign.
13. Edward Walsh, "Dukakis Camp Regroups, Regains Its Optimism," *Washington Post*, October 9, 1988, p. A18.
14. John Sasso was forced out as campaign manager because he approved the release of videos to the media that showed a rival candidate, Senator Joseph

Biden, using parts of a speech first given by British Labour party leader Neil Kinnock. Biden, who did not cite Kinnock in this address, dropped out of the campaign after the incident.

15. Lee Atwater, the architect of this strategy, stated in a 1985 interview: "When I first got into [politics], I just stumbled across the fact that candidates who went into an election with negatives higher than 30 or 40 points just inevitably lost." Quoted in Thomas B. Edsall, "Why Bush Accentuates the Negative," *Washington Post*, October 2, 1988, p. C4.

16. Gallup Poll conducted May 13–15, 1988, reported in Peter Goldman, Tom Mathews, et al. *The Quest for the Presidency: The 1988 Campaign* (New York: Simon and Schuster, 1989), p. 419.

17. Bush initially expressed some reluctance to engage in such a campaign against his opponent. He was persuaded to do so, however, by his aides, who showed him tapes of the Democratic convention, in which he was the subject of such attacks. Bush, who had taken a fishing vacation during that convention, had not previously seen the ridicule to which he had been subjected by Democratic speakers.

18. A political scientist, Steven J. Brams, and a mathematician, Morton D. Davis, have devised a formula for the most rational way to allocate campaign resources. They calculated that resources should be spent in proportion to the "3/2's power" of the electoral votes of each state. To calculate the 3/2's power, take the square root of the number of electoral votes and cube the result. Brams offers the following example: "If one state has 4 electoral votes and another state has 16 electoral votes, even though they differ in size only by a factor of four, the candidates should allocate eight times as much in resources to the larger state." In examining actual patterns of allocation between 1960 and 1972, Brams and Davis found that campaigns generally conformed to this rule. "The 3/2's Rule in Presidential Campaigning," *American Political Science Review* 68 (1974): 113.

19. Quoted in Lamb and Smith, *Campaign Decision-Making*, p. 95.

20. In devising an electoral college strategy, Reagan's strategists first calculated the odds of winning each state, using historical and current survey data. Information from polls was added as the campaign progressed. Those states in which the probability of winning was less than 70 percent but more than 30 percent were then ranked in order of population size and geographic area. Priority targets were identified among the large, middle, and small states. The initial calculations were made in March 1980. The targets were revised in June and over the course of the campaign. Richard Wirthlin, Vincent Breglio, and Richard Beal, "Campaign Chronicle," *Public Opinion* 4 (February/March 1981): 46.

21. Jerry Bruno and Jeff Greenfield, *The Advance Man* (New York: Morrow, 1971), p. 299.

22. Gerald M. Boyd, "Shielded from Demonstrations, Bush Assails Dukakis on Crime," *New York Times*, October 1, 1988, p. I8.

23. Another well-reported incident, this one involving Vice-President Nelson A. Rockefeller, occurred in 1976. It, too, was precipitated by heckling. The Republican vice-presidential candidate of that year, Senator Robert Dole, accompanied by Rockefeller, was trying to address a rally in Binghamton, New York. Constantly interrupted by the hecklers, Dole and then Rockefeller tried to restore order by addressing their critics directly. When this approach failed, Rockefeller grinned and made an obscene gesture, extending the mid-

dle fingers of his hands to the group. The vice-president's response was captured in a picture that appeared in newspapers and national magazines across the country, much to the embarrassment of the Republican ticket.

24. In 1976 Carter damaged his image by comments he made during an interview with *Playboy* magazine. In articulating his religious views, Carter quoted Christ as saying, "Anyone who looks on a woman with lust has in his heart already committed adultery." He went on to add, "I've looked on a lot of women with lust. I've committed adultery in my heart many times." *Playboy*, November 1976, p. 86.

25. Lloyd Bentsen, debate with Dan Quayle, Omaha, Nebraska, October 5, 1988, quoted in "Transcript of the Vice-Presidential Debate," *Washington Post*, October 6, 1988, p. A30.

26. Quoted in Edward Walsh, "Dukakis Is Wearing Ethnicity on His Sleeve," *Washington Post*, May 22, 1988, p. A7.

## SELECTED READINGS

Archer, J. Clark, Fred M. Shelley, Peter J. Taylor and Ellen R. White. "The Geography of U.S. Presidential Elections. *Scientific American* 259 (July 1988): 44–51.

Goldman, Peter, Tom Mathews, et al. *The Quest for the Presidency: The 1988 Campaign.* New York: Simon and Schuster, 1989.

Light, Paul C., and Celinda Lake. "The Election: Candidates, Strategies, and Decisions." In *The Elections of 1984*, edited by Michael Nelson, pp. 83–110, Washington, D.C.: Congressional Quarterly, 1985.

Melder, Keith. "The Whistlestop: Origins of the Personal Campaign." *Campaigns and Elections* 7 (May–June 1986): 46–50.

———. "The Whistlestop: The First Media Campaign." *Campaigns and Elections* 6 (Fall 1985): 62–68.

"Moving Right Along? Campaign '84's Lessons for 1988: An Interview with Peter Hart and Richard Wirthlin." *Public Opinion* 7 (December 1984/January 1985): 8–11.

Runkel, David R., ed. *Campaign for President: The Managers Look at '88.* Dover, Mass.: Auburn House, 1989.

White, Theodore H. *The Making of the President, 1960.* New York: Atheneum, 1988.

———. *The Making of the President, 1964.* New York: Atheneum, 1965.

———. *The Making of the President, 1968.* New York: Atheneum, 1969.

———. *The Making of the President, 1972.* New York: Atheneum, 1973.

———. *America in Search of Itself: The Making of the President, 1956–1980.* New York: Harper and Row, 1982.

# Chapter 7

# Image Building and the Media

## INTRODUCTION

Images are mental pictures that people rely on to make the world around them understandable. These pictures are stimulated and shaped by the environment as well as by personal attitudes and feelings. What is projected affects what is seen. Different people, however, also see the same thing differently; their attitudes color their perceptions. To some extent, beauty is in the eye of the beholder; to some extent, it is in the object seen.

The electorate forms different images of the parties, candidates, and issues. These perceptions help make and reinforce decisions on election day. The images of the party affect how the candidates and the issues are perceived. Strong party identifiers tend to see "their" candidate in a more favorable light than the opposition and perceive his or her position on the issues as closer to their own. Independents also apply their beliefs and feelings in the shaping of their perceptions of the candidates and the issues, although they are less likely to be encumbered by preconceived partisan perspectives in making their evaluations.

The importance of preconceptions should not imply, however, that what candidates say and do or how they appear is irrelevant. On the contrary, even strong party supporters can be influenced by what they see, read, and hear. George McGovern's poor showing among Democrats in 1972 and Walter Mondale's in 1984 dramatically illustrate how a candidate's image can adversely affect his partisan support. McGovern was perceived as incompetent and Mondale as ineffectual by much of the electorate.

Candidate images are short-term factors that are more variable than party images. In addition to being affected by partisan attitudes, they are also conditioned by specific situations. It is difficult to separate a candidate's image from the events of the real world. Incumbents, especially, tend to be evaluated on the basis of their performance in office. Richard Nixon's image improved between the elections of 1968 to 1972, as did Ronald Reagan's from 1980 to 1988, but Jimmy Carter's declined from 1976 to 1980. The changes were a consequence of the public's perception of these men's performance as president.

Personal qualities are also important. Perceived strength, moral integrity, seriousness of purpose, candor, empathy, and style all contribute to the impression people have of public figures. In fact, these personal characteristics are frequently cited as the reason for voting for or against a particular person.

In view of the weakening of party loyalties and the media's emphasis on personal factors, this emphasis on personal qualities is not surprising. For many, the images of the candidates provide a cognitive handle for interpreting the campaign and making a qualitative judgment. Candidates who enjoy a positive assessment have an advantage. They can use it to offset unpopular partisan, ideological, or issue positions.

The task for presidential candidates is to project as positive an image as possible of themselves and raise as many questions as they can about their opponents. Normally, just being a presidential candidate helps. The public's inclination to look up to the president usually extends to his opponent. Recent elections have provided exceptions to this rule, however. Carter and Reagan were perceived negatively by a majority of the electorate in 1980, as was Mondale four years later. Both Bush and Dukakis also had high negatives.

A favorable image, of course, cannot be taken for granted. It has to be created, or at least polished. To build a favorable image, the candidate and his campaign managers must first know what qualities voters look for in presidential candidates and how to project those qualities. The first section of this chapter discusses those traits that the public considers most desirable for the presidency, with recent campaigns used as examples. In the succeeding sections, the presentation and projection of positive and negative images in the media, primarily television, are explored. The increasing use of political advertisements, the attempts to shape campaign coverage, and the impact of that coverage on the electorate are assessed.

## PRESIDENTIAL TRAITS

The United States electorate has traditionally valued certain traits in its presidential candidates.[1] These reflect the public's psychological needs and its expectations of those in office. These traits also provide a model of an ideal president, one that is used to evaluate an incumbent and to rate a challenger.

Surveys of public opinion indicate that certain qualities are absolutely essential. The contemporary president is expected to be strong, assertive, dominant—a father figure to millions of Americans. He is expected to be skillful, knowledgeable, and analytic—a problem solver in an age of technology. He is also expected to be a person who can bring significant political, organizational, and managerial skills to bear on making the system work—the head of an effective government. Finally, the president should be able to empathize with the people as well as to embody their most cherished qualities. He must be understanding and inspiring, honest and honorable, reasonable and rational, respected and responsive—a leader who is sensitive to public values, needs, interests, and opinions. In presenting themselves to the voters, candidates must naturally try to project these traits and create the image of an ideal president or president-to-be.

Strength, boldness, and decisiveness are intrinsic to the public's conception of the office. During times of crisis or periods of social anxiety, these leadership characteristics are considered absolutely essential. The strength that Franklin Roosevelt was able to convey by virtue of his successful bout with polio, Dwight Eisenhower by his military command in World War II, and Ronald Reagan by his tough talk, clear-cut solutions, and consistent policy goals contrasted sharply with the perceptions of Adlai Stevenson in 1956, George McGovern in 1972, Jimmy Carter in 1980, and Walter Mondale in 1984 as weak, indecisive, and vacillating.

The presidency usually implies strength. When Gerald Ford and Jimmy Carter were criticized for their failure to provide strong leadership, their campaign organizations countered by focusing on their actions as president, emphasizing those situations in which they were in charge—giving orders, making decisions, announcing policies. George Bush's reelection campaign can be expected to present him in similarly assertive, official roles in 1992.

For nonincumbents, the task of seeming to be powerful, confident, and independent (one's own person) can best be imparted by a no-nonsense approach, a show of optimism, and a conviction that success is attainable. John Kennedy's rhetorical emphasis on activity in 1960 and Richard Nixon's tough talk in 1968 about the turmoil and divisiveness of the late 1960s helped to generate a take-charge impression. Kennedy and Nixon were perceived as leaders who knew what had to be done and would do it. Reagan's references to his economic and defense policies, combined with his "Can Do, America" appeal, were designed to convey a similar impression in 1980 and 1984. Michael Dukakis stressed his competence and integrity in 1988 to demonstrate that he could tackle the nation's toughest job.

In addition to seeming tough enough to be president, it is also important to exhibit sufficient knowledge and skills for the job. In the public's mind, personal experience testifies to the ability to perform. However, all experience is not equal. Having held an executive or legislative office at the national level is usually considered necessary, since the public does not think of the presidency as a position that a political novice could easily or adequately handle.

The advantage of incumbency is obvious. Presidents are presumed to be knowledgeable because they have been president. They have met with world leaders, dealt with national and international crises, and coped with the everyday problems of running the country. Even if they stumble on the facts, as Reagan did in his 1984 campaign, their incumbency testifies to their competency.

Incumbency can help a vice-president running for president as well if the administration of which that vice-president was a part has been perceived as successful. If it has not been, then being vice-president is apt to be a detriment. Bush benefited in 1988 from his eight years as Ronald Reagan's vice-president; Mondale was disadvantaged in 1984 from his four-year association with Jimmy Carter.

In general, nonincumbents face a difficult task. They have to show their presidential qualities without having been president or vice-president. Most candidates refer to some direct and relevant personal experience in presenting their qualifications for the office. In 1960, Kennedy pointed to his service in the Senate, particularly on the Foreign Relations Committee, as evidence of his knowledge of foreign affairs; in 1972, McGovern spoke of his years as an air force bomber pilot to lend credence to his patriotism and his opposition to the war in Vietnam; in 1976, Carter noted his involvement with the Trilateral Commission, a group of prominent individuals interested in United States relations with Western Europe and Japan, as an indication of his interest and proficiency in foreign relations; in 1980, Reagan talked about his governorship of California and in 1988 Dukakis referred to his experience as a two-term Massachusetts governor as qualifications for the executive duties of the presidency.

Citing figures and facts in a seemingly spontaneous manner is another tactic frequently employed by candidates to exhibit their knowledge, intelligence, and problem-solving skills. Nonincumbents in particular have used the forum of the debates to recite, without notes, statistics on the economy, foreign policy, and national security matters. Their objective is to equalize the information advantage that their opponents are perceived to have by virtue of their positions as vice-president or president. So concerned were Ford's supporters about the public's perception of his intellectual abilities that they released information about his academic record in college and law school. Reagan was frequently pictured in a librarylike setting during his 1980 campaign.

In addition to strength, decisiveness, knowledge, and competency, empathy is also an important attribute for presidential candidates. People want a president who can respond to their emotional needs, one who understands what and how they feel. As the government has become larger, more powerful, and more distant, empathy has become more important. Roosevelt and Eisenhower radiated warmth. Carter was particularly effective in 1976 in generating the impression that he cared, creating a vivid contrast with the conception of the imperial presidency and the stereotypical image of his Republican opponents. By comparison, McGovern, Nixon, and Dukakis appeared cold, distant, and impersonal. Unfortunately for Dukakis, he reinforced this image by his impersonal, matter-of-fact response to questions put to him during the campaign, particularly during the two presidential debates. (See "A Nonemotional Response.") Bush seemed to be the more personal and warm of the two candidates in 1988. His call for "a kinder and gentler America" was intended, in part, to give credibility to the human side of his public image and to counter the perception that he was the candidate of the rich.

Candor, integrity, and trust emerge periodically as important attributes in presidential image building. Most of the time these traits are taken for granted. Occasionally, however, a crisis of confidence, such as Watergate, dictates that political skills be downplayed and these qualities stressed. Such crises preceded the elections of 1952 and 1976.

In summary, candidates try to project images of themselves that are consistent with public expectations of the office and its occupant. Traits such as inner strength, decisiveness, competence, and experience are considered essential for the office, and others, such as empathy, sincerity, credibility, and integrity, are viewed as necessary for the individual. Which traits are considered most important varies to some extent with the assessment of the strengths and weaknesses of the incumbent. The negative attributes of the sitting president become the essential traits for the next one. In 1988 these traits were knowledge, energy, and empathy.

Candidates must constantly monitor public opinion to discern which qualities are most salient during a particular period. In 1988, the polling organizations that worked for Dukakis and Bush read adjective (trait) lists to people they were interviewing and asked them two basic questions: How important were these traits to a president? How well did these traits characterize each of the candidates?

Presidential nominees who seem to be lacking a major trait may have an image problem, but one that can be overcome. Candidates who appear to lack more than one, may be in more serious trouble. The next section discusses some of the ways in which presidential candidates have used media to try to overcome their image problems.

# A Nonemotional Response

The answer that really sealed Dukakis's technocratic, ice-man image was his cold and impersonal reply to the first question he was asked by correspondent Bernard Shaw during his second debate with George Bush:

*Q.* Governor, if Kitty Dukakis were raped and murdered, would you favor an irrevocable death penalty for the killer?

*Dukakis.* No, I don't, Bernard, and I think you know that I've opposed the death penalty during all of my life. I don't see any evidence that it's a deterrent and I think there are better and more effective ways to deal with violent crime. We've done so in my own state and it's one of the reasons why we have had the biggest drop in crime of any industrial state in America.

But we have work to do in this nation. We have work to do to fight a real war, and not a phony war, against drugs and that's something I want to lead, something we haven't had over the course of the past many years even though the Vice President has been at least allegedly in charge of that war. We have much to do to step up that war, to double the number of drug enforcement agents, to fight both here and abroad, to work with our neighbors in this hemisphere. And I want to call a hemispheric summit just as soon after the 20th of January as possible to fight that war.

But we also have to deal with drug education prevention here at home, and that's one of the things that I hope I can lead personally as the President of the United States. We've had great success in my own state, and we've reached out to young people and their families and been able to help them by beginning drug education and prevention in the early elementary grades.

So we can fight this war and we can win this war. And we can do so in a way that marshals our forces, that provides real support for state and local law enforcement officers, who have not been getting that kind of support; do it in a way which will bring down violence in this nation, will help our youngsters to stay away from drugs, will stop this avalanche of drugs that's pouring into the country and will make it possible for our kids and our families to grow up in safe and secure and decent neighborhoods.

*Source:* Transcript of the second debate between George Bush and Michael Dukakis, published in the *New York Times*, October 14, 1988, p. A14.

# CONTROLLED MEDIA

Candidates are marketed in both controlled and uncontrolled settings. When candidates can choose their medium, design their picture or message, and convey it in a direct and unaltered fashion, such as with advertising, they control media. When they cannot, when others such as reporters, camera crews, or even organizations intercede, their media is said to be uncontrolled.

The most powerful form of controlled media is political advertising. It is used to gain attention, make a pitch, and leave an impression. The end, of course, is to get the electorate to do something—vote for specific candidates on election day.

## *Organization*

To mount a successful advertising campaign a team of experts must be assembled and a plan put into effect. The magnitude of the task and the time constraints imposed normally dictate that outside experts be hired to supplement the regular campaign staff. In 1988 the Bush organization hired Roger Ailes, an experienced political consultant, to oversee its media efforts. Ailes had been in charge of advertising for Richard Nixon's campaign of 1968. His ads that year helped resurrect the image of Nixon, who had been defeated for president in 1960 and for governor of California in 1962. Ailes was given a similar assignment in 1988—develop a positive presidential image for George Bush and a negative one for his opponent, Michael Dukakis.

Ailes assembled a group of experienced advertising executives, many of whom had worked with him on previous Republican campaigns, including the Reagan-Bush effort in 1984. Ailes directed the operation, which included relations with the media as well as campaign advertising. He demanded and received direct access to Bush. A member of the small, inner circle of campaign directors, Ailes cleared his commercials with only a few top aides. He also had considerable input into the development of campaign strategy.

The Ailes group aired thirty-seven television ads. The total media budget for print, radio, and television was $35 million, of which $31.5 million was spent for television airtime. Additionally, associates of Ailes produced for television five national commercials and several regional ones for the Republican party. The GOP also spent $1 million on radio spots.[2]

Dukakis's media group was also composed of Madison Avenue advertising executives, but they were not nearly as cohesive or politically experienced as the Bush team. Nor did any member of the Dukakis group exercise the kind of influence over media operations that Ailes did for Bush's. In fact, there was considerable turnover among Dukakis's consultants and much wasted effort. One indication of the disarray was the number of scripts that were written and produced but never aired. Approximately $6.5 million of the $30 million spent on television advertising was for production, with the remainder for airing forty-seven different ads. Furthermore the Democrats did not supplement the Dukakis campaign with nearly as much party advertising for its candidates as the Republicans did for theirs. The Democrats expended only $1.5 million for national television commercials, in comparison to $12.5 million by the Republicans.[3]

## *Strategy*

At the beginning of the campaign, campaign managers generally design a media plan. The plan is a strategic blueprint, setting out the assumptions and objectives of the candidates. These include the personality traits that need to be emphasized, the issues that should be raised, and the images that have to be created. The plan, designed with the mood of the country in mind, outlines the form that the advertising should take and the way it should be marketed, targeted, and phased.

The assumptions of the plan relate to the environment and the candidate's position at the beginning of the campaign. The objectives indicate where the candidate would like to be at the end. The goal, of course, is to get there. Take the situation in which Bush found himself in the summer of 1988. He was perceived as weak, a vice-president in the shadow of a popular president, a person who had been the object of ridicule at the Democratic convention, and a candidate who was trailing his Democratic opponent by as much as 18 percent in public opinion poles taken in the summer preceding the election. The task, as his advisers saw it, was to change significant portions of his image and, in the process, to destroy his opponent's image. In the words of Bush's media director, Roger Ailes: "The strategy was simple. . . . It was basically [to present a] positive George Bush. . . . We always knew we would have to define Dukakis as well, and whichever of us defined the other and ourselves most effectively would win."[4]

The Bush advertising plan had three critical components. The first was to present a personable, likable candidate, one who would come across as an effective leader. As Janet Mullins, an official of the campaign's media group, put it, "We knew if people liked George Bush by seeing the George Bush we saw, they would like him."[5] Bush's early advertising pictured him as a family man playing with his grandchildren, in contrast to Dukakis's ads, which presented him as a state governor.

The second component of the Bush media strategy was to criticize Dukakis. Four issues on which Dukakis seemed particularly vulnerable were identified: crime, taxes, national security, and environmental cleanup. In each of these areas commercials were developed to distinguish Dukakis's beliefs from those of mainstream America and to challenge his competence to deal with these problems.

The third part of the Bush strategy was to present the Republican candidate as an effective leader of his party and as the person best able and most likely to maintain the peace and prosperity of the Reagan years. Here the White House was used as a backdrop, and Bush's role as vice-president was emphasized.

In contrast to the carefully planned television advertising that the Bush officials designed to supplement their campaign strategy, Dukakis's television commercials were inconsistent and inefficient. No plan built on campaign strategy was developed. Although some of the advertisements were individually competent, together they did not add up to a consistent message that reinforced the speeches and actions of the candidate on the campaign trail. Unlike the few Bush commercials that were repeated throughout the campaign, Dukakis's commercials changed constantly. Ads were produced that were not shown, shown but not tested, and aired but not repeated. As a consequence, Dukakis's advertising campaign did not achieve the impact that Bush's did.

## Technique

The advantage of advertising particularly on television is that there are no intermediaries. Nor is there any interference from television news analysts. Candidates can say and do what they want. The problem, however, is to make it look real. Candidate-sponsored programs are not unbiased, and the public knows it. Generating interest and convincing viewers are more difficult for advertisers than newscasters.

Thus, for advertising to be effective, it must be presented in a believable way. Having a candidate interact with people is one way of achieving credibility. The use of ordinary citizens rather than professional actors increases the sense of authenticity. Not only must media presentations appear authentic; they must seem realistic. When candidates are placed in situations in which they do not fit, visual media can do more damage than good. Such was the case when Dukakis's staff created a photo opportunity in which their candidate wore a helmet and rode in an army tank. The objective of the picture was to demonstrate Dukakis's sympathy for the military and his support for a strong defense. The situation, however, was so contrived and the candidate looked so silly that Roger Ailes produced a commercial for Bush in which the Dukakis photograph was featured. Ailes juxtaposed the picture of Dukakis in a tank with information about the Democratic candidate's opposition to a long list of military programs and weapons systems.

Underlining all television advertising is the need to maintain viewer interest, and interest is maintained by action: the ad must move. The

Carter campaign in 1976 was particularly skilled in creating viewer interest. Carter was seen walking on his farm, talking with local citizens, speaking to business and professional groups, and addressing the Democratic convention. His movement gave the impression of agility, of a person who was capable of meeting the heavy and multiple responsibilities of the presidency.

Political ads take many forms. The most popular ones from the perspective of the advertisers are the short spots of thirty and sixty seconds, which are interspersed with other commercials in regular programming. Longer advertisements that preempt part of the standard fare and full-length productions such as interviews, documentaries, and campaign rallies have also been employed. The primary benefits of the short spots are that they make a point, are cheaper to produce and air, and are usually viewed by a larger, more captive audience. Longer programs, which may go into greater detail about the candidate's career, qualifications, and beliefs, are generally seen by fewer people and usually the wrong ones—those who have already decided to vote for that candidate. While it may be necessary to energize these true believers and get them to the polls, the principal targets of most campaign advertising are the undecided and the indifferent. For them, the commercial must capture their attention, present a message, shape an image, and work toward motivating them to vote.

In addition to length, timing is also a critical consideration of campaign advertisers. When commercials are shown affects who will see them. Purchasing time slots is a specialized art, and campaign organizations hire experts to do it. Their object is to have the largest viewing audience or, in the jargon of the trade, the highest television rating.

For the candidate who appears to be ahead, the advertising should be scheduled at a steady rate over the course of the campaign to maintain the lead. Nixon in 1968 and 1972 and Carter in 1976 followed this practice. Reagan in 1984 and Bush in 1988 did not. Instead, with a lead in the polls and coverage in their official capacities, both decided to hold much of their advertising for the final weeks of the campaign, just in case a problem developed.[6] In contrast, Mondale and Dukakis were forced to run many of their commercials early and midway through their campaign to close the gap and improve their presidential images. If a candidate needs to catch up, however, a concentrated series of ads that builds toward the end of the campaign is more desirable, provided he is not too far behind. Humphrey in 1968 and Ford in 1976 adopted this approach.

Most campaign advertising must be sequenced as well. At the outset it is necessary to identify the candidate with information about his family, experience, and qualifications for the office. Once the personal dimension is established, the position of the candidate can be articulated in the second stage. In this argumentative phase the themes are presented and policy positions noted. In the third stage, the candidate frequently goes on the offensive. His campaign runs a series of negative ads in which the reasons not to vote for the opponent are stressed. Known as comparative or confrontational ads, they usually generate the most controversy, often leading to spirited defenses and counterattacks. Candidates like to end their campaign on a positive note. In the final phase, "feel good" commercials are shown. Replete with catchy and upbeat jingles, smiling faces, happy families, and much Americana, they strive to make voters feel good about supporting the candidate.[7]

Although most campaign advertising goes through these four stages, the periods frequently overlap. Different types of commercials are shown at the same time. In the 1988 elections, negative advertising was used by both candidates throughout the campaign to focus attention on the weaknesses of their opponents. There was so much emphasis on negative advertising in 1988 that negative ads themselves became an issue. The Dukakis campaign ran antinegative ads about Bush's negative advertising. In one such commercial Dukakis was pictured sitting in front of a television showing the Bush commercial that featured the photograph of Dukakis riding in a tank. Bush's commercial accused Dukakis of being against virtually every new weapons system. In the Dukakis commercial an angry Dukakis turned off the set and said: "I'm fed up with it. Haven't seen anything like it in twenty-five years of public life. George Bush's negative TV ads: distorting my record, full of lies, and he knows it." In general the candidate who is behind (as Bush was in the summer of 1988) uses negative ads to raise questions about the front-runner.

In addition to television advertising on the major networks, candidates usually supplement their appeals on radio, cable television, and in newspapers and magazines. Cheaper in cost, these communication vehicles normally reach a smaller but more clearly defined audience. As a consequence, advertisements on these media can be more effectively targeted to readers or listeners than can television commercials on the major networks. Computerized direct mail can be the most specific of all. It facilitates different people receiving different messages.[8]

## Content

The name of the game is image making. With the emphasis on leadership, it is essential to demonstrate those traits the public associates with the position. Three dimensions of presidential qualities are usually stressed: one has to do with character and persona, another with issue positions and basic values, and a third with the essential leadership skills of vision, charisma, and dispatch, the capability for getting things done. Positive campaign advertising is designed to project these qualities to bridge the gap between just another politician and one who is of presidential caliber.

**Positive Advertising.** Positive advertising emphasizes the strengths of a candidate. For presidents seeking reelection, or even vice-presidents running for the top office, one of those strengths is clearly experience in high office. Their advertising pictures them in a variety of presidential roles—meeting with the leaders of other governments, with members of Congress, and with their own top aides, presiding over official ceremonies, greeting visiting dignitaries, and working late and often alone in the Oval Office.

One of Jimmy Carter's most effective 1980 commercials showed him in a whirl of presidential activities ending as darkness fell over the White House. A voice intoned, "The responsibility never ends. Even at the end of a long working day there is usually another cable addressed to the Chief of State from the other side of the world where the sun is shining and something is happening." As a light came on in the president's living quarters, the voice concluded, "And he's not finished yet." Ronald Reagan in 1984 and George Bush in 1988 also took advantage of their positions as president and vice-president, respectively, in their presidential campaigns.

Comparisons are also important. While all candidates must demonstrate their presidential qualities, they also need to distinguish themselves from their opponents. In 1976, Carter emphasized his unusual leadership abilities. He was portrayed as a fresh, independent, people-oriented candidate who would provide new leadership. His slogan, "A leader, for a change," as well as his less formal appearance and even the deep green color of his literature in contrast to the traditional red, white, and blue, conveyed how different he was from the old-style Washington politician and the two previous Republican presidents.

In 1980 Reagan stressed his new solutions to the nation's old and persistent policy problems. In 1984 his commercials recounted his success: his strong leadership, defense buildup, and his no-nonsense attitude toward the Soviet Union. One of Mondale's difficulties in 1984 was that he could not claim to be new and different (as Carter could in 1976 and Reagan in 1980), nor could he match his opponent's perceived strong leadership and clear policy goals. Given the high performance ratings for President Reagan, Mondale was forced to focus on the future, contrasting his energy and flexibility with that of his seventy-four-year-old opponent.

Dukakis faced a similar predicament. He, too, needed to make the case for change; he, too, needed to stress his own capacity to lead the country effectively and in the right direction. He stressed his accomplishments as governor to demonstrate his ability to direct the country as president.

**Negative Advertising.** In addition to presenting a positive image, advertising may be designed to raise questions about an opponent. Ads that exploit an opponent's weaknesses by focusing on character deficiencies, issue inconsistencies, or false leadership claims are referred to as *confrontational* or *negative* advertising. This type of advertising has become a critical component of election strategy. In 1988, both candidates aired a great many negative ads. Of Bush's thirty-seven television ads, fourteen were negative. Forty percent of his television budget was spent on three of the most effective of these spots. Dukakis produced even more negative advertising. Almost half of his forty-seven ads that were scripted and aired for television were negative[9]

Criticism of the candidates, of course, is not new. In the past, the parties ritually sniped at each other's candidates and questioned their integrity, their experience, and their qualifications for the job. What seems to be different today is the increasing emphasis placed on these ads by the candidates; the extent to which they seem to have affected the tenor, agenda, and issues of the campaign; and the impact they are perceived to have on the electorate.

Instead of playing to a candidate's strength, negative advertising exploits the opposition's weaknesses. Perhaps the most famous (or infamous) negative political commercial was created by advertising executive Tony Schwartz in 1964 for use against Barry Goldwater. It was designed to reinforce the impression that Goldwater was a trigger-happy zealot who would not hesitate to use nuclear weapons against a communist foe. Pictured first was a little girl in a meadow plucking petals from a daisy. She counted to herself softly. When she reached nine, the picture froze on her face, her voice faded, and a stern-sounding male voice counted down from ten. When he got to zero there was an explosion, the little girl disappeared, and a mushroom-shaped cloud covered the screen. Lyndon Johnson's voice was heard: "These are the stakes—to make a world in which all of God's children can live, or go into the dark. We must either love each other, or we must die." The ad ended with an announcer saying, "Vote for President Johnson on November 3. The stakes are too high for you to stay home."

The commercial was run only once. Goldwater supporters were outraged and protested vigorously. Their protest kept the issue alive. In fact, the ad itself became a news item, and parts of it were shown on television newscasts. Schwartz had made the point stick.

In 1972 and 1976 the Republican candidates ran a series of very effective negative commercials. One showed a profile of McGovern, with an announcer stating a position that McGovern had taken and later changed. When the change in position was explained, another profile of McGovern, but one looking in the opposite direction, was flashed on the screen. This tactic of position change and profile rotation was repeated several times. Finally, when the announcer asked, "What about next year?" McGovern's face spun rapidly before viewers. A similar negative ad was directed against Carter in 1980.

In 1976, Ford's media advertisers created a very effective negative ad referred to as the "Man-in-the-Street" commercial. It began with interviews with a number of people in different areas of the country who indicated their preference for Ford. The focus then gradually changed. Some people were uncertain; others voiced reservations about Carter. Most convincing were the Georgia critics. "He didn't do anything," stated one man from Atlanta. "I've tried, and all my friends have tried, to remember exactly what Carter did as governor, and nobody really knows." The commercial concluded with an attractive woman, also from Georgia, saying, in a thick southern accent, "It would be nice to have a President from Georgia—but not Carter." She smiled. The ad ended.

The "Man-in-the-Street" commercial showed a contrast. It not only suggested that President Ford enjoyed broad support but also served to reinforce doubts about Carter, even among Georgians. Moreover, the fact that the people interviewed were not actors gave the ads more credibility. They seemed like news stories, and that was not coincidental. They were so effective, in fact, that most candidates now employ similar types of commercials in their primary and general election campaigns.

The presidential election of 1988 witnessed some of the most powerful and controversial negative advertising of recent presidential campaigns. It was powerful and controversial because it played on the fears and prejudices of the American people. It also stretched the truth and created false impressions.[10]

One ad in particular evoked a strong, emotional public response. It featured a mug shot of Willie Horton, a black prisoner who raped a white woman while on a weekend furlough from a Massachusetts jail. Directed at those who were fearful of crime, of blacks, and of liberals and their "do-good" social policies, the ad placed Dukakis squarely in the liberal, do-gooder camp. (See "The Willie Horton Ad: 'Weekend Passes.'")

Sponsored by a political action committee supporting Bush, not the official Bush campaign, this commercial was supplemented by other PAC ads featuring relatives of the victims of Horton's crimes, including a man whose wife had been raped by Horton and a woman whose brother had been stabbed by him. More than $2 million was spent by another pro-Bush PAC on speaking tours for these people who were personally touched by Horton's horrendous acts.[11]

The Bush campaign produced ads of its own to reinforce the crime issue and to differentiate Bush's and Dukakis's solutions to the problem. The most potent of these was called "Revolving Door." (See "The 'Revolving Door' Ad.")

The cumulative impact of Bush's crime ads was to leave the impression that Michael Dukakis released hardened criminals who then re-

# The Willie Horton Ad:
## "Weekend Passes"

| VIDEO | AUDIO |
|---|---|
| Side-by-side photographs | An announcer says, "Bush and Dukakis on Crime." |
| Photograph of Bush | "Bush supports the death penalty for first-degree murderers." |
| Photograph of Dukakis | "Dukakis not only opposes the death penalty, he allowed first-degree murderers to have weekend passes from prison." |
| Mug shot of Willie Horton | "One was Willie Horton, who murdered a boy in a robbery, stabbing him nineteen times." |

| | |
|---|---|
| Photograph of convict being arrested. | "Despite a life sentence, Horton received ten weekend passes from prison. Horton fled, kidnapped a young couple, stabbing the man and repeatedly raping his girlfriend." |
| Photograph of Dukakis | "Weekend prison passes. Dukakis on crime." |

*Source:* "A 30-Second Ad on Crime," *New York Times*, November 3, 1988, p. B20.

committed their heinous crimes on innocent victims. By the end of the campaign 25 percent of the electorate knew who Willie Horton was, what he did, and who furloughed him; 49 percent thought Dukakis was soft on crime.[12]

The negative ads seemed to have an effect. Unfavorable perceptions of Dukakis increased, while those of Bush remained relatively constant. Table 7–1 indicates the positive and negative perceptions of the candidates over the course of the campaign.

The increasing number of negative advertisements combined with their perceived effect on the voters has generated a debate over this type of campaign message. Media consultants argue that negative advertising serves an important purpose; it reveals information about a candidate that might portend problems in his presidency, such as a propensity to falsify information, or engage in unethical activities or illegal behavior. For a position in which character and leadership are inextricably intertwined, such as the presidency, such information is deemed necessary for the electorate to make an intelligent judgment about which candidate they consider to be the best qualified for the job.

Moreover, the people who subscribe to this argument also point out that mudslinging has been a part of the American political tradition since presidential campaigns have occurred. In an op-ed piece written for *The Washington Post*, Charlie Paul Freund points out that George Washington was called a philanderer and a thief; Andrew Jackson was accused of marrying a prostitute; at the outset of the Civil War Abraham

## TABLE 7–1
### Perceptions of the Candidates

| | Dukakis | | Bush | |
|---|---|---|---|---|
| Date | *Favorable* | *Unfavorable* | *Favorable* | *Unfavorable* |
| July 8–10, prior to the Democratic convention | 57 | 31 | 52 | 40 |
| August 5–7, prior to the Republican convention | 61 | 30 | 51 | 42 |
| September 5, after the Republican convention | 48 | 34 | 53 | 33 |
| October 1 | 42 | 41 | 52 | 34 |
| November 1 | 40 | 45 | 49 | 37 |
| Election day, November 8 | 45 | 44 | 53 | 37 |

*Source:* KRC Hotline, reprinted in Peter Goldman, Tom Mathews, et al. *The Quest for the Presidency: The 1988 Campaign* (New York: Simon and Schuster, 1989), pp. 420–22.

## The "Revolving Door" Ad

| VIDEO | AUDIO |
|---|---|
| A guard with a rifle climbs the circular stairs of a prison watchtower. The words "The Dukakis Furlough Program" are superimposed on the bottom of the prison visual. | Dissonant sounds are heard: a drum . . . music . . . metal stairs. An announcer says, "As governor, Michael Dukakis vetoed mandatory sentences for drug dealers." |
| A guard with a gun walks along a barbed wire fence. | "He vetoed the death penalty." |
| A revolving door formed by bars rotates as men in prison clothing walk in and back out the door in a long line. The words "268 Escaped" are superimposed. | "His revolving-door prison policy gave weekend furloughs to first-degree murderers not eligible for parole." |
| The camera comes in for a closer shot of the prisoners in slow motion revolving through the door. | "While out, many committed other crimes like kidnapping and rape." |
| The words "And Many Are Still At Large" are superimposed. | "And many are still at large." |
| The picture changes to a guard on a roof with a watchtower in the background. | "Now Michael Dukakis says he wants to do for America what he's done for Massachusetts." |
| A small color picture of Bush appears, and the words "Paid for by Bush/Quayle 88" appear in small print. | "American can't afford that risk!" |

*Source:* L. Patrick Devlin, "Contrasts in Presidential Campaign Commercials of 1988," *American Behavioral Scientist* 32, no. 4 (March/April 1989): 389.

Lincoln was charged with being illegitimate and black; Theodore Roosevelt was said to be a drunkard, Herbert Hoover a German sympathizer during World War I, and Franklin D. Roosevelt a lecher, lunatic, and a closet Jew whose real name was Rosenfeldt. Despite these allegations, the public was not duped and elected these individuals to the presidency.[13]

Opponents of negative campaigning, however, point to the damage that such advertising can do to the candidates, the electorate, and the political system. Negative campaigns can unfairly tarnish a candidate's reputation. They can distort the truth about a person, mislead the electorate, and divert its focus from important policy and partisan issues.

Their impact is often enlarged by the attention they receive. Scandalous attacks, frequently unsubstantiated, are regularly reported and prominently featured in the news. They become part of the campaign debate and affect short- and long-term public perceptions of the candidates. In 1988, rumors that Michael Dukakis had been twice treated for depression by a psychiatrist were spread and even given impetus by an off-handed joke that President Reagan uttered in which he referred to the Democratic candidate as "an invalid." Despite Reagan's apology and a statement by Dukakis's doctor that the candidate was in excellent health, Dukakis's ratings in the polls dropped 8 percent.[14]

In addition to damaging a candidate in the eyes of the voters and reducing the electoral support that candidate may receive, negative advertisements can have a wide-reaching, depressing effect on the electorate. They contribute to lower voter turnout, less confidence in political leaders, and less trust in government. In an era in which highly personalized, negative campaigning seems to be on the rise, is it any wonder that cynicism and apathy continue to plague the American people?

## UNCONTROLLED MEDIA

From the perspective of image building, political advertising gives the campaign the most control over what the voters see. The environment can be predetermined, the words and pictures can be created and coordinated, and the candidate can be rehearsed to produce the desired effect. Moreover, the message can be targeted.

News events are more difficult to influence. A candidate's media advisers do not control the environment, nor do they produce the product. In some cases, the message is partially mediated by the structure of the event. Interviews and debates provide a format that shapes but does not always direct the discussion. In other cases, the message and the image are directly affected by the media's orientation. Remarks are edited for the sake of the story. A candidate can be interrupted, his comments interpreted, and his policies evaluated. Major statements can even be ignored—especially when hecklers are present or if the candidate makes some goof, such as slipping or even bumping his head. Under these circumstances, aspirants for the presidency exercise much less leverage. They are not powerless, however.

## *Debates*

Candidates have viewed presidential debates as a way to improve their image and damage their opponent's image. The first series of televised debates occurred in 1960. Kennedy wanted to counter the impression that he was too young and inexperienced. Nixon, on the other hand, sought to maintain his stature as Eisenhower's knowledgeable and competent vice-president and the obvious person to succeed his "boss" in office. For a summary of presidential debates, see Table 7–2.

In the three elections that followed, Johnson and then Nixon, both ahead in the polls, saw no advantage in debating their opponents and refused to do so. Ford, however, trailed Carter in 1976. He saw debates

TABLE 7–2
### Presidential Debates, 1960–1988

| 1960 | John Kennedy v. Richard Nixon |
|---|---|
| September 26 | Chicago, Ill. |
| October 7 | Washington, D.C. |
| October 13 | Split screen: |
| | Kennedy in New York, N.Y. |
| | Nixon in Hollywood, Calif. |
| October 21 | New York City |
| **1976** | **Jimmy Carter v. Gerald Ford** |
| September 23 | Philadelphia, Pa. |
| October 6 | San Francisco, Calif. |
| October 15, Vice-presidental candidates: | Houston, Tex. |
| Walter Mondale v. Robert Dole | |
| October 22 | Williamsburg, Va. |
| **1980** | **Jimmy Carter v. Ronald Reagan** |
| October 18 | Cleveland, Ohio |
| **1984** | **Walter Mondale v. Ronald Reagan** |
| October 7 | Louisville, Ky. |
| October 11, Vice-presidential candidates: | Philadelphia, Pa. |
| Geraldine Ferraro v. George Bush | |
| October 21 | Kansas City, Mo. |
| **1988** | **Michael Dukakis v. George Bush** |
| September 25 | Winston-Salem, N.C. |
| October 5 | Omaha, Nebr. |
| October 13 | Los Angeles, Calif. |

as an opportunity to appear presidential and to chip away at his Democratic rival's "soft" backing. The Carter camp, on the other hand, saw them as a means of shoring up Carter's support. In 1980 the rationale was similar. From Reagan's perspective, it was a way to reassure voters about himself and his qualifications for office. For Carter, it was another chance to emphasize the differences between himself and Reagan, between their parties, and between their issue and ideological positions.

By 1984 presidential debates had become a recognized institution that even incumbents could not avoid without making their avoidance an issue. Thus Ronald Reagan was forced by the pressures of public opinion to debate Walter Mondale, even though he stood to gain little, and could have lost much, from their face-to-face encounter. And four years later, George Bush had to debate Michael Dukakis because debates had become part of the American political tradition.

One reason that debates have become such an integral component of the presidential electoral process is that they regularly attract great interest and many viewers, more than any other single event of the entire campaign. It is estimated that more than half the adult population of the United States watched all the Kennedy-Nixon debates and that almost 90 percent saw one of them.[15] The first Carter-Ford debate in 1976 attracted an estimated 90–100 million viewers, while the Carter-Reagan debate and Mondale-Reagan debates had audiences approaching 125 million. Audience estimates of the 1988 debates were much lower, in the range of 60 million.[16]

While presidential debates are here to stay, their number, scheduling, and format are still subject to considerable negotiation between the principal contenders and their staffs. In these negotiations incumbents and front-runners have an advantage. Carter refused to debate John Anderson in 1980; Reagan set the parameters for the debates with Mondale in 1984, as did Bush for the two meetings with Dukakis and the one between the vice-presidential candidates in 1988.[17]

Despite the appearance of spontaneity, debates are highly scripted. Careful preparation is now a must. Representatives of the candidates study the locations, try to anticipate the questions, and prepare written answers for their candidates. Mock studios are built and the debate environment simulated. The opponent's speeches and interviews are carefully studied for content, style, and other nuances. They are then used in dress rehearsals by stand-ins who imitate the opponent in debate. Here's how *Newsweek* reporters Goldman, Mathews, and others described Bush's preparation before his second meeting with his Democratic opponent:

> Bush's training camp . . . had a relaxed air, given the stakes. His homework was cooked down from a thick, tab-divided ring binder to fifty tight pages, plain-spoken enough to be accessible and thin

enough to be held together by a single clip at the top; there was less to read, but, as he would sheepishly let on to [Roger] Ailes long after, he gave it more time.

His dining room was once again converted into a sound stage for two mock debates, authentic down to the lecterns and the blue backdrop, and [Richard] Darman was waiting to play Dukakis, better, some thought, than the real thing. Bush showed up feeling offish and grumpy for the first run-through, cutting it short before the closing statements to go do a campaign event. But his performance was sharp and self-assured, ready . . . for prime time.[18]

In 1980 the elaborate preparation had taken a bizarre twist. The Reagan campaign obtained one of Carter's three briefing books. The book contained key lines, Reagan quotes, and pat answers. Knowing the quotes Carter would use, the questions he anticipated, and the answers he was advised to give helped Reagan's strategists prepare their responses to use in rebuttal. In general, all debate participants with the exception of Nixon, in his first debate with Kennedy, have been well prepared.[19] But not all have been feeling well. Nixon had bumped his knee on a car door going into the television studio for that first debate and was in pain during his first debate with Kennedy. Dukakis had a viral flu, with a fever of 101°F and a sore throat during his second debate with Bush.[20]

Much calculation goes into debate strategy. Candidates need to decide what issues to stress and how to stress them; how to catch their opponents off guard or goad them into an error; whether and how to respond to a personal attack and to criticism of their policy positions.

In his first debate with Bush, Dukakis had three strategic objectives: take the offensive and go after Bush; criticize Quayle as unqualified for the vice-presidency; and make the case for economic change.[21] Bush had two: paint Dukakis into a liberal corner, and convey himself as a warm and decent human being. Three weeks later, when they faced one another again with Bush still in the lead, the debate was seen as Dukakis's last opportunity to affect the outcome of the election. Dukakis had to win. All Bush needed to do, on the other hand, was to maintain the status quo. For him a satisfactory performance was one in which he made no mistakes, sounded confident, and gave acceptable but general responses—all of which he did.

In addition to their strategic emphases, candidates have also used style to achieve an effect. Kennedy and Carter talked faster than their opponents to create an action-oriented psychology in the minds of the viewers. Both tried to demonstrate their knowledge by citing many facts and statistics in their answers. Ford and Reagan spoke in more general terms, expressing particular concern about the size and structure of government. Reagan's wit and anecdotes in 1980 and Bush's manner in 1988 conveyed a human dimension with which viewers could identify in contrast to Carter's and Dukakis's all-business, rapid-fire, machinelike responses.

The reason style is so important is that the public reacts more to the overall performance of the candidates than to any of their specific arguments.[22] The media contribute to this reaction by their emphasis on controversy and on personality. In several instances, they have directly affected the images candidates were trying to project. By highlighting Ford's statement during his second debate with Carter that the Soviet Union did not dominate Eastern Europe, network commentators damaged the president's claim to be more capable and knowledgeable in foreign affairs; their reaction to Dukakis's response to the "what-if" question about his wife had a similar effect (see "A Nonemotional Response"). It reinforced his image as an "ice man."

The media have tended to assess debates in terms of winners and losers.[23] Their evaluation conditions how the public judges the results. Since most people do not follow the content very closely and do not put much faith in their own evaluation, media commentary can have a considerable impact on public opinion. It can modify the immediate impressions people have, moving the public's assessment in the direction of an acknowledged winner. This effect occurred in 1976 and again in 1980.

It is difficult to pinpoint precisely the impact of the debates on voting, however. Perceptions of the candidates change over the course of the campaign. Debates may contribute to these altered perceptions, but other factors contribute as well. It is easier to evaluate the short-run impact of debates on public opinion by conducting before-and-after surveys.

There seems to be a two-stage reaction. In stage one, which occurs in the twenty-four hours following the debate, opinions are influenced primarily by partisan orientations and previously held views. The tendency is to see one's own candidate in the more favorable light. In stage two, which occurs a day or two after the debate, the media's reporting of public reaction, combined with fading memories of the debate, can reinforce or alter the public's initial judgment. After that, the impact of the debate becomes more difficult to discern.

Ford's second debate with Carter is an excellent illustration of this second-stage effect. Surveys taken within the first twelve hours following the debate indicated that viewers, by almost 2:1 believed Ford had won. Few mentioned his remarks on Eastern Europe. Polls taken two to three days after the debate, however, presented a very different picture. By more than 2:1 Carter was perceived the winner. In 1980 the percentage of people believing Reagan to be the victor over Carter almost doubled within four days following their one debate. The Dukakis-Bush debates did not seem to have altered the general beliefs of the voters or their evaluation of the candidates. Although there is some evidence of a very modest, second-stage effect after the vice-presidential and second presidential debates in 1988. These effects faded, however, during the final weeks of the campaign. (See Table 7–3.)

With so many people watching, the shaping of perceptions about the candidates' personal attributes and their policy positions can influence the outcome of a close election. The effect of the debate, however, tends to vary with the attitudes and opinions of those watching it. For partisans, the debate tends to solidify support. Those who are more involved are more likely to watch the debates; those who are more knowledgeable are more likely to learn from them; those who are most

## TABLE 7–3
### Public Opinion during and after the 1988 Debates

| Stage | Date | Public Support of the Candidates | |
|---|---|---|---|
| | | *Dukakis* | *Bush* |
| **First Presidential Debate** | | | |
| I | September 25 | 38 | 50 |
| | September 26 | 38 | 50 |
| II | September 27 | 41 | 48 |
| | September 28 | 42 | 47 |
| | September 29 | 41 | 46 |
| | September 30 | | |
| **Vice-Presidential Debate** | | | |
| I | October 5 | 39 | 49 |
| | October 6 | 39 | 48 |
| II | October 7 | 39 | 49 |
| | October 8 | 40 | 48 |
| | October 9 | 42 | 48 |
| | October 10 | 41 | 48 |
| **Second Presidential Debate** | | | |
| I | October 13 | 41 | 47 |
| | October 14 | 40 | 48 |
| II | October 15 | 39 | 47 |
| | October 16 | 39 | 47 |
| | October 17 | 39 | 48 |
| | October 18 | 40 | 47 |
| | | 39 | 49 |

*Source:* KRC Hotline, reported in Peter Goldman, Tom Mathews, et al., *The Quest for the Presidency: The 1988 Campaign* (New York: Simon and Schuster, 1989), pp. 421–22.

partisan are more apt to be convinced by them. People root for their candidate. The debate confirms their perceptions. It makes them more likely to vote for their party's nominee.

For weaker partisans and independents, the debates can increase interest and can clarify, color, or even change perceptions. Before debating, Kennedy was thought by many to be less knowledgeable and less experienced than Nixon; Carter was seen as an enigma, as fuzzier than Ford; Reagan was perceived to be more doctrinaire and less informed than his first Democratic opponent, President Carter. The debates enabled each of these candidates to overcome these negative perceptions. In the end the debates proved to be important to the success of their candidacies.

Kennedy and Carter might not have won without the debates. Reagan probably would not have won by as much in 1980. In 1984 and again in 1988, the debates did not affect Reagan's and Bush's support in any appreciable way, although they did create the "age" issue in 1984, which might have become a factor had Reagan faltered during the second debate (which he did not do).

The experiences of Kennedy in 1960, Carter in 1976, and Reagan in 1980 suggest why debates tend to help challengers more than incumbents. Being less well-known, challengers have more questions raised about them, their competence, and their capacity to be president. The debates provide them with an opportunity to satisfy some of these doubts in a believable setting and on a comparative basis. By appearing to be at least the equal of their incumbent opponents, the challenger's image as a potential president is enhanced.

## News Coverage

News coverage is not likely to benefit a candidate in the same manner as debates or interviews do. The *modus operandi* of news reporting is to inform and interest the public. Rather than improve an image, news coverage can distort or destroy it.

Knowing how the media cover the campaign is critical to understanding how campaign organizations can affect the media. Most people follow presidential campaigns on television. It is the prime source of news for approximately two-thirds of the population.[24] Newspapers are a distant second, with only 20 percent of the population listing them as their principal source of news. Radio and magazines trail far behind.

News on television seems more believable. People can see what is happening. Being an action-oriented, visual medium, television reports the drama and excitement of the campaign. It does so by emphasizing the candidates and their campaign: How are they doing? What is their strategy? Who is ahead? It is the campaign as contest that provides the principal focus for television, as well as for the print medium.

This focus on the: "horse race" serves two primary purposes. It heightens viewers' interests; and higher interest, in turn, increases the audience and the profits, since advertising revenue is based on the estimated number of people watching a particular program. Second, it gives the media, both print and electronic, an aura of objectivity. Rather than presenting subjective reports of policy positions and their consequences, they can provide more objective data on the public's reaction to the campaign. One evidence of the attention given to the public during the election cycle is the increasing involvement of the major news organizations in the business of polling. But polling is expensive, so media that conduct polls regularly report them as news stories. During the primaries and caucuses, particularly at the beginning of the nomination process, polls are frequently the dominant story. In the general election other campaign issues, especially those that pertain to the candidates' characters, and strategies, and tactics, receive more attention.

This trend is not new. It predates television. Newspapers in the nineteenth and early twentieth centuries also covered campaigns as if they were sporting events, homing in on the contest between the combatants, not primarily on the policy issues and their impact on the country. One study of newspaper coverage in six elections over a hundred-year period, from 1888 to 1988, reported that the substance of campaign coverage had not changed all that much.[25]

Changes in media content have occurred. More empirical data have been provided by the emphasis on polling. With more people watching the campaign on television rather than reading about it in the press, there has been attention placed on personal images. But concern with who is going to win, how the candidates are doing, and how their campaigns reflect their capacity to govern has been a constant. In 1976 Thomas Patterson found about 60 percent of television election coverage and 55 percent of newspaper coverage devoted to the campaign as a contest.[26] Michael J. Robinson and Margaret Sheehan's analysis of "CBS Evening News" during the 1980 election revealed that five out of six stories emphasized the competition.[27]

Coverage in 1988 also reflected this general pattern. However, there were distinct differences between the primaries and the general election. In the primaries, the horse race was the dominant story. (See Chapter 4.) In the general election, issues of the campaign, such as Bush's attacks, Dukakis's ineffective responses, and Quayle's qualifications for vice-president, were the most frequent news stories. In a content analysis of 735 stories on the presidential election on the three major networks from August 19, 1988, to election day, Robert Lichter and his associates found the horse race had become less newsworthy than stories about the campaign itself and the candidates' barbs at one another.[28]

In contrast, policy issues have been relatively neglected. There is little in-depth analysis of the substantive policy questions. Nor is there much discussion of what difference it would make for the country who wins. The study of the "CBS Evening News" in 1980 revealed an average of only ninety seconds per program spent on issues of policy, approximately 20–25 percent of the total election coverage.[29] In 1984 no policy question received the attention that Geraldine Ferraro's finances or Ronald Reagan's age did.[30] In 1988, however, policy issues received more attention. Lichter and his associates identified 282 stories on policy issues on the evening news. Of these, crime, defense, and the economy were the primary focus.[31] That these were the issues that Bush emphasized in his speeches and commercials indicates that his campaign was successful in controlling the media's agents.

The dominance of campaign issues in media coverage encourages the candidates *not* to be spontaneous, *not* to be candid, *not* to make mistakes. It elevates the importance of image creation and reduces the incentive to provide much detailed, issue-specific information. This emphasis, in turn, practically forces the electorate to base its decision on candidate traits and general orientations more than on policy positions.

Not only do the media focus primarily on the candidates, they focus primarily on the major party candidates. As aspirants for the nomination, candidates receive coverage roughly in proportion to their popular standing, with the front-runners receiving the most. After the conventions are over, it becomes a two-person contest. Minority party and independent candidates receive little, if any, attention. The exception was independent candidate John Anderson in 1980. He obtained one-fourth the coverage given to Reagan and Carter.[32]

Once the general election campaign begins, both major party candidates get approximately the same amount of coverage. Contrary to popular belief, incumbents seeking reelection do not dominate the news.[33] However, when coverage is critical, incumbents do tend to receive more of it than do their challengers. In 1980, Jimmy Carter was treated more harshly than Ronald Reagan, and in 1984, Reagan was treated more harshly than Walter Mondale. Vice-President Bush fared the worst of all in that election. Maura Clancey and Michael Robinson's study of the evening news on the three major networks found no favorable story on Bush during the entire 1984 campaign![34]

Bush's coverage did not improve significantly in 1988. However, his opponent's coverage was equally unfavorable. Both received twice as many negative comments as positive ones. Quayle, however, received the worst coverage of all, particularly during the weeks following his nomination and after his debate with Democrat Lloyd Bentsen. Lichter and his associates report that only 21 percent of the stories on him were favorable.[35]

Notwithstanding the critical judgments of the print and electronic media, the vast majority of coverage tends to be neutral rather than critical. The media, particularly television, do not evidence an *ideological bias*.[36] Conservatives are treated neither better nor worse than liberals.

According to Clancey and Robinson, three out of four campaign stories in 1984 had no favorable or unfavorable "spin" at all.[37]

The media do, however, have a *journalistic bias,* an orientation to infuse politics with a sense of drama, to tap the human dimension, and to simplify and explain complex statements, issues, and events. As with the debates, this framework is couched in terms of winners and losers: how the candidates stand in the polls, how they interact with the voters, and how they differ from each other on a few major issues. Another reason policy questions do not generate the amount of coverage that candidate issues do is that they are not easily cast within such a framework. What is new and unexpected is newsworthy. What is old and predictable is not. A fresh face winning and an experienced candidate losing are news; an experienced one winning and a new one losing are not. Similarly, stump speeches and canned answers are not reported as frequently as are verbal slips, inconsistent statements, and mistakes. In fact, there has been an increase in the reporting of minor misstatements and slips of the tongue. Kiku Adatto reported that "only once in 1968 did a network even take note of a minor incident unrelated to the content of the campaign. In 1988 some twenty-nine reports highlighted trivial slips."[38]

Roger Ailes, Bush's media director, described the penchant of press to emphasize the foul-ups and mishaps as his "orchestra pit theory of politics":

> Let's face it, there are three things that the media are interested in: pictures, mistakes, and attacks. That's the one sure way of getting coverage. You try to avoid as many mistakes as you can. You try to give them as many pictures as you can. And if you need coverage, you attack, and you will get coverage.
>
> It's my orchestra pit theory of politics. If you have two guys on stage and one says, "I have a solution to the Middle East problem," and the other guy falls in the orchestra pit, who do you think is going to be on the evening news?[39]

Even a candidate's failure to provide the media with information or pictures they desire can be a source of admonishment. Take the comment that ABC correspondent Sam Donaldson made to Michael Dukakis, who was playing a trumpet with a local marching band in the midst of the 1988 presidential campaign. Donaldson reported, "He played the trumpet with his back to the camera." As Dukakis played the Democratic victory tune, "Happy Days Are Here Again," Donaldson could be heard saying off-camera, "We're over here governor."[40]

Television has an additional bias. As an action-oriented, visual medium, its content must move quickly and be capable of being projected as an image on a screen. It emphasizes pictures and de-emphasizes words; less attention is devoted to what candidates say and more to how people react to their words and images. The average length of a quotation from candidates on the evening news in 1968 was 42.3 seconds. In 1988, it was 9.8 seconds.[41]

Candidates and their advisers understand television's orientation toward action. They know they must take it into account when trying to affect the quantity and quality of coverage they receive. That is why they play the expectations game, why they speak in carefully calculated language, why they promise to solve the nation's problems but tend to do so without detailing their solutions.

The tactics used to influence the media are many and varied. They include the timing and staging of events, the access given to reporters, and the release of favorable information. Major announcements are made early enough to get on the evening news. Speeches are timed to maximize the viewing audience. Quiet periods, such as Saturday, are considered a good time to hold a press conference, schedule interviews, or provide a taped radio message. In addition to receiving same-day coverage by television, a Saturday event usually gets prominent treatment in the Sunday paper, which tends to have a larger circulation than do papers published on weekdays.

Campaign events are now carefully staged for television. Crowds are compacted. Excitement is generated. Complexity is simplified. Candidates talk in *media bites*—short, pithy statements that sound good and can be presented in the few seconds given to the candidate's remarks by television news. Catchy expressions such as "Where's the beef?" "It's morning in America," and "Read my lips" are used.

Access is a valuable commodity. So is the careful release of information, not only position papers but items on the personal lives of candidates and their families. To a large extent, those who report the news are dependent on this material. An analysis of news stories in twenty papers in 1968 found that candidates were the principal source of more than half of them.[42] Similar findings were reported in the 1980 campaign.[43]

In summary, there is both tension and cooperation between the media and the candidate. The tension is compounded by the media's need to highlight controversy and accentuate the negative and the candidate's desire to suppress unfavorable news. The cooperation is generated by the media's need for information and access and the candidate's desire to accentuate the positive. The key questions are: What impact does all this have on the voters? How does media coverage affect image creation during the campaign? The final section of this chapter proposes some answers to these questions.

## THE IMPACT OF THE MEDIA

The time, money, and energy spent on image building suggest that it has a major impact on voting behavior. Why else would so many resources be devoted to the media effort? Yet it is difficult to document the precise effect. There is little tangible evidence to support the propositions that television changes people's minds about the candidates and the issues, or that news programs raise the level of public knowledge, or that mass appeals affect many voting decisions.

Studies of campaigning in the 1940s indicated that the principal impact of the media was to activate predispositions and reinforce attitudes rather than to convert voters. Newspapers and magazines provided information, but primarily to those who were most committed. The most committed, in turn, used the information to support their beliefs. Weeding out opposing views, they insulated themselves from unfavorable news and from opinions that conflicted with their own.[44]

With the bulk of campaign information coming from printed matter in the 1940s, voters, particularly partisan voters, tended to minimize cross-pressures and to strengthen their own preexisting judgments. In contrast, the less committed also had less incentive to become informed. They maintained their ignorance by avoiding information about the campaign. The format of newspapers and magazines facilitated this kind of selective perception and retention.

Television might have been expected to change this. It exposes the less committed to more information and the more committed to other points of view. Avoidance is more difficult, since viewers are more captive to the picture than to the printed page.

While the same events get reported, the reports often differ. Robinson and Sheehan found the news on television to be "more mediating, more political, more personal, more critical, [and] more thematic than old-style print." Newspapers describe events. They indicate what candidates say and do. Television presents drama. It is more than entertaining. It provides a visual slice of reality, *not* a compendium of people, places, and things. In this way it mediates between candidates and the public more than newspapers do. It is also more analytic and more negative. Robinson and Sheehan report, "In the end, every major candidate in Campaign '80 got a more critical press on CBS than on UPI, explicitly or implicitly."[45]

The amount of coverage also differs. Television compartmentalizes. The evening news fits a large number of stories into a thirty-minute broadcast (which includes only twenty-three minutes of news). Of necessity, this time frame restricts the time that can be devoted to each item. Campaign stories average ninety seconds on the evening news, the equivalent of only a few paragraphs of a printed account. Their brevity helps explain why viewers do not retain much information from television coverage.

Two political scientists, Thomas E. Patterson and Robert D. Mc-Clure, who studied how television reported the news during the 1972 campaign, found:

1. Most election issues are mentioned so infrequently that viewers could not possibly learn about them.
2. Most issue references are so fleeting that they could not be expected to leave an impression on viewers.
3. The candidates' issue positions generally were reported in ways guaranteed to make them elusive.

"Television news adds little to the average voter's understanding of election issues," they concluded. "Network news may be fascinating. It may be highly entertaining. But it is simply not informative."[46]

Nonetheless, network news is still important. Along with the written press, it helps set the agenda for the campaign. Its emphasis or lack of emphasis on certain issues affects the content of the debate, the attention that the candidates must give to specific policy questions, and, to some extent, the kinds of responses they have to provide. Emphasis on the network news can be particularly significant for certain types of issues, such as foreign affairs, space exploration, or even the behavior of public officials, that do not have as direct an impact on the voters as do certain domestic issues, particularly those that pertain to economic well-being and personal security. Unlike these domestic concerns, the other types of issues might not seem as salient had they not been stressed by the media.

The need to emphasize the contest affects which issues are covered when issues *are* covered. The media focus on those issues that provide clear-cut differences between the candidates, those that provoke controversy, and those that can be presented in a simple, straightforward manner. Although policy positions of the candidates may be reported, these positions are not usually described in detail, much less analyzed. Nor are personal histories or public records of the principal candidates explored in any depth. With the great emphasis on the horse race and hoopla, it is no wonder that people learn so little about their voting choices from the news.

Where, then, do people receive information? One of the most interesting findings of the Patterson and McClure study is that people actually get more information from the advertisements they see on television than from the evening news. The reason seems to be that ads are more repetitive, more compact, and more focused than the news. When placed with other commercials during popular shows, they are difficult to avoid.[47] In fact, studies have shown that television watchers pay about twice as much attention to political advertisements as they do to other kinds of commercials.[48]

The amount of attention people devote to ads relates to their partisanship as well. According to political scientist Diana Owen, partisans are apt to be more attentive to commercials of their own party's candidates than to those of their opponents. Similarly, they tend to evaluate their candidate's commercials more favorably. Owen also found differences in levels of exposure and attention between supporters of the leading and trailing candidates, with those backing the losing candidate more informed. She speculated that supporters of the underdog needed to validate their candidate preferences with more information.[49]

Do the media affect the election? Do they influence the vote? The answer is yes. They do so by setting the agenda. They do so by providing the criteria by which much of the electorate evaluates the candidates, primarily their potential for leadership. But the influence of the media is limited by the stability of public beliefs and political attitudes, by the compartmentalization of the news and the neutrality of the reporting, and by the lack of attention given to the media by much of the general public.

In general, the effect varies with preexisting beliefs. It tends to reinforce the loyalties of strong partisans rather than challenge those loyalties. The campaign is simply too short, the defenses of these partisans too resilient, and the news too vacuous for large-scale changes of attitude to occur. For those without strong partisan identities, and those who are marginally interested in the election but have limited knowledge about the candidates and issues, television in particular may alter perceptions, although it usually does not change opinions or even improve knowledge of substantive policy issues. What happens is that some people begin to see the candidates in a different light. They are persuaded to vote for or against a particular individual.

The media are apt to be more influential during the preconvention period, when less is known about the candidates and when partisan affiliation is not a factor. However, with the decline of strong partisanship in the electorate and the increase in the number of independents, the audience that may be affected in this manner during the general election has become larger and is potentially more malleable for a longer period. Consequently campaigns spend a great deal of time and energy on media advertising from the very beginning of the electoral cycle and try to affect news coverage of their candidates throughout the campaign.

## SUMMARY

The presentation and projection of images are important to a presidential campaign because the electorate's assessment of the candidates, issues, and parties affects its voting behavior. Influencing that assessment is the goal of the image makers. They work on the assumption that what candidates say affects their image and that their image, in turn, affects their chances of winning the election.

The increasing dependence on television as a communications medium has forced greater emphasis to be placed on candidate images and less on the party and policy issues. Candidates try to project images that embody traits people desire in their presidents. These include the strong, decisive, intelligent, and knowledgeable leadership endemic to the office plus the warmth, empathy, sincerity, candor, and integrity desirable for the individual who occupies it.

Images must be conveyed primarily through the media. Relatively few people come into direct contact with the candidates. The objective of the campaign organizations in communicating information is, of course, very different from that of the media in covering the campaign. Thus the task from the candidate's perspective is to get the message across as clearly, as frequently, and as cogently as possible.

The easiest (and also the most costly) way to get the message across is to air an advertisement that sells the candidate much as any product is marketed (frequently by the same people who market those products). Advertising can tap positive or negative dimensions of personality. It can be targeted and timed to maximize its impact. It can even be made to look like news. The more credible the ad, the more the appeal resonates with the electorate's perceptions, beliefs, and values, the more likely it will have an effect.

Candidates try to distinguish their message by its thematic content. Presidents Kennedy and Carter stressed activity and decisiveness in the aftermath of conservative Republican years. Johnson and Nixon promised mainstream politics, in contrast to their more reactionary or radical opponents. Ford pointed to his decency and honesty in a not-so-subtle contrast to his Republican predecessor. Reagan and Bush articulated basic values, utilized traditional symbols, and advocated conservative policies as the best way to meet the country's economic and military needs. Both criticized the liberalism of their opponents who tried to make the case for change and for their greater competence to deal with future problems.

In addition to political advertising, there are other ways of influencing perceptions through the media. Candidates exercise considerable discretion in the words they use and the demeanor they present in interviews, in debates, and even on the news. Despite the appearance of spontaneity, their comments are carefully prepared and well rehearsed. In fact, throughout the entire campaign, public utterances are almost always made and actions taken with the press in mind.

How the media cover campaigns affects how candidates attempt to influence that coverage. The media emphasize the contest. They highlight drama and give controversial statements and events the most attention. There is little a campaign organization can do to affect that focus or divert attention from major blunders and conflicts. There is much, however, it can do to affect the regular reporting of everyday events of the campaign. Its release of information, its timing and staging of activities, and even the access provided the candidate and his senior aides can influence the quantity and quality of coverage and thereby affect the image that is projected to the public.

The overall impact of the media varies with the type of communication. The print medium tends to attract a smaller but better-educated, higher-income, more professional audience than do radio and television. Newspapers and magazines require more active involvement of their readers than television does of its viewers, but they also facilitate selective perception to a larger extent. Television, on the other hand, has a more captive and passive audience.

None of the media emphasizes policy issues. Instead they focus on the principal candidates in action, capsuling the major events of their day. To some extent paid media coverage compensates for this focus by providing more substantive information in addition to the favorable or unfavorable profiles it presents. The debates also convey the candidate's general orientation on policy matters.

What effect does the media have on the voters? The literature suggests that newspapers and magazines work primarily to activate and reinforce existing attitudes. For strong party identifiers, television does the same. For weaker partisans and independents, however, television can alter perceptions of the candidates, although it is unlikely in the short run to change political attitudes or affect issue positions. How many people are actually influenced is difficult to measure. In a close election, however, even a small number can change the results. Few campaign managers would be willing to discount the impact of the media. This impact explains why candidates are very careful about what they say and how they appear whenever reporters and cameras are around.

## NOTES

1. An excellent examination of presidential traits appears in Benjamin I. Page, *Choices and Echoes in Presidential Elections* (Chicago: University of Chicago Press, 1978), pp. 232–65. The following discussion draws liberally from Professor Page's description and analysis.
2. L. Patrick Devlin, "Contrasts in Presidential Campaign Commercials of 1988," *American Behavioral Scientist* 32, no. 4 (March/April 1989): 391, 403, 404.

    In its advertising campaign, the Ailes group benefited from considerable data that had been collected on public perceptions, opinions, and attitudes by pollsters working for the Republican National Committee during the Reagan presidency and for Bush during his quest for the nomination. This data revealed the vulnerabilities of the Democrats and the strengths of the Republicans. The Republican polling operations also provided the techniques for assessing the strengths and weaknesses of Dukakis and Bush in 1988. The focus groups on which the Bush campaign depended for designing its media strategy were conceived and sophisticated by the Republicans during this early period.

3. Ibid., pp. 409, 406, 403.
4. Quoted in Steven W. Colford, "Ailes: What He Wants Next," *Advertising Age,* November 14, 1988, p. 67.
5. Quoted in Devlin, "Contrasts in Commercials," p. 393.
6. In the words of George Bush's media director, Roger Ailes, "We were always trying to maximize our dollars because we decided we wanted to have plenty for the end. We wanted to keep a certain amount of contingency and we didn't want to have to go dark from Labor Day on at any time." Quoted in David R. Runkel, ed., *Campaign for President: The Managers Look at '88* (Dover, Mass.: Auburn House, 1989), p. 154.
7. Edwin Diamond and Stephen Bates, "The Ads," *Public Opinion* 8 (December 1984/January 1985): 55–57, 64.
8. Each party spent a considerable amount of its soft money in the key, battleground states of the Midwest on mailing their message to voters. The Republican communications tended to be fancier, longer, and more complex than the Democratic mailings. They were also more directly targeted to voters who had been identified by telephone surveys as more likely to split their tickets, Reagan Democrats in particular. In one such mailing, voters in Missouri received a four-page brochure. On the cover was a hand behind bars holding a small card that said, "Get out of jail free, compliments of Michael Dukakis." In the brochure, Dukakis was accused of allowing convicts to leave jail on weekend passes during which time they once again committed the rapes, murders, and drug deals for which they were imprisoned. The Democrats sent simpler mailings, en masse, to voters in key precincts. Illinois voters, for example, received an enlarged postcard that stated on one side "Ronald Reagan appointed George Bush to run America's war against drugs" and pictured a young girl smoking marijuana on the other with the caption "and we're losing." Thomas B. Edsall, "Negative Election Mailings Set to Reach Peak," *Washington Post,* October 31, 1988, p. A5.
9. Devlin, "Contrasts in Commercials," p. 406.
10. Kathleen Hall Jamieson, "For Televised Mendacity, This Year's Race Is the Worst Ever," *Washington Post,* October 30, 1988, C 1, 2.
11. M. Hailey, "Crime Victims Condemn Dukakis," *Austin-American Statesman,* October 11, 1988, B3.
12. Edwin Diamond and Adrian Marin, "Spots," *American Behavioral Scientist* 32, no. 4 (March/April 1989): 386.
    The Bush campaign also ran highly successful negative ads on Dukakis as Massachusetts governor. In one entitled "Harbor," Dukakis's environmental policy was contrasted with his environmental performance. The ad graphically illustrated the pollution in Boston Harbor. It pictured garbage floating on the beach, pipes that were leaking sewage, and a "Danger/Radiation Hazard/No Swimming" sign.
    Dukakis's most effective ad was called "Handlers." It featured Bush advisers hypocritically and unscrupulously manipulating the facts and appealing to emotions as they scripted the campaign. The ad implicitly implied that Bush was a captive of his handlers, a pawn in their plan to win the White House.
13. Charles Paul Freund, "What's New? Mud Slinging Is an American Tradition," *Washington Post,* October 30, 1988, C 1, 2.
14. Peter Goldman, Tom Mathews, et. al. *The Quest for The Presidency: The 1988 Campaign* (New York: Simon and Schuster, 1989), p. 360.

15. Elihu Katz and Jacob J. Feldman, "The Debates in the Light of Research: A Survey of Surveys," in *The Great Debates*, ed. Sidney Kraus (Bloomington, Ind.: Indiana University Press, 1962), p. 190.

16. John Carmody, "The TV Column," *Washington Post*, September 28, 1988, p. C 10.

17. At the time of the negotiations for the debate, Bush was only slightly ahead in the public opinion polls, but momentum had clearly shifted in his direction. Thus his advisers were in a stronger position than Dukakis's advisers to influence the number, format, and timing of the meetings. With a lead in the polls and a candidate who was not a great debater, the Bush campaign wanted to minimize the effects of debate. His advisers initially proposed only one debate (they actually wanted two) on any evening between September 25 and October 17—when it would compete with the Olympics, the World Series, and Monday Night Football—with a traditional meet-the-press format. Naturally Dukakis wanted more debates and wanted to hold them closer to election day. He also wanted them held with only a single moderator so that the candidates would confront each other more directly with less diversions. In the end, however, Dukakis was forced to accept Bush's terms or face the possibility of no debates. He chose the debates.

18. Goldman, Mathews, et al. *The Quest for Presidency*, p. 390.

19. Nixon had closeted himself alone in a hotel before his first debate with Kennedy. He received only a ten-minute briefing.

20. Theodore H. White, *The Making of the President, 1960* (New York: Atheneum, 1988), p. 285; Goldman, Mathews, et al., *Quest for the Presidency*, p. 387.

21. Goldman, Mathews, et al., *Quest for the Presidency*, p. 387.

22. The public also reacts to physical appearance. In 1960 Nixon's pallid complexion and patronizing manner in his first debate with Kennedy contrasted sharply with his opponent's more polished appearance and aggressive style. The differences were not nearly so noticeable in their subsequent meetings. Height can also be an issue. In 1976 and again in 1980 Jimmy Carter insisted that cameras be positioned so as not to show that his opponents were taller.

23. Responding to criticism that their evaluation influenced public judgments, the networks deliberately avoided picking a winner in the first two debates of 1988. They did, however, report public reaction. One network, ABC, even conducted its own instant poll and aired the results following the debate. In the third debate, however, a general consensus emerged. According to most network commentators, Dukakis needed to win but had not. Some of them, in fact, declared Bush the victor.

24. Harold W. Stanley and Richard G. Niemi, *Vital Statistics on American Politics* (Washington, D.C.: Congressional Quarterly, 1988), p. 58.

25. Lee Sigelman and David Bullock, "Candidates, Issues, Horse Races, and Hoopla: Presidential Campaign Coverage, 1888–1988," *American Politics Quarterly* (forthcoming).

26. Thomas E. Patterson, "Television and Election Strategy," in *The Communications Revolution in Politics*, ed. Gerald Benjamin (New York: Academy of Political Science, 1982), p. 30.

27. Michael J. Robinson and Margaret A. Sheehan, *Over the Wire and on TV: CBS and UPI in Campaign '80* (New York: Russell Sage Foundation, 1983), p. 148.

28. S. Robert Lichter, Daniel Amundson, and Richard E. Noyes, "Election '88: Media Coverage," *Public Opinion* 11 (January/February 1989): 18.

29. Robinson and Sheehan, *Over the Wire and on TV*, p. 146.

30. Thomas E. Patterson and Richard Davis, "The Media Campaign: Struggle for the Agenda," in *The Elections of 1984*, ed. Michael Nelson (Washington, D.C.: Congressional Quarterly, 1985), p. 119.
31. Lichter, Amundson, and Noyes, "Media Coverage," p. 52.
32. Robinson and Sheehan, *Over the Wire and on TV*, p. 74.
33. James Glen Stovall, "Incumbency and News Coverage of the 1980 Presidential Election Campaign," *Western Political Quarterly* 37 (1984): 628.
34. Maura Clancey and Michael J. Robinson, "The Media in Campaign '84— General Election Coverage: Part I," *Public Opinion* 8(December 1984/January 1985): 49–50.
35. Lichter, Amundson, and Noyes, "Media Coverage," p. 52.
36. Michael J. Robinson, "The Media in Campaign '84, Part II: Wingless, Toothless, and Hopeless," *Public Opinion* 8(February/March 1985): 47–48.
37. Clancey and Robinson define spin as "the way the correspondent interprets or embellishes the facts in a story." Spin involves *tone*, the part of the reporting that extends beyond hard news. On October 12, for example, Ronald Reagan's train trip through western Ohio was hard news. But when Dan Rather chose to label the ride "a photo-opportunity train trip, chock full of symbolism and treading on Harry Truman's old turf," Rather added "spin." "General Election Coverage," p. 50.
38. Kiku Adatto, "The Incredible Shrinking Sound Bite," *New Republic*, May 28, 1990, p. 22.
39. Quoted in Runkel, *Campaign for President*, p. 136.
40. Quoted in Adatto, "Sound Bite," p. 22.
41. Ibid., p. 20.
42. Doris A. Graber, "Presidential Images in the 1968 Campaign" (Paper delivered at the annual meeting of the Midwest Political Science Association, Chicago, April 30–May 2, 1970), p. 3.
43. Robinson and Sheehan, *Over the Wire and on TV*, p. 184.
44. Paul Lazarsfeld, Bernard Berelson, and Hazel Goudet, *The People's Choice* (New York: Columbia University Press, 1948); Barnard Berelson, Paul Lazarsfeld, and William McPhee, *Voting: A Study of Opinion Formation in a Presidential Campaign* (Chicago: University of Chicago Press, 1954).
45. Robinson and Sheehan, *Over the Wire and on TV*, pp. 9, 271.
46. Thomas E. Patterson and Robert D. McClure, *The Unseeing Eye* (New York: G. P. Putnam's Sons, 1976), pp. 58, 54.
47. Patterson and McClure, *Unseeing Eye*, pp. 109, 122.
48. Patterson, "Television and Election Strategy," p. 32.
49. Diana Owen, *Media Messages in American Presidential Elections* (New York: Greenwood Press, 1991), pp. 59, 88.

## SELECTED READINGS

Adatto, Kiku. "The Incredible Shrinking Sound Bite." *New Republic*, May 28, 1990, pp. 20–33.
Crouse, Timothy. *The Boys on the Bus: Riding with the Campaign Press Corps*. New York: Random House, 1973.
Devlin, L. Patrick. "Contrasts in Presidential Campaign Commercials of 1988." *American Behavioral Scientist* 32, no. 4 (March/April 1989): 489–514.
Diamond, Edwin, and Adrian Marin. "Spots." *American Behavioral Scientist* 32, no. 4 (March/April 1989): 382–388.

————, and Stephen Bates. *The Spot.* Cambridge, Mass.: MIT Press, 1984.

Jamieson, Kathleen Hall, and David S. Birdsell. *Presidential Debates.* New York: Oxford University Press, 1988.

Litcher, S. Robert, Daniel Amundson, and Richard E. Noyes. "Election 88: Media Coverage." *Public Opinion* 11 (January/February 1989): 18–19, 52.

————, ————, and ————. *The Video Campaign: Network Coverage of the 1988 Primaries.* Washington, D.C.: American Enterprise Institute, 1988.

McGinnis, Joe. *The Selling of the President, 1968.* New York: Trident Press, 1969.

Owen, Diana. *Media Messages in American Presidential Elections.* New York: Greenwood Press, 1991.

Page, Benjamin I. *Choices and Echoes in Presidential Elections.* Chicago: University of Chicago Press, 1978.

Patterson, Thomas E., and Robert D. McClure. *The Unseeing Eye.* New York: Putnam, 1976.

Payne, J. Gregory, John Marlier, and Robert A. Baukus. "Polispots in the 1988 Presidential Primaries." *American Behavioral Scientist* 32, no. 4 (March/April 1989): 365–81.

Robinson, Michael J., and Margaret A. Sheehan. *Over the Wire and on TV: CBS and UPI in Campaign '80.* New York: Russell Sage Foundation, 1983.

# PART IV

# The Election

Celebrated cartoonist Thomas Nast created
the symbol of the Democratic party—the
donkey—in 1870. Nast also was the first
to draw the elephant, which represented the
Republican party, in 1874.

# Chapter 8

# The Vote and Its Meaning

## INTRODUCTION

Predicting the results of an election is a favorite American practice. Politicians do it; the media do it; even the public anticipates the outcome far in advance of the event. It is a form of entertainment—somewhat akin to forecasting the winner of a sporting event.

Presidential elections are particularly prone to such predictions. Public opinion polls report on the choices of the American public at frequent intervals during the campaign. Television projects a winner long before most of the votes are counted. Election day surveys of voters exiting from the polls assess the mood of the electorate and present the first systematic analysis of the results. Subsequently, more in-depth studies reveal shifts in opinions and attitudes.

Predictions and analyses of the electorate based on survey data are not conducted solely for their entertainment or news value, although many are. They also provide important information to candidates running for office and to those who have been elected. For the nominees, surveys of public opinion indicate the issues that can be effectively raised and those that should be avoided. They also suggest which audience would be most receptive to what policy positions. For the successful candidates, analyses of voter preferences, opinions, and attitudes provide an interpretation of the vote, indicate the range and depth of public concern on the key issues, and signal the amount of support a newly elected president is likely to receive as he begins his administration.

This chapter examines the presidential vote from three perspectives.

The first section deals with predictions. It discusses national polls, describes their methodology, and evaluates their effect on the conduct of the campaign. The election eve predictions of the media are also described.

The next section turns to an examination of the vote itself. After alluding to the election day surveys, it reports on the National Election Studies conducted since 1952 by the Survey Research Center and the Center for Political Studies at the University of Michigan. These studies—surveys of the national electorate—provide the basic data that scholars have used to analyze elections and understand voting behavior. The principal findings of these analyses are summarized for each presidential election since 1952.

The final section of the chapter discusses the relationship between campaigning and governing, between issue debates and public policy making, between candidate evaluations and presidential style. Do the campaign issues determine the form of agenda building? Does the projected or perceived image of the candidate affect the tone of his presidency or his actions as president? Can an electoral coalition be converted into a governing party? Does the selection process help or hinder the president in meeting the expectations it creates? These questions will be explored in an effort to determine the impact of the election on the operation of the office, the behavior of the president, and the functioning of the political system.

## PREDICTING PRESIDENTIAL ELECTIONS

### *Public Opinion Polls*

The most popular question during a campaign is, Who is going to win? The public is naturally interested in the answer, and the media and candidates are obsessed with it, although for different reasons. In focusing on the campaigns, the media feel compelled to report who is ahead and, to a lesser extent, on the issues that are dividing the voters. In forging a winning coalition, candidates and their organizations need to know how the electorate is reacting to these issues and to their positions on them. Both require this information at frequent intervals during the campaign. Waiting until it is all over is obviously too late.

Many of these data can be obtained from surveys of the population. Since 1916 there have been nationwide assessments of public opinion during elections. The largest and most comprehensive of the early surveys were the straw polls conducted by the *Literary Digest*, a popular monthly magazine. The *Digest* mailed millions of ballots and questionnaires to people who appeared on lists of automobile owners and in telephone directories. In 1924, 1928, and 1932, the poll correctly predicted the winner of the presidential election. In 1936, it did not: a huge Alfred Landon victory was forecast, and a huge Franklin Roosevelt victory occurred.

What went wrong? The *Digest* mailed 10 million questionnaires over the course of the campaign and received 2 million back. As the ballots were returned, they were counted and the results totaled. This procedure tended to cloud, not highlight, trends in the responses. But the tabulation procedure was not the major problem. That problem was the sample of people who responded; it was not representative of the total voting population. Automobile owners and telephone subscribers were simply not typical voters in 1936, since most people did not own cars or have telephones. This distinction mattered more in 1936 than it had in previous years, because of the Great Depression. There was a socio-economic cleavage within the electorate. The *Literary Digest* sample did not reflect this cleavage; thus its results were inaccurate.[1]

While the *Digest* was tabulating its 2 million responses and predicting that Landon would be the next president, a number of other pollsters were conducting more scientific surveys and correctly forecasting Roosevelt's reelection.[2] The polls of George Gallup, Elmo Roper, and Archibald Crossley differed from the *Digest*'s in two principal respects: they were considerably smaller, and their samples approximated the characteristics of the population as a whole.

The *Digest* went out of business, but Gallup, Roper, and Crossley continued to poll and to improve their sampling techniques. In 1940, Gallup predicted Roosevelt would receive 52 percent of the vote; he actually received 55 percent. In 1944, Gallup forecast a 51.5 percent Roosevelt vote, very close to his actual 53.2 percent. Other pollsters also correctly predicted the results. As a consequence, public confidence in election polling began to grow.

The confidence was short-lived, however. In 1948, all major pollsters forecast a Thomas Dewey victory. Their errors resulted from poor sampling techniques, from the premature termination of polling before the end of the campaign, and from incorrect assumptions about how the undecided would vote.

In attempting to estimate the population in their samples, the pollsters had resorted to filling quotas. They interviewed a certain number of people with different sexual, religious, ethnic, economic, and social characteristics until the percentage of these groups in the sample resembled that percentage in the population as a whole. However, simply because the percentages were approximately equal did not mean that the sample was representative of the population. For example, interviewers avoided certain areas in cities, and the results were consequently biased.

Moreover, the interviewing stopped several weeks before the election. In mid-October, the polls showed that Dewey was ahead by a substantial margin. Burns Roper, son of Elmo Roper, polling for *Fortune* magazine, saw the lead as sufficiently large to predict a Dewey victory without the need for further surveys. A relatively large number of people, however, were undecided. Three weeks before the election, Gallup concluded that 8 percent of the voters had still not made up their minds. In estimating the final vote, he and other pollsters assumed that the undecided would divide their votes in much the same manner as the electorate as a whole. This assumption turned out to be incorrect. Most of those who were wavering in the closing days of the campaign were Democrats. In the end, most voted for Truman or did not vote at all.

The results of the 1948 election once again cast doubt on the accuracy of public opinion polls. Truman's victory also reemphasized the fact that surveys reflect opinion at the time they are taken, not necessarily days or weeks later. Opinion and voter preferences may change.

To improve the monitoring of shifts within the electorate, pollsters changed their method of selecting people to be interviewed. They developed more effective means of anticipating who would actually vote. They polled continuously to identify more precisely and quickly shifts in public sentiment and reactions to campaign events. They also extended their surveys to the day before the election to get as close to the time people actually voted as they could. These changes, plus the continued refinement of the questions, have produced more accurate forecasts. (See "How Polls Are Conducted.")

Between 1936 and 1950, the average error of the final Gallup Poll was 3.6 percent; between 1952 and 1960, it fell to 1.7 percent; between 1962 and 1970, it declined to 1.6 percent; and between 1972 and 1988, it decreased even further to 1.4 percent.[3] (See Table 8–1.) Very close elections in 1960, 1968, and 1976, however, resulted in several pollsters making wrong predictions. In 1980 the size of Reagan's victory was substantially underestimated in many nationwide polls.

Some of the problems in 1980 were similar to those in 1948. Polling stopped too early. With partisan ties weakening, voting behavior has in recent years become more volatile. The electorate tends to make up its mind later in the campaign and seems more susceptible to influence by candidates, issues, and events. In 1980 there were a large number of undecided voters. The CBS News/*New York Times* Poll estimated that approximately 20 percent of the electorate made up its mind in the final week of the campaign; many voters did so on the final day. Since most of the public polls were completed by November 1, four days before the election, they did not detect the large surge for Reagan. The candidates' polls, which continued until the eve of the election, did.

In contrast, the 1988 election posed fewer problems for pollsters. The electorate displayed much less volatility than in the 1980 election. Most voters had decided before the final week whom they would support.[4] Typically, one-half to two-thirds of the electorate makes that de-

TABLE 8–1

## Final Preelection Polls and Results, 1948–1988

| Year | Gallup Poll[a] | Roper CBS/*New York Times* Polls[b] | Harris Poll | Actual Results[c] |
|---|---|---|---|---|
| *1948* | | | | |
| Harry Truman | 44.5 | 37.1 | | 49.6 |
| Thomas Dewey | 49.5 | 52.2 | | 45.1 |
| Others | 6.0 | 4.3 | | 5.3 |
| *1952* | | | | |
| Dwight Eisenhower | 51.0 | | | 55.1 |
| Adlai Stevenson | 49.0 | | | 44.4 |
| *1956* | | | | |
| Dwight Eisenhower | 59.5 | 60.0 | | 57.4 |
| Adlai Stevenson | 40.5 | 38.0 | | 42.0 |
| *1960* | | | | |
| John Kennedy | 51.0 | 49.0 | | 49.7 |
| Richard Nixon | 49.0 | 51.0 | | 49.5 |
| *1964* | | | | |
| Lyndon Johnson | 64.0 | | 64.0 | 61.1 |
| Barry Goldwater | 36.0 | | 36.0 | 38.5 |
| *1968* | | | | |
| Richard Nixon | 43.0 | | 41.0 | 43.4 |
| Hubert Humphrey | 42.0 | | 45.0 | 42.7 |
| George Wallace | 15.0 | | 14.0 | 13.4 |
| *1972* | | | | |
| Richard Nixon | 62.0 | | 61.0 | 60.7 |
| George McGovern | 38.0 | | 39.0 | 37.5 |
| *1976* | | | | |
| Jimmy Carter | 48.0 | 51.0 | 46.0 | 50.1 |
| Gerald Ford | 49.0 | 47.0 | 45.0 | 48.0 |
| Others | 3.0 | 2.0 | 3.0 | 1.9 |
| Undecided | | | 6.0 | |
| *1980* | | | | |
| Ronald Reagan | 47.0 | | 46.0 | 50.7 |
| Jimmy Carter | 44.0 | | 41.0 | 41.0 |
| John Anderson | 8.0 | | 10.0 | 6.6 |
| Others | | | | 1.7 |
| Undecided | 1.0 | | 3.0 | |
| *1984* | | | | |
| Ronald Reagan | 59.0 | | 56.0 | 59.0 |
| Walter Mondale | 41.0 | | 44.0 | 41.0 |
| Others/Undecided | | | 2.0 | |
| *1988* | | | | |
| George Bush | 53.0 | 48 | 51.0 | 53.4 |
| Michael Dukakis | 42.0 | 40 | 47.0 | 45.6 |
| Others/Undecided | 5.0 | 12 | 2.0 | 1.0 |

[a] The Gallup polls estimate of the major party vote in 1988 gave Bush 56 percent and Dukakis 44 percent. The actual two-party vote gave Bush 53.9 percent and Dukakis 46.1 percent.

[b] For 1988, figures are from CBS/*New York Times* Poll.

[c] The percentage of minor candidate votes is not noted in the elections of 1952–1964 and 1972.

*Source:* "Record of Gallup Poll Accuracy," *The Gallup Report*, November 1988, pp. 5 and 33.

## How Polls Are Conducted

The typical media poll is conducted on the telephone. Numbers, randomly selected, are dialed, and random selection is also used to determine the voter in the household to be interviewed. The average length of such an interview is fifteen to twenty minutes, during which voters are asked to evaluate the candidates, issues, the parties, and frequently, the campaign itself. Information on the demography of the voter (race, age, sex, religion, education, and income) is also solicited. These demographic data can be weighted to reflect the population in the country as a whole.

Interviews are conducted over a one- to three-day period. The number of respondents vary. The total surveyed range anywhere from six hundred to twenty-four hundred. The larger samples, while more costly, are also more accurate. They have the added benefit of allowing analysts to break down the sample into smaller demographic groupings for the purposes of analyzing the vote.

cision before or during the national nominating conventions.[5] As a result, the polls conducted in September are likely to be close to the final election results. Most tend to be within 4 points of the actual total. In "trial heats" conducted by the Gallup organization the candidate who was ahead in early September won in nine of eleven elections since 1948, and the person ahead at the end of September won ten of eleven times, Truman being the only exception.[6] (See Table 8–2.)

The accuracy of polls and their newsworthiness have increased the number of polls and thrust the media into the polling business. In 1988 there were 144 public polls plus those conducted by and for the campaign organizations themselves, compared to 100 four years earlier.[7] In 1984 one study of newspapers reported that one out of every five campaign stories referred to polls.[8] An analysis by Scott C. Ratzan of the *Washington Post* and *New York Times* in the month before the 1988 election revealed that more than 40 percent of the front page election stories mentioned polls and one-half of these stories featured them as the primary subjects of the article.[9] (See "Why Polls Are Accurate.")

### Television Forecasts

Predictions continue right to the end, until all the votes are tabulated. The final projections are presented by the major television networks during the night of the election. In broadcasting the results the news

TABLE 8–2
**Early Deciders
in Presidential Elections,
1960–1988**

| Year | Percentage |
|------|-----------|
| 1960 | 62% |
| 1964 | 66 |
| 1968 | 59 |
| 1972 | 62 |
| 1976 | 54 |
| 1980 | 58 |
| 1984 | 66 |
| 1988 | 60 |

*Source:* James E. Campbell and Kenneth A. Wink, "Trial-Heat Forecasts of the Presidential Vote," *American Politics Quarterly* 18 (July 1990): 257.

media have three objectives: to report the vote, to forecast the winners, and to analyze the returns.

To accomplish the first of these objectives, the major networks and news services have established a consortium known as the News Election Service (NES). Operating on election night to report the results, the NES assigns thousands of reporters to precincts and county election boards around the country. Their job is to telephone the presidential, congressional, and gubernatorial vote to a center, which feeds the returns into a central computer. Each of the networks (ABC, CBS, NBC, and CNN) and news services (Associated Press and United Press International) that participate in the consortium have terminals indicating how the vote is progressing.[10]

If all the media wished to do were report the results of the vote as rapidly as possible, the NES system would suffice. However, in close elections, the winners and losers might not be obvious for some time. Moreover, the initial reports on who is ahead and likely to win might be misleading. The NES results do not reveal which precincts have reported, whether they tend to be Democratic or Republican, or how their returns compare with those of past elections.

Since accuracy and speed are paramount, the networks developed exit polls to anticipate the results and to analyze them. Exit polls work in the following manner. A large number of precincts across the country are randomly selected. The random selection is made within states in such a way that principal geographic units (cities, suburbs, and rural areas), size of precincts, and their past vote are taken into account. Representatives of the networks, often college students, administer the

# Why Polls Are Accurate

The main reason polls have become increasingly accurate is the improvement in sampling procedures. Since the objective of surveying is to generalize from a small number, it is essential that the people interviewed be representative of the population. The odds of the sample's being representative can be estimated when it is randomly selected.

Random selection does not mean haphazard choice. Rather, it means that every element in the population (in this case, the eligible electorate) has a known and usually equal chance of being included in the sample, and the choice of any one element is independent of the choice of any other. The *Literary Digest* sample of 1936 and the quota sample of 1948 were not random. There was no way to determine whether the people interviewed were typical. As it turned out, they were not—at least not of those who voted on election day.

Random selection is thus the key to sampling. There are several ways of conducting it. Most pollsters employ what is known as a *stratified cluster random sample*. In such a sample, the population is divided into geographic units and then grouped (stratified) on the basis of the size of communities. Within each stratum, smaller and smaller units are then randomly selected until a block in a city or part of a township is isolated. Then, a number of interviews are conducted according to a carefully prescribed procedure at each of these sampling points. Interviewers have no choice whom they interview or where they conduct the interviews. In 1988 the Gallup organization randomly selected three hundred fifty sampling points and held about five interviews at each.

Since sampling is based on probability theory, the likelihood of being right or wrong can be calculated. In a random sample the odds of being right are determined primarily by the size of the sample. The larger the sample is, the more likely it is that it will be accurate, and more confidence can be placed in the results. For national surveys, a sample of approximately eleven hundred will yield an error of plus or minus 3 percent in 95 percent of the polls conducted. In other words, the population as a whole will not differ by more than 3 percent in either direction from the results of the sample, 95 percent of the time.

The way to improve the accuracy of a sample is to enlarge it.

poll to voters who are chosen in a systematic way (for example, every fourth or fifth person) as they leave the voting booths. Voters are asked to complete a short questionnaire (thirty to forty items) which is designed to elicit information on voting choices, political attitudes, candidate evaluations and feelings, as well as demographic characteristics

However, enlarging it adds to its cost. At some point a law of diminishing returns sets in. For example, to increase the accuracy of a nationwide sample to plus or minus 2 percent, a total of approximately twenty-four hundred randomly selected respondents would be needed, as opposed to about ninety-six hundred for plus or minus 1 percent and six hundred for plus or minus 4 percent.

The accuracy of a poll in measuring public opinion is also affected by the questionnaire and the relationship between the interviewer and the respondent. A survey is only as good as its questions: how they are worded and what order they are in. If they suggest a particular answer, then they force opinion rather than reflect it.

The focus of the questions is normally dictated by the objectives of the study. Public polls, such as those conducted by independent research organizations like Gallup and Harris and syndicated to newspapers and magazines, usually focus on who is ahead and on how different groups of people feel about the candidate. "If the election were held today, for whom would you vote?" is the key question.

In addition to random selection and sample size, the likelihood of those interviewed actually voting must also be considered. Pollsters regularly ask respondents a series of questions to differentiate potential voters from nonvoters. Those whose answers suggest that they probably will not vote are eliminated or separated from the others when analyzing the results.

Finally, pollsters and candidates alike are interested in the currency of their polls. A survey measures opinion only during the time in which interviews were conducted. To monitor changes as rapidly as possible, a technique known as *tracking* is used. Instead of simply interviewing the entire sample in one or two days and then analyzing the results, interviews are conducted continuously. As new responses are added, old ones are dropped. This procedure produces a rolling sample. Continuous analyses of this sample can identify emerging issues, monitor a candidate's strength among various constituencies, and evaluate the impact of the candidate's media advertising.

of those who voted. Three times over the course of the day, the questionnaires are collected, tabulated, and their results telephoned to a central computer bank.[11] After most or all of the election polls in a state have been completed, the findings of the exit poll are broadcast.

The survey is usually very accurate. Because it is conducted over the course of the day, there is no time bias that would under- or over-represent certain types of voters. Moreover, the large number of voters sampled, anywhere from ten to fifteen thousand or even more, reduces the error to much less than that of the national surveys conducted by Gallup, Harris, and the Center for Political Studies of the University of Michigan. Moreover, it provides a sample of sufficient size to enable analysts to discern the attitudes, opinions, and choices of smaller groups (such as Jews, black males, and unmarried, college-educated women) within the electorate.

All three networks have depended on exit polls in recent years to analyze the vote. It was not until the 1980s, however, that they also began to rely on them to forecast the winner of a presidential election. Current technology and survey techniques enable more rapid projections than ever before. But the costs of conducting a massive voter survey have also increased. To reduce their costs, the major networks, newspapers, and wire services pooled their resources to conduct one large national exit poll in the 1990 congressional elections.[12] They plan to do so again in 1992.

Early projections of the presidential election winner have generated considerable criticism, primarily on the grounds that they discourage turnout and affect voting in states in which the polls are still open. This controversy was heightened in 1980. When the early returns and private polls all indicated a Ronald Reagan landslide, the networks projected a Reagan victory early in the evening while polls were still open in most parts of the country. At 9:30 P.M. Eastern Standard Time, President Jimmy Carter appeared before his supporters and acknowledged defeat. His concession speech was carried live on each of the major networks. Almost immediately Carter's early announcement incurred angry protests, particularly from defeated West Coast Democrats, who alleged that the president's remarks discouraged many Democrats from voting. It is difficult to substantiate their claim, however.

In general, turnout declined more in the East and Midwest than it did in the Far West in 1980. Even if there was a decline after Carter's concession, there is little evidence to suggest that Democrats behaved any differently from Republicans and independents. Hawaii, the last state to close its polls, voted for Carter.

A number of researchers have studied the impact of television projections on voting at all levels. They have found a small reduction in turnout in the West, which they associated with the election night predictions.[13] They did not, however, find evidence of voting switching as a result of the early projections of who was likely to win.[14]

The minimal effect of the election reporting on the outcome seems to be related to the fact that relatively few people watch the broadcasts and then vote. Only 7 percent said that they did in 1988.[15] Most people vote first and watch the returns later in the evening. Perhaps this pattern of voting and then watching or listening to the returns explains why George Bush's projected victory on the networks in 1988 did little to change the results in three out of four Pacific states (Washington, Oregon, and Hawaii) that went for Michael Dukakis.

Despite the absence of much evidence to support the proposition that media projections affect voting, the networks have continued to receive much criticism for their early night predictions. In 1989 the House of Representatives considered a bill that would have established a uniform poll-closing time for the continental United States. Although this legislation was not enacted into law, media representatives promised that their networks would not project winners in any election within a state until a majority of its polls had closed.

## INTERPRETING THE ELECTION

In addition to predicting the results, the television networks also provide an instant analysis of them on election night. This analysis, based primarily on exit polls, relates voting decisions to the issue positions, ideological perspectives, and partisan preferences of the electorate. Patterns among demographic characteristics, issue stances, and electoral perceptions and choices are noted and used to explain why people voted for particular candidates.

Exit polls present a detailed picture of the electorate on election day. They do not, however, provide a longitudinal perspective. To understand changes in public attitudes and opinions, it is necessary to survey people over the course of the campaign, asking the same questions and, if possible, reinterviewing the same people before and after they vote. The nationwide polls conducted by Gallup and Harris often repeat questions, but they do not repeat respondents. The National Election Studies conducted by the University of Michigan do. They reinterview respondents and ask them some of the same questions they posed to them earlier. This interview-reinterview technique has enabled social scientists to discern opinion changes and the factors that have contributed to those changes over the course of the campaign. The wealth of data that these studies have produced has served as a basis for political scientists to construct theories of why people vote as they do.

### Models of Voting Behavior

There are two basic models of voting behavior: the *prospective model*, which emphasizes the issues and looks to the future; and the *retrospective model*, which emphasizes the candidates and looks to the past.

In the prospective voting model, voters compare their beliefs and policy preferences with those of the parties and their nominees. They make a determination of which party and which candidate espouse positions that are closer to their own and thus would more likely pursue those positions if elected. In other words, voters make a judgment on the prospects of obtaining future policy they desire based on the current positions of the candidates.

In the retrospective voting model, voters also make a judgment about the future but do so primarily on the basis of the party's candidate's performance in the past. How they evaluate that performance is critical to the voting choice they will make on election day.

While a variety of factors are considered in performance evaluations, external conditions—how good or bad things seem to be—are almost always a major part of that analysis. If the economy is strong, society harmonious, and the nation perceived as secure, people assume that their leaders, particularly the president, must be doing a good job. If conditions are not, then the president gets much of the blame. Thus the key question that voters ask themselves when making a retrospective evaluation is: Am I better off now than I was before the party now in power and its presidential candidate won control of the White House?

There is another component to a retrospective voting decision. It involves a comparison between the principal contenders over which is more likely to do well in the future.[16] It is not sufficient to evaluate an incumbent, even one seeking reelection, if the candidate for the opposition is thought to be markedly better or worse.

In both models, partisanship is apt to be an important influence on the evaluations people make to arrive at their voting decision. As noted in Chapter 3, a partisan orientation provides voters with a lens through which the campaign is filtered, the candidates and issues are evaluated, and electoral judgments are made.

In the retrospective model, partisanship itself is the consequence of evaluations of the past performance of parties. It therefore functions as a summary judgment of how the parties and the candidates have performed, and as a basis for anticipating how they will perform in the future. Partisans who make a retrospective evaluation are more apt to rate presidents of their party more favorably and those of the other party less favorably. Similarly, partisans tend to be closer to their candidate's positions on the issues than to their opponent's, although most people do not necessarily arrive at their position by virtue of their partisanship alone.

Since the identification people make with political parties is the most stable and resilient factor affecting the voting decision, it is considered to be the single most important long-term influence on voting. Orientations voters have toward the candidates and issues are short-term factors that fluctuate more rapidly from election to election. If strong enough, they can, of course, cause people to vote against their partisan inclinations or, over time, change those inclinations. Usually, however, they do not. In most cases they serve as an inducement and a rationalization for supporting the party and its candidates.

Since a majority of the electorate identifies with a political party or leans in a partisan direction, the candidate of the dominant party should be advantaged—all things being equal. But all things are never equal. Candidates change, issues change, public moods change, and even the partisan identity of voters can shift, although not as rapidly as these other factors. How the electorate evaluates these changes, how the candidates and issues are perceived, and how these perceptions interact with the partisan inclinations of the voters affect their voting decisions and the election outcomes. The next sections discuss the interplay of these components in presidential elections since 1952.

## 1952–1956:
## The Impact of Personality

In 1952 the Democrats were the dominant party, but the Republicans won the presidential election and gained a majority in both houses of Congress. The issues of that election—the fear of communism at home and abroad, the presence of corruption in high levels of government, and United States involvement in the Korean War—benefited the GOP, as did the popularity of its presidential candidate, General Dwight D. Eisenhower. These short-term factors offset the Democrat's longer-term, partisan advantage and enabled the Republicans to win.[17] The electorate saw the Republicans as better able to deal with the problems of fighting communism, promoting efficiency in government, and ending the war. Eisenhower was also perceived in a more favorable light than his opponent, Adlai Stevenson. While the public still regarded Democrats as more capable of handling domestic problems, the appeal of Eisenhower, combined with the more favorable attitude toward the Republican party in the areas of foreign affairs and government management, resulted in the victory of the minority party's candidate.

President Eisenhower's reelection four year later was also a consequence of his personal popularity, not his party's. Eisenhower was positively evaluated by voters. His opponent, Adlai Stevenson, was not. However, the Republicans did not win control of Congress as they had in 1952. Their failure to do so in 1956 testified to the continuing partisan advantage that the Democrats enjoyed among the American electorate during this period.

## 1960–1972:
## The Increasing Importance of Issues

Beginning in the 1960s, the issues of the campaign seemed to play a more important role in the election's outcome than they had since the New Deal realignment. Noneconomic policy issues undercut the impact of a partisanship forged since the 1930s on economic ties. In general, these issues contributed to the defection of Democrats from their party's presidential candidates in 1960, 1968, and 1972, and to defections by Republicans (and southern Democrats) from theirs in 1964.

John Kennedy's Catholicism was a primary concern to many voters in 1960 and helps explain the closeness of the election. Despite the Democrats' dominance within the electorate, Kennedy received only 115,000 more votes than Richard Nixon, 0.3 percent more of the total vote.

Kennedy's Catholicism cost him votes. He lost about 2.2 percent of the popular vote, or approximately 1.5 million votes, because he was a Catholic.[18] The decline in Democratic voting was particularly evident in the heavily Protestant South. However, outside the South, Kennedy picked up Democratic votes because of the massive support he received from Catholics. Almost 80 percent of the Catholic vote, 17 percent more than the Democrats normally obtained, went to Kennedy. In fact, the concentration of Catholics in the large industrial states may have contributed to the size of his electoral college majority.[19]

Although Kennedy barely won in 1960, Lyndon Johnson won by a landslide four years later. Short-term factors also explain the magnitude of the Johnson victory.[20] Barry Goldwater was perceived as a minority candidate within a minority party, ideologically to the right of most Republicans. Moreover, he did not enjoy a favorable public image, as Johnson did. Policy attitudes also favored the Democrats, even in foreign affairs. Goldwater's militant anticommunism scared many voters. They saw Johnson as the peace candidate.

Goldwater's strong ideological convictions, coupled with his attempt to differentiate his policy positions from Johnson's, undoubtedly contributed to a greater issue awareness. Although most policy conscious voters had their views on the issues reinforced by their partisan attitudes, two groups within the electorate did not. White southern Democrats, fearful of their party's civil rights initiatives, cast a majority of their votes for Goldwater, while northern Republicans, who disagreed with their candidate's policy positions, voted for Johnson. For the first time since the New Deal realignment, five states in the solid Democratic South (plus Goldwater's home state of Arizona) went Republican, auguring the major regional realignment that was to occur.

The impact of issues on voting grew in 1968. With the Vietnam War, urban riots, campus unrest, and civil rights dividing the nation and splitting the Democratic party, partisan desertions increased. The Democratic share of the vote declined 19 percent, while the Republican proportion increased 4 percent. The third party candidacy of George Wallace accounted for much of the difference.

Wallace's support was much more issue based than support for Hubert Humphrey or Richard Nixon. The Alabama governor did not have as much personal appeal for those who voted for him as did his policy positions.[21] Unhappy with the Democratic party's handling of a wide range of social issues, white Democratic partisans, particularly in the South but to a limited degree in the urban North as well, turned from their party's presidential candidate, Hubert Humphrey, to vote for Wallace, who received 13.5 percent of the vote. Had Wallace not run, the Republican presidential vote undoubtedly would have been larger, since Nixon was the second choice of most Wallace voters.

The results of the 1968 presidential election thus deviated from the partisan alignment of the electorate primarily because a significant number of Democrats had grievances against their party and against Lyndon Johnson's conduct of the presidency and expressed them by voting for Wallace and, to a much lesser extent, for Nixon. A decline in the intensity of partisanship and a growth in the number of independents contributed to the amount of issue voting that occurred in 1968. Had it not been for the Democrats' large partisan advantage and the almost unanimous black vote that Humphrey received,[22] the presidential election would not have been nearly so close.

The trend away from partisan presidential voting for the Democratic candidate continued in 1972. With a nominee who was ideologically and personally unpopular, the Democrats suffered their worst presidential defeat since 1920. Richard Nixon enjoyed a better public image than George McGovern. He was seen as the stronger presidential candidate. The electorate reacted to him personally in a positive manner, although less so than in 1960.[23] McGovern, on the other hand, was viewed negatively by non-Democrats and neutrally by Democrats. These perceptions, positive for Nixon and negative for McGovern, contributed to Nixon's victory, as did his stands on most of the issues. Most of the electorate saw the Republican standard-bearer as closer to their own positions than the Democratic candidate. McGovern was perceived as liberal on all issues and ideologically to the left of his own party. Thus Democrats defected in considerable numbers, but Republicans did not.[24]

## *1976–1988:*
### *The Evaluation of Performance*

**1976.** Issue differences narrowed in 1976. Neither Gerald Ford nor Jimmy Carter emphasized the social and cultural concerns that played a large role in the previous presidential contest. Both focused their attention on trust in government and on domestic economic matters. In the wake of Watergate and a recession that occurred during the Ford presidency, it is not surprising that these issues worked to the Democrats' advantage.

Carter was also helped by a slightly more favorable personal assessment than that given to Ford.[25] Normally, an incumbent would enjoy an advantage in such a comparison. However, Ford's association with the Nixon administration, highlighted in the public mind by his pardon of the former president, his difficult struggle to win his own party's nomination, and his seeming inability to find a solution to the country's economic problems adversely affected his image as president.

Nonetheless, Ford was probably helped more than hurt by being the incumbent. He gained in recognition, reputation, and stature. He benefited from having a podium with a presidential seal on it. His style and manner in the office contrasted sharply with his predecessor's— much to Ford's advantage. As the campaign progressed, his presidential image improved.[26] It just did not improve quickly enough to allow him to hold on to the office.

With sociocultural issues muted and the Vietnam War over, economic matters divided the electorate along partisan lines. This shift put the candidate of the dominant party into the driver's seat. Democrats had more faith in their party's ability to improve the economy. Carter won primarily because he was a Democrat and secondarily because his personal evaluation was more favorable than Ford's.

Carter was also helped by being a southerner. He received the electoral votes of every southern state except Virginia. In an otherwise divided electoral college, this support proved to be decisive.

**1980.** When Carter sought reelection in 1980, being a Democrat, an incumbent, and a southerner was not enough. Poor performance ratings overcame the advantage partisanship and incumbency normally bring to a president of the dominant party. In 1976, Carter was judged on the basis of his potential *for* office. In 1980 he was judged on the basis of his performance *in* office. As the results of the election indicate, that judgment was very harsh. Carter's vote fell behind his 1976 percentages in every single state, and in approximately half the states it dropped at least 10 percent. Why did he lose so badly?

Personal evaluations of Carter and assessments of his policies were not nearly so favorable as they had been four years earlier. Starting the campaign with the lowest approval rating of any president since the ratings were first begun in 1952, Carter saw his performance in office approved by only 21 percent of the adult population in July 1980. Personal assessments of Ronald Reagan were also low—although, in contrast to Carter's ratings, they became more favorable as the campaign unfolded.

Economic conditions also seemed to benefit Reagan. Concerns about the economy, persistently high inflation, large-scale unemployment, and the decreasing competitiveness and productivity of American industry all worked to the out-party's advantage. For the first time in many years, the Republicans were seen as the party better able to invigorate the economy, return prosperity, and lower inflation. The Democrats, and particularly Carter, were blamed for the problems.

Dissatisfaction with the conduct of foreign affairs, culminating in frustration over the Soviet invasion of Afghanistan and failure of the United States to obtain the release of American hostages in Iran contributed to Carter's negative evaluation and to changing public attitudes toward defense spending and foreign affairs. In 1980 most Americans supported increased military expenditures, a position with which Reagan was closely identified, combined with a less conciliatory approach and a stronger posture in dealing with problems abroad.

These issues, together with the negative assessment of Carter as president, explain why he lost even though he was the dominant party's candidate. Twenty-seven percent of the Democrats who had supported Carter in 1976 deserted him in 1980. Approximately 80 percent of these deserters voted for Reagan. They represented all ideological groups, not just conservatives. And Carter's share of the independent vote declined substantially.

Independent John Anderson benefited from the disaffected voters. He was a protest candidate who drew equally from Democrats and Republicans. Anderson was unable, however, to attract a solid core of supporters. Nor was he able to differentiate his policy positions sufficiently from Carter's and Reagan's to generate an issue-oriented vote. In the end, his failure to win any electoral votes and only 6.5 percent of the popular vote demonstrates the resiliency of the major parties and the legitimacy that their labels provide candidates for office.

In summary, Carter was repudiated by the voters because of how they retrospectively evaluated his presidency. In 1980 it was Reagan who offered greater potential. He won primarily because he was the option that had become acceptable. He did not win because of his ideology or his specific policy positions. While there was a desire for change, there was little direct ideological or issue voting.[27] Nor did Reagan's personal appeal in 1980 contribute significantly to his victory.[28]

**1984.** Four years later, Reagan's personal appeal did contribute to his victory. In 1984 voters rewarded President Reagan for what they considered to be a job well done with a landslide victory. What factors contributed to Reagan's impressive victory? Was his landslide primarily a product of his ideology, his issue stands, or his performance in office?

Ideology did not work to Reagan's advantage in 1984 any more than it did in the previous election. In 1984, the average voter considered himself or herself to be a moderate, holding issue positions slightly closer to the liberal Mondale than to the conservative Reagan.[29] This moderate perspective, however, did not easily translate into presidential voting. As a consequence, it did not adversely affect Reagan; nor did it help Mondale.

There was a potential for issue voting in 1984. The electorate did perceive a choice between the two candidates on a range of domestic matters. But it was conditions more than positions that seemed to influence the electorate's judgment. A resurgent economy, strengthened military, and renewed feelings of national pride brought the president broad support. Although voters agreed with Mondale more than with Reagan on many of the specific problems confronting the nation, they viewed Reagan as the person better able to deal with them.

Leadership was a dominant concern. Voters evaluated Reagan much more highly than Mondale in this regard. Reagan was seen as the stronger and more independent of the two candidates, less beholden to special and parochial interests. When leadership was combined with the ability to deal with the most pressing problems, Reagan won hands down.

Reagan won a retrospective vote. The electorate supported him primarily for his performance in office. In other words, they voted *for* him in 1984 just as they had voted *against* Carter four years earlier.

**1988.** The trend of retrospective voting continued in 1988. George Bush won because the electorate evaluated the Reagan administration positively, associated Bush with that administration, and concluded that he, not Michael Dukakis, would be better able and more likely to maintain the good times and the policies that produced them.[30] That Bush was not as favorably evaluated as Reagan had been four years earlier partially accounts for his narrower victory.[31] Bush received 53 percent of the popular vote and 426 electoral votes, compared to Reagan's 59 percent and 535 electoral votes.

Partisanship affected voting behavior more in 1988 than it had in any election since 1960.[32] Partisan identifiers hewed their party line and stuck with its presidential candidates. The CBS News/*New York Times* exit poll indicates that Dukakis received 82 percent of the Democratic vote and Bush 91 percent of the Republican vote.[33] In the past a high correlation between partisan identities and voting behavior would have worked to the Democrats' advantage. In 1988 it did not. A decline in Democratic allegiances and an increase in Republican allegiances among the voters produced an almost evenly divided electorate. There were slightly more Democrats but greater turnout and less defection among Republicans. In the end neither candidate was appreciably advantaged by partisan voting. Among independents, Bush enjoyed a solid lead of 12 percent. (See Table 8–3 and also Table 3–4, which contains comparable data from the Gallup poll on the 1988 vote for president.)

Ideological orientations worked to reinforce partisan voting patterns in 1988, with the Republican candidate, Bush, winning overwhelmingly among Republicans and conservatives and the Democratic candidate, Dukakis, doing almost as well among Democrats and liberals. The problem for Dukakis, however—and any liberal for that matter—is that the proportion of the electorate that considers itself liberal has declined substantially. In 1988 almost twice as many people who voted considered themselves conservative rather than liberal. (See Table 8–3.)

In addition to ideology and party, the 1988 vote also evidenced clear class distinctions. Bush did better among the more privileged, establishment groups, among white-collar workers, and among those who were better educated (except for people with postgraduate education). Dukakis maintained the traditional support Democrats receive from those in the lower economic, educational, and social groupings.

Race, gender, and generational differences continued to persist as well, although generational differences were somewhat muted. The Republican candidate received a predominantly white vote, with substantially more support from men than from women. Youth, who preferred Reagan by substantial margins in 1984, also preferred Bush in 1988. In contrast, the Democratic candidate did best with the oldest age group, a legacy of the Roosevelt revolution when the Democrats became the majority party. Dukakis also did well among minority racial groups, particularly blacks and Hispanics. (See Tables 8–3 and 3–4.)

Issues also affected voting behavior in 1988, although like party identification, they did not work to the advantage of either candidate. In general the electorate took a more moderate stance on most issues than did Bush or Dukakis. The exception was the role of women, where a majority of voters sided with Dukakis.[34] Had that been the dominant issue, it would have helped the Democratic candidate, but it was not. Other concerns from defense spending to foreign competition, from budget deficits to a sluggish economy, from clean air to constraints on business divided the electorate and positioned them between the candidates. As a result the impact of issues was muted.

With neither partisanship nor issues producing a clear advantage for either candidate, the retrospective evaluation of the Reagan presidency seemed to be the deciding factor, the one that best explains the election outcome. Sixty percent of the electorate approved of how Reagan was handling his job, and of them, almost 80 percent voted for Bush.[35] Thus it is only a slight exaggeration to say that Reagan won the 1988 election. He won it for George Bush. In the light of this conclusion, Bush's decision to tie his fate inextricably and unalterably to the Reagan administration during the campaign proved to be a wise choice.

Finally, the voting patterns in 1988 suggest a continuation of the trends that have characterized presidential voting in the last two decades. They show the evenness of the major partisan coalitions within the electorate. No longer is there a unified dominant majority sufficient to dictate the outcome. For the presidency, the critical factors remain economic, social, and national security conditions and how those conditions reflect on the demonstrated or potential leadership qualifications of the candidates. In 1988 those conditions in the aggregate were seen as favorable by a majority of the voters. Over the course of the campaign they helped shape the perception that the incumbent vice-president, Bush, was more experienced, competent, and personally caring than his Democratic challenger, Dukakis, and thus more likely to maintain the perceived gains of the previous eight years. For most Republican and many independent voters, for most of those who had prospered during the Reagan presidency, for those who believed in the values that the Republicans and their candidates articulated—personal security, individual economic freedom, and God, family, and country—the Bush

TABLE 8–3
Portrait of the Electorate

| % of 1988 Total | | Vote in 1980 | | | Vote in 1984 | | Vote in 1988 | |
|---|---|---|---|---|---|---|---|---|
| | | Reagan | Carter | Anderson | Reagan | Mondale | Bush | Dukakis |
| — | TOTAL | 51% | 41% | 7% | 59% | 40% | 53% | 45% |
| 48 | Men | 55 | 36 | 7 | 62 | 37 | 57 | 41 |
| 52 | Women | 47 | 45 | 7 | 56 | 44 | 50 | 49 |
| 85 | Whites | 55 | 36 | 7 | 64 | 35 | 59 | 40 |
| 10 | Blacks | 11 | 85 | 3 | 9 | 89 | 12 | 86 |
| 3 | Hispanics | 35 | 56 | 8 | 37 | 61 | 30 | 69 |
| 69 | Married | — | — | — | 62 | 38 | 57 | 42 |
| 31 | Not married | — | — | — | 52 | 46 | 46 | 53 |
| 20 | 18–29 years old | 43 | 44 | 11 | 59 | 40 | 52 | 47 |
| 35 | 30–44 years old | 54 | 36 | 8 | 57 | 42 | 54 | 45 |
| 22 | 45–59 years old | 55 | 39 | 5 | 59 | 39 | 57 | 42 |
| 22 | 60 and older | 54 | 41 | 4 | 60 | 39 | 50 | 49 |
| 8 | Not a high school graduate | 46 | 51 | 2 | 49 | 50 | 43 | 56 |
| 27 | High school graduate | 51 | 43 | 4 | 60 | 39 | 50 | 49 |
| 30 | Some college education | 55 | 35 | 8 | 61 | 37 | 57 | 42 |
| 35 | College graduate or more | 52 | 35 | 11 | 58 | 41 | 56 | 43 |
| 19 | College graduate | — | — | — | — | — | 62 | 37 |
| 16 | Postgraduate education | — | — | — | — | — | 50 | 48 |
| 48 | White Protestant | 63 | 31 | 6 | 72 | 27 | 66 | 33 |
| 28 | Catholic | 49 | 42 | 7 | 54 | 45 | 52 | 47 |
| 4 | Jewish | 39 | 45 | 15 | 31 | 67 | 35 | 64 |
| 9 | White fundamentalist or evangelical Christian | 63 | 33 | 3 | 78 | 22 | 81 | 18 |
| 25 | Union household | 43 | 48 | 6 | 46 | 53 | 42 | 57 |

| | | | | | | | |
|---|---|---|---|---|---|---|---|
| Family income under $12,500 | 12 | 42 | 51 | 6 | 45 | 54 | 37 | 62 |
| $12,500–24,999 | 20 | 44 | 46 | 7 | 57 | 42 | 49 | 50 |
| $25,000–$34,999 | 20 | 52 | 39 | 7 | 59 | 40 | 56 | 44 |
| $35,000–$49,999 | 20 | 59 | 32 | 8 | 66 | 33 | 56 | 42 |
| $50,000 and over | 24 | 63 | 26 | 9 | 69 | 30 | 62 | 37 |
| $50,000–$100,000 | 19 | — | — | — | — | — | 61 | 38 |
| Over $100,000 | 5 | — | — | — | — | — | 65 | 32 |
| From the East | 25 | 47 | 42 | 9 | 52 | 47 | 50 | 49 |
| From the Midwest | 28 | 51 | 40 | 7 | 58 | 40 | 52 | 47 |
| From the South | 28 | 52 | 44 | 3 | 64 | 36 | 58 | 41 |
| From the West | 19 | 53 | 34 | 10 | 61 | 38 | 52 | 46 |
| Republicans | 35 | 86 | 8 | 4 | 93 | 6 | 91 | 8 |
| Democrats | 37 | 26 | 67 | 6 | 24 | 75 | 17 | 82 |
| Independents | 26 | 55 | 30 | 12 | 63 | 35 | 55 | 43 |
| Liberals | 18 | 25 | 60 | 11 | 28 | 70 | 18 | 81 |
| Moderates | 45 | 48 | 42 | 8 | 53 | 47 | 49 | 50 |
| Conservatives | 33 | 72 | 23 | 4 | 82 | 17 | 80 | 19 |
| Professional or manager | 31 | 57 | 32 | 9 | 62 | 37 | 59 | 40 |
| White-collar worker | 11 | 50 | 41 | 8 | 59 | 40 | 57 | 42 |
| Blue-collar worker | 13 | 47 | 46 | 5 | 54 | 45 | 49 | 50 |
| Full-time student | 4 | — | — | — | 52 | 47 | 44 | 54 |
| Teacher | 5 | 46 | 42 | 10 | 51 | 48 | 47 | 51 |
| Unemployed | 5 | 39 | 51 | 8 | 32 | 67 | 37 | 62 |
| Homemaker | 10 | — | — | — | 61 | 38 | 58 | 41 |
| Agricultural worker | 2 | 36 | 59 | 4 | — | — | 55 | 44 |
| Retired | 16 | — | — | — | 60 | 40 | 50 | 49 |

*Note:* 1988 data based on questionnaires completed by 11,645 voters leaving polling places around the nation on election day. 1984 data based on questionnaires from 9,174 voters; 1980 data based on questionnaires from 15,201 voters. Those who gave no answers are not shown. Dashes indicate that a question was not asked in a particular year.

Family income categories in 1980: Under $10,000, $10,000–14,999, $15,000–24,999, $25,000–49,999, and $50,000 and over. "Fundamentalist or evangelical Christian" was labeled "born-again Christian" in 1980 and 1984. Male and female college graduates include postgraduate education.

*Source:* "Portrait of the Electorate," from *The New York Times,* November 10, 1988, p. B6.

campaign struck a responsive cord. All of these factors helped Bush to win.

# CONVERTING ELECTORAL CHOICE INTO PUBLIC POLICY

## *The President's Imprecise Mandate*

It is not unusual for the meaning of the election to be ambiguous. The reasons that people vote for a president vary. Some do so because of his party, some because of his issue stands, some because of their assessment of his potential or his performance. For most, a combination of factors contributes to their voting decision. This combination makes it difficult to discern exactly what the electorate means, desires, or envisions by its electoral choice.

The president is rarely given a mandate for governing. For a mandate to exist the party's candidates must take discernible and compatible policy positions, and the electorate must vote for them because of those positions. Moreover, the results of the national election must be consistent. If one party wins the White House and another the Congress, it would be difficult for a president to claim a mandate for governing.

Few elections meet these criteria for a mandate. Presidential candidates usually take a range of policy positions, often waffle on a few highly divisive and emotionally charged issues, may differ from their party and its other candidates for national office in their priorities and their stands, and rarely have coattails long enough to sweep others in with them. In fact, they may run behind their congressional candidates, as Bush did in 1988.

Mandates may not exist, but presidents have been successful in claiming them. They need to do so. They need to be sensitive to public wants and needs when fashioning their policy programs, and they need to obtain public support to get others in government, including members of Congress and federal executives, to back their initiatives.

For these reasons elections are important for governing. They help an administration define its initial goals, but they do not dictate priorities or long-term policy decisions. They provide the basis for a governing coalition, but one that must be constantly nurtured if it is to endure. Presidents and their staffs have to do the nurturing.

Assuming that party is an influence on voting behavior, what cues can a president cull from his partisan connection? Party platforms normally contain a large number of positions and proposals, the 1988 Democratic platform being the exception (see Chapter 5), but there are problems in using the platform as a guide for new administrations. First and foremost, the presidential candidate may not have exercised a major influence on the platform's formulation. Or, second, he may have had to accept certain compromises in the interests of party unity. It is not unusual for a nominee to disagree with one or several of the platform's positions or priorities. Carter personally opposed his party's abortion stand in 1980 and had major reservations about a $12-billion jobs program that the Democratic platform endorsed.

In addition to containing items the president-elect may oppose, the platform may omit some that he favors, particularly if they are controversial. There was no mention of granting amnesty to Vietnam draft dodgers and war resisters in the 1976 Democratic platform, although Carter had publicly stated his intention to do so if he was elected.

Another limitation to using a platform as a guide to the partisan attitudes and opinions of the public is that many people, including party rank and file, are unfamiliar with most of its contents. The platform per se is not the reason people vote for their party's candidates on election day.

On the other hand, presidential nominees usually do exercise influence over the contents of the platform, as Bush and Dukakis did in 1988. Incumbents, in particular, exercise a lot. In 1964, 1972, and 1984, party platforms were crafted by White House aides and approved by the president himself. Thus it is not surprising that a considerable number of party positions and campaign promises find their way into public policy.

Political scientist Jeff Fishel found that from 1960 to 1984 presidents "submitted legislation or signed executive orders that are broadly consistent with about two-thirds of their campaign pledges." Of these, a substantial percentage were enacted into law, ranging from a high of 89 percent of those proposed during the Johnson administration to a low of 61 percent during the Nixon years.[36] Although these figures do not reveal the importance of the promise, its scope, or its impact, they do suggest that, in general, campaign platforms and candidate pledges are important. They provide a foundation from which an administration's early policy initiatives emanate.

One reason campaign promises are important is that they are part of the public record; candidates and parties can be held accountable for them. Another is that they represent the interests of a significant portion of the population. To gain public approval, a president must respond to these interests. In addition, organized groups, to whom promises have been made, have clout in Congress and in the bureaucracy. The president can either mobilize them to help him achieve his campaign promises or be thwarted by them if he fails to do so. George Bush ran into this problem in 1990 when he recanted on his pledge not to raise taxes. Conservative Republican members of Congress, who opposed tax increases in their own campaigns for office, voted against the budget compromise that contained a tax increase, a compromise that the president supported.

## Expectations and Performance

When campaigning, candidates also try to create an aura of leadership, conveying such attributes as assertiveness, decisiveness, compassion, and integrity. Kennedy promised to get the country moving, Johnson to continue the New Frontier–Great Society program, Nixon to "bring us together," Bush to maintain the Reagan policies that produced peace and prosperity. These promises created expectations of performance regardless of policy stands. In the 1976 election, Jimmy Carter heightened expectations by his constant reference to the strong, decisive leadership he intended to exercise as president. His decline in popularity stemmed in large part from his failure to meet these expectations. In contrast, Reagan's high approval before, during, and after his reelection indicate that most of the public believed that he had provided the strong leadership he had promised in his 1980 and 1984 campaigns.

All new administrations, and to some extent most reelected ones, face diverse and often contradictory desires. By their ambiguity, candidates encourage voters to see what they want to see and to believe what they want to believe. Disillusionment naturally sets in once a new president begins to make decisions. Some supporters feel deceived, while others may be satisfied.

One political scientist, John E. Mueller, has referred to the disappointment groups may experience with an administration as "the coalitions of minorities variable." In explaining declines in popularity, Mueller notes that the president's decisions inevitably alienate parts of the coalition that elected him. This alienation, greatest among independents and supporters who identify with the other party, produces a drop in popularity over time.[37]

The campaign's emphasis on personal and institutional leadership also inflates expectations. By creating the aura of assertiveness, decisiveness, and potency, candidates help shape public expectations of their performance in office. Jimmy Carter contributed to the decline in his own popularity by promising more than he could deliver. Carter's problem was not unique to his presidency. It is one that other successful candidates have and will continue to face. How can the promise of leadership be conveyed during the campaign without creating unrealistic and unattainable expectations of the candidate's performance as president?

## The Electoral Coalition and Governing

Not only does the selection process inflate performance expectations and create a set of diverse policy goals, it also *decreases* the president's power to achieve them. His political muscle has been weakened by the decline in the power of party leaders and the growth of autonomous state and congressional electoral systems.

In the past, presidential candidates were dependent on the heads of the state parties for delegate support. Today, they are not. In the past, the state party organizations were the principal means for conducting the general election campaign. Today, they are not. In the past, partisan ties united legislative and executive officials more than they currently do.

Today, presidential candidates are more on their own. They essentially designate themselves to run. They create their own organizations, mount their own campaigns, win their own delegates, and set their own convention plans. They pay a price for this independence, however. By winning the party's nomination a candidate gains a label but not an organization. In the general election, he must expand his prenomination coalition, working largely with his own advisers. Planning a strategy, developing tactics, writing speeches, formulating an appeal, organizing interest groups, and, perhaps with the help of the party, conducting a grass-roots registration and a get-out-the-vote effort are all part of seeking the presidency.

The personalization of the presidential electoral process has serious implications for governing. To put it simply, it makes coalition building more difficult. The electoral process provides the president with fewer political allies in the states and in Congress. It makes his partisan appeal less effective. It fractionalizes the bases of his support.

The establishment of candidate campaign organizations and the use of out-of-state coordinators have weakened the state parties. These practices have created competition, not cooperation. The competition cannot help but deplete the natural reservoir of partisan support a president needs to tap when he alienates parts of his electoral coalition.

Moreover, the democratization of the selection process has also resulted in the separation of state, congressional, and presidential elections. In the aftermath of Watergate, Jimmy Carter made much of the fact that he did not owe his nomination to the power brokers within his party, nor did he owe his election to them or to members of Congress. The same could be said for members of Congress and, for that matter, governors and state legislators. The independence of congressional elections from the presidential election decreases legislators' political incentives to follow the president's lead.

The magnitude of the president's problem is compounded by public expectations of his leadership. Yet that leadership is difficult to achieve because of the constitutional and political separation of institutions. Thus the weakening of party ties during the electoral process carries over to the governing process, with adverse consequences for the president.

Finally, personality politics has produced factions within the parties. It has created a fertile environment for the growth of interest group pressures. Without strong party leaders to act as brokers and referees, groups vie for the nominee's attention and favor during the campaign and for the president's after the election is over. This group struggle provides a natural source of opposition and support for almost any presidential action or proposal. It enlarges the arena of policy making and contributes to the multiplicity of forces that converge on most presidential decisions.

## *Personality Politics and Presidential Leadership*

What is a president to do? How can he meet public expectations in light of the weakening of partisanship and the increased sharing of policy-making powers? How can a president lead, achieve his goals, and satisfy pluralistic interests at the same time?

Obviously, there is no set formula for success. Forces beyond the president's control may affect the course of events. Nonetheless, there are certain maxims that presidents would be wise to follow in their struggle to convert promises into performance and perhaps also get reelected.

1. A president must define and limit his own priorities rather than have them defined and expanded for him.
2. A president must build his own coalitions rather than depend solely or even mostly on existing partisan or ideological divisions.
3. A president must take an assertive posture rather than let words and actions speak for themselves. He must actively shape public opinion. He must lead while also appearing to follow.

Priority setting is a necessary presidential task. Without it, an administration appears to lack direction and leadership. People question what the president is doing and have difficulty remembering what he has done. The absence of clear, achievable priorities at the beginning of the Carter administration, combined with the president's perceived inconsistency in some of his economic and foreign policy decisions affected Carter's approval ratings in the public opinion polls and contributed to his defeat in 1980. The Reagan administration understood this lesson and limited the issues, controlled the agenda, and, most important, focused the media on the president's principal policy objectives during his first term in office.

Presidents have discretion in deciding on their priorities. Reagan used this discretion at the beginning of his first term when he jettisoned his conservative social agenda in favor of major economic reforms. Bush chose to emphasize foreign policy and de-emphasize domestic issues in the first three years of his administration, despite his campaign's emphasis on domestic concerns and his own promise to build a kinder and gentler America.

Beyond establishing priorities and positions, the president has to get them adopted. His electoral coalition does not remain a cohesive entity within the governing system. The inevitable shifting of that coalition forces him to build and rebuild his own alliances around his policy objectives. Constructing these alliances requires organizing skills different from those used in winning an election.

Public appeals are often necessary to maintain a high level of support on potentially divisive national issues and to use that support to influence public officials to back the president's initiatives. The Reagan administration effectively marshaled public support in 1981 and 1982. The president took to the airwaves to explain his program to the American people and rally them behind it, particularly his budget and tax proposals. The White House then orchestrated the first favorable response, directing it toward members of Congress. Bush was much less successful in convincing the public to support the budget and tax agreement that his aides negotiated with the Democratic leadership of Congress. One of the reasons he was less successful was the message itself: Sacrifice and pay more taxes. Another was the failure of the White House to organize a favorable response to the president's urgent request. Bush was far more successful in gaining and maintaining public support for United States involvement in the Persian Gulf war. The threat posed by the Iraqi invasion of Kuwait to international peace and American interests, the bipartisan nature of the issue, particularly after the congressional vote authorizing the president to use force, and the quick and overwhelming success of the coalition military effort produced extremely high levels of public approval for the president's actions.

In addition to mobilizing external forces, presidents need to employ other inducements and tactics to convince public officials, who have their own constituencies and must be responsive to them, to back presidential policy. This effort requires time, energy, and help. The president cannot do it alone.

As campaign organizations are necessary to win elections, so, too, are governing organizations necessary to gain support for presidential policies. Several offices within the White House have been established to provide liaison and backing for the president on Capitol Hill, in the bureaucracy, and with outside interest groups. By building and mending bridges, a president can improve his chances for success. He can commit, convince, cajole, and otherwise gain cooperation despite the constitutional and political separation of institutions and powers.

Unlike winning the general election, making and implementing public policy are not all-or-nothing propositions. Assessments of performance are based on expectations, somewhat as they were in the primaries.

Part of the president's image problem results from the contrast between an idealized concept of what his powers are or ought to be and his actual ability to get things done. The gap explains why a president needs a public relations staff and why some grandstanding is inevitable.

If a president cannot achieve what he wants, he can at least shift the blame for failure. He can at least look good trying, and perhaps he can even claim partial success. And finally, he can always change his public priorities to improve his batting average. Public appeals may or may not generate support within the governing coalition, but they can boost support outside it, and within the electoral coalition the next time around.

## SUMMARY

Americans are fascinated by presidential elections. They want to know who will win, why the successful candidate has won, and what the election augurs for the next four years. Their fascination stems from four interrelated factors: elections are dramatic, they are decisive, they are participatory, and they affect future policy and leadership.

These factors suggest why so much attention has been devoted to predicting and analyzing presidential elections. Public opinion polls constantly monitor the attitudes and views of the electorate. They reflect and, to some extent, contribute to public interest through the hypothetical elections they continuously conduct and the media report. Private surveys also record shifts in popular sentiment, helping the candidates who pay for them know what to say, to whom to say it, and, in some cases, when and even how to say it.

Polls have become fairly accurate measures of opinion at the time they are taken. They provide data that can be employed to help explain the meaning of the election: the issues that were most salient, the positions that were most popular, the hopes and expectations that are initially directed toward the elected leaders of government.

The personality of the candidates, the issues of the campaign, and the retrospective evaluation of the previous administration and the party that has controlled it have dominated recent elections and the voting decisions of the electorate. Singularly and together, these factors, along with partisanship, explain the outcome of the vote. In 1960, it was Kennedy's religion that seemed to account for the closeness of the popular vote despite the large Democratic majority in the electorate. In 1964, it was Goldwater's uncompromising ideological and issue positions that helped provide Johnson with an overwhelming victory in all areas but the deep South. In 1968, it was the accumulation of grievances against the Democrats that spurred the Wallace candidacy and resulted in Nixon's triumph. In 1972, ideology, issues, and the perception of McGovern as incompetent split the Democratic party and culminated in Nixon's landslide. In 1976, however, partisanship was reinforced by issue, ideological, and personal evaluations to the benefit of the dominant party's nominee. In 1980 and 1984 it was not. Dissatisfaction with Carter's performance in office and satisfaction with Reagan's overcame the Democrats' decreasing numerical advantage within the electorate, causing voters to cast their ballots for Reagan as the person they thought best qualified to lead. By 1988 the Democrats had lost their partisan advantage. The issues, while important, did not favor one candidate at the expense of the other. This balance left the retrospective evaluation of the Reagan years as the critical factor. A majority of voters evaluated these years favorably and believed that Bush, not Dukakis, would be better able and more likely to continue them.

When combined, the influences on voting create a diverse and inflated set of expectations for a new president. That these expectations may be conflicting, unrealistic, or in other ways unattainable matters little. Presidents are expected to lead, to achieve, and to satisfy the interests of a heterogeneous coalition. Their failure or success will depend in large part on their ability to fulfill these expectations.

Newly elected presidents have a problem. The election provides them with an open-ended mandate that means different things to different people, including to the presidents themselves, but does not provide them with the political clout to get things done.

Parties seem to exercise less influence over public officials than they did in the past. Electoral systems have become more autonomous. Candidates now have to create their own organizations to win the election, and presidents have to build their own alliances to govern. In the past, the electoral and governing coalitions were more closely connected by partisan ties than they are today.

This situation has presented serious governing problems for recent presidents. To overcome them they must establish their own priorities, construct their own policy alliances, articulate their appeals clearly, and convey them forcefully to those outside the government.

# NOTES

1. Michael Wheeler, *Lies, Damn Lies, and Statistics* (New York: Dell, 1976), p. 84. Moreover, the 2 million people who returned the questionnaire were not necessarily even typical of those who received it. By virtue of responding, they displayed more interest and concern than the others.
2. Archibald Crossley predicted that Roosevelt would receive 53.8 percent of the vote, George Gallup estimated that he would receive 55.7 percent, and Elmo Roper forecast 61.7 percent. Roosevelt actually received 62.5 percent.
3. *The Gallup Report* (Wilmington, Del.: Scholarly Resources, 1989), p. xiv.
4. According to the CBS News/*New York Times* exit poll, 84 percent of the electorate had already made its voting decision before the last week of the campaign. Reported in *Public Opinion* 11 (January/February 1989): 27.

5. The survey data of the National Election Studies indicate a persistent pattern of early deciders before or during the nominating conventions.

6. James E. Campbell and Kenneth A. Wink, "Trial-Heat Forecasts of the Presidential Vote," *American Politics Quarterly* 18 (July 1990): 257.

7. Ed Rollins, quoted in David R. Runkel, ed., *Campaign for President: The Managers Look at '88* (Dover, Mass.: Auburn House, 1989), p. 166.

8. James Glen Stovall, "Coverage of the 1984 Campaign," *Journalism Quarterly* 65 (Summer 1988): 443–49, 484.

9. Scott C. Ratzan, "The Real Agenda Settles," *American Behavioral Scientist* 32, no. 4 (March/April 1989): 451–63.

10. Paul Wilson, "Election Night 1980 and the Controversy over Early Projections," in *Television Coverage of the 1980 Presidential Campaign*, ed. William C. Adams (Norwood, N.J.: Ablex, 1983). Joan Bieder, "Television Reporting," in *The Communications Revolution in Politics*, ed. Gerald Benjamin (New York: Academy of Political Science, 1982), pp. 37–41.

11. Kathleen A. Frankovic, "Media Polls: Monitoring Changes in Public Opinion," *ICPSR Bulletin* (February 1990): 1–3.

12. Unfortunately for participants in this project, a glitch in the computer program delayed the early projections and analyses so that neither the networks during their election night broadcasts nor the newspapers in their morning editions could report them.

13. Raymond Wolfinger and Peter Linquiti, "Tuning In and Turning Out," *Public Opinion* 4 (February/March 1981), 57–59.

14. Harold Mendelsohn and Irving Crespi, *Polls, Television, and the New Politics* (Scranton, Pa.: Chandler, 1970), pp. 234–36; William C. Adams, "Early Projections in 1984: How the West Deplored But Ignored Them" (Paper presented at the annual meeting of the American Association of Public Opinion Research, Princeton, New Jersey, 1985).

15. Gallup survey for the Times Mirror Company, reported in *Public Opinion* 11 (January/February 1989): 35.

16. This view of retrospective voting was advanced by Anthony Downs, *An Economic Theory of Democracy* (New York: Harper and Row, 1957). Downs suggests that people evaluate the past performance of parties and elected officials in order to anticipate how they will perform in the future compared to their opponents. If this concept were applied to 1988, then it could be hypothesized that one of the reasons Michael Dukakis lost was that he was unsuccessful in convincing voters that he would be able to handle the problems the country faced more effectively than George Bush.

17. For an analysis of the components of the 1952 presidential election, see Angus Campbell, Philip E. Converse, Warren E. Miller, and Donald E. Stokes, *The American Voter* (New York: Wiley, 1960), pp. 524–27.

18. Philip E. Converse, Angus Campbell, Warren E. Miller, and Donald E. Stokes, "Stability and Change in 1960: A Reinstating Election," in *Elections and the Political Order*, ed. Angus Campbell, Philip E. Converse, Warren E. Miller, and Donald E. Stokes (New York: Wiley, 1966), p. 92.

19. Kennedy's Catholicism may have enlarged his electoral college total by 22 votes. See Ithiel de Sola Pool, Robert P. Abelson, and Samuel Popkin, *Candidates, Issues, and Strategies* (Cambridge, Mass.: MIT Press, 1965), pp. 115–18.

20. For a discussion of the 1964 presidential election, see Philip E. Converse,

Aage R. Clausen, and Warren E. Miller, "Electoral Myth and Reality: The 1964 Election," *American Political Science Review* 59 (1965): 321–36.

21. Philip E. Converse, Warren E. Miller, Jerrold G. Rusk, and Arthur C. Wolfe, "Continuity and Change in American Politics: Parties and Issues in the 1968 Election," *American Political Science Review* 63 (1969): 1097. Wallace claimed that there was not a dime's worth of difference between the Republican and Democratic candidates. He took great care in making his own positions distinctive. The clarity with which he presented his views undoubtedly contributed to the issue orientation of his vote. People knew where Wallace stood.

22. Converse, Miller, Rusk, and Wolfe, "Continuity and Change," p. 1085.

23. Warren E. Miller and Teresa E. Levitin, *Leadership and Change* (Cambridge, Mass.: Winthrop, 1976), p. 164.

24. Arthur H. Miller, Warren E. Miller, Alden S. Raine, and Thad A. Brown, "A Majority Party in Disarray: Policy Polarization in the 1972 Election," *American Political Science Review* 70 (1976): 753–78.

25. Arthur H. Miller and Warren E. Miller, "Partisanship and Performance: 'Rational' Choice in the 1976 Presidential Elections" (Paper presented at the annual meeting of the American Political Science Association, Washington, D.C., September 1–4, 1977).

26. Ibid., p. 99.

27. Ibid., p. 7; Warren E. Miller, "Policy Directions and Presidential Leadership: Alternative Interpretations of the 1980 Presidential Election" (Paper presented at the annual meeting of the American Political Science Association, New York, September 3–6, 1981).

28. According to Arthur H. Miller and Martin P. Wattenberg, "Reagan was the least positively evaluated candidate elected to the presidency in the history of the National Election Studies, which date back to 1952." "Policy and Performance Voting in the 1980 Election" (Paper presented at the annual meeting of the American Political Science Association, New York, September 3–6, 1981), p. 15.

29. Paul R. Abramson, John H. Aldrich, and David W. Rohde, *Change and Continuity in the 1984 Elections* (Washington, D.C.: Congressional Quarterly, 1986), pp. 171–80.

30. J. Merrill Shanks and Warren E. Miller, "Alternative Interpretations of the 1988 Election" (Paper presented at the annual meeting of the American Political Science Association, Atlanta, Georgia, August 31–September 3, 1989), p. 58.

31. Paul R. Abramson, John H. Aldrich, and David W. Rohde, *Change and Continuity in the 1988 Elections* (Washington, D.C.: Congressional Quarterly, 1990), p. 195.

32. Ibid., p. 212.

33. "Portrait of the Electorate," *New York Times*, November 10, 1988, p. B6.

34. Abramson, Aldrich and Rohde, *Change and Continuity in the 1988 Elections*, p. 169.

35. Ibid., pp. 195, 198, 193.

36. Jeff Fishel, *Presidents and Promises* (Washington, D.C.: Congressional Quarterly, 1985), pp. 38, 42–43.

37. John E. Mueller, *War, Presidents, and Public Opinion* (New York: Wiley, 1973), pp. 205–8, 247–49.

# SELECTED READINGS

Abramson, Paul R., John H. Aldrich, and David W. Rohde. *Change and Continuity in the 1988 Elections.* Washington, D.C.: Congressional Quarterly, 1989.

Dahl, Robert A. "Myth of the Presidential Mandate." *Political Science Quarterly* 105 (Fall 1990): 355–72.

Fiorina, Morris. *Retrospective Voting in American National Elections.* New Haven, Conn.: Yale University Press, 1981.

Fishel, Jeff. *Presidents and Promises.* Washington, D.C.: Congressional Quarterly, 1985.

Kelley, Stanley. *Interpreting Elections.* Princeton, N.J.: Princeton University Press, 1983.

Miller, Arthur H. "The Majority Party Reunited? A Comparison of the 1972 and 1976 Elections." In *Parties and Elections in an Anti-Party Age,* edited by Jeff Fishel, pp. 127–40. Bloomington, Ind.: Indiana University Press, 1978.

———, and Martin P. Wattenberg. "Throwing the Rascals Out: Policy and Performance Evaluations of Presidential Candidates, 1952–1980." *American Political Science Review* 79 (1985): 359–72.

Miller, Warren E. *Without Consent: Mass-Elite Linkages.* Lexington, Ky.: University Press of Kentucky, 1989.

Nelson, Michael, ed. *The Elections of 1988.* Washington, D.C.: Congressional Quarterly, 1989.

Pomper, Gerald M., et al. *The Election of 1988.* Chatham, N.J.: Chatham House, 1989.

Shanks, J. Merrill., and Warren E. Miller. "Alternative Interpretations of the 1988 Elections." Paper presented at the annual meeting of the American Political Science Association, Atlanta, Georgia, August 31–September 3, 1989.

———. "Policy Direction and Performance Evaluation: Complementary Explanations of the Reagan Elections." *British Journal of Political Science* 20 (April 1990): 143–235.

Wattenberg, Martin P. *The Rise of Candidate-Centered Politics.* Cambridge: Harvard University Press, 1991.

This campaign poster was used in the 1816 campaign of Democrat James Monroe, who ran against Rufus King.

## Chapter 9

# Reforming the Electoral System

## INTRODUCTION

The American political system has evolved significantly in recent years. Party rules, finance laws, and media coverage are very different from what they were thirty years ago. The composition of the electorate has changed as well, with the expansion of suffrage to all citizens eighteen years of age or older and the reduction of legal obstacles to voting, particularly in the South in the 1960s. And the electoral college certainly does not function in the manner in which it was originally designed to do so.

Have these changes been beneficial? Has the system been improved? Are further structural or operational changes desirable? These questions have elicited a continuing, and sometimes spirited, debate.

Critics have alleged that the electoral process is too long, too costly, and too burdensome, that it wears down candidates and numbs voters, resulting in too much style and too little substance, too much rhetoric and too little debate. They have said that many qualified people are discouraged from running for office and much of the electorate is discouraged from participating in the election. Other criticisms are that the system benefits the rich, encourages factionalism, weakens parties, overemphasizes personality and underemphasizes policy, and that it is unduly influenced by the media. It has also been contended that voters do not receive the information they need to make intelligent, rational decisions on election day.

In contrast, proponents argue that the political system is more dem-

277

ocratic than ever. More, not fewer, people are involved, especially at the nomination stage. Candidates, even lesser-known ones, have ample opportunity to demonstrate their competence, endurance, motivation, and leadership capabilities. Parties remain important as vehicles through which the system operates and by which governing is accomplished. Those who defend the process believe voters do receive as much information as they desire and that most people can make intelligent, informed, rational judgments.

The old adage "where you stand influences what you see" is applicable to the debate about electoral reform. No political process is completely neutral. There are always winners and losers. To a large extent the advantages that some enjoy are made possible only by the disadvantages that others encounter. Rationalizations aside, much of the debate about the system, about equity, representation, and responsiveness, revolves around a very practical, political question: Who gains and who loses?

Proposals to change the system need to be assessed in the light of this question. They should also be judged on the basis of how such changes would affect the operation of the political system and impact on governance. This chapter will discuss some of these proposals and the effect they could have on the road to the White House. The chapter is organized into two sections; one dealing with the more recent developments in party rules, campaign finance, and media coverage; and the other examining the long-term, democratic issues of participation and voting.

## MODIFYING RECENT CHANGES

### *Party Rules*

Of all the changes that have recently occurred in the nomination process, none has caused more persistent controversy than the reforms governing the selection of delegates. Designed to encourage grass-roots participation and broaden the base of representation, these reforms have also lengthened the nominating period, made the campaign more expensive, generated candidate-based organizations, weakened state party leaders, converted conventions into coronations, and loosened the ties between the parties and their nominees. As a consequence, governing has been made more difficult.

Since 1968, when the Democrats began to rewrite their rules for delegate selection, the parties have suffered from these unintended repercussions. Each succeeding presidential election has seen new changes to the Democratic party's rules, changes that have attempted to reconcile expanded participation and representation with the traditional need to unify the party for a national campaign. While less reform conscious than the Democrats, the Republicans have also tried to steer a middle course between greater rank-and-file involvement and more equitable representation on the one hand and the maintenance of successful electoral and governing coalitions on the other.

How to balance these oft-competing goals has been a critical concern. Those who desire greater public participation have lauded the trend toward having more primaries and a larger percentage of delegates selected in them. Believing that the reforms have opened up the process and made it more democratic, they favor the continued selection of pledged delegates based on the proportion of the popular vote their candidate receives. In contrast, those who believe that greater control by state and national party leaders is desirable argue that the reforms have gone too far. They would prefer fewer primaries, a smaller percentage of delegates selected in them, and more unpledged delegates, elected officials, and party leaders attending the nominating conventions. They would also favor a larger involvement by the national party organizations in the presidential campaign. Giving federal funds to the party, and not to the candidate, has been proposed as one way to achieve the latter objective. The continuation of the soft money loophole, which allows the national party to raise money for its state affiliates, is another.

Strong party advocates appear to be in the ascent, although the Democrats did agree to Jesse Jackson's proposal to allocate delegates only by straight proportional voting in 1992, a procedure that could encourage more candidates to run and to stay in the race longer, thereby delaying a consensus on the party's nominee.

There has been widespread public support for shortening the process. Several proposals have been made in this regard and even introduced in the form of legislation in Congress. One would limit the period during which primaries or caucuses could be held; a second would cluster primaries and caucuses geographically, forcing states in designated regions to hold their elections on the same day; a third would create a national primary.

Having an official period during the spring of the election year for primaries and caucuses has been suggested as a way to reduce the impact the early contests have had on the nomination. A second but equally important objective has been to reduce the media's influence on public opinion during these initial stages of the process.

The Democratic party has attempted to achieve these goals since 1984 by imposing its own window period during which primaries and caucuses could be held. Opposition from several states, however, including Iowa and New Hampshire, has forced the party to grant them exceptions to the imposed time frame. The exceptions, in turn, continue to produce the problem that generated the proposal in the first place—

the holding of early contests that receive extensive media coverage and for that reason are disproportionately important to the candidates.

Theoretically, if the parties do not or will not impose a primary period, Congress can. Legislation has been proposed that would require all states to schedule their contests between the second Tuesday in March and the second Tuesday in June.

One problem with Congress's establishing such a period is that it would involve the national government in an area traditionally reserved for the states. Another difficulty is that it might produce an effect precisely the opposite to the one intended. Instead of shortening the campaign and decreasing the media's influence, the imposition of a window, combined with the front-loading of the caucuses and primaries at the beginning of the period, might actually increase the time needed by candidates to develop their organization, raise money, and mount large-scale media efforts. No longer would candidates have the luxury of waiting until after the early caucuses and primaries had boosted their national recognition to provide the basis for a simultaneous multistate campaign.

To allow states to retain some discretion yet encourage them to hold primaries and concentrate them at specific points in the nominating process, a system of regional or interregional primaries has been suggested. Although the proposals differ in specifics, they agree in the basic essentials:

1. Divide the country into contiguous regions.
2. Require states within those regions to hold primaries (if they have one) on the same day.
3. Randomly choose the dates for the regional election.
4. Schedule the regional votes two to four weeks apart.

A regional primary system would undoubtedly compress the process and better focus public attention in the area where the vote occurred. This concentration might encourage turnout, which would also be spurred by the likelihood of a regional media blitz. The allocation of delegates in regional primaries would probably reflect the popularity of the candidates within the region. Under such a system, conventions would still be necessary to choose among the leading candidates or to ratify the selection of the winner, as well as to perform their other traditional functions—writing a platform, rallying the faithful, making a public appeal.

On the negative side, regional primaries might exacerbate sectional rivalries, encourage sectional candidates, and produce more organizations to rival those of the state and national parties. Moreover, like straight proportional voting, they could impede the emergence of a consensus candidate, thereby extending the process through the convention and increasing, not decreasing, costs, time, and media attention. Finally, a system of regional primaries that was imposed on the states would deny them the option of setting their own dates. For this reason alone, some state officials and their congressional representatives, especially those from Iowa and New Hampshire, have consistently opposed the idea.

Other state leaders, on the other hand, believe a regional primary system would enhance their state's influence and give them a greater voice in the selection of the nominee and the issues the candidates address. Southern Democrats, in particular, unhappy over their party's standard-bearers in 1972 and 1984, over their party's national image, and over its recent platforms, regarded regional primaries as an opportunity to stamp the ticket with a southern imprint. These leaders convinced their state legislatures—all incidentally controlled by the Democrats—to hold primaries on the same day in 1988 (the second Tuesday in March) and caucuses the following weekend. Thus the first regional elections were established, without congressional legislation or mandated changes in party rules.

The results of the Southern regional primaries and caucuses, however, were mixed from the perspective of its sponsors. The regional elections did not produce a consensus nominee whose views were consistent with those of the more conservative Democratic South than with the more liberal, northern wing of the Democratic party. Rather, it produced a division among the three principal candidates, reflecting the pluralism of the party's southern rank and file. It did produce a consensus Republican candidate, George Bush, which may indicate the existence of a more homogeneous southern Republican party than Democratic party.

The multistate regional campaign had to be media based, and thus it was costly. That advantaged the best-organized and best-financed candidate, who did not happen to come from the South or be a conservative, Governor Michael Dukakis of Massachusetts. On the other hand, turnout was up in most of the region. It was higher in most southern states in 1988 than in 1984 or 1980, although turnout in the South still lagged the nation as a whole.[1] But whether the increase in southern turnout occurred because the election was held within the same region on the same day, because that date was so early in the nomination process, or because of a factor peculiar to that geographic area, is unclear.

Unhappy with the outcome of the election and fearful that the vote would be divided once again, several prominent southern Democratic officials have recommended that their states not participate in another regional election in 1992.

Instead of having regional elections, another option, and the one that would represent the most sweeping change, would be to institute a national primary. While party leaders, including members of the reform commissions, have opposed such a proposal and Congress has been cool to the idea, the general public seems to be more favorably disposed. Gallup Polls taken over the last twenty years indicate that about two-thirds of the electorate would prefer such an election to the present system.[2]

Most proposals for a national primary call for a one-day election to be held during the summer. Candidates who wished to enter their party's primary would be required to obtain a certain number of signatures, equal to approximately 1 percent of the vote in the last presidential election. Any aspirant who won a majority would automatically receive the nomination. In some plans a plurality would be sufficient, provided it was at least 40 percent. In the event that no one received 40 percent, a runoff election would be held several weeks later between the top two finishers. Nominating conventions would continue to select the vice-presidential candidates and to decide on the platforms, although they might have to convene after the national primary was completed.

A national primary would be consistent with the "one person, one vote" principle that guides most aspects of the U.S. electoral system. All participants would have an equal voice in the selection. No longer would those in the early, small primary and caucus states exercise disproportionate influence.

It is likely that a national primary would stimulate turnout. The attention given to such an election would provide greater incentive for voting than currently exists, particularly in those states that hold their nomination contests after the apparent winner has emerged. A national primary would probably result in nomination by a more representative electorate than is currently the case.

A single primary for each party would accelerate a nationalizing trend. Issues that affect the entire country would be the primary focus of attention. Thus candidates for the nation's highest office would be forced to discuss the problems they would most likely address during the general election campaign and would most likely confront as president.

Moreover, the results of the election would be clear-cut. The media could no longer interpret primaries and caucus returns as they saw fit. An incumbent's ability to garner support through the timely release of grants, contracts, and other spoils of government might be more limited in a national contest. On the other hand, such an election would undoubtedly discourage challengers who lacked national reputations. No longer would an early victory catapult a relatively unknown aspirant into the position of serious contender and jeopardize a president's chances for renomination. In fact, lesser-known candidates such as George McGovern, Jimmy Carter, and even Michael Dukakis, might find it extremely difficult to raise money, build an organization, and mount a national campaign. These difficulties would improve the chances that competent, experienced political leaders would be selected as their party's standard-bearers—or, depending on one's perspective, that older, tired, Washington-based politicians would be chosen.

From the standpoint of a party, a national primary would further weaken the ability of its leaders to influence the selection of the nominee. A successful candidate would probably not owe his victory to party officials. Moreover, a postprimary convention could not be expected to tie the nominee to the party, although it might tie the party to the nominee at least through the election. The trend toward personalizing politics would probably continue. At the very least, the successful candidate would have to wage a media campaign, further emphasizing image, probably at the expense of substantive policy issues.

Whether the primary winner would be the party's strongest candidate is also open to question. With a large field of contenders, those with the most devoted supporters might do best. On the other hand, candidates who do not arouse the passions of the diehards but who are more acceptable to the party's mainstream might not do as well. Everybody's second choice might not even finish second, unless a system of approval voting, which allows the electorate to list their top two or three choices in order, were used. But such a system would complicate the election, confusing the result and adding to the costs of conducting it.

In addition to weakening the party, a national primary could lessen the ability of states to determine when and how their citizens would participate in the presidential nomination process. The ability of state party leaders and elected officials to affect the process and influence the outcome would suffer. These likely consequences have made it difficult to mobilize wide support for such a plan despite the general appeal of the idea to the general public.

## Finance Laws

Closely related to the period and process of delegate selection are the new finance laws. Enacted in the 1970s in reaction to secret and sometimes illegal bequests to candidates, to the disparity in contributions and spending among them, and to the spiraling costs of modern campaigns, particularly the costs of television advertising, these laws were designed to improve accountability, subsidize nominations, and fund the general election. Some of these objectives have been achieved, but in the process other problems have been created.

The laws have taken campaign finance out of the back rooms and put much of it into the public spotlight. They have also, however, generated a nightmare of compliance procedures and reporting requirements. Detailed records of practically all contributions and expenditures of the presidential campaign organizations must now be kept and periodically reported to the Federal Election Commission. A good accountant and attorney are now as necessary as a pollster, image maker, and grass-roots organizers. Moreover, the soft money amendment of 1979 has now created a gigantic loophole in the law that permits large contributions and expenditures on the presidential race to go unreported.

The amount wealthy individuals can donate to presidential nominating campaigns, but not the amount they can spend independently, is limited by law. This situation has created incentives for obtaining broad-based public support but not decreased the need for frequent appeals for funds. It has not only eliminated the burden of raising money during the general election but has also created severe budget constraints on the candidates. The influence of PACs, particularly those that can mobilize their members and sympathizers on behalf of a particular candidate has been increased.

Nor have federal funds equalized the financial status of the major party candidates. Republicans still enjoy an advantage by virtue of their party's superior organizational and financial base at the national, state, and local levels. Incumbents are also benefited by their capacity to make news, affect events, and use the perquisites of office.

The law has also increased the amount of money that the campaign organizations can legally spend but not the total amount that is spent on presidential elections. The spending ceilings within the states, particularly those states that hold the earliest primaries and caucuses, have been routinely circumvented, and in a close and extended contest the overall ceiling would be subjected to similar practices. Moreover, the soft money provision has permitted both parties to raise and spend millions of dollars on their presidential campaign in addition to the federal funds provided the candidate.

Several changes have been proposed to alleviate these problems. Compliance procedures could be eased for the presidential campaigns. For example, the size of the contribution that must be reported could be increased, and the number of reports might be reduced. This change would relieve campaign organizations of some of the burdens of record keeping but would also mean that less detailed information would be available less promptly to the public.

The soft money amendment, which has created such a gigantic loophole in the Federal Election Campaign Act, could be repealed. If it were, expenditures of the parties and their candidates would be equal, and overall campaign spending would be reduced. Repealing the amendment, however, would damage party-building efforts in the states. It could also adversely affect turnout, the raison d'etre for the amendment. Turnout is lower today than it was when the amendment was enacted into law.

Independent spending, another cause of escalating costs and unequal expenditures, cannot be prevented, but there are ways in which its impact could be moderated. Congress could require television stations to allow candidates free time to respond to advertising paid for by PACs. Had such a requirement been in effect in 1988, Dukakis would have been permitted to reply without cost to the Willie Horton ad that was sponsored by a pro-Bush PAC.

A law that forced the media to provide free time might actually reduce the amount of public communications during the campaign. Television and radio stations would undoubtedly be discouraged from selling time to nonparty groups and individuals if they were under obligation to provide it free to the person or party who was the object of the commercial. A decrease in media advertising would reduce the information available to the public and increase the electorate's dependence on the candidates and the media for it.

Another way to decrease the influence of PACs is to prohibit or reduce the amount of money that they could contribute to federal elections, and increase the contribution limits for individual donors. These changes would benefit the party organizations and provide them with more incentive to create and maintain a structure that could mobilize the vote for their nominees. The problem with increasing the amount individuals could give is that the wealthy would gain greater influence, as they have with the soft money provision, and grass-roots solicitation might suffer.

Similarly, the spending limits in the nomination process might be increased and the per-state ceilings eliminated altogether. This change would reduce the practices and accounting procedures that evade the law, but it would also increase campaign costs and accentuate the financial advantage that the better-known candidates currently enjoy.

Finally, more money could be given by the federal government, if more money were available. With less than 20 percent of the population now contributing to the campaign fund, however, a large increase would require more money and probably require another method of funding, placing election funds in competition with other programs. As it stands, unless Congress provides alternative funding, or the public education campaign of the FEC is successful, there will not be sufficient funds to meet the expenses of both the 1992 nominations and general elections.

Although many lawmakers see problems with the finance laws, they cannot agree on solutions. The difficulty with amending the law lies in ensuring that no one party benefits or suffers at the expense of the other. Maintaining this objective, however, decreases the partisan motive for passing the legislation.

In addition to the question of political equity, there is an even more fundamental issue for a democratic society. Competing needs have created contradictory goals. Freedom of speech implies the right to advance beliefs by contributing to the candidates and party of choice and spending independently on their behalf. However, in a democratic political system in which the vote and presumably the voice of all citizens should be equal, the wealthy should not be advantaged. Yet appeals to a large segment of the electorate are very expensive. The difficulty of ensuring sufficient funds, protecting freedom of speech, and promoting political equality—all without partisan advantage—has generated considerable debate in the halls of Congress in recent years, but few easy or quick solutions.[3]

## Media Coverage

A third significant change in the electoral process concerns the way in which information about the campaign is communicated to the voters. Beginning in the 1950s, television became the principal medium through which candidates made their appeals and by which those appeals were assessed. Since then, television's emphasis on the contest, the drama, and the style of campaigning has affected public perceptions of the candidates and influenced the images they sought to create.

Changes in party rules and finance laws have also contributed to the media's impact. The increasing number and complexity of preconvention contests have provided the media with greater inducements to cover these events and interpret their results. The desire of the party to obtain maximum exposure for its nominating convention has further extended such coverage and interpretation. The limited money available to presidential candidates who accept federal funding has also increased the importance of news about the election and may have contributed to its impact on the voters. Today candidates do not leave their coverage to chance. They attempt to influence it by carefully releasing favorable information, by staging events, and by paying for many commercial messages.

Is the coverage adequate? Do voters receive sufficient information from the news media to make an intelligent decision? Many believe they do not. Academics, especially, have urged that greater attention be paid to policy issues and less to the horse race and other campaign issues. One proposal would have the networks and wire services assign special correspondents to cover the issues of the campaign, much as they assign people to report on its color, drama, and personal aspects. Another would be to assign a reporter to campaign coverage itself and to assess the accuracy of the statements and advertising claims of the candidates. Some major newspapers such as the *Washington Post* and the *New York Times* do, but they are the exception, not the rule.

In addition to criticizing the media's treatment of the issues and its watchdog function in the campaign, academics and others have frequently called into question the amount and accuracy of election reporting. The law states that if the networks provide free time to some candidates, they must provide equal time to all running for the same position, including those of fringe parties. This "equal time" provision has in fact resulted in no or little free time, although coverage of debates between candidates for their party's nomination and later, between candidates of the major parties in the general election, is permitted. Networks are also required to be impartial in their coverage. Station licenses can be challenged and even revoked if biases are consistently evident in the presentation of the news.

Other than requiring fairness, preventing obscenity, and ensuring that public service commitments are met, there is little the government can do to ensure adequate coverage without impinging on the freedom of the press. The media are free to choose which elections and candidates to emphasize, what kind of coverage to provide, how to interpret the results of primaries and caucuses, and even to predict who will win before the election is concluded.

Projecting the returns on election night has caused particular controversy. Since 1964, when a Lyndon Johnson landslide was predicted before the polls on the West Coast had closed, proposals have been advanced to limit or prohibit these glimpses into the immediate future. One proposal, sponsored by the League of Women Voters, would request the networks and wire services to refrain voluntarily from making any forecasts until voting across the country has been completed. Beginning in 1984 the networks consented to a variation of this proposal, agreeing not to predict the outcome in any one state until a majority of its polls had closed. This voluntary restriction, however, did not rectify the four-time-zones problem in which voting ends in the East hours before it does in the West. Thus, in 1984 all the networks had projected President Ronald Reagan the winner by 8:30 P.M. Eastern Standard Time and in 1988 two of the three networks projected a George Bush sweep by 9:20 P.M., two hours and forty minutes before the polls closed on the West Coast.

A second proposal, which has been introduced in the form of legislation, would establish a uniform hour at which all polls in the continental United States would close. To provide as long a voting day as possible in the West, the plan would extend daylight-saving time in Pacific states until the Sunday following each presidential election but revert to standard time in the rest of the country. Under such a system, the polls would then remain open until 7:00 P.M. Pacific Daylight Time and 9:00 P.M. Eastern Standard Time. The House has enacted this legislation three times since 1986, but the Senate has not.

A third proposal, the most far-reaching, would eliminate the polls altogether and have all votes cast by mail. Ballots would be distributed by the state to all eligible voters within that state. They would have to be returned (postmarked) by a specific date.

Each of these proposals has encountered criticism. Could the networks be expected to wait until voting ended across the nation, given the competitive character of news reporting? Even if there was a uniform poll closing for the entire country, there still would be no guarantee that early forecasts could be eliminated. Forecasts could still be made on the basis of exit polling. Moreover, a law, such as the one which the House of Representatives passed in 1989, would have forced thirty-nine states to change their voting hours, reducing their constitutional prerogative to conduct elections for federal officials. Eight states, including California, would have had to reduce the hours during which people could vote, conceivably contributing to lower turnout. Other states, which would have had to increase their hours, would face additional costs. And the third proposal, voting by mail, would be expensive, time-consuming, and potentially most subject to fraud.

In addition to the obvious First Amendment problems that such proposals would engender, the restrictions on the media might meet other objections. Americans seem to want their election returns reported rapidly. After a lengthy campaign, workers and sympathizers are eager to know the results and to celebrate or commiserate. Moreover, exit polls have value. Knowledge about the beliefs, attitudes, and motivations of the voters is useful information, particularly for those who are elected. In a democracy, it is essential to get as clear a reading of the pulse of the electorate as possible. At the very least this reading prevents mythical mandates from being claimed and implemented.

## ENHANCING ELECTORAL CHOICE

### *Turnout*

While suffrage has expanded, the proportion of those eligible actually turning out to vote has declined. It has declined in part because the number of eligible voters has increased, and it takes a while for newer voters to accustom themselves to the electoral process and vote with the same regularity as those who have had the franchise before. The strength of partisan attitudes, also a motivation for voting, has decreased. Finally, a number of other factors, including legal obstacles, continue to confound and confuse would-be voters. As a result only a little over 50 percent of the electorate exercises its franchise and votes during presidential elections, with lower turnout during nonpresidential elections.

This relatively low turnout in a free and open society has been a source of embarrassment to the United States and of concern to its public officials. How can a president legitimately claim a public mandate with the electoral support of only about one-quarter of those eligible to vote? Bush's percentage was 27 in 1988. How can the government claim to be representative if half the electorate chooses not to participate in its selection?

Concern over low turnout has generated a number of proposals for remedying it. One proposal would make election day in presidential years a holiday. Presumably this change would prevent work-related activities from interfering with voting for the bulk of the population. Many countries follow this practice or hold their elections on Sunday. The problem here is that another national holiday would cost employers millions of dollars in lost productivity, with no guarantee that turnout would be increased. For workers in certain service areas the holiday might be a workday anyway.

Another proposal would be to facilitate registration. Since approximately 80 percent of those who register vote, easier registration would increase the percent of voters.[4] In fact, political scientists Raymond E. Wolfinger and Steven J. Rosenstone have estimated that abolishing the requirement, practiced in many states, that registration be completed thirty days prior to the election would increase turnout 3–9 percent for the nation as a whole.[5]

The 101st Congress (1989–1990) considered a "motor-voter" bill that would have permitted people to register to vote at the time they applied to obtain or renew their driver's licenses. The legislation enacted by the House of Representatives would have also permitted voter registration at libraries, schools, and other public offices. Antifraud provisions to require states to confirm address and "clean" their voter registration lists were also part of the bill.

Proponents of the legislation saw it as an easy, workable solution to the registration problem, one which could add millions of new voters. Opponents, however, including President Bush, decried the federal government's intrusion into constitutionally designated state activity and the costs and procedural burdens that it would place on the states. Critics of the legislation also pointed to the potential for fraud because mail-in applications would not be required to be notarized. There was also an underlying partisan issue on this and other legislation to ease registration. Since a larger proportion of those who are not registered have less education and lower incomes, Republicans fear that the higher turnout that might be achieved through higher registration would benefit the Democrats.

Other proposals that have been advanced from time to time include making registration automatic, as it is in many European countries where turnout is much higher, or extending it to election day itself. The states with the highest turnout in 1984 and 1988 (Minnesota, Maine, and Wisconsin) permit election day registration. In general the states with the least restrictive laws have higher turnouts.

But there are a number of problems with automatic registration or simultaneous registration and voting. The potential for voting fraud might be increased; the ability of states to monitor federal elections could be impaired; and citizens' responsibilities might be lessened. Should it be the duty of the national government or the states to conduct elections? The Constitution specifies that the states hold elections for national officials, although amendments extending suffrage have limited a state's authority to determine who is eligible to vote. Should it be a responsibility of the federal government to oversee the electoral process and an obligation of the citizenry to participate in it?

The most radical proposal would be to simply compel people to vote: to force them to go to the polls and cast a ballot. Penalties would be imposed on those who refused to do so. Australia, Belgium, and Italy require voting, and their turnout is, not surprisingly, very high.[6]

If everybody who was eligible had to vote, parties and candidates would have to broaden their appeal. They would have to address the needs and desires of all the people and not concentrate on those who were most likely to vote. Those who have not participated as frequently in the current voluntary system of voting—the poorer, less educated, less fortunate—would receive more attention not only from candidates for office but from elected officials in office. More equitable policies might result. The ideal of a government of, by, and for the people might be a step closer to reality.

One obvious problem with compelling people to vote is the compulsion itself. Some may be physically or mentally incapable of voting. Others may not care, have little interest, and have very limited information. They might not even know the names of the candidates. Would the selection of the best-qualified person be enhanced by the participation of these uninformed, uninterested, uncaring voters? Might demagogy be encouraged, or even slicker and more simplistic advertising develop? Would government be more responsive and more popular, or would it be more prone to what British philosopher John Stuart Mill referred to as "the tyranny of the majority"? Finally, is it democratic to force people to vote? If the right to vote is an essential component of a democratic society, then what about the right not to vote? Should it be protected as well?

## The Electoral College

In addition to the problem of who votes, another source of contention is how the votes should be aggregated. Theoretically, the Constitution allows electors chosen by the states to vote as they please. In practice, all votes are cast for the popular vote winner in the state. The reason for this outcome is simple. The vote for president and vice-president is actually a vote for competing slates of electors selected in all but two states on a state wide basis. The slate that wins is the slate proposed by the winning candidate's party. Naturally the electors are expected to vote for their party's nominees.

This de facto system has been criticized as undemocratic, as unrepresentative of minority views within states, and as potentially unreflective of the nation's popular choice. Over the years, there have been numerous proposals to alter it. The first was introduced in Congress in 1797. Since then, there have been more than five hundred others.

In urging changes, critics have pointed to the electoral college's archaic design, its electoral biases, and the undemocratic results it can produce. (See Chapter 1.) In recent years, four major plans—automatic, proportional, district, and direct election—have been proposed as constitutional amendments to alleviate some or all of these problems. The following sections will examine these proposals and the impact they could have on the way in which the president is selected.

**The Automatic Plan.** The actual electors in the electoral college have been an anachronism since the development of the party system. Their role as partisan agents is not and has not been consistent with their exercising an independent judgment in choosing a president. In fact, sixteen states plus the District of Columbia prohibit such a judgment by requiring electors to cast their ballots for the winner of the state's popular vote. Although probably unenforceable because they seem to clash with the Constitution, these laws strongly indicate how electors should vote.

The so-called automatic plan would do away with the danger that electors may exercise their personal preferences. First proposed in 1826, it has received substantial support since that time, including the backing of Presidents John Kennedy and Lyndon Johnson. The plan simply keeps the electoral college intact but eliminates the electors. Electoral votes are automatically credited to the candidate who has received the most popular votes within the state.

Other than removing the potential problem of faithless or unpledged electors, the plan would do little to change the system. It has not been enacted because Congress has not felt the problem to be of sufficient magnitude to justify a constitutional amendment. There have in fact been only eight faithless electors, who failed to vote for their party's nominees—six since 1948.[7] Additionally, one Democratic West Virginia elector in 1988 reversed the order of the nominees, voting for Lloyd Bentsen for president and Michael Dukakis for vice-president.

**The Proportional Plan.** Electing the entire slate of presidential electors has also been the focus of considerable attention. If the winner of the state's popular vote takes all the electoral votes, the impact of the majority party is increased within that state and the larger, more competitive states, where voters are more evenly divided, are benefited.

From the perspective of the minority party or parties within the state, this winner-take-all system is not desirable. In effect, it disenfranchises people who do not vote for the winning candidate. And it does more than that: it discourages a strong campaign effort by a party that has little chance of winning the presidential election in that state. Naturally the success of other candidates of that party is affected as well. The winner-take-all system also works to reduce voter turnout.

One way to rectify this problem would be to have proportional voting. Such a plan has been introduced on a number of occasions. Under a proportional system, the electors would be abolished, the winner-take-all principle would be eliminated, and a state's electoral vote would be divided in proportion to the popular vote the candidates received within the state. A majority of electoral votes would still be required for election. If no candidate obtained a majority in the electoral college, most proportional plans call for a joint session of Congress to choose the president from among the top two or three candidates.

The proportional proposal would have a number of major consequences. It would decrease the influence of the most competitive states and increase the importance of the least competitive ones, where voters are likely to be more homogeneous. Under such a system, the *size* of the victory would count. To take a dramatic example, if the electoral votes of Vermont and New York in 1960 had been calculated on the basis of the proportional vote for the major candidates within the states, Richard Nixon would have received a larger margin from Vermont's 3 votes (1.759 to 1.240) than John Kennedy would have gotten from New York's 45 (22.7 to 22.3). Similarly, in 1968, George Wallace's margin over Nixon and Hubert Humphrey in Mississippi, which had 7 electoral votes, would have been larger than Humphrey's over Nixon in New York, which had 43.

While the proportional system rewards large victories in relatively homogeneous states, it also seems to encourage competition within those states. Having the electoral vote proportional to the popular vote provides an incentive to the minority party to mount a more vigorous campaign and establish a more effective organization. However, it might also cause third parties to do the same, thereby weakening the two-party system.

The proportional plan contains a pattern of biases far different from the one found in the electoral college. As noted in Chapter 1, the electoral college benefits the very smallest and, to a greater extent, the very largest states. Within the larger and more competitive states, the system favors geographically concentrated groups with cohesive voting patterns. A proportional system, however, would advantage smaller, homogeneous states, disadvantage larger, heterogeneous ones, and would not benefit geographically concentrated groups nearly as much as the current system does.[8]

Finally, operating under a proportional plan would in all likelihood make the electoral college vote much closer, thereby reducing the president's claim to broad public backing for him, his new administration, and the policy proposals he has advocated during his campaign. George Bush would have defeated Michael Dukakis by only 43.1 electoral votes in 1988, Jimmy Carter would have defeated Gerald Ford by only 11.7 in 1976, and Richard Nixon would have won by only 6.1 in 1968. (See Table 9–1.)

In at least one recent instance, a proportional electoral vote in the states might have changed the election results. Had this plan been in effect in 1960, Richard Nixon would probably have defeated John Kennedy by 266.1 to 265.6. However, it is difficult to calculate the 1960 vote precisely because the names of the Democratic presidential and vice-presidential candidates were not on the ballot in Alabama and because an unpledged slate of electors was chosen in Mississippi.

**The District Plan.** The district electoral system is another proposal aimed at reducing the effect of winner-take-all voting. While this plan has had several variations, its basic thrust would be to keep the electoral college but to change the manner in which the electoral votes within the state are determined. Instead of selecting the entire slate on the basis of the statewide vote for president, only two electoral votes would be decided in this manner. The remaining votes would be allocated on the basis of the popular vote within individual districts (probably congressional districts). A majority of the electoral votes would still be necessary for election. If the vote in the electoral college were not decisive, then most district plans call for a joint session of Congress to make the final selection.

For the very smallest states, those with three electoral votes, all three electors would have to be chosen by the state as a whole. For others, however, the combination of district and at-large selection would probably result in a split electoral vote. On a national level, this change would make the electoral college more reflective of the partisan division of the newly elected Congress rather than of the popular division of the national electorate.

The losers under such an arrangement would be the large, competitive states and, most particularly, the organized, geographically concentrated groups within those states. The winners would include small states. Third and minority parties might also be aided to the extent that they were capable of winning specific legislative districts. It is difficult to project whether Republicans or Democrats would benefit more from such an arrangement, since much would depend on how the legislative districts within the states were apportioned. If the 1960 presidential vote were aggregated on the basis of one electoral vote to the popular vote winner of each congressional district and two to the popular vote winner

## TABLE 9–1
### Voting for President, 1952–1988:
### Four Methods for Aggregating the Votes

| Year | Electoral College | Proportional Plan | District Plan | Direct Election (percentage of total vote) |
|---|---|---|---|---|
| *1952* | | | | |
| Eisenhower | 442 | 288.5 | 375 | 55.1% |
| Stevenson | 89 | 239.8 | 156 | 44.4 |
| Others | 0 | 2.7 | 0 | .5 |
| *1956* | | | | |
| Eisenhower | 457 | 296.7 | 411 | 57.4 |
| Stevenson | 73 | 227.2 | 120 | 42.0 |
| Others | 0 | 7.1 | 0 | .6 |
| *1960* | | | | |
| Nixon | 219 | 266.1 | 278 | 49.5 |
| Kennedy | 303 | 265.6 | 245 | 49.8 |
| Others | 0 | 5.3 | 0 | .7 |
| *1964* | | | | |
| Goldwater | 52 | 213.6 | 72 | 38.5 |
| Johnson | 486 | 320.0 | 466 | 61.0 |
| Others | 0 | 3.9 | 0 | .5 |
| *1968* | | | | |
| Nixon | 301 | 231.5 | 289 | 43.2 |
| Humphrey | 191 | 225.4 | 192 | 42.7 |
| Wallace | 46 | 78.8 | 57 | 13.5 |
| Others | 0 | 2.3 | 0 | .6 |
| *1972* | | | | |
| Nixon | 520 | 330.3 | 474 | 60.7 |
| McGovern | 17 | 197.5 | 64 | 37.5 |
| Others | 1 | 10.0 | 0 | 1.8 |
| *1976* | | | | |
| Ford | 240 | 258.0 | 269 | 48.0 |
| Carter | 297 | 269.7 | 269 | 50.1 |
| Others | 1 | 10.2 | 0 | 1.9 |
| *1980* | | | | |
| Reagan | 489 | 272.9 | 396 | 50.7 |
| Carter | 49 | 220.9 | 142 | 41.0 |
| Anderson | 0 | 35.3 | 0 | 6.6 |
| Others | 0 | 8.9 | 0 | 1.7 |
| *1984* | | | | |
| Reagan | 525 | 317.6 | 468 | 58.8 |
| Mondale | 13 | 216.6 | 70 | 40.6 |
| Others | 0 | 3.8 | 0 | .7 |
| *1988* | | | | |
| Bush | 426 | 287.8 | 379 | 53.4 |
| Dukakis | 111 | 244.7 | 159 | 45.6 |
| Others | 1 | 5.5 | 0 | 1.0 |

*Source:* Figures on Proportional and District Vote for 1952–1980 were supplied to the author by Joseph B. Gorman of the Congressional Service, Library of Congress. Calculations for 1984 and 1988 were completed by Mark Drozdowski and Erik Pages, respectively, on the basis of data reported in the *Almanac of American Politics* (Washington, D.C.: National Journal, 1985 and 1989).

of each state, Nixon would have defeated Kennedy 278 to 245 with 14 unpledged electors. In 1976 the district system would have produced a tie, with Carter and Ford each receiving 269 votes. (See Table 9–1.) In 1988, Bush would have defeated Dukakis, 379 to 159. The states of Maine and Nebraska are the only ones that presently choose their electors in this manner.

**The Direct Election Plan.** Of all the plans to alter or replace the electoral college, the direct popular vote has received the most attention and support. Designed to eliminate the college entirely and count the votes on a nationwide basis, it would elect the popular vote winner provided the winning candidate received a certain percentage of the total vote. In most plans, 40 percent of the total vote would be necessary. In some, 50 percent would be required.[9] In the event that no one got the required percentage, a runoff between the top two candidates would be held to determine the winner.[10]

A direct popular vote would, of course, remedy a major problem of the present system—the possibility of electing a nonplurality president. It would better equalize voting power both among and within the states. The large, competitive states would lose some of their electoral clout by the elimination of the winner-take-all system. Party competition within the states and perhaps even nationwide would be increased. Turnout should also improve. Every vote would count in a direct election.

However, a direct election might also encourage minor parties, which would weaken the two-party system. The possibility of denying a major party candidate 40 percent of the popular vote might be sufficient to entice a proliferation of candidates and produce a series of bargains and deals in which support was traded for favors with a new administration. Moreover, if the federal character of the system were changed, it is possible that the plurality winner might not be geographically representative of the entire country. A very large sectional vote might elect a candidate who trailed in other areas of the country. This result would upset the representational balance that has been achieved between the president's and Congress's electoral constituencies.

The organized groups that are geographically concentrated in the large industrial states would have their votes diluted by a direct election. Take Jewish voters, for example. Highly supportive of the Democratic party since World War II, Jews constitute approximately 3 percent of the total population but 14 percent in New York, the state with the second largest number of electoral votes. Thus the impact of the New York Jewish vote is magnified under the present electoral college arrangement.[11]

The Republican party has also been reluctant to lend its support to direct election. Republicans perceive that they benefit from the current arrangement, which provides more safe Republican states than Democratic ones. While Republican Benjamin Harrison was the last non-plurality president to be elected, Gerald Ford came remarkably close in 1976. On the other hand, Richard Nixon's electoral college victory in 1968 could conceivably have been upset by a stronger Wallace campaign in the southern border states.

A very close popular vote could also cause problems with a direct election. The winner might not be evident for days, even months. Voter fraud could have national consequences. Under such circumstances, large-scale challenges by the losing candidate would be more likely.

The provision for the situation in which no one received the required percentage of the popular vote has its drawbacks as well. A runoff election would extend the length of the campaign and add to its cost. Considering that some aspirants begin their quest for the presidency many years before the election, a further protraction of the process might unduly tax the patience of the voters and produce an even greater numbing effect than currently exists. Moreover, it would also cut an already short transition period for a newly elected president and would further drain the time and energy of an incumbent seeking reelection.

There is still another difficulty with a contingency election. It could reverse the order in which the candidates originally finished. This result might undermine the ability of the eventual winner to govern successfully. It might also encourage spoiler candidacies. Third parties and independents seeking the presidency could exercise considerable power in the event of a close contest between the major parties. Imagine Wallace's influence in 1968 in a runoff between Humphrey and Nixon.

Nonetheless, the direct election plan is supported by public opinion and has been ritualistically praised by contemporary presidents. Gallup Polls conducted over the last three decades have consistently found the public favoring a direct election over the present electoral system by substantial margins.[12] Carter and Ford have both urged the abolition of the electoral college and its replacement by a popular vote.

In 1969 the House of Representatives actually voted for a constitutional amendment to establish direct election for president and vice-president, but the Senate refused to go along. Despite this support, it seems unlikely that sufficient impetus for such a change that requires a constitutional amendment will occur until the issue becomes salient to more people. It may take the election of a nonplurality president or some other electoral crisis to produce the public outcry and political momentum needed to change the electoral college system.

The difficulty of generating change speaks to the resiliency of the electoral college system and perhaps also to its perceived success in choosing the president. Despite the complaints that are ritualistically voiced during the election period that the candidates are no good, that there is very little difference between them, and that the campaigns are mean, superficial, and irrelevant, the electorate has not demanded that its congressional representatives change the system beyond extending suffrage to all citizens. Similarly, the reforms in finance laws and party rules have been designed to achieve the democratic goals of encouraging more people to support the candidates and to participate in their campaigns. The electoral system may not be perfect, but it has functioned with public support for over 200 years, a significant achievement in itself. This achievement is cited by those who oppose changing it on the grounds that "if it ain't broke, it don't need fixing."

## SUMMARY

There have been changes and continuities in the way we select a president. In general the changes have made the system more democratic. The continuities link the system to its republican past.

The nomination process has been affected more than the general election. Significant modifications have occurred in the rules for choosing delegates, in the laws regulating contributions and spending, and in the media through which appeals are made. The composition of the electorate has been altered as well. In contrast, the electoral college has continued to function in much the same way for the last century and a half, although certainly not as the framers intended.

Have these changes been beneficial or harmful? Have they functioned to make the system more efficient, more responsive, and more likely to result in the choice of a well-qualified candidate? Political scientists disagree in their answers.

Much of the current controversy over campaign reform has focused on party rules. Designed to encourage greater rank-and-file participation in the selection of delegates, the new rules have helped democratize presidential nominations. In the process, however, they have also fractionalized and personalized the parties, weakened the position of their leadership, and in the case of the Democrats, disadvantaged their presidential candidates in the general election. These unintended consequences have stimulated a debate over the merits of the changes.

A consensus seems to be emerging that some of the reforms have gone too far and that stronger party control over the nomination process is needed. The Democrats have tried to move in this direction, modifying some of their reforms but not others. In fact their imposition of straight proportional voting in 1992 may factionalize the party still further and prevent or delay agreement on the nominee until later in the process. The Republicans continue to allow their state parties to determine the rules by which their caucuses and primaries are conducted.

Despite the inclinations of Democratic leaders to retrench and of some members of Congress to control the undesirable effects of the nomination process by legislating when caucuses and primaries can be held, a majority of the electorate would go even further—but in the opposite direction. They would have more participatory democracy, not less. They would abolish the present patchwork of state caucuses and primaries and replace it with a single, national primary.

The new finance legislation has also been designed to improve accountability, equalize contributions, and control spending. This legislation has enhanced public information, but it has done so only by increasing the burden on candidate organizations to keep detailed records and submit frequent reports. The law has reduced but not eliminated the influence of large donors, particularly through the soft money amendment. It has also contributed to the factionalizing of parties, encouraging multiple candidacies for the nomination. By giving the bulk of federal funds directly to the candidates, it has encouraged the development of separate candidate organizations and provided incentives for political action committees. Whether the end result has been to lessen the advantage of wealth and effectively open the process to a much larger group of aspirants is difficult to say. No consensus on how to improve the law is apparent.

Media coverage has also been the subject of considerable controversy. Television has made more people aware of presidential candidates than in the past, but that awareness has also tended to be indirect and passive. The reporting of information about personalities and campaign events far exceeds that of substantive policy issues. Television, in particular, is often blamed for the average voter's low level of knowledge and for exercising undue influence on the electorate.

Whether or not this accusation is accurate, it is widespread and has generated persistent criticism. Few changes are likely, however, in the short run because the public is less concerned about media coverage than are the candidates, and any nonvoluntary attempt to affect coverage is apt to run up against the guarantees of the First Amendment.

Who votes and how the votes should be aggregated continue to prompt debate and elicit concern. The expansion of suffrage has made the election process more democratic in theory, but the decline in turnout and lower rates of participation have called this theoretical improvement into question. While the failure of almost one-half of the electorate to exercise the franchise has been a source of embarrassment and dismay, there is little agreement on how to deal with this problem in a federal system that values individual initiative and individual fulfillment of civic responsibility.

Finally, the equity of the electoral college has also been challenged, but none of the proposals to alter or abolish it, except by the direct election of the president, has received much public support. With no outcry for change, Congress has been reluctant to alter the system by amending the Constitution and seems unlikely to do so until an electoral crisis or unpopular result forces its hand. ·

Does the electoral process work? Yes. Can it be improved? Of course.

Will it be changed? Probably, but if the past is any indication, there is no guarantee that the changes will produce only, or even, the desired effect. If politics is the art of the possible, then success is achieved by those who can adjust most quickly to the change and turn it to their advantage.

# NOTES

1. Barbara Norrander, "Turnout in Super Tuesday Primaries: The Composition of the Electorate" (Paper presented at annual meeting of the American Political Science Association, Atlanta, Georgia, August 31–September 3, 1989), p. 2.
2. *Gallup Report*, no. 226 (July 1984): 23.
3. Legislation debated by the Congress included voluntary limits on campaign spending for congressional elections, restrictions on out-of-state contributions, and limiting or eliminating PAC contributions.
4. Curtis Gans, director of the Committee for the Study of the American Electorate, estimated that a universal election day registration would increase voter turnout by 6 million voters. Quoted in Martha Angle, "Low Voter Turnout Prompts Concern on the Hill," *Congressional Quarterly, Weekly Report*, April 2, 1988, p. 862. Other estimates have been as high as 13 million.
5. Raymond E. Wolfinger and Steven J. Rosenstone, *Who Votes?* (New Haven, Conn.: Yale University Press, 1980), p. 130.
6. Turnout was over 93 percent in Australia and Belgium and almost 90 percent in Italy during the 1980s. Ibid., p. 863.
7. There is some controversy whether three other electors in 1796 might also have gone against their party when voting for president. They supported John Adams although they were selected in states controlled by the Democratic-Republicans. However, the fluidity of the party system in those days, combined with the weakness of party identification, makes their affiliation (if any) difficult to establish.
8. Lawrence D. Longley and James D. Dana, Jr., "New Empirical Estimates of the Biases of the Electoral College for the 1980s," *Western Political Quarterly* 33 (1984): 172–73.
9. Abraham Lincoln was the only plurality president who failed to attain the 40 percent figure. He received 39.82 percent, although he probably would have received more had his name been on the ballot in nine southern states.
10. Other direct election proposals have recommended that a joint session of Congress decide the winner. The runoff provision was contained in the resolution that passed the House of Representatives in 1969. A direct election plan with a runoff provision failed to win the two-thirds Senate vote required to initiate a constitutional amendment in 1979.
11. John Kennedy carried New York by approximately 384,000 votes. He received a plurality of more than 800,000 from precincts that were primarily Jewish. Similarly, in Illinois, a state he carried by less than 9,000, Kennedy had a plurality of 55,000 from the so-called Jewish precincts. Mark R. Levy and Michael S. Kramer, *The Ethnic Factor* (New York: Simon and Schuster, 1972), p.104.
12. A 1980 Gallup Poll found 67 percent favoring direct election over the present system, with only 19 percent opposed and the rest undecided. In Gallup

surveys dating back to 1966, similar majorities have supported direct election and the elimination of the electoral college. George H. Gallup. *The Gallup Poll* (Wilmington, Del.: Scholarly Resources, 1981), pp. 258–260.

## SELECTED READINGS

Alexander, Herbert E. "Campaign Finance Reform." *Proceedings of the Academy of Political Science* 37 (1989): 123–40.

Best, Judith. *The Case against Direct Election of the President: A Defense of the Electoral College*. Ithaca, N.Y.: Cornell University Press, 1975.

Caeser, James W. *Reforming the Reforms: A Critical Analysis of the Presidential Selection Process*. Cambridge, Mass.: Ballinger, 1982.

Heard, Alexander. *Made in America: The Nomination and Election of Presidents*. New York: Harper Collins, 1991.

Longley, Lawrence D., and Alan G. Braun. *The Politics of Electoral College Reform*. New Haven, Conn.: Yale University Press, 1975.

Peirce, Neal R., and Lawrence D. Longley. *The People's President*. New Haven, Conn.: Yale University Press, 1981.

Polsby, Nelson W. *Consequences of Party Reform*. New York: Oxford University Press, 1983.

Sundquist, James L. *Constitutional Reform*. Washington, D.C.: Brookings Institution, 1986.

PART
V

Appendixes

# Appendix A

## Results of Presidential Elections, 1860–1988

| Year | Candidates Democrat | Candidates Republican | Electoral Vote Democrat | Electoral Vote Republican | Popular Vote Democrat | Popular Vote Republican |
|---|---|---|---|---|---|---|
| 1860(a) | Stephen A. Douglas Herschel V. Johnson | Abraham Lincoln Hannibal Hamlin | 12 4% | 180 59% | 1,380,202 29.5% | 1,865,908 39.8% |
| 1864(b) | George B. McClellan George H. Pendleton | Abraham Lincoln Andrew Johnson | 21 9% | 212 91% | 1,812,807 45.0% | 2,218,388 55.0% |
| 1868(c) | Horatio Seymour Francis P. Blair Jr. | Ulysses S. Grant Schuyler Colfax | 80 27% | 214 73% | 2,708,744 47.3% | 3,013,650 52.7% |
| 1872(d) | Horace Greeley Benjamin Gratz Brown | Ulysses S. Grant Henry Wilson | | 286 78% | 2,834,761 43.8% | 3,598,235 55.6% |
| 1876 | Samuel J. Tilden Thomas A. Hendricks | Rutherford B. Hayes William A. Wheeler | 184 50% | 185 50% | 4,288,546 51.0% | 4,034,311 47.9% |
| 1880 | Winfield S. Hancock William H. English | James A. Garfield Chester A. Arthur | 155 42% | 214 58% | 4,444,260 48.2% | 4,446,158 48.3% |
| 1884 | Grover Cleveland Thomas A. Hendricks | James G. Blaine John A. Logan | 219 55% | 182 45% | 4,874,621 48.5% | 4,848,936 48.2% |
| 1888 | Grover Cleveland Allen G. Thurman | Benjamin Harrison Levi P. Morton | 168 42% | 233 58% | 5,534,488 48.6% | 5,443,892 47.8% |
| 1892(e) | Grover Cleveland Adlai E. Stevenson | Benjamin Harrison Whitelaw Reid | 277 62% | 145 33% | 5,551,883 46.1% | 5,179,244 43.0% |

| Year | Candidate / Running Mate | Electoral Vote | % | Popular Vote | % |
|---|---|---|---|---|---|
| 1896 | William J. Bryan / Arthur Sewall | 176 | 39% | 6,511,495 | 46.7% |
|  | William McKinley / Garret A. Hobart | 271 | 61% | 7,108,480 | 51.0% |
| 1900 | William J. Bryan / Adlai E. Stevenson | 155 | 35% | 6,358,345 | 45.5% |
|  | William McKinley / Theodore Roosevelt | 292 | 65% | 7,218,039 | 51.7% |
| 1904 | Alton B. Parker / Henry G. Davis | 140 | 29% | 5,028,898 | 37.6% |
|  | Theodore Roosevelt / Charles W. Fairbanks | 336 | 71% | 7,626,593 | 56.4% |
| 1908 | William J. Bryan / John W. Kern | 162 | 34% | 6,406,801 | 43.0% |
|  | William H. Taft / James S. Sherman | 321 | 66% | 7,676,258 | 51.6% |
| 1912(f) | Woodrow Wilson / Thomas R. Marshall | 435 | 82% | 6,293,152 | 41.8% |
|  | William H. Taft / James S. Sherman | 8 | 2% | 3,486,333 | 23.2% |
| 1916 | Woodrow Wilson / Thomas R. Marshall | 277 | 52% | 9,126,300 | 49.2% |
|  | Charles E. Hughes / Charles W. Fairbanks | 254 | 48% | 8,546,789 | 46.1% |
| 1920 | James M. Cox / Franklin D. Roosevelt | 127 | 24% | 9,140,884 | 34.2% |
|  | Warren G. Harding / Calvin Coolidge | 404 | 76% | 16,133,314 | 60.3% |
| 1924(g) | John W. Davis / Charles W. Bryant | 136 | 26% | 8,386,169 | 28.8% |
|  | Calvin Coolidge / Charles G. Dawes | 382 | 72% | 15,717,553 | 54.1% |
| 1928 | Alfred E. Smith / Joseph T. Robinson | 87 | 16% | 15,000,185 | 40.8% |
|  | Herbert C. Hoover / Charles Curtis | 444 | 84% | 21,411,991 | 58.2% |
| 1932 | Franklin D. Roosevelt / John N. Garner | 472 | 89% | 22,825,016 | 57.4% |
|  | Herbert C. Hoover / Charles Curtis | 59 | 11% | 15,758,397 | 39.6% |
| 1936 | Franklin D. Roosevelt / John N. Garner | 523 | 98% | 27,747,636 | 60.8% |
|  | Alfred M. Landon / Frank Knox | 8 | 2% | 16,679,543 | 36.5% |

# Appendix A

## Results of Presidential Elections, 1860–1988 (*continued*)

| Year | Candidates Democrat | Republican | Electoral Vote Democrat | Republican | Popular Vote Democrat | Republican |
|---|---|---|---|---|---|---|
| 1940 | Franklin D. Roosevelt<br>Henry A. Wallace | Wendell L. Wilkie<br>Charles L. McNary | 449<br>85% | 82<br>15% | 27,263,448<br>54.7% | 22,336,260<br>44.8% |
| 1944 | Franklin D. Roosevelt<br>Harry S Truman | Thomas E. Dewey<br>John W. Bricker | 432<br>81% | 99<br>19% | 25,611,936<br>53.4% | 22,013,372<br>45.9% |
| 1948(h) | Harry S Truman<br>Alben W. Barkley | Thomas E. Dewey<br>Earl Warren | 303<br>57% | 189<br>36% | 24,105,587<br>49.5% | 21,970,017<br>45.1% |
| 1952 | Adlai E. Stevenson<br>John J. Sparkman | Dwight D. Eisenhower<br>Richard M. Nixon | 89<br>17% | 442<br>83% | 27,314,649<br>44.4% | 33,936,137<br>55.1% |
| 1956(i) | Adlai E. Stevenson<br>Estes Kefauver | Dwight D. Eisenhower<br>Richard M. Nixon | 73<br>14% | 457<br>86% | 26,030,172<br>42.0% | 35,585,245<br>57.4% |
| 1960(j) | John F. Kennedy<br>Lyndon B. Johnson | Richard M. Nixon<br>Henry Cabot Lodge | 303<br>56% | 219<br>41% | 34,221,344<br>49.8% | 34,106,671<br>49.5% |
| 1964 | Lyndon B. Johnson<br>Hubert H. Humphrey | Barry Goldwater<br>William E. Miller | 486<br>90% | 52<br>10% | 43,126,584<br>61.0% | 27,177,838<br>38.5% |
| 1968(k) | Hubert H. Humphrey<br>Edmund S. Muskie | Richard M. Nixon<br>Spiro T. Agnew | 191<br>36% | 301<br>56% | 31,274,503<br>42.7% | 31,785,148<br>43.2% |

| Year | Candidate (President / Vice President) | Electoral vote | % | Popular vote | % |
|---|---|---|---|---|---|
| 1972(l) | George McGovern / Sargent Shriver | 17 | 3% | 29,171,791 | 37.5% |
| | Richard M. Nixon / Spiro T. Agnew | 520 | 97% | 47,170,179 | 60.7% |
| 1976(m) | Jimmy Carter / Walter F. Mondale | 297 | 55% | 40,828,657 | 50.1% |
| | Gerald R. Ford / Robert Dole | 240 | 45% | 39,145,520 | 48.0% |
| 1980 | Jimmy Carter / Walter F. Mondale | 49 | 10% | 35,483,820 | 41.0% |
| | Ronald Reagan / George Bush | 489 | 90% | 43,901,812 | 50.7% |
| 1984 | Walter F. Mondale / Geraldine Ferraro | 13 | 2% | 37,577,137 | 40.6% |
| | Ronald Reagan / George Bush | 525 | 98% | 54,455,074 | 58.8% |
| 1988(n) | Michael S. Dukakis / Lloyd Bentsen | 111 | 21% | 41,809,074 | 45.6% |
| | George Bush / Dan Quayle | 426 | 79% | 48,886,097 | 53.4% |

*Source: Congress and the Nation* (Washington, D.C.: The Congressional Quarterly, 1985), Vol. VI, pp. 1090–1091, updated by the author. Copyrighted material reprinted with permission of Congressional Quarterly Inc.

(a) 1860; John C. Breckinridge, Southern Democrat, polled 72 electoral votes; John Bell, Constitutional Union, polled 39 electoral votes.

(b) 1864; 81 electoral votes were not cast.

(c) 1868; 23 electoral votes were not cast.

(d) 1872; Horace Greeley died after election, 63 Democratic electoral votes were scattered. 17 were not voted.

(e) 1892; James B. Weaver, People's party, polled 22 electoral votes.

(f) 1912; Theodore Roosevelt, Progressive party, polled 88 electoral votes.

(g) 1924; Robert M. LaFollette, Progressive party, polled 13 electoral votes.

(h) 1948; J. Strom Thurmond, States' Rights party, polled 39 electoral votes.

(i) 1956; Walter B. Jones, Democrat, polled 1 electoral vote.

(j) 1960; Harry Flood Byrd, Democrat, polled 15 electoral votes.

(k) 1968; George C. Wallace, American independent, polled 46 electoral votes.

(l) 1972; John Hospers, Libertarian party, polled 1 electoral vote.

(m) 1976; Ronald Reagan, Republican, polled 1 electoral vote.

(n) 1988; Lloyd Bentsen, the Democratic vice-presidential nominee, polled 1 electoral vote for president.

# Appendix B

## 1988 Presidential Election Results*

| State | Electoral Vote Rep. | Electoral Vote Dem. | Electoral Vote Other | Total Vote | Republican | Democratic | Other | Plurality | Percentage Total Vote Rep. | Percentage Total Vote Dem. | Percentage Major Vote Rep. | Percentage Major Vote Dem. |
|---|---|---|---|---|---|---|---|---|---|---|---|---|
| Alabama | 9 | | | 1,378,476 | 815,576 | 549,506 | 13,394 | 266,070 R | 59.2% | 39.9% | 59.7% | 40.3% |
| Alaska | 3 | | | 200,116 | 119,251 | 72,584 | 8,281 | 46,667 R | 59.6% | 36.3% | 62.2% | 37.8% |
| Arizona | 7 | | | 1,171,873 | 702,541 | 454,029 | 15,303 | 248,512 R | 60.0% | 38.7% | 60.7% | 39.3% |
| Arkansas | 6 | | | 827,738 | 466,578 | 349,237 | 11,923 | 117,341 R | 56.4% | 42.2% | 57.2% | 42.8% |
| California | 47 | | | 9,887,065 | 5,054,917 | 4,702,233 | 129,915 | 352,684 R | 51.1% | 47.6% | 51.8% | 48.2% |
| Colorado | 8 | | | 1,372,394 | 728,177 | 621,453 | 22,764 | 106,724 R | 53.1% | 45.3% | 54.0% | 46.0% |
| Connecticut | 8 | | | 1,443,394 | 750,241 | 676,584 | 16,569 | 73,657 R | 52.0% | 46.9% | 52.6% | 47.4% |
| Delaware | 3 | | | 249,891 | 139,639 | 108,647 | 1,605 | 30,992 R | 55.9% | 43.5% | 56.2% | 43.8% |
| Florida | 21 | | | 4,302,313 | 2,618,885 | 1,656,701 | 26,727 | 962,184 R | 60.9% | 38.5% | 61.3% | 38.7% |
| Georgia | 12 | | | 1,809,672 | 1,081,331 | 714,792 | 13,549 | 366,539 R | 59.8% | 39.5% | 60.2% | 39.8% |
| Hawaii | | 4 | | 354,461 | 158,625 | 192,364 | 3,472 | 33,739 D | 44.8% | 54.3% | 45.2% | 54.8% |
| Idaho | 4 | | | 408,968 | 253,881 | 147,272 | 7,815 | 106,609 R | 62.1% | 36.0% | 63.3% | 36.7% |
| Illinois | 24 | | | 4,559,120 | 2,310,939 | 2,215,940 | 32,241 | 94,999 R | 50.7% | 48.6% | 51.0% | 49.0% |
| Indiana | 12 | | | 2,168,621 | 1,297,763 | 860,643 | 10,215 | 437,120 R | 59.8% | 39.7% | 60.1% | 39.9% |
| Iowa | | 8 | | 1,225,614 | 545,355 | 670,557 | 9,702 | 125,202 D | 44.5% | 54.7% | 44.9% | 55.1% |
| Kansas | 7 | | | 993,044 | 554,049 | 422,636 | 16,359 | 131,413 R | 55.8% | 42.6% | 56.7% | 43.3% |
| Kentucky | 9 | | | 1,322,517 | 734,281 | 580,368 | 7,868 | 153,913 R | 55.5% | 43.9% | 55.9% | 44.1% |
| Louisiana | 10 | | | 1,628,202 | 883,702 | 717,460 | 27,040 | 166,242 R | 54.3% | 44.1% | 55.2% | 44.8% |
| Maine | 4 | | | 555,035 | 307,131 | 243,569 | 4,335 | 63,562 R | 55.3% | 43.9% | 55.8% | 44.2% |
| Maryland | 10 | | | 1,714,358 | 876,167 | 826,304 | 11,887 | 49,863 R | 51.1% | 48.2% | 51.5% | 48.5% |
| Massachusetts | | 13 | | 2,632,805 | 1,194,635 | 1,401,415 | 36,755 | 206,780 D | 45.4% | 53.2% | 46.0% | 54.0% |
| Michigan | 20 | | | 3,669,163 | 1,965,486 | 1,675,783 | 27,894 | 289,703 R | 53.6% | 45.7% | 54.0% | 46.0% |
| Minnesota | | 10 | | 2,096,790 | 962,337 | 1,109,471 | 24,982 | 147,134 D | 45.9% | 52.9% | 46.4% | 53.6% |
| Mississippi | 7 | | | 931,527 | 557,890 | 363,921 | 9,716 | 193,969 R | 59.9% | 39.1% | 60.5% | 39.5% |
| Missouri | 11 | | | 2,093,713 | 1,084,953 | 1,001,619 | 7,141 | 83,334 R | 51.8% | 47.8% | 52.0% | 48.0% |

| | | | | | | | | | | | | |
|---|---|---|---|---|---|---|---|---|---|---|---|---|
| Montana | 4 | | | 365,674 | 190,412 | 168,936 | 6,326 | 21,476 R | 52.1% | 46.2% | 53.0% | 47.0% |
| Nebraska | 5 | | | 661,465 | 397,956 | 259,235 | 4,274 | 138,721 R | 60.2% | 39.2% | 60.6% | 39.4% |
| Nevada | 4 | | | 350,067 | 206,040 | 132,738 | 11,289 | 73,302 R | 58.9% | 37.9% | 60.8% | 39.2% |
| New Hampshire | 4 | | | 451,074 | 281,537 | 163,696 | 5,841 | 117,841 R | 62.4% | 36.3% | 63.2% | 36.8% |
| New Jersey | 16 | | | 3,099,553 | 1,743,192 | 1,320,352 | 36,009 | 422,840 R | 56.2% | 42.6% | 56.9% | 43.1% |
| New Mexico | 5 | | | 521,287 | 270,341 | 244,497 | 6,449 | 25,844 R | 51.9% | 46.9% | 52.5% | 47.5% |
| New York | | 36 | | 6,485,683 | 3,081,871 | 3,347,882 | 55,930 | 266,011 D | 47.5% | 51.6% | 47.9% | 52.1% |
| North Carolina | 13 | | | 2,134,370 | 1,237,258 | 890,167 | 6,945 | 347,091 R | 58.0% | 41.7% | 58.2% | 41.8% |
| North Dakota | 3 | | | 297,261 | 166,559 | 127,739 | 2,963 | 38,820 R | 56.0% | 43.0% | 56.6% | 43.4% |
| Ohio | 23 | | | 4,393,699 | 2,416,549 | 1,939,629 | 37,521 | 476,920 R | 55.0% | 44.1% | 55.5% | 44.5% |
| Oklahoma | 8 | | | 1,171,036 | 678,367 | 483,423 | 9,246 | 194,944 R | 57.9% | 41.3% | 58.4% | 41.6% |
| Oregon | | 7 | | 1,201,694 | 560,126 | 616,206 | 25,362 | 56,080 D | 46.6% | 51.3% | 47.6% | 52.4% |
| Pennsylvania | 25 | | | 4,536,251 | 2,300,087 | 2,194,944 | 41,220 | 105,143 R | 50.7% | 48.4% | 51.2% | 48.8% |
| Rhode Island | | 4 | | 404,620 | 177,761 | 225,123 | 1,736 | 47,362 D | 43.9% | 55.6% | 44.1% | 55.9% |
| South Carolina | 8 | | | 986,009 | 606,443 | 370,554 | 9,012 | 235,889 R | 61.5% | 37.6% | 62.1% | 37.9% |
| South Dakota | 3 | | | 312,991 | 165,415 | 145,560 | 2,016 | 19,855 R | 52.8% | 46.5% | 53.2% | 46.8% |
| Tennessee | 11 | | | 1,636,250 | 947,233 | 679,794 | 9,223 | 267,439 R | 57.9% | 41.5% | 58.2% | 41.8% |
| Texas | 29 | | | 5,427,410 | 3,036,829 | 2,352,748 | 37,833 | 684,081 R | 56.0% | 43.3% | 56.3% | 43.7% |
| Utah | 5 | | | 647,008 | 428,442 | 207,343 | 11,223 | 221,099 R | 66.2% | 32.0% | 67.4% | 32.6% |
| Vermont | 3 | | | 243,328 | 124,331 | 115,775 | 3,222 | 8,556 R | 51.1% | 47.6% | 51.8% | 48.2% |
| Virginia | 12 | | | 2,191,609 | 1,309,162 | 859,799 | 22,648 | 449,363 R | 59.7% | 39.2% | 60.4% | 39.6% |
| Washington | | 10 | | 1,865,253 | 903,835 | 933,516 | 27,902 | 29,681 D | 48.5% | 50.0% | 49.2% | 50.8% |
| West Virginia | | 5 | 1 | 653,311 | 310,065 | 341,016 | 2,230 | 30,951 D | 47.5% | 52.2% | 47.6% | 52.4% |
| Wisconsin | | 11 | | 2,191,608 | 1,047,499 | 1,126,794 | 17,315 | 79,295 D | 47.8% | 51.4% | 48.2% | 51.8% |
| Wyoming | 3 | | | 176,551 | 106,867 | 67,113 | 2,571 | 39,754 R | 60.5% | 38.0% | 61.4% | 38.6% |
| Dist. of Col. | | 3 | | 192,877 | 27,590 | 159,407 | 5,880 | 131,817 D | 14.3% | 82.6% | 14.8% | 85.2% |
| United States | 426 | 111 | 1 | 91,594,809 | 48,886,097 | 41,809,074 | 899,638 | 7,077,023 R | 53.4% | 45.6% | 53.9% | 46.1% |

*Source: Richard M. Scammon and Alice V. McGillivray, eds. (Washington, D.C.: Congressional Quarterly, 1989). p. 7.*

* Total popular vote: 91,594,809; Bush's plurality: 7,077,023

# Appendix C
## Tentative Presidential Primary and Caucus Dates, 1992 (in Chronological Order by Date)*

| Date | State | Method |
|---|---|---|
| *February* | | |
| 10 | Iowa | Caucus |
| 18 | New Hampshire | Primary |
| 23 | Maine | Caucus |
| 25 | South Dakota | Primary |
| *March* | | |
| 3 | Colorado | Primary |
| | Georgia | Primary |
| | Maryland | Primary |
| | Minnesota | Caucus |
| (Democrats) | Idaho | Caucus |
| (Democrats) | Utah | Caucus |
| (Democrats) | Washington | Caucus |
| (Democrats) | North Dakota | Caucus |
| 7 | Arizona | Caucus |
| | South Carolina | Primary |
| | Wyoming | Caucus |
| 8 | Nevada | Caucus |
| 10 | Delaware | Caucus |
| | Florida | Primary |
| | Hawaii | Caucus |
| | Louisiana | Primary |
| | Massachusetts | Primary |
| | Mississippi | Primary |
| | Missouri | Caucus |
| | Oklahoma | Primary |
| | Rhode Island | Primary |
| | Tennessee | Primary |
| | Texas | Primary |
| 17 | Illinois | Primary |
| | Michigan | Primary |
| 24 | Connecticut | Primary |
| 26 (Democrats) | Louisiana | Caucus |
| 31 | Vermont | Caucus |
| *April* | | |
| 2 (Democrats) | Alaska | Caucus |
| 5 | Puerto Rico | Primary |
| 7 | Kansas | Primary |
| (Republicans) | Minnesota | Primary |
| | New York | Primary |

*(continued)*

# Appendix C
## Tentative Presidential Primary and Caucus Dates, 1992 (*continued*)

|  |  |  |
|---|---|---|
|  | Wisconsin | Primary |
| 11 | Virginia | Caucus |
| 27 (Republicans) | Utah | Caucus |
| 28 | Pennsylvania | Primary |

| *May* |  |  |
|---|---|---|
| 5 | District of Columbia | Primary |
|  | Indiana | Primary |
|  | North Carolina | Primary |
|  | Ohio | Primary |
| 9 (Democrats) | Michigan | Caucus |
| 12 | Nebraska | Primary |
|  | West Virginia | Primary |
| 19 | Oregon | Primary |
|  | Washington | Primary |
| 26 | Arkansas | Primary |
|  | Kentucky | Primary |
| (Republicans) | Idaho | Primary |

| *June* |  |  |
|---|---|---|
| 2 | Alabama | Primary |
|  | California | Primary |
|  | Montana | Primary |
|  | New Jersey | Primary |
|  | New Mexico | Primary |
| 9 (Republicans) | North Dakota | Primary |

*Source:* Democratic and Republican National Committees.

\* Several state parties had yet to decide on a date at the time this appendix was prepared (April 10, 1992).

# Acknowledgments *(continued from p. iv)*

# Index

**311**